LAL KITAB
of
ASTROLOGY

*(English version of a very famous and rare book
'LAL KITAB' originally published in Urdu)*

Prof. U.C. Mahajan
M.A., M.Phil.

PUSTAK MAHAL®
Delhi • Bangalore • Mumbai • Patna • Hyderabad

Publishers
Pustak Mahal®, Delhi

J-3/16, Daryaganj, New Delhi-110002
☎ 23276539, 23272783, 23272784 • *Fax:* 011-23260518
E-mail: info@pustakmahal.com • *Website:* www.pustakmahal.com

London Office
5, Roddell Court, Bath Road, Slough SL3 OQJ, England
E-mail: pustakmahaluk@pustakmahal.com

Sales Centre
10-B, Netaji Subhash Marg, Daryaganj, New Delhi-110002
☎ 23268292, 23268293, 23279900 • *Fax:* 011-23280567
E-mail: rapidexdelhi@indiatimes.com

Branch Offices
Bangalore: ☎ 22234025
E-mail: pmblr@sancharnet.in • pustak@sancharnet.in
Mumbai: ☎ 22010941
E-mail: rapidex@bom5.vsnl.net.in
Patna: ☎ 3294193 • *Telefax:* 0612-2302719
E-mail: rapidexptn@rediffmail.com
Hyderabad: *Telefax:* 040-24737290
E-mail: pustakmahalhyd@yahoo.co.in

© **Reserved**

ISBN 978-81-223-0884-6

Revised & Enlarged Edition : August 2006
Reprint : October 2007

Printed at : Param Offsetters, Okhla, New Delhi-110020

Humble Dedication

Dedicated to the sacred memory of my revered parents,
Late Shrimati Maya Devi and Late Shri Ghamir Chand
of Sujanpur Tira (H.P.)

—*Prof. U.C. Mahajan*

Preface to the Third Edition

The third edition of this immortal book before the students of astrology and its publication in such a short span of time, i.e., one year and a few months is a testimony to the unprecedented success it enjoys.

There are a plethora of books, critical comments and analytical discourses on the various aspects of astrology in the market but I do genuinely feel proud in having offered an entirely new and unique bouquet of astrological gems in the form of this book. Let me bow my head in reverence to the original authors of *Lal Kitab* in Urdu who inspired and guided me from heaven to perpetuate their memory in this translation. Earlier this book had been gathering dust because of the poor knowledge of Urdu after the partition of India and my translation has given a new lease of life. The English knowing students of astrology have now a rare ancient book on ancient wisdom before them. Let me express my thanks to all well wishers, relatives, friends and especially, Shri R.A. Gupta (M.D.), Shri S. Roy (Executive Editor), M/S Pustak Mahal Publisher, Daryaganj, New Delhi for the grand success of this book.

I have added a few more charts to make the book more comprehensive. I hope this edition will receive the same response from the lovers of astrology as the previous edition.

—**Prof. U.C. Mahajan**
Vivek Nagar, Pir Nigah Road
Una (H.P.) – 174303

Contents

Lal Kitab And Its Astrological Significance

1. What is Lal Kitab (Red Book)

This rare book on astrology was written by the renowned astrologer, Rup Lal, in the late nineteenth century and was published from Lahore in pre-partitioned India. It was in Urdu, as during that time both the Hindus as well as the Muslims read Urdu. It was the language of the court and was, in fact, the first language of the pre-partitioned Punjab, extending from Delhi to the borders of Afghanistan. This book is not available now, but Pandit Girdhari Lal, resident of Pheruwala, Noormahal, District Jallandhar published it in 1952, and almost simultaneously, Pandit Atma Ram of village Rahan of Nurpur Tehsil, District Kangra also published an edition of Lal Kitab. The former is the exact copy of the earlier book and comprises 1,173 pages. It is quite a voluminous book, whereas the latter book by Pandit Atma Ram contains only 380 pages and is a simplified version of the earlier voluminous book. It has an admixture of Punjabi and Pahari dialects, but the fundamentals are the same.

This rare book was quite popular in north-west India, Pakistan, Iran and many other countries. It would have been completely forgotten but for the efforts of these two great astrologers mentioned above. Sh. Rup Lal, the original author of this book, was not only an astrologer of great repute but also a sage who could see through the veil of unknown future.

2. Salient Features of Lal Kitab

बीमारी का बगैर दवाई भी इलाज है
मगर मौत का कोई इलाज नही
दुनियावी हिसाब-किताब है
कोई दावा-ए-खुदाई नही

Without medicines, diseases are curable,
But death is inevitable;
It is just the worldly account,
We do not claim Godhood.

These are the opening lines of this great book. This *inter alia* means that disease is curable by adopting the remedies suggested in this book, but there is no remedy against death; hence, the great astrologer does not claim to be God. Here are certain important points to be noted:

1. *SAADE-SAATI* OF SATURN – According to ancient astrology, Saturn exercises its malefic effect in three cycles of two-and-a-half years each, totalling seven years-and-a-half. But according to Lal Kitab, Saturn's obnoxious effect is to be adjudged from such mishaps as

stinging by a snake, damage to the house or its sale or auction, problem in eyesight, sickness of relatives, loss of machinery etc. are proofs that Saturn is indeed malefic. In other words, Sun's *antardasha* or *saade-saati* of Saturn is having its malefic effect. Results are, of course, the same.

2. To find remedies, refer to the annual charts which can be prepared in a few minutes. The catalogue of annual charts and how to prepare and understand them is explained in the book.

3. Remedies are easy to follow, cheap and affordable. It has been observed that these are quite effective.

4. Remedies for most obnoxious diseases such as T.B., epilepsy, rheumatism etc. are indicated; of course, man has no control over death, which is inevitable.

5. In ancient astrology, *Rahu* and *Ketu* are always at 180 degrees to each other. If Rahu is in house no. 1, Ketu will obviously occupy house no. 7 in the birth chart as well as in the annual chart, but in Lal Kitab, this distinction has been done away with. They can be in different houses and even in the adjacent ones in the annual chart of Lal Kitab. It is also likely that Mercury, which is usually closer to Sun, may drift away in the annual chart of Lal Kitab.

6. **This book should be bound in a red cover which should not be very bright. All other colours will bring misfortune.**

7. This book should be read like a novel many a time; the secrets of fate will unfold themselves automatically.

8. The most important thing about this book is that *Raashis* (Signs), *Nakshatras*, *Panchangs* (Ephemerides) have been done away with. The Ascendant (*Lagna*) has been assigned *Aries* (Raashi No. 1). Thus, the first house belongs to *Aries*, the second to *Taurus* and so on and so forth. The ancient astrologer may assign any Raashi to the Ascendant but according to Lal Kitab, the Ascendant will be assigned no. 1.

Here is an example:

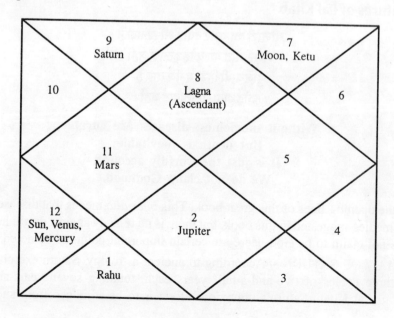

Now remove all the figures such as 8, 9, 10 etc. and assign no. 1 to the Lagna i.e. the first house, no. 2 to the second house etc. Here is the birth chart according to Lal Kitab.

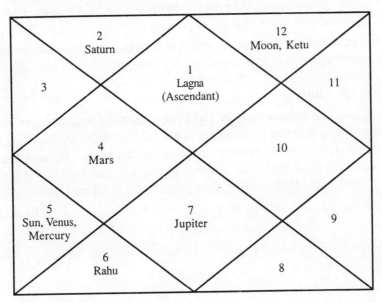

In this way, we have done away with the cycle of 12 Raashis, 28 Nakshatras and the complicated details of Panchang.

राशि छोड़ नक्षत्र भूला
नाहीं कोई पंचाग लिया
मेष राशि खुद लगन को गिनकर
बारह पक्के घर मान लिया

**We have done away with Raashis, Nakshatras,
and the intricacies of Panchang.
Lagna is assigned *Aries* and
so are 12 houses given *Aries, Taurus, Gemini, Cancer*
and so on and so forth.**

Some Points to be Remembered

1. It is true that Lal Kitab dispenses with Raashis and Nakshatras, but in its broader spectrum, it does refer to their importance at many places. Raashis do have their effect – malefic as well as benefic. For example, Jupiter in house no. 1 in *Capricorn*, i.e. Raashi no. 10, becomes malefic and must be read under bad effect in Jupiter in house no. 1 and also in house no. 10.

2. Further, certain planets in some particular houses do have Raashi effect, e.g. Moon, Mars and Jupiter in house no. 6 and Moon in house no. 7 etc. These have been indicated against the relevant houses.

3. Lal Kitab does attach some importance to the Nakshatras as well; otherwise it would not have recommended remedies for 43 days i.e. 28 days for 28 Nakshatras and 12 days for 12 Raashis and 3 days as the grace period. The total comes out to be 43 days. It also refers to the 'mahadasha' cycle of 120 years, though in passing.

4. The 120-year cycle of the planets of deception is very important in order to arrive at the exact conclusions regarding good or bad times.

Predictions from Lal Kitab

It has been noticed that a thorough study of Lal Kitab can make an astrologer perfect in making predictions. Even time and date can be correctly predicted. Lal Kitab is, therefore, not an ordinary book on astrology, but God's words on man's sojourn on this planet. By adopting the affordable remedies suggested in this great book, one can lead a better and healthier life. It is a ready reckoner in which all the problems and their solutions are presented and effectively solved.

–**Prof. U.C. Mahajan**

Astrology & Human Life

1. Astrology and its Influence on Human Life

Astrology can be defined as "the study of the real or supposed relationship between the Heavens and the people on the earth". It is, in fact, the science of divination, which calculates the supposed influence of planets upon human affairs and aims at foretelling the events on earth by their movements, positions and aspects. In simple words, *it is the ancient science of predicting the course of human destiny with the help of indications deduced from the positions and movements of heavenly bodies.** It can be best summarised up in the saying, "As above, so below". Astrologers believe that the Universe is the manifestation of 'Divine Will' and hence, is subject to interpretation. The basic premise of Astrology, therefore, is that the events in the Heavens correspond to those on earth.

2. Horoscope/Birth Chart

Just as a soldier cannot fight without a gun, similarly an astrologer must have the horoscope or "The map of the Hour" as his chief weapon. Separate chapters have been assigned to the 'Casting of a horoscope', Zodiac hours, signs, constellations etc. for the convenience of the readers and to facilitate exact interpretation of the birth chart.

3. Sun-sign

The earth revolves around the sun once in a year and it appears to make a circle of the Zodiac. The sign or constellation against which the sun appears to rise on the day of birth is called the 'Sun-sign'. In parties we often hear people telling each other, "I am a Leo, are you a Virgo?" Thus the sun-sign is the most important factor in the birth chart as the Sun represents the creative life force.

4. Ascendant or Rising Sign (Lagna)

As the earth rotates on its axis once a day, we have the second daily cycle of the zodiac. The sign at the time of birth of an individual is called the 'Rising Sign' and the sunrise point itself is called the 'Ascendant'. This is equally important in the interpretation of a horoscope. The 'Ascendant' further determines the division of the horoscope into twelve houses.

5. Three Broad Classifications of Astrology

There are three broad classifications of astrology, viz. Natal Astrology, Mundane Astrology and Horary Astrology:

    (a) **Natal Astrology:** Natal Astrology aims at analysing the character of the individual and predicting his future on the basis of horoscope.

---
* Webster's Third International Dictionary.

11

(b) **Mundane Astrology:** It deals with Universal phenomena such as wars, natural calamities, earthquakes, floods, famines, political turmoil and natural upheavals etc.

(c) **Horary Astrology:** It is based upon the assumption that the horoscope of any given moment can determine the meaning and significance of that moment. A question is put to an astrologer at a particular moment and he prepares the chart for that moment when the particular question is asked. He accordingly makes his predictions.

We will dwell upon the native Astrology, as the other two branches of Astrology are beyond the scope of this book.

It may be noted that the astrologer must base his predictions taking into account the sun-sign, ascendant, planets within their signs, aspects between the planets – both favourable & unfavourable etc. in order to arrive at an exact conclusion. In other words, horoscope should be read in its entirety.

Planets and their equivalent names in Hindi and Urdu

S. No.	English Name	Hindi Name	Urdu Name	Colour
1.	Sun	Ravi	Shamsh	Copper red
2.	Moon	Chandra	Qamar	Milky white
3.	Mars	Kuja, Mangal or Bhaum	Mariakh	Red (blood like)
4.	Jupiter	Guru or Brihaspeti	Mushtri	Yellow
5.	Saturn	Shani	Zuhal	Black
6.	Mercury	Budh	Attaroo	Green
7.	Venus	Shukra or Bhrigu	Zohra	White (Curd like)
8.	Dragon's head	Rahu	Raas	Blue
9.	Dragon's tail	Ketu	Zunab	Black & white

Signs (Raashis) and their equivalent names in Hindi

S. No.	Name of Raashi in English	Hindi Name
1.	Aries	Mesh
2.	Taurus	Vrish
3.	Gemini	Mithun
4.	Cancer	Kark
5.	Leo	Singh
6.	Virgo	Kanya
7.	Libra	Tula
8.	Scorpio	Vrishchik
9.	Sagittarius	Dhanu
10.	Capricorn	Makar
11.	Aquarius	Kumbh
12.	Pisces	Meen

Note: "Sign" means "Raashi".

Astrological symbols of the signs (Raashis) of Zodiac

Name of Sign	Permanent No.	Astrological Symbol
Aries	1	☉
Taurus	2	♉
Gemini	3	II
Cancer	4	♋
Leo	5	♌
Virgo	6	♍
Libra	7	♎
Scorpio	8	♏
Sagittarius	9	♐
Capricorn	10	♑
Aquarius	11	♒
Pisces	12	♓

ooo

The Time

Time and its Interpretation

In Hindu Astrology, Sun's position is the most significant. It enters 'Aries' in 1st Baisakh, which approximately falls on 13th April. Further division of time is calculated in terms of 'Ghatis' and 'Pals'. Each 'Ghati' is equivalent to 24 minutes and 60 'Pals' make one 'Ghati'. In other words, 2½ ghatis are equal to one hour and there are 60 ghatis in one day (24 hours). Duration of Sun per Raashi (Sign) per day is indicated in the following chart:

Names–English Months	Names–Hindi Months	Duration of Sun per Raashi (Sign) per day	Remarks
13 April to 12 May	Baisakh	3 Ghatis (72 Mts.)	(1) Aries
13 May to 12 June	Jeth	4 Ghatis (96 Mts.)	(2) Taurus
13 June to 12 July	Ashar	5 Ghatis (120 Mts.)	(3) Gemini
13 July to 12 August	Sawan	6 Ghatis (144 Mts.)	(4) Cancer
13 August to 12 September	Bhado	6 Ghatis (144 Mts.)	(5) Leo
13 September to 12 October	Asuj	6 Ghatis (144 Mts.)	(6) Virgo
13 October to 12 November	Kartik	6 Ghatis (144 Mts.)	(7) Libra
13 November to 12 December	Magher	6 Ghatis (144 Mts.)	(8) Scorpio
13 December to 12 January	Posh	6 Ghatis (144 Mts.)	(9) Sagittarius
13 January to 12 February	Maagh	5 Ghatis (120 Mts.)	(10) Capricorn
13 February to 12 March	Phagun	4 Ghatis (96 Mts.)	(11) Aquarius
13 March to 12 April	Chaitra	3 Ghatis (72 Mts.)	(12) Pisces

Raashi No. 1 & 12 ⇒ 72 Mts. each = 144 Mts.
Raashi No. 2 & 11 ⇒ 96 Mts. each = 192 Mts.
Raashi No. 3 & 10 ⇒ 120 Mts. each = 240 Mts.
Raashi No. 4,5,6,7,8 and 9 ⇒ 144 Mts. each = 864 Mts.
Total ⇒ = **1440 Mts. = 24 Hrs.**

Planets & Their Significance

I. Solar System and Planets

Sun is the central focus of the Solar System. This system primarily includes Sun and nine planets such as Mercury, Venus, Moon (a satellite of earth), Saturn, Uranus, Neptune and Pluto. We may conveniently ignore Uranus, Neptune and Pluto as their effect is negligible on human life. Our seers and sages referred only to the seven planets including Moon in their astrological calculations as Uranus, Neptune and Pluto are recent discoveries. We will obviously take into consideration Sun and other six planets for our calculations alongwith two nodes – Rahu (Dragon's Head) and Ketu (Dragon's Tail) as the ancient sages felt that these two nodes exercised tremendous influence on human life.

We would like to distinguish between the terms 'Planet' and 'Star'. Term planet is derived from Greek word 'Planets' meaning 'Wanderers'. Thus they shift their positions and sometimes disappear from view. They are named after gods such as Jupiter, Mercury, Venus, Mars, and Saturn etc. Rotating on their axes these planets revolve round Sun in long elliptical orbits. 'Stars' on the other hand are visible in their fixed positions.

1. **Sun:** It is the centre of solar system. Its mass is approximately 740 times as much as that of all the planets put together. For our purpose, it is Lord Vishnu who supports, sustains and nurtures life. Its main period lasts for 6 years in a total span of 120 years.

2. **Jupiter:** It is the great Guru. It is 'Lord Brahma', the creator of life. Its main period extends to 16 years in a total life span of 120 years.

3. **Moon:** It represents mother earth, who bestows all her bounties on her children. It also refers to mind, heart and mother. Its main period lasts for 10 years in a total life span of 120 years.

4. **Venus:** It is goddess Laxmi, bestowing happiness and wealth on the couple. It refers to husband/wife and lasts for 20 years.

5. **Mars (benefic):** It refers to Lord Hanuman, the reliever of pain and sorrows. It bestows power on the man and its total period is 7 years along with Mars (malefic).

6. **Mars (malefic):** It refers to the terrible aspect of Mars. It creates terror and works havoc. It dances the dance of death and bloodshed.

7. **Mercury:** It is all-powerful goddess Durga. Its main period lasts for 17 years.

8. **Saturn:** It represents Lord Bhairon, a poisonous snake and 'Yama', the lord of death. Its main period extends to 19 years.

9. **Rahu:** It refers to goddess 'Saraswati' and is the guide and friend of the downtrodden. Its main period extends to 18 years. It is not a planet, but a node called 'dragon's head'.

10. **Ketu:** It is a far-sighted dog that leads people to the shrine of a sage. It also represents son. Its main period lasts for 7 years. It is not a planet, but a node called 'dragon's tail'. It is always at the beck and call of its master, Rahu. Rahu is the master and Ketu is its slave.

II. Nature of Auspicious and Inauspicious Planets

1. **Sun:** It is hot, short-tempered and quick-witted. Its habitat is jungle and is related to four-footed animals.

2. **Moon:** It is jovial, always smiling and sweet-tongued. It is phlegmatic and is related to watery and wet places.

3. **Mars:** It is short-tempered, peevish and outspoken with a perverted mind and fiery temper.

4. **Jupiter:** It is very wise, jovial, scholarly, learned and popular. It is phlegmatic and dwells at sacred places or places of worship.

5. **Mercury:** It is learned, well-read, jovial and liberal. It is phlegmatic and quick-tempered and is related to sacred places.

6. **Venus:** It is jovial with a smiling face, sweet-tongued, sexy and easily attracted towards other sex and it leads a life of luxury. It is phlegmatic and is related to wet and watery places.

7. **Saturn:** It is short-tempered with a perverted mind, hisses and stings like a snake; has a venomous tongue. Its habitat is deserted and secluded places.

The above are the attributes of auspicious and inauspicious planets.

III. Exalted Planets and their Significance

1. **Sun:** This planet is the king of all planets. It is the ruler of body and soul. All other planets derive light from it and are sub-servient to it.

2. **Moon:** This planet is the Prince of Wales or heir apparent to the throne. It is, in fact, the viceroy; the royal representative and powerful minister.

3. **Jupiter:** This planet is a man of letters and scholarship; learned; pious; noble; dependable; generous; specialist in languages; reliable and knowledgeable adviser and treasurer.

4. **Venus:** This planet is a jeweller, trader; fond of music, dance and beautiful women; and full of zest for sexual life.

5. **Mars:** This planet is the Commander-in-chief; General of army; police chief; rich having a large retinue of servants; head of an organisation; industrialist.

6. **Mercury:** This planet is the writer; man of letters; doctor; mathematician; astrologer, astronomer; trader, and auditor general.

7. **Saturn:** This planet is the leader of a panchayat; rich owner of lands; administrator of treasury; lands and estates.

8. **Rahu & Ketu:** They are mean and perform mean and base acts.

IV. Debilitating or Malefic Planets and their Significance

1. **Malefic Sun:** Jealous, rival, always ready to obey others, man born to serve.

2. **Malefic Moon:** Poor man, spy, undependable, full of mean thoughts.

3. **Malefic Jupiter:** Poor sadhu, beggar, irreligious, ignoble, given to self-praise, hypocrite.

4. **Malefic Venus:** Lover of women, undependable, lustful, keeps company of mean and sinful people.

5. **Malefic Mars:** Thief, instigator of riots, butcher, sinful, lustful, notorious.

6. **Malefic Mercury:** Talkative, talks and speaks meaningless things, flatterer, cheap and useless learning, knowledge and wit.

7. **Malefic Saturn:** Lack of knowledge, labourer, factory worker, miserly, slave, full of bad and mean thoughts.

8. **Rahu & Ketu:** Perform mean and base acts.

V. Vakri (Retrograde) and Margi (Straight Moving) Planets

Astrologers often mention 'Vakri' or 'Margi' against the planets in the life chart of an individual. 'Vakri' refers to a planet, which moves backwards and becomes retrograde instead of moving forward. For example, a planet occupying 'Leo' in the birth chart moves backwards to 'Cancer' instead of 'Virgo' after completing its course, is called 'Vakri'.

'Margi' is just the opposite of 'Vakri'. It is a planet, which moves ahead and forward. For example, a planet occupying 'Leo' in the birth chart moves forward to 'Virgo' and then to 'Libra' and so on and so forth, is called 'Margi'.

Sun and Moon always move straight, hence 'Margis'. Mars, Mercury, Jupiter, Venus and Saturn sometimes become 'Margi' and sometimes 'Vakri'. Rahu and Ketu are always 'Vakri'. A 'Margi' planet achieves its aim and destination, whereas a 'Vakri' planet is deprived of its destination. In simple words straight movement of planets is called 'Margi' and their backward movement is called 'Vakri'.

VI. Rising and Setting Planets

Some planets are awake i.e. they are full of power and light; whereas others are asleep i.e. they are setting or sinking planets and are dead for all intents and purposes.

A setting planet is one which is in conjunction with Sun or is at a distance of 6 degrees (Ansh) from Sun. Sun combusts such a planet and destroys its power and potential. Setting or combusting Venus is the most malefic, but this cannot be said of Mercury. According to some astrologers, Sun cannot combust and destroy Mercury as it always resides near the Sun. If Sun is the monkey, then Mercury is its tail. Since animals residing in a river or an ocean are never drowned by water, so is the case with Mercury. Mercury may become dim in the presence of Sun, but is never destroyed.

A setting planet brings misery and disease, whereas a rising planet is the source of happiness, health and prosperity. A setting planet is like a diseased person on the brink of death and a rising planet is like a healthy man who enjoys all the pleasures of life. A setting planet becomes very weak and malefic during Solar/Lunar eclipse. Besides any enemy planet in association with or in adverse aspect of Rahu/Ketu becomes inauspicious, malefic and debilitating. For example, Rahu in 3rd house destroys Sun in the 9th house, howsoever powerful it may be or Sun in association with Rahu is eclipsed. Similarly, Moon in conjunction with Ketu or directly aspected by it is completely eclipsed and afflicted.

VII. Planets/Raashis and Degrees (Ansh)

Heavenly sphere consists of 360 degrees and each sign (Raashi) comprises 30 degrees – making the total 360 degrees. To know on what degree a particular planet or Raashi is situated, astrologers indicate it in the birth chart after studying the Panchang (ephemerides) or Jantri of that particular year.

For information of readers, it is mentioned here that a planet having 3 to 9 degrees is a child and adolescent; from 10 to 22 degrees, it is powerful and young and from 23 to 28 degrees, it is old and from 29 to 2 degrees (i.e. 29, 30, 1 and 2), it is dead.

VIII. Characteristics and Articles of Planets

Planet	Presiding Lord	Characteristics	Main Features
Sun (Self, giver of life)	Vishnu	Bold, sustains life	Fire, anger, body, knowledge, intelligence
Moon (Mother, earth)	Shiva	Compassion, mercy, peace, mother, heart, water, inherited property	Happiness, comfort, mother's blessing and love, heart, legacy
Jupiter (Father, Great Guru)	Brahma	Teacher, a noble guide and leader	Air, soul, breath, father, teacher, mental happiness
Mars {Exalted}, Brother	Hanuman	Bravery	Courageous, fighter
Mars {Malefic} (man-eater)	Evil spirits	Butcher	Mean, enemy, conspirator, cheat, terrorist
Mercury (Sister, aunt)	Goddess Durga	Sycophant, flatterer	Power of speech, brain, skill, specialisation, advice, popularity among people
Venus (Spouse)	Goddess Laxmi	Lover, beloved, flirt	Wife or husband, domestic happiness, lustful spouse
Saturn (Son opposed to father & paternal uncles)	Bhairon	Mechanic, skilled worker, ironsmith, carpenter, but foolish & obstinate	Death, disease, cunning-ness, black magic and power to observe & watch
Rahu (In-laws)	Goddess Saraswati	Cunning person, cheat, mean, cruel	Dirty thoughts, fear electricity, enmity, earthquake
Ketu (Son, dog)	Lord Ganesha	Coolie, labourer	Hearing, movement of feet

Animal	Tree	Articles	Precious Stones and Minerals	Power
Monkey	Tej-bill (tooth-ache tree)	Wheat, jaggery, skylight	Ruby, copper, shilajeet	Full of heat and fire (Sun)
Horse, peacock	Green poppy full of milk	Rice, milk, natural fountain well	Pearl (milky white), silver	Mother's blessings, love and service of ancestors (Moon)
Lion	Peepal	Saffron, chana daal, turmeric etc.	Topaz, gold	Officer/subordinate having power to rule, guide and help (Jupiter)
Tiger	Neem	Masur daal, honey, sugar, saunf (fennel), Arms	Red coral or Ruby (not bright)	Army/police officer, brother, patriot, fighting wars (Mars exalted)
Camel, deer	Dek tree (Dhak)	Arms & Ammunition	Bright red stone	Corrupt officer, exploiting & terrorising people [Mars (malefic)]
Goat	Banana	Moong, green things	Emerald, diamond	Intelligent, gift of gab (public speaking), power of convincing & befriending others, skilled worker, dentist, doctor, engineer etc. (Mercury)
Cow, ox	Cotton	Curd, camphor, butter, sand	Pearl (curd like) or diamond	Life of luxury, lover of women, music, dance, poetry and fine arts (Venus)
Buffalo, snake	Palm, keekar, (acacia), palm tree or madar (swallow wart)	Urad, iron, leather, coal, almonds, wine etc.	Sapphire, iron, steel	Occult, tantric, evil, perfomer of black magic to harass others (Saturn)
Elephant, rat	Palm	Mustard (sarson), coconut, barley	Sapphire or gomed (Zircon), lead	Guide to tease, torture and harass others (Rahu)
Dog, donkey, pig	Imli (tamarind), sesame (til)	Sesame (til), black & white blanket, banana, black & white dog	Vaidrya (cat's eye), Lahsunya, black & white stone	Movement, walking, meeting others (Ketu)

19

Day & Time	Parts of Body
Sunday 8:00 AM to 10:00 PM	The whole body, right side.
Moon-lit fortnight (Poornima) Monday 10:00 AM to 11:00 AM	Heart (left side).
Thursday 6:00 AM to 8:00 AM	Neck, nose, forehead.
Tuesday 11 AM to 1 PM	Liver, upper lip.
Tuesday 11 AM to 1 PM	Liver, lower lip.
Wednesday 4 AM to 6 PM	Brain, teeth, arteries, the whole body without head.
Friday or dark fortnight (Amavasya) 1.00 PM to 3.00 PM	Cheeks (upper part).
Saturday night	Eyesight, eyelids, hair.
Thursday evening, twilight	Chin, head part only (shadow without body).
Sunday, early morning	Ears, feet, urinary tract, body without head, spinal cord, knees.

IX. Symptoms and Remedies Concerning Malefic & Inauspicious Planets

Planet	Malefic Symptoms	Remedies
1. Sun	Loss of power of moving the limbs of the body, numbness of limbs, continuous flowing of froth from mouth.	Take a little 'Mishri' or sugar & then take a few sips of water before doing auspicious work.
2. Moon	Drying up of wells & water fountains, death of milk yielding animal, loss of feeling & sensation.	Seek the blessings of elders.
3. Jupiter	Instant & automatic falling of hair at the top of head, loss of gold, habituated to wearing beads around the neck, loss of reputation through rumours & mud-slinging, disruption in studies.	Put yellow dot on forehead, start work after blowing out the nose, wear gold chain or yellow thread around the neck.
4. Venus	Skin disease.	Take care of your clothes and personal hygiene.
5. Mercury	Destruction & loss of teeth, insensitive to foul & good smell, loss of virility.	Pierce the nose; keep teeth clean; use alum while cleaning teeth.

Planet	Malefic Symptoms	Remedies
6. Mars	Loss of child after his birth, loss of one eye, impurities in blood i.e. loss of movements in joints, pale body, not competent to produce a child in spite of being sexually potent & virile.	For remedy please refer to 'Malefic Mars' in house no. 4, also use white *surma*.
7. Saturn	Loss & destruction of house, death of buffaloes, incidence of fire, falling of hair around eyes, especially eyebrows and eyelids.	Use 'Mesvak' – Indian datun made of fibrous tree such as Keekar (acacia) and Neem for cleaning teeth.
8. Rahu	Death or loss of black dog, peeling off nails of fingers, insanity, surrounded by enemies for no fault.	Live in joint family; don't spoil relations with in-laws; don't be overconfident and overliberal.
9. Ketu	Peeling off nails of toes, diseases of urine, joints & limbs, problems regarding children.	Pierce the ears; tie pure white silk thread in toes; keep or feed a dog.

X. Miscellaneous Information about Planets

(i) Exalted and Perfect Planets

A planet which occupies its permanent houses and is in its own Raashi and is not adversely aspected by enemy planets is the most exalted planet e.g. Jupiter in house no. 9 and in Sagittarius (Raashi no. 9).

(ii) Planet's own Raashi/House

A planet occupying its own sign (Raashi) is called a planet in its own house/Raashi e.g. Mercury in Virgo.

(iii) Enemy Planets

A weak and debilitating planet occupying an enemy's house and enemy's Raashi is the worst planet e.g. Saturn in Aries in house no. 1.

(iv) Wicked Planets

Saturn, Rahu and Ketu are wicked and sinful.

(v) Masculine Planets

Jupiter, Sun, Mars and Saturn. They govern soul, body, blood and minerals respectively.

(vi) Feminine Planets

Moon (mother) and Venus (spouse).

(vii) Eunuchs

Mercury which affects earth and vegetation. Rahu and Ketu are not planets. They are nodes affecting head and feet.

(viii) Exalted/Weak Planets

When a planet is in a Raashi which is exalted/weak, it is called exalted/weak planet.

(ix) Neutral Planets or Planets having Equal Strength

Refer to the chart indicating friendship and enmity of planets.

(x) Blind Horoscope

When house no. 10 is being destroyed by two enemy planets, such a horoscope is called Blind Horoscope. Even exalted Saturn fails to help. Other planets, however benefic they may be, also fail to redeem it.

(xi) Partially Blind Planets

A partially blind horoscope is one when Sun is in house no. 4 and Saturn is in house no. 7.

(xii) Religiously Inclined (Noble) Planets

Rahu and Ketu, the most wicked planets in house no. 4 take a vow before Moon (the mother) to shun their evil ways and Saturn, the most sinful planet in house no.11 takes a solemn pledge before Jupiter (the great guru) to give up its wickedness. In other words, if Rahu and Ketu are in house no. 4 or in any house in conjunction with Moon and if Saturn is in house no. 11 or in any house along with Jupiter, such a horoscope will not fall a prey to the evil designs of wicked planets. All planets will become noble and pious.

(xiii) Enemies Shedding Hatred and becoming Friends

When planets (exalted or debilitated according to Raashis or Houses) exchange places, they shed their mutual hatred and help each other. For example:

    (a) If Saturn is in Aries and Mars is in Capricorn, the two enemies exchange their Raashis and do not harm each other.

    (b) Sun in house no. 10 (Saturn's house) and Saturn in house no. 5 (Sun's house).

    (c) Jupiter in house no. 7 and Venus in house no. 12.

    (d) Saturn in house no. 1 and Mars in house no. 10.

    (e) Jupiter in Libra (Raashi no. 7) and Venus in Sagittarius (Raashi no. 9).

(xiv) Enemy Planets

    (a) Sun is Saturn's enemy, Venus is Sun's enemy, Venus is Jupiter's enemy, Jupiter is Mercury's enemy, Ketu is Moon's enemy, Mars (malefic) is Ketu's enemy.

    Above all, Rahu is Sun's, Venus's, Moon's and Mars's enemy.

    (b) Friendly planets

    Sun's friend is Moon; Moon's friend is Jupiter; Mars's (benefic) friend is Jupiter; Rahu's friend is Mercury; Mercury's friend is Saturn; Saturn's friend is Venus; and Venus's friend is Ketu.

In other words, the planets mentioned above are enemies or friends. The leader of enemy planets is Rahu and leader of friendly planets is Ketu. Rahu represents head and Ketu feet.

Yoga for Eminence: If all the planets are in quick succession and no house is vacant, it constitutes Eminent Yoga. He achieves distinction in life. It is like a necklace around the neck.

Example:

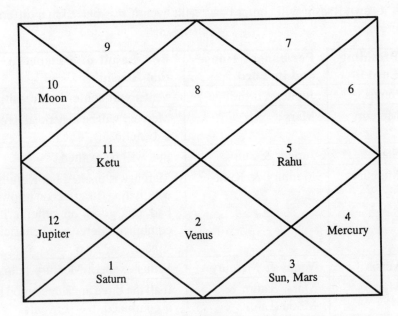

Fig. 1

XI. Scapegoat Planets which are Sacrificed

(a) **Saturn:** Whenever there is a clash between Saturn (Son) and Sun (Father), Venus (Spouse) is sacrificed, e.g. Sun in house no. 6 and Saturn in house no. 12. In that case, wife suffers.

(b) **Rahu and Ketu:** They are Saturn's agents and are employed to ward off attacks from enemies.

(c) **Jupiter:** Ketu is sacrificed when Jupiter faces trouble.

(d) **Sun:** It also sacrifices Ketu when in trouble.

(e) **Moon:** It sacrifices Jupiter, Sun and Mars when it faces trouble.

(f) **Venus:** It sacrifices Moon (Mother); e.g. when Venus and Moon are opposite to each other, mother becomes blind.

(g) **Mars:** Malefic Mars (Brother) sacrifices Ketu (Son) e.g. Mars in house no. 10 and Sun in house no. 6, Son suffers or dies.

XII. Exalted Raashis (Sign) of a Planet and their effect on a Permanent House

Every planet in its own Raashi will confer best result even if it is placed in a different permanent house:

Raashi No.	Presiding Lord	Permanent House and its Lord	Best Result of a Planet in that Raashi
2	Venus	Jupiter	Venus will confer best result.
3	Mercury	Mars	Mercury will be beneficial, provided Mars is benefic.
5	Sun	Jupiter & Sun	Sun will be exalted.
6	Mercury	Mercury & Ketu	Mercury is exalted but Ketu is weak and debilitating. Its effect on its own articles is bad but good on others; if both are combined, Mercury is beneficial but Ketu is bad.
7	Venus	Venus & Mercury	Venus exalted; Mercury helps others.
8	Mars	Mars, Saturn & Moon (Life)	If all the three are alone, good results, and if combined, worst results.
11	Saturn	Jupiter	Saturn exalted; other planets outwardly good, but are, in fact, bad and stifling like wild and unripe 'Ber' (Jujubes).

XIII. Life Span of Planets

Whenever a planet is exalted or debilitating and is not aspected by any other planet, it will give its effect throughout its whole span e.g. Jupiter 16 years, Sun 22 years, Moon 24 years etc. If friends or enemies affect a particular planet, then Jupiter, Sun, Moon will last for 6 years, 2 years and 1 year etc. The following chart is self-explanatory:

S.No.	Planet & its age (Years)	Span of 35 years	Mahadasha period 120 years	Total years 275	Time of effect	Speed	Days in a year	Effect
1.	Jupiter (75 yrs)	6 yrs	16 yrs	16 yrs	In the Middle	Lion	32 days	16 days wild cow & 16 days fish
2.	Sun (100 yrs)	2 yrs	6 yrs	22 yrs	Beginning	Chariot	22 days	Lion
3.	Moon (85 yrs)	1 yr	10 yrs	24 yrs	End	Horse	24 days	Crab
4.	Venus (85 yrs)	3 yrs	20 yrs	25 yrs	Middle	Bull	50 days	25 days bull & 25 days scales

No.	Planet							
5.	Mercury (80 yrs)	2 yrs	17 yrs	34 yrs	Always same	Ram	68 days	34 days couple & 34 days girl
6.	Saturn (90 yrs)	6 yrs	19 yrs	36 yrs	End	Fish	72 days	36 days crocodile and 36 days fish
7.	Mars (benefic) & Mars (malefic) (90 years)	3 years + 3 years = 6 years	3 years + 4 years = 7 years	13 years + 15 years = 28 years	Beginning (without Sun, Mars is malefic)	Stag, Leopard (man-eater)	24 days and 32 days = 56 days	28 days Ram and 28 days scorpion (death)
8.	Rahu (90 years)	6 years	18 years	42 years	End	Elephant	40 days	Fish (41 days)
9.	Ketu (80 years)	3 years	7 years	48 years	End	Pig	43 days	Girl
Total		35 years	120 years	275 years			367 days	

Note: Every planet confers its effect:

(1) During the half and $1/4^{th}$ of its total span.

(2) During solar eclipse or lunar eclipse, life may be reduced by three years.

(3) Saturn confers good results during the 10th, 19th, and 36th years regarding wealth and prosperity.

XIV. Thirty-five Year Cycle of Planets

All planets complete their full cycle in 35 years. Planets that give bad effect during the first 35 years will not be malefic during their second cycle of 35 years. There is a difference in the 35-year cycle of a planet and 35 years of man's life. This difference must be clearly understood. For example, if Jupiter starts with one's birth the whole cycle will be completed in 35 years i.e. Jupiter: 6 years, Sun: 2 years, Moon: 1 year, Venus: 3 years, Mars: 6 years, Mercury: 2 years, Saturn: 6 years, Rahu: 6 years and Ketu: 3 years. Please refer to Col. 3 of life span of planets. It is possible that man's first planet is Saturn instead of Jupiter and it starts from 7th year instead of birth date. Now all planets will complete the cycle in 35 years but when last planet's last day comes, at that time it will be 35 years plus 6 years. (When Saturn's first planet had not started as yet, man's age at that time would be 41 years, which means that then the second cycle of 35 years would have started.)

XV. Life Span of Intervening Planets in a 35-year Cycle of Planet

Planet's Term	Jupiter (6 years)	Sun (2 years)	Moon (1 year)	Venus (3 years)	Mars (6 years)	Mercury (2 years)	Saturn (6 years)	Rahu (6 years)	Ketu (3 years)
Beginning	Ketu (2 years)	Sun (8 months)	Jupiter (4 months)	Mars (1 year)	Mars (2 years)	Moon (8 months)	Rahu (2 years)	Mars (2 years)	Saturn (1 year)
Middle	Jupiter (2 years)	Moon (8 months)	Sun (4 months)	Venus (1 year)	Saturn (2 years)	Mars (8 months)	Mercury (2 years)	Ketu (2 years)	Rahu (1 year)
End	Sun (2 years)	Mars (8 months)	Moon (4 months)	Mercury (1 year)	Venus (2 years)	Jupiter (8 months)	Saturn (2 years)	Rahu (2 years)	Ketu (1 year)

XVI. Intervening Planets in a Year

Divide the year into three: every part will consist of 4 months which will have the effect of an intervening planet as per chart given below:

Suppose Jupiter is in house no. 5 in the annual chart; the first four months will give the effect of Ketu – whether good or bad – as it is placed in the annual chart. The second four months will have Jupiter's own effect according to its placement in the annual chart and finally the last four months will have the Sun's effect according to its position in the annual chart. So is the case with other planets:

Intervening Planets and their Effect in a Year

Permanent House	Beginning (4 Months)	Middle (4 Months)	End (4 Months)
Jupiter	Ketu	Jupiter	Sun
Sun	Sun	Moon	Mars
Moon	Jupiter	Sun	Moon
Venus	Mars	Venus	Mercury
Mars	Mars	Saturn	Venus
Mercury	Moon	Mars	Jupiter
Saturn	Rahu	Mercury	Saturn
Rahu	Mars	Ketu	Rahu
Ketu	Saturn	Rahu	Ketu

Effect of a Benefic Planet, if Alone

S.No.	Planet (if alone)	Effect
1.	Jupiter	Will never have bad effect on the native.
2.	Sun	Will be self-made rich.
3.	Moon	Compassionate and polite like Moon; will definitely have a son.
4.	Venus	Will never be bad, provided it is not instigated or destroyed by a malefic planet.
5.	Mars	Like a tiger in a zoo or a tiger among goats.
6.	Saturn	If alone with Sun, it will give the effect of Mercury.
7.	Rahu	Will dominate all planets and will save the native from enemies.
8.	Ketu	Will always serve its master i.e. Rahu.

Effect of Combined Planets

The following combined planets, irrespective of their placement in House, give the effect of the Houses mentioned against them:

S.No.	Combined Planets	Effect of the House
1.	Sun – Mars	House No. 1
2.	Jupiter – Venus	House No. 2
3.	Mars – Mercury	House No. 3
4.	Mars – Venus	House No. 4
5.	Sun – Jupiter	House No. 5
6.	Mercury – Ketu	House No. 6
7.	Venus – Mercury	House No. 7
8.	Mars – Saturn – Moon	House No. 8
9.	Mercury – Saturn (according to their personal traits)	House No. 9
10.	Saturn	House No. 10
11.	Jupiter – Saturn	House No. 11
12.	Jupiter – Rahu	House No. 12

Effect of Planets on other Planets

House No.	Planet	Effect on another Planet
1	Ketu	Sun will confer best results.
1	Rahu	Sun will be destroyed & eclipsed, whatever house it may occupy.
2	Mercury	Jupiter will be destroyed.
4	Mercury	Moon will be destroyed.
6	Mars	Sun will confer best results, but Ketu will be destroyed.
11	Rahu	Jupiter will be destroyed.
11	Ketu	Moon will be destroyed if Mercury is in house no. 9.
11	Jupiter	Rahu will be destroyed if Mercury is debilitated or malefic.
12	Moon	Ketu will be destroyed.

Additional Information about the Effects of Planets

(i) Every planet in its own or a friend's Raashi will confer best results.

(ii) An exalted planet will never give bad effect, even if it is destroyed by an enemy planet although it may not confer good effect i.e. it will neither be bad nor good, just neutral.

(iii) A planet whether good or bad in a horoscope will give its good or bad effect when it occupies the same house or Raashi. For example, Jupiter in Cancer, in House No. 4 is the most exalted. Its best results will be available when it occupies house no. 4 or 2 (Permanent House). A malefic planet will be all the more malefic, if it occupies house no. 8 (the House of Death & Disease).

(iv) An exalted planet in a house where it is considered exalted, will never harm its associate enemy planet or a planet that is aspected by it, though it may not help the enemy. In other words, an auspicious planet will never give up its goodness.

Example

S.No.	Planet	House No.	Enemy Planet	House No.
1.	Jupiter	4	Venus & Mercury	10
2.	Sun	1	Venus & wicked planets (Spouse may have ill-health)	7
3.	Moon	2	Mercury & wicked planets	6 & 12
4.	Venus	12	Sun, Moon & Rahu	2
5.	Mars	10	Mercury & Ketu	2
6.	Mercury	6	Moon	12
7.	Saturn	7	Sun, Moon & Mars	7
8.	Rahu	3 & 6	Venus, Sun & Mars	12
9.	Ketu	9 & 12	Moon & Mars	2

If all the planets in the horoscope are bad, such a person will have the strength to fight against the whole world alone. Such a person is indeed very bold and hence good results. ooo

28

Zodiac*

Zodiac is a Greek phrase, which actually means "Circle of Animals". That is why the ancient Hindus and Egyptians assigned names to the various signs of the Zodiac from the animal kingdom and agriculture. According to Dr Norbert Schiller, the ancient sages divided the year into spring, summer, autumn and winter and assigned to each season the constellation through which the Sun passed. They gave Aries (Ram) to the constellation after March 21, because this was the time when sheep produced their young. To the constellation that followed in the middle of April, they gave the name of Taurus (Bull) who tilled the land. Next came the Gemini (Twins), as the goats usually produce two young ones at the end of May. On June 21, when the Sun turned back towards the equator, they assigned the name Cancer (Crab) – the animal that crawls backwards. To the constellation with the Sun at its Zenith, they gave the name Leo (lion). They chose the sign of the Virgo (Virgin) for the harvest time, when girls glean the ears of corn. In the month of August, they assigned Libra (scale) to the period when the day and night are of equal length.

As the retreat of the Sun in the October gives rise to all types of diseases, the name of Scorpio (Scorpion) was aptly given to this constellation. Then came the hunting time with the symbol of Archer (Sagittarius). On December 21, the Sun starts rising higher in the sky under the sign of the ibex (Goat) i.e. Capricorn. In January it rains heavily, hence sign of water carrier (Aquarius) and in the end, we have the time of fishing, hence the name Pisces (Fish).

Zodiac is an imaginary belt in the heavens usually 18 degrees wide that encompasses the apparent paths of all the principal planets except Pluto and it is divided into 12 constellations of signs, each taken for astrological purposes to extend to 30 degrees of longitude. In simple words, it is a diagram that represents the circular movements of the planets. It is divided into twelve equal signs or Raashis, which are Aries, Taurus, Gemini, Cancer, Leo, Virgo, Libra, Scorpio, Sagittarius, Capricorn, Aquarius and Pisces. Their description is as follows:

(1) **Aries (Ram):** It is the first sign of the Zodiac and covers the first 30° (degree) from March 21 to April 20. Its ruling planet is Mars and refers to Head.

(2) **Taurus (Bull):** It is the second sign of the Zodiac and covers the next 31°-60° from April 21 to May 21. Its ruling planet is Venus and operates on neck and face.

(3) **Gemini (Twins):** It is the third sign of the Zodiac extending from 61°-90° from May 22 to June 21. Its ruling planet is Mercury and covers arms and chest.

(4) **Cancer (Crab):** It is the fourth sign of the Zodiac extending from 91°-120° from June 22 to July 23. Its ruling planet is Moon and operates on heart and chest.

---

*Note: Although this chapter does not form an integral part of "Lal Kitab", yet it is essential for learning the fundamentals of Astrology.

(5) **Leo (Lion):** It is the fifth sign of Zodiac extending from 121°-150° from July 24 to August 23. Its Lord is Sun and refers to stomach.

(6) **Virgo (Virgin):** It is the sixth sign of the Zodiac comprising 151°-180° from August 24 to September 23. Its ruling planet is Mercury and covers waist and back.

(7) **Libra (Scales):** It is the seventh sign of the Zodiac extending from 181°-210° from September 24 to October 23. Its Lord is Venus and covers intestines and stomach.

(8) **Scorpio (Scorpio):** It is the eighth sign of the Zodiac covering 211°-240° from October 24 to November 23. Its ruling planet is Mars and operates on private parts i.e. penis & vagina.

(9) **Sagittarius (Archer):** It is the ninth sign of the Zodiac extending from 241°-270°, from November 24 to December 23. Its Lord is Jupiter and covers thighs and legs.

(10) **Capricorn (Goat):** It is the tenth sign of the Zodiac covering 271°-300°, from December 23 to January 20. Its ruling planet is Saturn and covers thighs and knees.

(11) **Aquarius (Pitcher full of water or water carrier):** It is the eleventh sign of Zodiac extending from 301°-330° from January 21 to February 19. Its ruling planet is Saturn and covers feet and hips.

(12) **Pisces (Fish):** It is the twelfth sign of Zodiac extending from 331°-360°, from February 20 to March 20. Its ruling planet is Jupiter and covers part of feet.

(i) Mobile and Fixed Raashis (signs)

(a) Mobile Raashis (char in Hindi) – Aries, Cancer, Libra and Capricorn.

(b) Fixed Raashis (sthir in Hindi) – Taurus, Leo, Scorpio and Aquarius.

(c) Partially mobile and partially fixed Raashis (Dodhabhao in Hindi) – Gemini, Virgo, Sagittarius and Pisces.

(ii) Male and Female Raashis (signs)

(a) Male Raashis – All odd Raashis i.e. Aries, Gemini, Leo, Libra, Sagittarius and Aquarius.

(b) Female Raashis – All even Raashis i.e. Taurus, Cancer, Virgo, Scorpio, Capricorn and Pisces.

(iii) Day and Night Raashis

Aries, Gemini, Leo, Libra, Sagittarius and Aquarius are called Night Raashis; whereas Taurus, Cancer, Virgo, Scorpio, Capricorn and Pisces are called Day Raashis.

(iv) Odd and Even Raashis

(a) Aries, Gemini, Leo, Libra, Sagittarius and Aquarius are called Odd signs.

(b) Taurus, Cancer, Virgo, Scorpio, Capricorn and Pisces are called Even signs.

Male Planets are powerful in Odd Raashis and Female Planets are powerful in Even Raashis.

(v) Nature of Auspicious and Inauspicious Signs

Taurus, Cancer, Libra, Sagittarius and Pisces are auspicious signs; whereas Aries, Scorpio, Capricorn and Aquarius are inauspicious signs. Auspicious planets are powerful in auspicious signs and wicked planets are powerful in inauspicious signs. On the contrary, auspicious planets are weak in inauspicious signs but wicked planets become very powerful in auspicious signs. Gemini and Virgo are neutral and Leo is cruel.

	Nature	Sign		Nature	Sign
1.	Inauspicious	Aries	7.	Auspicious	Libra
2.	Auspicious	Taurus	8.	Inauspicious	Scorpion
3.	Neutral	Gemini	9.	Auspicious	Sagittarius
4.	Auspicious	Cancer	10.	Inauspicious	Capricorn
5.	Cruel (Inauspicious)	Leo	11.	Inauspicious	Aquarius
6.	Neutral	Virgo	12.	Auspicious	Pisces

Constellation (Nakshatras or Lunar Mansions or Asterisms)

According to Hindu Astrology system Zodiac is divided into 27 Nakshatras (Constellations), each extending 13°20' of arc. They are grouped into groups of three and each is ruled by a planet–Ketu, Venus, Sun, Moon, Mars, Rahu, Jupiter, Saturn and Mercury in that order.

Lal Kitab, a rare book on Astrology in Urdu on which my whole premise is based, has done away with Nakshatra and nowhere it recognises them, but it does make occasional reference to total span of 120 years and Mahadasha cycle of various planets viz. Sun–6yrs; Moon–10yrs; Mars–7yrs; Rahu–18yrs; Jupiter–16yrs; Saturn–19yrs; Mercury–17yrs; Ketu–7yrs and Venus–20yrs. It naturally means that Nakshatras cannot be summarily dismissed as they form the very basis of Mahadasha cycle of planets on which the whole Hindu Astrology is based. My research and experience in the subject extending to more than a decade also vouchsafes for the importance of 'Nakshatras and Raashis'.

Dasha at the time of birth is calculated from the position of Moon at birth. Each constellation, as explained covers 13°20' of arc of 800'. The Moon may occupy any degree or minute in a 'Nakshatra' at epoch. The Ruling Planets of various constellations are as under:

	Constellation		Planet	Duration
Ashwani	Magha	Moola	Ketu	7 years
Bharni	P.Phaguni	P.Shada	Venus	20 years
Kritika	U.Phaguni	U.Shada	Sun	6 years
Rohini	Hastha	Shravana	Moon	10 years
Mrigshira	Chitra	Dhanishta	Mars	7 years
Ardra	Swathi	Shatbhisha	Rahu	18 years
Punarvasu	Visakha	P.Bhadra	Jupiter	16 years
Pushya	Anuradha	U.Bhadra	Saturn	19 years
Ashlesha	Jyeshta	Revati	Mercury	17 years

Thus, the first Mahadasha of a planet at birth is calculated from the position of Moon in particular 'Nakshatra' and its lord. Suppose Moon at birth is in 'Magha Nakshatra' the first Mahadasha will be that of Ketu, as Ketu is the lord of Magha. If the Moon is passing through the Karitika the initial Mahadasha period will be that of Sun.

The duration of first Mahadasha is to be calculated from the distance covered by Moon in the particular 'Nakshtra'. If the Moon has first entered 'Kritika' the person will have full span of 6 years of Sun's Mahadasha. Suppose Moon has covered 3°20' of Kritika (the total span of each constellation is 3°20') naturally one quarter of 6 years has already elapsed and 1 year and 6 months should be deducted from 6 years. Sun's Dasha at birth will therefore be 4 years and 6 months; next will be that of Moon (10yrs.); Mars (7yrs.) and so forth.

The above Mahadasha cycle is for 'Vimshotri' cycle, which has total duration of 120 years and is prevalent in North India. For details of Dasha intervening (Antardasha/sub periods/Pratantar Dasha) please refer to the appendix**.

Ready Reckoner

How to calculate the Antardasha (Intervening Period) or sub-period

Suppose we want to calculate the Antardasha of Jupiter in the Mahadasha of Jupiter. The following method may be adopted:

16 (Mahadasha of Jupiter) × 16 (Mahadasha of Jupiter) = 256

The first two digits signify the no. of months. The third digit should be multiplied by 3 to get the no. of days. Thus, 256 means 25 months and 6 × 3 = 18 i.e., 2 years 1 month and 18 days.

How to calculate Pratantar Dasha (sub-sub period)

First Method: Suppose we want to calculate Jupiter's Pratantar in Rahu's Mahadasha and Moon's Antardasha adopt the following formula:

16 (Jupiter's Period) × 18 (Rahu's Period) × 10/Moon's period) = 2880 days

Divide it by 40 : 2880 ÷ 40 = 72 days i.e. 2 months 12 days.

Second Method for computing Antardasha:

Co-efficient of Mahadasha Lord = Mahadasha years × 3 days.

Sun's Coefficient is 6 × 3 = 18 days
Moon's .... 10 × 3 = 30 ......
Mars's .... 7 × 3 = 21 ......
Rahu's .... 18 × 3 = 54 ......
Jupiter's .... 16 × 3 = 48 ......
Saturn's .... 19 × 3 = 57 ......
Mercury's .... 17 × 3 = 51 ......
Ketu's .... 7 × 3 = 21 ......
Venus's .... 20 × 3 = 60 ......

**Note: For greater details, please refer to chapter no. 7 of my book *Horoscope Reading* published by M/s Pustak Mahal, Daryaganj, New Delhi.

Now if you want to know the Antardasha/sub-period of a particular planet in the Mahadasha of another planet, adopt the following method:

Example

(a) Antardasha of Sun in Sun → 6 × 18 = 108 days.

(b) .... Jupiter in Sun → 16 × 18 = 288 days.

(c) .... Jupiter in Rahu →16 × 54 = 864 days i.e. 28 months = 24 days.

(d) .... Saturn in Rahu →19 × 54 = 1026 days i.e. 34 months 6 days (2 years 10 months 6 days).

(e) .... Saturn in Venus → 19 × 60 = 1140 i.e. 38 months = 3 years 2 months only.

But the method at no. 1 is simple and easy to understand. For the convenience of readers, comprehensive table showing periods of Mahadasha, Antardasha and Pratantar Dasha are given in the attached appendix.

Ashtottari System of Mahadasha

This system of calculating Mahadasha is in vogue in some parts of South India, but the Astrologers prefer the Vimshottari system (as discussed in detail in the preceding pages). In this system the wheel of life is fixed at 108 years and every planet has been allotted certain years of span:

Planet	Sun	Moon	Mars	Mercury	Saturn	Jupiter	Rahu	Venus
Duration	6 yrs.	15 yrs.	8 yrs.	17 yrs.	10 yrs.	19 yrs.	12 yrs.	21 yrs.

Dasha at the time of birth is calculated from the position of Moon at birth, as is the case with Vimshottari system.

How to determine 'Antardasha' in Ashtottari System

Suppose we want to calculate the Antardasha of Jupiter in the Mahadasha of Moon. We adopt the following formula:

Example no. 1: 15 (Moon's Mahadasha) × 19 (Jupiter's Mahadasha) + 108 (Total wheel of life)

$$= \frac{15 \times 19}{108} = \frac{285}{108} \text{years}$$

$$= \frac{285}{108} \times 12 = 31 \text{ months} = 20 \text{ days i.e. 2 years 7 months 20 days.}$$

Example no. 2: Antardasha of Moon in Saturn

$$\frac{15 \times 10 \times 12}{108} = \frac{50}{3} \text{ months} = 16 \text{ months} = 20 \text{ days i.e.1 year 4 months 20 days.}$$

As regards the results, the same predictions may be made, as is the case with 'Vimshottari' system. An exalted planet will obviously show better results during its Mahadasha, whereas, a debilitating planet will bring misfortune.

Horoscopes in South India are prepared in clockwise direction

12 Pisces	1 Aries	2 Taurus, Saturn	3 Gemini, Ketu	4 Cancer, Venus
11 Aquarius				5 Leo, Sun, Mercury, Mars (Lagna)
10 Capricorn	9 Sagittarius, Rahu, Jupiter	8 Scorpio	7 Libra	6 Virgo, Moon

In other parts of India, horoscopes are prepared in the anticlockwise direction.

The following is the birth chart of the above sample according to North Indian system:

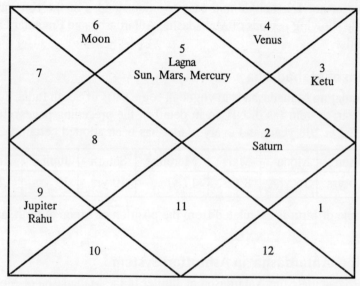

Fig. 2

Important Points to remember while making predictions on the basis of Mahadasha etc.

(i) During the Antardasha of a benefic or a friendly planet in the main Dasha of an exalted planet, one gets promotion, happiness and physical well being.

(ii) During the Antardasha of a debilitating/malefic planet in the Mahadasha of a benefic planet results are partially good and partially bad.

(iii) During the Antardasha of a malefic planet in the Mahadasha of a benefic planet, one suffers a lot.

(iv) During the Antardasha of a benefic planet in the Main Dasha of a malefic planet, results are partially good and partially bad.

(v) During the Antardasha of an enemy planet in an otherwise Mahadasha of an exalted planet, results are partially good and partially bad. One may achieve one's goal but after facing opposition.

34

Constellation (Nakshatras') Information

S.No.	Name of Nakshatras	Shape
1.	Ashwani	Face of horse
2.	Bharni	Yoni (Vagina)
3.	Kartika	Curved knife
4.	Rohini	Cart
5.	Mrigshira	Face of deer
6.	Ardra	Jewel
7.	Punarvarsha	House
8.	Pushya	Arrow
9.	Ashlesha	Circular
10.	Magha	House
11.	Purva phaguni	Raised seat (Dais)
12.	Uttar phaguni	Small cot
13.	Hast	Hand
14.	Chitra	Pearl
15.	Swati	Coral
16.	Vishakha	Arched doorway
17.	Anuradha	A fold of wrinkle
18.	Jyeshtha	Circular earring
19.	Moola	Tail of a lion
20.	Purvashada	Tusk of an elephant
21.	Uttarashada	Dais or raised seat
22.	Shravana	Aeroplane
23.	Dhanishtha	Bagpiper (Musical instrument)
24.	Shatbhisha	Elliptic
25.	Purva bhadrapad	Raised seat
26.	Uttar bhadrapad	Twins
27.	Revati	Drum

Beside these 27 Nakshatras, there is another one named 'Abhijit'. It occupies the last 15 ghatis (15×24 = 360 minutes i.e. 6 hours) of Uttarshada Nakshatra. The first four ghatis (4×24 = 96 minutes = 1 hour 36 minutes) of Shravana Nakshatra. Abhijit occupies only 19 ghatis i.e. 456 minutes. Ordinarily one Nakshatra has a life of 60 ghatis i.e. 24 hours.

Constellations and their stages

Every constellation has been divided into four stages or 'Charanas', such as 1st, 2nd, 3rd, & 4th stages. The following chart elucidates the various stages of each sign (Raashi).

S.No.	Name of sign (Raashi)	Stages of Constellation
1.	Aries	All the four stages of 'Ashwani', 'Bharni' & one quarter of 'Kartika'.
2.	Taurus	The remaining three stages of 'Kartika', all the four stages of 'Rohini' and the first two stages of 'Mrigshira'.
3.	Gemini	Last two stages of 'Mrigshira', all the four stages of 'Ardra' and the first three stages of 'Punarvasu'.
4.	Cancer	The last two stages of 'Punarvasu' and all the four stages of 'Pushya' and 'Ashlesha'.
5.	Leo	All the four stages of 'Magha' and 'Purva phaguni' and the first stage of 'Uttar phaguni'.
6.	Virgo	The last three stages of 'Uttar phaguni', all the four stages of 'Hast' and the first two stages of 'Chitra'.
7.	Libra	The last two stages of 'Chitra', all the four stages of 'Swati' and the first three stages of 'Vishakha'.
8.	Scorpio	The last quarter of 'Vishakha'; all the four of 'Anuradha' and 'Jyeshtha'.
9.	Sagittarius	All the four stages of 'Moola' and 'Purushadha' and the first quarter of 'Uttarashada'.
10.	Capricorn	The last three stages of 'Uttarashada', all the four stages of 'Shravana' and the first two stages of 'Dhanishtha'.
11.	Aquarius	The last two stages of 'Dhanishtha', all the four stages of 'Shatbhisha' and the first three stages of 'Purva bhadrapad'.
12.	Pisces	The last quarter of 'Purva bhadrapad', and all the four stages of 'Uttar bhadrapad' and 'Revati'.

'Abhijit' constellation is counted in the Capricorn sign.

Jurisdiction of a constellation

Zodiac is divided into 27 constellations and each constellation has a jurisdiction of 13°20' of longitude. Formula is very simple. Divide 360° (heavenly sphere being 360°) by 27 (number of constellations), it comes out to 13°20'.

Jurisdiction of each constellation, therefore, is as under:

S.No.	Constellation	From (Degree & Minutes)	To (Degree & Minutes)
1.	Ashwani	0°0'	13°20'
2.	Bharmi	13°20'	26°40'
3.	Kartika	26°40'	40°0'
4.	Rohini	40°0'	53°20'
5.	Mrigshira	53°20'	66°40'
6.	Ardra	66°40'	80°0'
7.	Punarvarsha	80°0'	93°20'
8.	Pushya	93°20'	106°40'
9.	Ashlesha	106°40'	120°0'
10.	Magha	120°0'	133°20'
11.	Purva phaguni	133°20'	146°40'
12.	Uttra phaguni	146°40'	160°0'
13.	Hast	160°0'	173°20'
14.	Chitra	173°20'	186°40'
15.	Swati	186°40'	200°0'
16.	Vishakha	200°0'	213°20'
17.	Anuradha	213°20'	226°40'
18.	Jyeshtha	226°40'	240°0'
19.	Moola	240°0'	253°20'
20.	Purvashada	253°20'	266°40'
21.	Uttarashada	266°40'	280°0'
22.	Shravana	280°0'	293°20'
23.	Dhanishtha	293°20'	306°40'
24.	Shatbhisha	306°40'	320°0'
25.	Purva bhadrapad	320°0'	333°20'
26.	Uttar bhadrapad	333°20'	346°40'
27.	Revati	346°40'	360°0'

Further, each constellation has four stages or feet (charanas); it may be divided by four i.e. 13°20' ÷ 4 = 3°20', starting from zero. In other words, every stage or charana has jurisdiction over 3°20', totalling 13°20' for each constellation.

Example

Sign/Raashi	Degree & Minutes	Constellation Stage
Aries	0°0'	Ashwani (1)
Aries	3°20'	Ashwani (2)
Aries	6°40'	Ashwani (3)
Aries	10°0'	Ashwani (4)
Aries	13°20'	Bharni (1)
Aries	16°40'	Bharni (2)
Aries	20°0'	Bharni (3)
Aries	23°20'	Bharni (4)
Aries	26°40'	Kartika (1)

And so on and so forth. Next comes Taurus, then Gemini etc.

Appendix

Ready-reckoner showing the Mahadasha period and the Antardasha periods (sub-periods) of a planet:

Main Lord	1. Sun (6 years)				2. Moon (10 years)				3. Mars (7 years)			
		yrs	mths	days		yrs	mths	days		yrs	mths	days
Sub-period	Sun	0	3	18	Moon	0	10	0	Mars	0	4	27
	Moon	0	6	0	Mars	0	7	0	Rahu	1	0	18
	Mars	0	4	6	Rahu	1	6	0	Jupiter	0	11	6
	Rahu	0	10	24	Jupiter	1	4	0	Saturn	1	1	9
	Jupiter	0	9	18	Saturn	1	7	0	Mercury	0	11	27
	Saturn	0	11	12	Mercury	1	5	0	Ketu	0	4	27
	Mercury	0	10	6	Ketu	0	7	0	Venus	1	2	0
	Ketu	0	4	6	Venus	1	8	0	Sun	0	4	6
	Venus	1	0	0	Sun	0	6	0	Moon	0	7	0

Main Lord	4. Rahu (18 years)				5. Jupiter (16 years)				6. Saturn (19 years)			
		yrs	mths	days		yrs	mths	days		yrs	mths	days
Sub-period	Rahu	2	8	12	Jupiter	2	1	18	Saturn	3	0	3
	Jupiter	2	4	24	Saturn	2	6	12	Mercury	2	8	9
	Saturn	2	10	6	Mercury	2	3	6	Ketu	1	1	9
	Mercury	2	6	18	Ketu	0	11	6	Venus	3	2	0
	Ketu	1	0	18	Venus	2	8	0	Sun	0	11	12
	Venus	3	0	0	Sun	0	9	18	Moon	1	7	0
	Sun	0	10	24	Moon	1	4	0	Mars	1	1	9
	Moon	1	6	0	Mars	0	11	6	Rahu	2	10	6
	Mars	1	0	18	Rahu	2	4	24	Jupiter	2	6	12

Main Lord	7. Mercury (17 years)				8. Ketu (7 years)				9. Venus (20 years)			
		yrs	mths	days		yrs	mths	days		yrs	mths	days
Sub-period	Mercury	2	4	27	Ketu	0	4	27	Venus	3	4	0
	Ketu	0	11	27	Venus	1	2	0	Sun	1	0	0
	Venus	2	10	0	Sun	0	4	6	Moon	1	8	0
	Sun	0	10	6	Moon	0	7	0	Mars	1	2	0
	Moon	1	5	0	Mars	0	4	27	Rahu	3	0	0
	Mars	0	11	27	Rahu	1	0	18	Jupiter	2	8	0
	Rahu	2	6	18	Jupiter	0	11	6	Saturn	3	2	0
	Jupiter	2	3	6	Saturn	1	1	9	Mercury	2	10	0
	Saturn	2	8	9	Mercury	0	11	27	Ketu	1	2	0

For greater details, please refer to my book *Horoscope Reading* published by M/s Pustak Mahal Publishers, Daryaganj, New Delhi.

OOO

Birth Chart (Horoscope)*

Horoscope – Map of the Hour – is the chief operational aid of an astrologer. Just as a soldier cannot fight without a gun and the bullets, so is the case with the astrologer. He needs the following equipment to cast the birth chart of a child born at a particular time, date and place:

1. Date of birth
2. Time of birth
3. Longitude and Latitude of place of birth
4. Ephemeris

Before casting a horoscope, convert the Indian Standard Time into Local Mean Time. Conversion method is very simple.

Suppose, a child is born in Mumbai at 10:00 AM IST. First calculate the difference between 72°50' East (longitude of Mumbai) and 82°30' East (central meridian for whole of India). It comes out to be 9°40'. Thereafter multiply 9°40' by 4 minutes which is equal to 38 minutes and 40 seconds. In this case, the local mean time is (10 hrs. 00 min. 00 sec.) – (00 hrs. 38 min. 40 sec.) = (09 hrs 21 min. 20 sec.). Thus the local mean time is = 9:21:20 AM.

Note: (1) If the longitude of the place is more than central meridian, then add the difference and if it is less, then subtract.

(2) The difference in sunrise is 15 minutes for a difference of 1° longitude with same latitude.

We will not go into the details as 'computerized horoscopes' give complete information on the birth chart, Raashi chart, constellations, mahadasha, and intervening dashas. Similarly, complete and readymade material is available in all the Panchangs/Jantris (ephemerides). One can cast a horoscope with complete information from Panchangs.

We have, nevertheless, discussed in detail constellations, Mahadasha periods and placement of planets in chapters 3 & 4.

***Note:** For exact casting of Horoscope, please refer to chapter no. 6 of my book *Horoscope Reading* published by M/s Pustak Mahal Publishers, Daryaganj, New Delhi.

OOO

Houses

Distinction between the houses and signs (Raashis) should be clearly understood. Here is a birth chart, which will explain their relationship:

Right Side: I to VI Houses and **Left Side:** VII to XII Houses

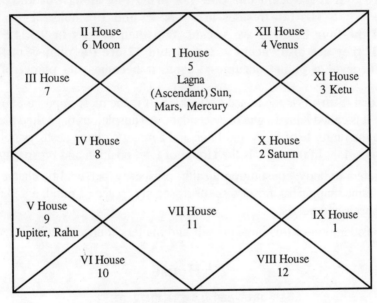

Fig. 3

Lagna or Ascendant is the First House, No. 5 indicates the sign (Raashi). It means that Sun, Mars and Mercury are occupying the first house in Leo sign (Raashi No. 5). Moon occupies the 2nd House in Virgo (Sign No. 6) and so on and so forth.

In all, there are twelve houses and each house has its own distinctive nature and function.

1st House (Lagna or Ascendant)

घर पहला है तख़्त हज़ारी ग्रह-फल राजा कुंडली का
ज्योतिष में इसे लग्न भी कहते झगड़ा मनुष है माया का
लग्न यदि ख़ुद ख़ाली होवे किस्मत साथ न आई हो
किस्मत उसकी सातवें बैठे या घर चौथे दसवें हो
मुठ्ठी के घर चारों ख़ाली नौ-तीन-ग्यारह पांचवें हो
यह घर भी ख़ाली होवें दो-छः-आठवें हों।
किस्मत का वह मालिक होगा बैठा तख़्त पर उसके जो हों।

It is king's throne, master of all that it surveys.
It is called Lagna (Ascendant) in astrology –
And governs both the soul and worldly affairs.
If it is vacant one does not bring fate alongwith him
His fate resides in 7th & 4th and 10th houses.
If all the four kendras are vacant, fate then resides in 9,3,11,5 houses.
If they are also vacant – 2, 6, 8 and 12 are the planets of fate.
Whenever a planet occupies Lagna, it becomes the planet of fate.

Presiding Lord (Sun): It is the house of the king. It is the most important house in the birth-chart, that is why it is called King Lagna or Ascendant. An auspicious or exalted planet in the house raises the man to the pinnacle of glory and fame and a malefic planet destroys not only health but also wealth and position. In fact, this is the House of fate, position and prosperity.

This house refers to body, constitution, health, prosperity, personality, character, appearance, glory, name and fame, happiness, misery, status in society, peace of mind, age, knowledge etc. It represents head, neck and pelvis.

The chief consideration of this house is self and matters connected with it.

2nd House

घर पक्का दूजा गुरु ब्रह्मगाय स्थान है।
मिलता जहां पर है इकट्ठा मान व ज़र ससुराल है।
घर चल कर जो आवे दूजे ग्रह किस्मत बन जाता है।
अगर घर दसवां ख़ाली होवे सोया हुआ कहलाता है।
पाप की बैठक घर गुरु के गृहस्थ शुक्र बन जाता है।

It is a permanent house where resides Jupiter, the great Guru.
It is the temple where dwell Brahma and holy cow.
It confers all wealth and comforts, esteem, respect and money from in-laws
Planet occupying this house becomes the planet of fate.
If No. 10 is vacant, it becomes asleep.
Even sinners like Rahu shun their evil ways.
And Venus sheds her enmity and offers marital comforts.

Presiding Lord (Jupiter): It is the sacred temple of God; hence it denotes domestic happiness, personal fate, honour, wealth, prosperity, old age, precious metal etc. It also governs face, right eye, mouth, right shoulder and quality of speech. It also refers to one's faith in God, truth versus falsehood, generosity or miserliness, oratory etc.

Being God's dwelling place, even Rahu and other wicked planets give up their evil designs & deeds and bow before the great Guru i.e. Jupiter. This house, therefore, is very important for predicting promotion, happiness, prosperity and better status. It is the abode of goddess Laxmi, showering wealth and happiness upon the person. It confers wealth and respect from in-laws. The planet in this house becomes exalted provided house no. 8 is vacant. In the case of Jupiter, it remains dormant or asleep, if there is no planet in house no. 8.

House no. 2 does not aspect house no. 8, but it aspects house no. 6 in a friendly manner (house no. 8 aspects house no. 2). In this house, Moon, Venus and Saturn give Raashi (Sign) results. House no. 9 is the ocean full of monsoons and house no. 2 is just like series of mountains where the monsoons hover and bless the hills & valleys with beneficent rains.

It is made all the more exalted if it is occupied by Moon.

3ʳᵈ House

घर तीजा है पक्का मंगल धन-दौलत के जाने का।
ख़्वेशो अकारब भाई अपने या चोरी-अय्यारी का।
इस घर का जो रंग है ख़ूनी असर होता भी ख़ूनी है।
ग्रह जो इस घर बदी पे होवे कहलाता वह कष्टी है।

Mars being its Lord signals wealth's exit
Refers to relatives, brothers, theft and cunningness.
Being bloody in colour; its effect is gory.
When it resorts to evil; it gives all types of bloody trouble.

Presiding Lord (Mars): This house is reserved for real brothers, sisters, relatives, servants, valour, both physical and moral death of parents, right ear, throat, neck, right arm, upper part of chest, illness, road to the other world, and above all, an outlet for wealth i.e. expenditure.

Moon in the House confers life and saves man from misfortunes, provided it is not destroyed by Saturn from House no. 8. If house no. 11 is the house of income, house no. 3 is the house of expenditure. If house no. 3 is occupied by malefic planets and no. 6 and no. 8 are also malefic, there will be a death like situation, but the saving grace will be the planet in house no. 12, whether friend or enemy of the planet in house no. 3. For example: Mars in no. 12 and Ketu in no. 3 (although both of them are enemies) will confer wealth. Similarly, Mercury in no. 12 and Jupiter or Saturn in no. 3 will bestow wealth and honour, although Mercury is Jupiter's enemy.

If Venus and Rahu are in no. 12, and Saturn is in no. 3, Rahu will not be able to harm Venus, as Venus will be aspected by a friend i.e. Saturn. It has been often noticed that Rahu-Venus in house no. 12 often leads to separation between husband and wife or death of the spouse, if it is not aspected by Saturn from house no. 3. If there are two or more planets in house no. 3, the planets of house no. 12 will have individual effect – good or bad.

4th House

चौथे चन्द्र को पेट माता और - ठंडी रोशनी माना है।

चार तरफ का पानी दुनिया - दूध समुद्र दरिया है।

दिल सफर माता, धरती, घोड़ा तरफ शमाली मशरिक है

चरिन्दे चावल दूध पिलाते बज़ाज़ी मुर्गे आबी है।

राहु-केतु घर चौथे में - पाप से हरदम डरते हैं।

तारें खा न तारें मरज़ी - कसम पाप की करते हैं।

Moon, the presiding goddess refers to
mother's womb and refreshing cool silvery light.
An ocean surrounded on all four sides by overflowing milk and not water.
She presides over heart, travel, mother, earth and horse.
It refers to north-eastern horizon.
It also means birds, rice, milk and water birds – duck and swan.
Rahu-Ketu are scared of mother.
And vow to shun evil in her domain.

Presiding Lord (Moon): It refers to education, conveyances, mother, landed property, treasure, intelligence, house, righteous conduct, nobility of soul, piety, perfumes, clothes, right portion of nose, thighs, good reputation, ancestral property, abundance of rice and milk etc. It denotes 'mother's lap and her blessings'. It fills man's coffer with wealth, ocean of milk, and makes his life comfortable and easy. Even Rahu and Ketu shun their evil designs and take oath before the moon (mother) not to indulge in diabolical acts. Planets in this house always help the man at the time of distress, especially old age.

In this house Venus, Mars and Ketu confer 'Raashi effect'. Saturn is like a poisonous snake and Mars in Cancer is malefic. Benefic Jupiter gives exalted results only when it occupies house no. 2 and 4 in the annual chart. Naturally this house denotes God's plenty by Mother's grace.

When any planet occupies house no. 4 and moon is malefic in a house outside the four kendras (1,4,7,10), the planets in house no. 4, whether friends or foes, will not adversely affect Moon. For example, if Ketu is in house no. 4 and Moon is in house no. 8 or 11, Ketu will no longer be malefic. It may also be noted that if house no. 3, 6 and 8 are malefic in the birth chart, then house no. 4 becomes the excuse for death. Further, Moon exercises good influence if house no. 4 is vacant and Moon does not occupy any of the four kendras i.e. 1,4,7 & 10. Even if exalted Jupiter occupies house no. 4, which confers wealth & prosperity, it will be dormant and asleep if house no. 10 is vacant.

5th House

घर पांचवां है ज्ञान गुरु का - तेज तपस्या होता है।

हवा, रोशनी, लड़के, पोते - वक्त आईंदा होता है।

औलाद जन्म ताउमर बुढ़ापा - महल, बचत औलाद के हैं।

अक्ल ज्ञान, समझ हो साया, इल्म, सबर, ईमान भी है।

रवि गुरु दोनों से कोई घर दसवें जा बैठा हो।

पांचवें घर खा दोस्त इसका ज़हरी दुश्मन होता है।

Presided over by Sun, it refers to Guru's knowledge, fame & penance.
Air, brightness, sons, grandsons, future progeny.
Children, life from birth to old age and mansions left for offspring.
Knowledge, intelligence, fame, faith and spiritualism.
Sun or Jupiter occupying 10th house completely destroys planet of this
House, whether friend or foe.

Presiding Lord (Sun and Jupiter): This house refers to children (sons and daughters) and their fate and future, knowledge, eminence, wisdom, intelligence, legacy of good actions, writing of books, right cheek, right side of heart and right thigh, honesty, integrity, hot temper etc. In fact, this house is the repository of knowledge and bright children.

If house no. 10 is occupied by Jupiter or Sun or both, they will strike at the very roots of the planet in house no. 5 and fill it with poison, even though house no. 5 is occupied by a friend of Jupiter or Sun. Remedy lies in burying the articles concerning the enemies of planet in house no. 5, in the foundation of the house or in the earth. An enemy planet in house no. 6 also destroys the planet in house no. 5, in that case, bury the articles pertaining to the enemy in the earth, if house no. 8 is malefic.

If malefic planets occupy house no. 3, 4 or 9, they will exercise malefic influence on house no. 5. Further, malefic Saturn and Venus exercise bad effect but that effect is minimised and nullified if Moon is exalted. If Sun-Venus or Sun-Jupiter are placed in house no. 5 in the horoscope, man suffers from ill health whenever any wicked planet or Venus occupies house no. 1 in the Annual Chart. But if Venus, Mercury or any wicked planet is in house no. 5 in the birth chart, then man also suffers from ill health when Sun or Jupiter occupies house no. 1 in the annual chart.

6th House

घर छठे में पाताल में बैठे केतु-बुध (लड़का-लड़की) इकट्ठे हों
दुश्मन गो वह बाहम होते इसजा वह नहीं लड़ते हैं।
केतू लड़का तो बुध है लड़की - दुम (बुध) कुत्ते (केतू) की साथी है।
रिश्तेदार हों माता-पिता के अक्ल, सफर खुद ख़ाकी है।
पाताल ख़ाली घर जब तक रहता नेक असर कुल देता है।

Ketu (Son), Mercury (daughter) together in this nether world.
Though sworn enemies never quarrel.
Both are like the tail (Mercury) and dog (Ketu); Living together perforce.
Relatives of parents; intelligence and travels on land are governed by this house.
Vacant 6th house confers good results.

Presiding Lord (Mercury and Ketu): This house refers to the **underworld** (Lord Yama and Pluto – the God of death), maternal uncles, worries, enemies, secret, help, compassion, litigation, the right side of calf, chest and jaws, disease, venereal diseases, fear, misfortunes, wounds, opposition and enmity.

House no. 2 helps house no. 6. Mars and Saturn in this house always give 'Raashi' effect. Saturn in no. 6 adversely aspects house no. 2 and destroys it even though occupied by a friend. Mars in no. 4 will not be malefic, if Sun and Moon are in house no. 6. Rahu and Mercury will never give bad results in no. 6. Except Sun, Moon and Jupiter (which will give 'Raashi' result), all other planets in this house will confer their own planet's effect.

If Mercury and Ketu jointly occupy this house, Ketu (son) becomes debilitating and Mercury (daughter) is exalted in this house and will never adversely aspect house no. 2 and kendras (1,4,7,10).

7th House

घर सातवां है पक्का शुक्र – घूमता बुध (आकाश) ऊपर का है।

दोनों इकट्ठे चक्की चलती – निचला (धरती) शुक्र माना है।

बुध सातवें का चक-घुमारां – मिट्टी शुक्र होती है।

शुक्र-बुध जब दो हों इकट्ठे – शनि भी उमदा होता है।

अन्न दौलत की कमी न कोई – घी मिट्टी से निकलता है।

Sky (Mercury) and earth (Venus) are the potter's wheels, conferring all benefits. Mercury is the touchstone of intelligence and making the mud pot is the Venus. When both are together, Saturn too becomes benefic. No dearth of wealth and gains. Both turning mud into ghee and gold.

Presiding Lord (Venus): This house denotes domestic happiness or domestic discord, marriage, spouse (husband or wife), sexual desires, extra-marital affairs, journey to distant places, the mouth, navel, and two feet, good perfumes, partaking of delicious foods, soft drinks, couple of sweethearts or wives, urinary troubles, sex organs. Passion, marriage, love and marital happiness are the hallmarks of this house. It is, in fact, the house of goddess Laxmi (the goddess of wealth).

Saturn, Venus and Mercury are exalted, whereas Sun (except in Leo) is malefic. When Venus or Moon (female planet) in this house is associated with two or more planets, its effect will be visible on male planet. In other words, instead of wife (Venus) or mother (Moon) effect will be felt on Jupiter (father) or Mars (brother) or Sun (self) – whether good or bad.

Jupiter, Sun (debilitating), Moon and Rahu give 'Raashi' results in this house.

8th House

घर आठवां है मौत नागहानि – मंगल बद ही लेते हैं।

ग्रह नर में से कोई हो आठवें – मौत टली ही लेते हैं।

घर आठवां जब बदी पे आवे – दो-छ: भी आ मिलते हैं।

बारह खाह दूर ही बैठा – फैसला इसका लेते हैं।

Mars malefic is the Lord of inevitable death. If a male planet occupies it; one evades death. When the planet of this house resorts to destruction and evil 2 & 6 also aid and abet it. But planet in 12 becomes the final arbitrator.

Presiding Lord (Mars – debilitating): It is the house of disease and death, cruel and callous justice, longevity of life, diseases of genitals, anus, urinary troubles, debts, loans, cremation ground i.e. death, bad name, notoriety, ill-fame. Scorpio, the lord of this sign, is the symbol of disease & death and, hence, malefic.

This house is the house of cruel and inhuman justice i.e. tit for tat or tooth for a tooth and eye for an eye. It knows no compassion or mercy. If Sun or Moon or Jupiter individually or collectively occupy this house, they remain confined to this house and will not aspect no. 12 or no. 2. They will conquer death. Further, Saturn or Mars or Moon are always good if alone in this house. But, if two or all three of them are conjunct, they will spell disease and death. Moon will destroy mental health and wealth and Mars (malefic) will wreak havoc. Mercury or Mars in no. 8 is always malefic, but Mercury and Mars together in house no. 8 are good, provided Saturn does not occupy house no. 2, otherwise Mars will be malefic and will lead to death.

Moon will give its 'Raashi' effect in the house. A weak or malefic Moon in this house leads to epilepsy, depression, insanity and palpitation of heart.

9th House

घर नौवां है गुरुबजुर्गी – जड़ बुनियाद ग्रह नौ की ।

मकान जदी जो होवे अपना – परोपकार बुजुर्गों का ।

उमर दादा या बाप हो अपनी – ज़माना है खेल-खिलाड़ी का ।

घर कच्चा ख़ाह पक्का होवे – हाल है दुनिया ग़ैबी का ।

घर नौवां मरकज़ है कुंडली – धरती का जो मैहवर है ।

जिसम में रूह की हरकत गिनते – हाकम सब ही ग्रह का है ।

Jupiter, its Lord, refers to ancestral blessings and is the foundation of all nine planets. Ancestral house confers ancestral benefactions.
It refers to father's, grandfather's and even one's own age.
House whether pucca or of mud speaks of blessings of God.
This House, being the centre of horoscope, is the fulcrum around which fate revolves.
It enlivens body with soul and is the master of all planets.

Presiding Lord (Jupiter): This house deals with inherited property, lands and legacy left by ancestors, religious inclination, piety, fame, nobility, good deeds, charitable acts, visit to holy places, long life of parents/grandparents, goodness inherited from ancestors, foundation of one's own fate, comforts, previous birth, left cheek, left side of heart and knees. It is, in fact, Jupiter's abode and temple. If Jupiter is exalted, best results are available and if malefic, results are not to one's desires. Mercury or Venus or malefic Mars will confer bad results. Saturn will bestow best results for sixty years. Ketu, Sun, Moon, Mars (benefic) will give exalted results. Exalted Jupiter alone in this house, without any adverse aspect, confers royal status on man. Jupiter acts as 'Huma' – a legendary bird, which makes a man king, if it flies over his head.

Further references and explanations

House no. 9 means the foundation of fate and is like a boundless ocean. House no. 2 is the foundation of all the nine planets and no. 4 is the foundation of house no. 2. When house no. 3 and 9 are vacant, no. 9 is awakened by house no. 2. Further, when a dormant planet of horoscope occupies house no. 9 in the annual chart, it becomes active and confers good results.

(a) Sun in house no. 8 occupies house no. 9 during 22nd year, hence its good results for 22 years i.e. up to 44th year.

(b) Moon in house no. 8 occupies house no. 9 during 24th year, hence its best results from 24th to 48th year.

(c) Mars in house no. 2 occupies house no. 9 during 28th year, hence its good results from 28th to 56th year.

(d) Jupiter in house no. 2 occupies house no. 9 during 16th year, hence its good results from 16th to 32nd year.

(e) Saturn in house no. 8 occupies house no. 9 during 36th year, hence its good results from 36th to 72nd year.

(f) Mercury in house no. 3 occupies house no. 9 in 17th year, hence its bad results from 17th to 34th year.

(g) Venus in house no. 12 occupies house no. 9 in 25th year, hence its bad results only during 25th year, if it is adversely aspected by house no. 3 or 5. Otherwise good results.

(h) Rahu in house no. 4 occupies house no. 9 in 42nd year, hence its good results from 42nd to 84th year.

(i) Ketu in house no. 8 occupies house no. 9 in 48th year, hence its good results from 48th to 96th year.

10th House

घर दसवां है शनि का अपना – खुद वरासत लाता है ।
सुख पिदर को या उसे होवे – साल मकां इकत्तीस रहता है ।
चार तरफ की चीज़ें दुनियां – चालाकी मक्कारी हो ।
रिश्तेदार हों गैर-हकीकी – दुःख ज़हमत बीमारी हो ।
सांप का घर और आंख की पुतली – रंग स्याह भी होते हैं ।
गाय-भैंस हो लोहे रंगी – दुम ज़हरीले होते हैं ।
ग्रह पापी उस टेवे में जैसे कहीं भी उसके बैठे हों ।
फल वैसे ही घर दसवें के उस टेवे में होते हैं ।

It's Saturn's own house and is the architect of its own fate.
Refers to father's delight and house which he often builds.
And also it has four eyes and is full of evil and cunningness.
Relations – real or distant – grief and sickness it governs.
Being snake's dwelling, like eye's retina it is all black.
Iron coloured like cows and buffaloes its sting is fatal.
Sinful planets residing in any house give the same result in 10th house.

Presiding Lord (Saturn): It refers to rank, status, profession, position, honour from state, ruling authority, father's patronage, means of livelihood, field of action, trade, commerce, general success in life, the left nostril, left thigh etc. If malefic, man is cunning and sly like a fox or a wounded snake.

Mars is exalted in this house provided it is all alone and is not adversely aspected by another planet. If this house is adversely aspected or destroyed by enemy planets, the whole horoscope is termed 'blind horoscope' and even exalted Saturn fails to redeem it.

It is also the house of deception. Whenever a planet occupies this house in the annual chart, refer to 8th and 2nd house. If house no. 8 is malefic, this house will be doubly malefic and if house no. 2 is benefic, it will be doubly benefic. If house no. 8 and house no. 2 are vacant, then look to house no. 3, 5 and 11 for help. If they are also vacant, Saturn's position will decide the final verdict – whether good or bad.

Role of Rahu, Ketu and Mercury is suspicious in this house. In that case, if Saturn is benefic, results are good, otherwise bad. If mutually hostile planets occupy house no. 10, such a horoscope is like a blind man finding his way with difficulty. In that case, benefic Moon helps.

11th House

घर ग्यारह का शनि है – मालिक – पर दरबार गुरु का है ।
घड़ा भरा पानी है बेशक – बरतता तो गुरु ही है ।
फकीर की झोली की किस्मत गिनते – जन्म वक्त खुद आमद है ।
शनि गुरु का हल्फ उठावे – फैसला करता बाद में है ।
धन-दौलत है ग्यारह आता – घर तीजे से जाता है ।
मंगल कुंडली कहीं हो बैठा – फैसला इसका होता है ।
बुध-गुरु नहीं इस घर अच्छे – या के चंद्र बैठा हो ।
पाप अकेला असर अकेला – तीन, पांच, नौ, ग्यारह ।
शनि वली का साथ मिले तो – असर बढ़े गुना ग्यारह ।

Saturn may be its Lord, but it is Jupiter's Durbar.
Though pitcher is full of water, is governed by Jupiter.
It's the faqir's bag taking out with sleight of hand fate at birth.
Saturn swears by Jupiter but decides later
House of wealth it is, but 3rd House signals its exit.
Mars situated anywhere is the final arbitrator.
Mercury, Jupiter here are not good and else the Moon.
Sinner gives effect singly in 3, 5, 9, 11 houses.
But, when Saturn joins, its effect is multiplied manifold.

Presiding Lord (Jupiter/Saturn): Saturn is the Lord of this house, but, Jupiter holds its 'Durbar' here. Hence, Saturn vows before the great guru i.e. Jupiter to shun its evil ways.

This is the house of income, gains, acquisition of gold, jewels, all items of luxury, fulfilment of cherished desires, field of fate, luxurious living, houses, left ear, arm and left testicles.

This is the house of gains and income and not that of expenditure. House no. 3 denotes expenditure. Exalted Mars in this house decides about wealth. Exalted Rahu, Ketu and Saturn confer best results in this house. These wicked planets in this house become the planets of fate when they occupy 1st house in the annual chart (23,36,48,57,72,84 etc.). Malefic planets, however, bring misery and destruction and even lead to accidents.

An exalted Mars in this house is like the honeybee, which fills the beehives with honey. In other words, his coffers will overflow with wealth. Ketu in house no. 11 in the annual chart bestows son, provided Moon and Jupiter are not in house no. 5. Further, if house no. 3 is occupied by Sun, Moon, Mars (friend of Jupiter), house no. 11 will give best results. House no. 3 aspects house no. 11 and if there are planets in both the houses, house no. 11 will be deemed to be awake. Ketu in this house destroys Moon and Jupiter destroys Rahu and vice-versa.

It may be noted that only wicked planets, if exalted, confer best results in this house. However, if a planet of house no. 11 occupies house no. 8 or house no. 11 in the annual chart, results are not to the liking of the individual. In order to ward off the evil effects, one should not buy material pertaining to that planet. If one has to purchase the material, one should simultaneously purchase a toy or sports material. It will help. Suppose, a man with Saturn in house no. 11 purchases machinery shoes and leather goods, that year (20,34,45,53,67,79 etc.) he must buy toys or sports material also.

The appended table highlights the effects of planets in this house:

Results of Planets in House no. 11:

Name of Planet in House no. 11	Good Results	Bad Results
Sun	The nobler, the more honest and more pious he is, the more exalted status he enjoys for self and children.	If he takes meat and wine, he will be ruined; must shun evil and refrain from drinking.
Moon	There will be abundance of wealth and happiness from children, during the lifetime of mother, provided Jupiter and Ketu are exalted.	Mother may not see the grandson during her lifetime.
Mars	Like a brave tiger crossing all hurdles and achieving his destination and fulfilling all his desires through nobler means and courage of conviction.	Like Hanuman's burnt tail destroying everything i.e. there is dearth of money and livelihood for which he may have to run from pillar to post.
Jupiter	As long as he lives in the joint family, even Saturn will pay respect to Jupiter. Everything fine during father's lifetime.	Most malefic results and loss of income, if he is of bad and loose character and lives separately from father. Lustful conduct will ruin him.
Saturn	Will have the courage to fight against enemies; man of faith and determination; noble; Saturn protects and blesses him with a son.	Most malefic results; may even forsake his children and leave them in lurch when they need him the most.
Mercury	Will keep the needy and the distressed; will save and revive a drowning man; victorious and bold.	Foolish and shortsighted; will destroy others and himself be destroyed.

Name of Planet in House no. 11	Good Results	Bad Results
Venus	Lot of wealth if Mars is exalted or wife's brothers are alive.	Cowardly, chicken-hearted, simpleton, and eunuch, impotent; may incur loss of money.
Rahu	Self-respecting, having faith in his powers; will not demand a penny from parents and in-laws; may lose inherited gold; but self-made rich.	May ruin parents and everything.
Ketu	Ketu's effect 11 times exalted; will have a son when Ketu is in house no. 11, provided Moon and Jupiter are not in house no. 5.	Very bad results regarding son; even Moon and Saturn will give worst results.

12th House

घर बारह है सुख गृहस्थी – गुरु राहू दो बैठे हैं।
मछली ढूंढ़े पानी बादल का – वचन श्राप इकट्ठे हैं।
ख़रचा जाति दिमाग़ की हरकत मर्द औरत का तलुक होता है।
शनि गुरु और राहू टेवे कहीं भी उसके बैठे हों।
फल वैसे ही घर बारह के उस टेवे में होते हैं।

It's house of conjugal bliss, but occupied by Jupiter and Rahu both.
Fish craving for rains from clouds, fulfilment of promise and curse both together.
Personal expenses, brain's movement and relationship of wife-husband.
Saturn, Jupiter and Rahu, in whatever position they are,
Confer similar results in this house.

Presiding Lord (Jupiter and Rahu): This house refers to expenditure, financial losses, final hour of death, conjugal happiness, pleasures of bed, happiness from spouse, bad names, dreams, imprisonment, mental agony, poetic justice, left eye, shoulder, and left part of sexual organs.

Rahu in this house is malefic, and Ketu is exalted. It is the house that listens to all appeals and arbitrates on all appeals, but final appeal lies with house no. 2.

Summary of Lords of Houses and their Nature and Significance

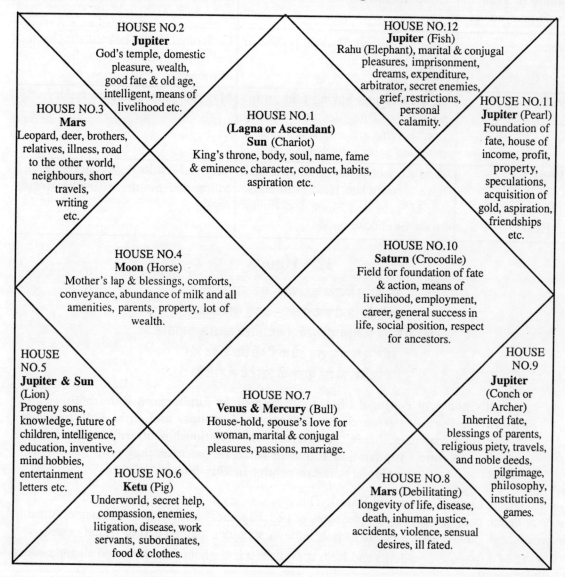

HOUSE NO.2
Jupiter
God's temple, domestic pleasure, wealth, good fate & old age, intelligent, means of livelihood etc.

HOUSE NO.12
Jupiter (Fish)
Rahu (Elephant), marital & conjugal pleasures, imprisonment, dreams, expenditure, arbitrator, secret enemies, grief, restrictions, personal calamity.

HOUSE NO.3
Mars
Leopard, deer, brothers, relatives, illness, road to the other world, neighbours, short travels, writing etc.

HOUSE NO.1
(Lagna or Ascendant)
Sun (Chariot)
King's throne, body, soul, name, fame & eminence, character, conduct, habits, aspiration etc.

HOUSE NO.11
Jupiter (Pearl)
Foundation of fate, house of income, profit, property, speculations, acquisition of gold, aspiration, friendships etc.

HOUSE NO.4
Moon (Horse)
Mother's lap & blessings, comforts, conveyance, abundance of milk and all amenities, parents, property, lot of wealth.

HOUSE NO.10
Saturn (Crocodile)
Field for foundation of fate & action, means of livelihood, employment, career, general success in life, social position, respect for ancestors.

HOUSE NO.5
Jupiter & Sun (Lion)
Progeny sons, knowledge, future of children, intelligence, education, inventive, mind hobbies, entertainment letters etc.

HOUSE NO.7
Venus & Mercury (Bull)
House-hold, spouse's love for woman, marital & conjugal pleasures, passions, marriage.

HOUSE NO.9
Jupiter (Conch or Archer)
Inherited fate, blessings of parents, religious piety, travels, and noble deeds, pilgrimage, philosophy, institutions, games.

HOUSE NO.6
Ketu (Pig)
Underworld, secret help, compassion, enemies, litigation, disease, work servants, subordinates, food & clothes.

HOUSE NO.8
Mars (Debilitating)
longevity of life, disease, death, inhuman justice, accidents, violence, sensual desires, ill fated.

Fig. 4

ooo

Interpret a Birth Chart

Birth Chart: Here is the horoscope of an individual who was born ...e in Himachal Pradesh and rose to an eminent position in his own ...

...rth–27/4/1939; Horoscope as prepared by Astrology:

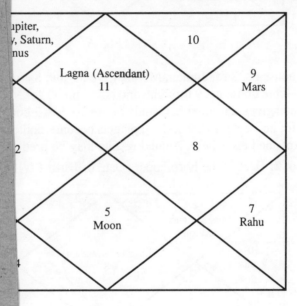

upiter,
y, Saturn,
nus

Lagna (Ascendant)
11

10

9
Mars

2

8

5
Moon

7
Rahu

4

Fig. 5

...irth chart; according to *Lal Kitab*, considering the Lagna as in 1st ...e Raashis.

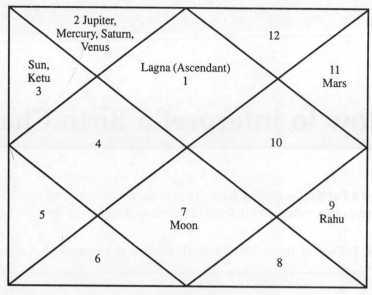

Fig. 6

Now study house no. 2 for Jupiter, Mercury, Venus and Saturn; house no. 3 for Sun and Ketu; house no. 7 for Moon; house no. 9 for Rahu and house no. 11 for Mars. Also study the Raashi effect; for example, Moon gives Raashi effect; study house no. 5 & 7 both for Moon; similarly, Rahu may be studied both for house no. 7 & 9. In fact, planets become exalted/debilitated according to Raashi and house as explained elsewhere. Annual results may be predicted from the annual chart.

Example no. 2: Here is the horoscope: (Date of Birth–20/12/1941)

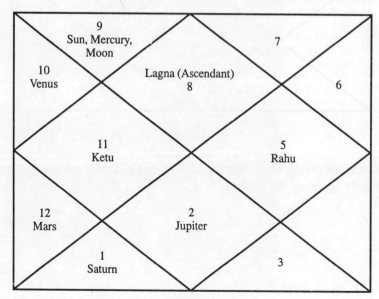

Fig. 7

Convert it into the following giving house no. 1 to Lagna or Ascendent.

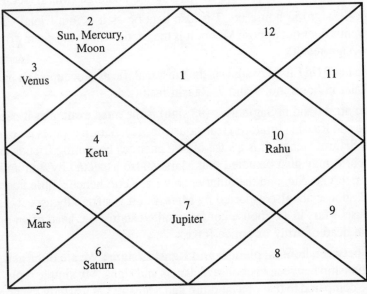

Fig. 8

The above horoscope is the 'Yoga of Eminence' (Rajayog). The native occupies the most important office in his profession. Study the effect on all planets in house no. 2,3,4,5,6,7 and 10.

Here Sun, Moon, Venus, Mars are benefic, but Saturn is the most debilitated; it strikes back at house no. 2; even Jupiter is weak, being in enemy's house and Raashi; Saturn aspects Venus; hence, rich. Jupiter makes him restless for brothers whom he helps, but without any returns; rather, he is opposed by some of them. Ketu in 4th house makes him honest and noble.

Study the horoscope in all its aspects. It will be noticed that Rahu destroys Mars (see permanent house no. 5). Annual results may be accordingly predicted from the planets occupying houses in the annual chart for that particular year.

How to interpret this birth-chart: (Example No. 1):

1. 1st house or Lagna is occupied by Aquarius (11th sign) and is vacant.

2. 2nd house is occupied by Jupiter, Venus, Saturn and Mercury in Pisces i.e. 12th sign. Jupiter is the Lord of both the 2nd house and Pisces. Hence, Jupiter is very exalted, but it loses its glitter and brightness, as house no. 8 is vacant. (See permanent house no. 2). Further, Saturn and Venus in Jupiter's sign and Jupiter's house are also exalted. (See house no. 2). Mercury in Pisces is the most malefic as it is Jupiter's worst enemy. Here it occupies Jupiter's house and Jupiter's sign (12th sign); hence very bad results. But, when Jupiter and Saturn are together in any house, Mercury's bad effect is mitigated to some extent (see Mercury house no. 12–Raashi result).

3. Sun – Ketu in 3rd house in Aries: Mars is the Lord of 3rd house and also the Lord of Aries (1st Raashi), hence, Sun being in a friend's house, friend's sign is exalted but it is to be dimmed by Ketu. Hence, its effect is somewhat lessened; but, it is revived because it is aspected by

55

Mars from 11th house (see Sun house no. 3 and also house no. 1 Raashi result). Ketu is debilitating and bad as it occupies its enemy's house and sign (Mars) (see Ketu house no. 3).

4. Moon (in Leo/5th sign) in house no. 7 is also benefic as it is in a friend's Raashi and house. Remember, Venus does not oppose Moon. It is the Moon who is the enemy of Venus (see Moon in 7th house – sign result).

5. Rahu in house no. 9 (in Libra/7th sign) is the most malefic as it occupies an enemy's Raashi and house (see Rahu in house no. 9 and 7–Raashi result).

6. Mars in house no. 11 and in Sagittarius (9th sign) is the most exalted as it occupies an intimate friend's house and Raashi (Jupiter's) (see house no. 11). Saturn aspects it i.e. its own house and Mars aspects Saturn. Hence, it is a case of two enemies becoming friends and shaking hands to become rich. It may also be noted that Mars is also aspected by Sun and Ketu both (50% aspect), one friend i.e. Sun and the other enemy i.e. Ketu; hence a little late rise. Further, Sun and Ketu in 3rd house are also aspected by Mars, but it is a friendly aspect, hence good results for the 3rd house. Mars in 11th house confers exalted status viz. head of an organization, chief executive, and head of army or police force.

Relationship between houses, planets and Raashis/signs: We are often asked the question as to what is the relationship between the houses, planets and signs. My simple reply is that their inter-relationship can be compared to that of a landlord and a tenant. Let us study the horoscope (example no. 1).

1. Jupiter is the Lord of the 2nd house and Pisces (12th house), hence, in this case, Jupiter is occupying his own house in all his glory and power, hence the most exalted.

2. Jupiter is the Lord of 11th house and Sagittarius (9th sign). Mars is occupying a friend's house in a friendly sign, hence exalted.

3. Rahu is occupying Jupiter's house (no. 9) in an enemy's Raashi (7th), hence, here a rogue is the tenant torturing and troubling the landlord and the other occupant, hence most malefic.

Similarly, Mercury is occupying the enemy's house/enemy's sign, hence worst results. The conclusion to be drawn is as under:

(a) If the landlord is his own tenant, his life is happy and comfortable. (Planet occupying his own house and Raashi).

(b) If an intimate friend is occupying the friend's house, life will be equally comfortable/a friend occupying a friend's house in his own sign or friend's sign : Venus in Capricorn in house no. 10).

(c) If the rogue is the tenant, life will be miserable i.e. a wicked enemy's sign occupying a weak enemy's house e.g. Saturn in Aries in house no. 1 or Rahu in Sagittarius in house no. 9.

(d) If landlord is a rogue and the tenant is weak and poor, life for the tenant is the most miserable. Jupiter in house no. 10 and 10th sign Capricorn is landlord i.e. Saturn is destroying Jupiter.

(e) A weak planet in his own house in enemy's sign also suffers and destroys his own house (Saturn in Aries in house no. 10).

This is how the interrelationship between the houses, planets and signs is to be interpreted. But, do not forget to see the aspects – friendly and adverse – Saturn in Aries in house no. 1 is malefic if Mars occupies house no. 10 in Capricorn. Saturn will no longer remain malefic. It is a case of two bitter enemies shaking hands to avoid confrontation.

Another Explanation: Sun in house no. 9 is, of course, exalted but, if it is aspected by Rahu from house no. 3, it is eclipsed and destroyed. Notwithstanding friendly or adverse planetary aspects, the following points may also be remembered for exalted or good and debilitating or weak planets:

(a) Exalted (good and strong) planets:

(1) Planet in his own house and Raashi.

(2) Planet in a friend's house and own Raashi.

(3) Planet in a friend's house and friend's Raashi.

Results are mutually benefic.

(b) Partially good and partially weak:

(1) An exalted planet in an enemy's house.

(2) An exalted planet in a neutral planet's house.

(3) A planet in a neutral house and neutral Raashi.

(c) Debilitating/malefic planets:

(1) A debilitating planet in enemy's house and enemy's Raashi.

(2) A malefic planet in its own house but in an enemy's Raashi.

Information regarding vacant houses: When the houses are vacant, they are deemed to be occupied by their respective signs (Raashis). In the case of house no. 6, both Mercury and Ketu are the lords and in the case of house no. 12, both Jupiter and Rahu are the presiding lords. Hence, in both these cases, following points may be remembered:

(a) If Mercury occupies its other sign (Raashi) i.e. house no. 3 (Gemini), Ketu will be the lord of vacant house no. 6

(b) If Jupiter occupies its other sign (Raashi) i.e. house no. 9 (Sagittarius), Rahu will be the lord of vacant house no. 12.

Further, if Mercury does not occupy sign no. 3 or 6, both Mercury and Ketu will be considered joint lords of vacant house no.6, but, it may be noted that where Mercury is strong and exalted, Ketu will be weak and debilitated. In such a case, the lord of house no.6 will either be Mercury or Ketu – the planet which is strong and benefic in the birth chart will be its lord – as house no. 6, if vacant is regarded good-intentioned in the horoscope, the weak cannot be its lord.

Similarly, when Jupiter does not occupy sign no.9 or 12, both Rahu and Jupiter will be considered vacant in house no.12. We, therefore, come to the conclusion that Jupiter will be the lord of vacant house no. 9 and Mercury that of vacant house no. 6.

In all other vacant houses, the lords of their Raashis (signs) will be considered as their lords.

○○○

Planets & Signs

मेष वृश्चिक मालिक मंगल – तुला वृष शुक्र की है।

कन्या मिथुन का बुध है मालिक – कुंभ मकर दोनों शनि की है।

गुरु मालिक है धन मीन का – कर्क चंद्र की होती है।

सिंह अकेला गर्जे दुनिया – राशि जो सूरज की है।

केतु बैठे घर कन्या राशि – राहु नवासी मीन का है।

पाप चढ़ा आसमान के ऊपर – जड़ जिसकी पाताल में है।

Mars is the Lord of Aries (1) & Scorpio (8) – Venus of the Libra (7) and Taurus (2)
Mercury is Lord of Gemini (3) and Virgo (6) – Saturn of Capricorn (10) and Aquarius (11)
Jupiter is Lord of Sagittarius (9) and Pisces (12) – Moon of Cancer (4)
Lion roars alone in world – It is Sun's Raashi Leo (5)
Ketu resides in Virgo (6) – Rahu dwells in Pisces (12)
The Sinner (Rahu) ascends over the sky (12) – whose roots (6) are in nether world.

Most important information about houses, planets, signs (Raashis) aspect – favourable or unfavourable, friendship or enemity of planets, planets of fate etc.

Please go through this chapter thoroughly as it contains the most vital information which is fundamental to the learning of astrology.

Information Regarding Planets and Signs

S.No.	Sign (Raashi)	Symbol	Colour	Effect	Nature	Presiding Lord	Exalted Results	Debili-tating (Worst)
1.	Aries	Ram	Red	Hot & Dry	Fiery	Mars	Sun	Saturn
2.	Taurus	Bull	White (Curd)	Cool	Earthly	Venus	Moon	Nil
3.	Gemini	Couple (Man & Woman)	Green	Hot & Wet	Windy	Mercury	Rahu	Ketu
4.	Cancer	Crab	Milky White	Cool	Watery	Moon	Jupiter	Mars

5.	Leo	Lion	Copper Red	Hot & Dry	Fiery	Sun	Nil	Nil
6.	Virgo	Girl	Green & Coloured	Cool & Dry	Earthly	Mercury & Ketu	Mercury & Rahu	Ketu
7.	Libra	Scales	White (Curd)	Hot & Wet	Windy	Venus	Saturn	Sun
8.	Scorpio	Scorpion	Red	Cold & Wet	Fiery	Mars	Nil	Moon
9.	Sagittarius	Cow & Archer	Yellow	Hot & Wet	Fiery	Jupiter	Ketu	Rahu
10.	Capricorn	Crocodile	Black	Cold & Dry	Earthly	Saturn	Mars	Jupiter
11.	Aquarius	Pitcher full of Water	Black	Hot & Wet	Windy	Saturn	Nil	Nil
12.	Pisces	Fish	Blue & Yellow	Cold & Wet	Watery	Jupiter & Rahu	Venus & Ketu	Mercury & Rahu

Friendship and Enmity of Planets

S.No.	Planet	Neutral or Equal Powers	Friends	Enemies
1.	Jupiter	Saturn, Rahu, Ketu	Sun, Moon, Mars	Venus, Mercury
2.	Sun	Mercury (Combust), Ketu (Dims Sun)	Jupiter, Moon, Mars	Venus, Saturn, Rahu (Solar Eclipse)
3.	Moon	Saturn, Venus, Mars, Jupiter	Sun, Mercury	Ketu (Lunar Eclipse), Rahu (Dims Moon)
4.	Venus	Mars, Jupiter	Saturn, Mercury, Ketu	Sun, Moon, Rahu
5.	Mars	Saturn, Venus, Rahu (Ineffective)	Sun, Moon, Jupiter	Mercury, Ketu
6.	Mercury	Saturn, Ketu, Mars, Jupiter	Sun, Venus, Rahu	Moon
7.	Saturn	Ketu, Jupiter	Mercury, Venus, Rahu	Moon, Sun, Mars
8.	Rahu	Jupiter, Moon (Dimmed)	Mercury, Saturn, Ketu	Venus, Sun (Solar Eclipse), Mars
9.	Ketu	Jupiter, Saturn, Mercury, Sun (Dimmed)	Venus, Rahu	Moon (Lunar Eclipse), Mars

Notes:

(a) Moon and Mercury are friends but it is Moon, which opposes Mercury.

(b) Moon and Venus are friends but Moon is inimical to Venus.

(c) Venus and Jupiter are of equal strength, but Venus opposes Jupiter.

(d) Mars and Saturn are of equal strength, but Mars is Saturn's enemy.

(e) When Rahu and Jupiter are combined in house no. 2, Jupiter dominates Rahu.

(f) Although Mercury is Jupiter's enemy and Moon is Mercury's enemy, yet in house no. 2 & 4, Mercury and Moon give up their animosity and monetarily help each other.

(g) Further, it is the planet that harbours ill will and enmity suffers and not the other. Shakespeare says, "O beware jealousy, it is the green-eyed monster which doth mock at the meat it feeds on".

Thus, enmity like jealousy harms the one who harbours it e.g. Moon is the loser and not Mercury, as it is the former who opposes the latter and not vice-versa.

Information about Houses, Aspects and Signs

The following tables and graphs are very important and may be read carefully:

Twelve Houses, Raashis and their Descriptions

S.No.	Raashi	Lord	Exalted (Best)	Malefic (Worst)	Permanent house	Bringer of luck	Result of planet	Raashi effect
1.	Aries	Mars (Benefic)	Sun	Saturn	Sun (Benefic)	Mars	Mars	Rahu
2.	Taurus	Venus	Moon	Nil	Jupiter	Moon	Rahu, Ketu	Nil
3.	Gemini	Mercury	Rahu	Ketu	Mars	Mercury	Saturn	Saturn
4.	Cancer	Moon	Jupiter	Mars	Moon	Moon	Moon	Venus, Mars, Ketu
5.	Leo	Sun	Nil	Nil	Jupiter	Sun	Sun, Jupiter	Nil
6.	Virgo	Mercury, Ketu	Mercury, Rahu	Ketu	Ketu	Rahu	Ketu, Mercury	Sun, Mars, Jupiter, Saturn (Retro-grade)
7.	Libra	Venus	Saturn	Sun	Venus, Mercury	Venus	Venus	Sun, Jupiter, Rahu
8.	Scorpio	Mars (Malefic)	Nil	Moon	Mars (Malefic), Saturn	Moon	Mars (Malefic)	Nil
9.	Sagitta-rius	Jupiter	Ketu	Rahu	Jupiter	Jupiter	Jupiter	Saturn

60

10.	Capri-corn	Saturn	Mars	Jupiter	Saturn	Saturn	Saturn	Mercury, Ketu
11.	Aquarius	Saturn	Nil	Nil	Jupiter	Jupiter	Jupiter, Saturn	Nil
12.	Pisces	Jupiter, Rahu	Venus, Ketu	Mercury, Rahu	Rahu	Ketu	Rahu	Mercury

Table for Exalted and Malefic Planets

	Sun	Moon	Mars	Mercury	Jupiter	Venus	Saturn
Exaltation	Aries	Taurus	Capricorn	Virgo	Cancer	Pisces	Libra
Malefic	Libra	Scorpio	Cancer	Pisces	Capricorn	Virgo	Aries

Aspects of Planets

	Sun	Moon	Venus	Mercury	Rahu	Ketu	Jupiter	Mars	Saturn
100% Aspect	7th	7th	7th	7th	7th	7th	7th, 5th, 9th	7th, 4th, 8th	7th, 3rd, 10th

- Ketu is always at the behest of Rahu who dominates Ketu, who has no identity of its own.
- Partially i.e. 50% – All planets aspect the 5th house and are friends e.g. 2nd aspecting the 6th.
- Planets aspect 25% – 8th aspect 6th, 2nd aspect 12th (25%) and vice-versa.
- 8th house aspects the 2nd 100% and not the 2nd aspecting the 8th.

Graph for aspects

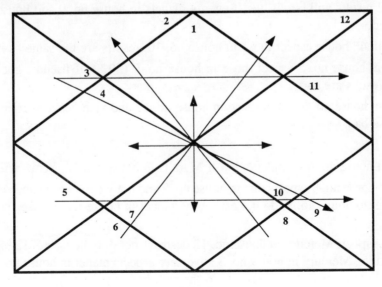

Fig. 9

61

Beginning of Arrow	1st house	3rd house	4th house	5th house	6th house	8th house
End of Arrow	7th house & vice-versa	9th house (100%), 11th house (50%)	10th house & vice-versa	9th house (50%)	12th house (100%)	2nd house (100%)

Notes:

- 5th house does not aspect the 11th house.
- 2nd house does not aspect the 8th house.
- If the planet is aspected by a friendly planet, the results are benefic, otherwise malefic.
- Mercury in the 12th house adversely aspects the 6th and from 9th it adversely aspects the 3rd (refer to Mercury no.12).
- Saturn in the 6th house is retrograde, it adversely aspects the 2nd house and destroys it even though it is occupied by Venus, its great friend.

Further Explanations: The above graph clearly shows:

House no. 1 aspects house no. 7 (100%); if they are friends, planets in house no. 1 will help those in house no. 7 and if planet in house no. 1 is the enemy of planet in house no. 7, it will have adverse effect. But, in no case, planet in house no. 7 will have any effect on planet in house no. 1. Planet in house no.1 will give the effect of sugar in milk for the planet in house no. 7.

Example:

(a) Sun in house no. 1 will brighten Venus or Mercury in house no. 7, but in that case, wife will suffer from ill health.

(b) Planets in house no. 3 will aspect that of planet in house no. 9 (100% aspect) and that of house no. 11 (50% aspect). If planet of house no. 3 is the friend of those in house no. 9 and 11, good results will be visible; if enemy planets in house no. 9 and house no. 11 will be destroyed.

(c) Planets in 4th house aspect those in house no. 10, results are the same as in number (a).

(d) Planets in house no. 5 aspect those in house no. 9 (50%), if friends, good results and if enemy, results are bad.

(e) Planets in house no. 6 aspect those in house no. 12 and vice-versa. If friends, best results, otherwise bad.

Example:

(f) Venus in house no. 6 is malefic, but if Mars is in house no. 12, Venus will help Mars.

(g) Planet in house no. 8 aspects that in house no. 2 and not vice-versa. (Sun, Moon and Jupiter, of course, in house no. 8, do not aspect the planet in house no. 2 – (see permanent house no. 8).

Mercury's Aspect: Mercury in house no. 12 destroys not only house no. 12 but also planet in house no. 6. Further, Mercury in house no. 3 adversely aspects planet in house no. 9 and Mercury in house no. 9 destroys planet in house no. 6 through house no. 12. Mercury destroys all such planets even though they may be exalted.

25% Aspects: House no. 8 aspects house no. 2 and house no. 2 aspects house no. 6; in other words, house no. 8 aspects house no. 6 (25%); similarly, house no. 6 aspects house no. 12 and house no. 8 aspects house no. 12 (50%) and house no. 2 (100%); obviously, house no. 2 aspects house no. 12 (25%).

100% Aspects of Kendras: As regards the kendras i.e. 1-7, 4-10 houses, the aspect is 100%. Planets in house no. 1 aspect those of house no. 7 and planets in house no. 4 aspect those of house no. 10 and aspects are 100%. (Please note planets and not vacant houses). They merge their effect into those of house no. 7 and house no. 10, like sugar into milk. It is called Merger of Mercury. But, planets in house no. 1 and house no. 4 will not lose their identity and effect i.e. they will continue to have their own individual effect – good and bad.

Examples:

(a) Suppose Sun is in house no. 1 and Venus & Mercury are in house no. 7. Sun will merge its effect and brightness into the planets of house no. 7 i.e. the planets in house no. 7 will become exalted and bright. As Venus is Sun's enemy, the spouse may suffer from ill health.

(b) Suppose Venus is in house no. 6, which is malefic and Mars is in house no. 12. Now Venus will merge its effect into Mars and Mars will give exalted results i.e. his brothers will have a fine time but his spouse will suffer.

Sudden loss or accident (of life or property or both)

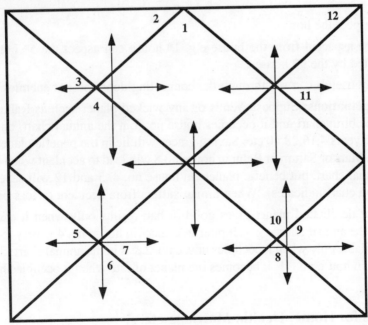

Fig. 10

Whether friends or enemies, life or property is destroyed. It happens without warning e.g. suppose Rahu in the first house moves to the 3rd or vice-versa, it may entail loss of property or life. If it is aspected by Sun or Moon or Jupiter etc., person will survive.

Chart showing friendship, enmity, deception & sudden loss, accident etc.

House no.	Aspect	Mutual aid	Basic aspect	Enmity	Deception	Connecting door	Sudden loss or injury or accident
1	A-B	5-9	7-7	8-6	10-4	2-12	73 & 11
2	A-B	6-10	8-8	9-7	11-5	1-11	4
3	A-B	7-11	9-9	10-8	12-6	4-2	1
4	A-B	8-12	10-10	11-9	1-6	5-3	10,6
5	A-B	9-1	11-11	12-10	2-7	6-4	7
6	A-B	10-2	12-12	1-11	3-9	7-5	4
7	A-B	11-3	1-1	2-12	4-10	8-4	1,5,9
8	A-B	12-4	2-2	3-1	5-11	9-7	10
9	A-B	1-5	3-3	4-2	6-12	10-8	7
10	A-B	2-6	4-4	5-3	7-1	1-7	4,8,12
11	A-B	3-7	5-5	6-4	8-2	12-10	1
12	A-B	4-8	6-6	7-5	9-3	1-11	10

Notes: A. Can aspect the house.

    B. Can be aspected from the house e.g. 1st house can aspect the 5th house and it can be aspected by the 9th house.

    • Only friends can see through the connecting door and not enemies.

Further Explanations: Suppose Venus or any wicked planet such as Rahu/Saturn etc. is in house no. 1 in the birth chart and it occupies house no. 3 in the annual chart, one may meet with an accident in the years 4,16,28,40 etc. Saving graces will lie in the benefic planets in house no. 5, 9,7,11. Similarly, Mars or Saturn or Rahu in house no.8 will lead to accident when it occupies house no. 10 in the annual chart, but benefic planets in house no. 4, 5 and 12 will save the person. The last column of the chart indicates, "When a man suffers from accident or loss or injury".

An exalted or debilitated planet gives good or bad results only when it occupies the house reserved for it in the annual chart e.g. – Jupiter in Cancer in house no. 4 is very exalted; its exalted result will be available only when it occupies house no. 2 & 4 in the annual chart. Similar is the case with other planet in house no. 11; it becomes the planet of fate when it occupies house no. 1 in the annual chart.

Special aspects for Home, Health, Marriage etc.

(1) House no. 3 will befriend house no. 5, whether friend or foe.

(2) If house no. 5 will look at house no. 7 and house no. 7 at house no. 9; their relationship will be friendly or inimical according to the position of planets. If friends, good results, if enemies, bad results.

(3) House no. 6 and house no. 8 and house no. 8 and house no. 10 will be inimical to each other except the Sun in house no. 9 that will be like benign rain.

(4) House no. 10 will aspect house no. 5 and destroy it, whether friend or foe. (Refer to permanent house no. 5).

(5) Regarding kendras, i.e., 1, 4, 7, 10 houses, please go through the graph of aspects and explanation thereupon.

Planets which mislead (Planets of deceptions): Deceptions here do not mean to deceive or to cheat, but it means the planet may lead to better results or mislead to worse results. It can both be a boon or a curse.

When a planet occupies house no. 10 in the annual chart, it becomes the planet of deception; if a malefic planet occupies house no. 8, the results will be doubly bad. If an exalted planet occupies house no. 2, results are the best.

Examples: (1) If a planet in house no. 2 (house of personal fate) occupies house no. 11 (house of fate and income), it will lead the person to a better position.

(2) Suppose the malefic Moon occupies house no. 10 in the annual chart and house no. 8 is occupied by another malefic planet, i.e., Rahu etc., the person will face unexpected loss or reverse. (For details, please refer to the permanent house no. 10)

(3) In order to find out the deceiving planet, add 9 to the planet in a particular house, e.g. 2+9 = 11; 3+9 = 12 and 4+9 = 13, etc.

(4) A planet in house no. 10 in the Birth chart occupying house no. 7 in the Annual chart will bring bad luck to the native that year.

Here is the chart of planets of deception

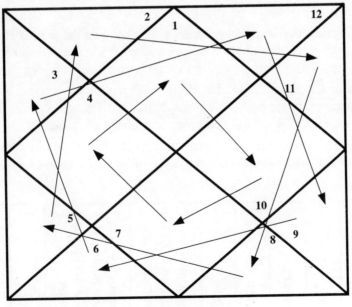

Fig. 11

20-year cycle of misleading planets

According to Hindu astrology, a person's span of life has been fixed at 120 years. The following chart may be prepared by multiplying 12×10 = 120 (house no. 10 is the house of deception and there are 12 houses in the birth) – Birth chart with Sun in house no. 1 (search for misleading planets).

Sun House 1	Moon House 2	Ketu House 3	Mars House 4	Mercury House 5	Saturn House 6	Rahu House 7	Planet of House 8 (House of Death) i.e. Saturn & Mars	Planet of House 9 i.e. Jupiter	Jupiter House 10	Venus House 11	Planet of House 12 i.e. Jupiter
1	2	3	4	5	6	7	8	9	10	11	12
13	14	15	16	17	18	19	20	21	22	23	24
25	26	27	28	29	30	31	32	33	34	35	36
37	38	39	40	41	42	43	44	45	46	47	48
49	50	51	52	53	54	55	56	57	58	59	60
61	62	63	64	65	66	67	68	69	70	71	72
73	74	75	76	77	78	79	80	81	82	83	84
85	86	87	88	89	90	91	92	93	94	95	96
97	98	99	100	101	102	103	104	105	106	107	108
109	110	111	112	113	114	115	116	117	118	119	120

(Figures under the planets indicate the age of the person and house no. is mentioned above the name of the planet).

Write 'Sun' against the year Sun occupies house no. 1 in the annual chart for the first time, and complete it as above. For example: Sun is in house no. 5 in the birth chart, it will occupy house no. 1 in the 5th year. Write 'Sun' at no.5 in the above chart and complete the cycle in that order.

As already stated, house no. 10 is the 'House of deception'– benefic or malefic – when planet in house no. 10 occupies house no. 10 in annual chart, it will become a planet of deception – doubly good or doubly malefic. (For details, see permanent house no. 10).

As stated above, if planet is auspicious and benefic, it will doubly bless the person. If it is malefic, it will be doubly devastating. Here is the order in which such misleading or deceiving planets appear.

Sun	Moon	Ketu	Mars	Mercury	Saturn	Rahu	Planet of house no.8 (Death) Saturn & Mars	Planet of house no.9 (Ancestral planet) Jupiter	Jupiter	Venus	Planet of house no.12 (end of Raashi) i.e. Jupiter

66

Whenever the planet in no.10 of birth chart occupies house no. 10 again in the annual chart, its effect will be doubly good or bad. Even if it proves to be the planet of deception in no.10, according to the above chart, such a planet will definitely mislead (good or bad) the individual.

If no.8, 9, 12 are vacant in the birth chart, then read Mars-Saturn for no.8 and Jupiter for no.9 and 12. One must not worry if the same planet appears twice.

How to find out the planet of deception or misleading planet

Man's average span of life has been fixed for 120 years. Prepare the following chart by multiplying 12 × 10 = 120 years.

If the Sun is in house no. 1 in the birth chart, it may be placed in no.1. Under Sun, thereafter Moon under no.2, then Ketu, Mars, Mercury etc. in that order. It may be, however, noted that Sun no.6 should be written under no.9; Sun no.9 may be indicated under no.6 and Sun no.7 under no.5 provided house no.1 is vacant; otherwise Sun in 7 will be under no.7.

Suppose, if the Sun is in house no. 3 in the birth chart, it will be written under 'Column no.3', Moon under 4, Ketu under 5 etc.

The 120-year cycle of deception in the whole life for all individuals

Mars	Mercury	Saturn	Rahu	Mars & Saturn	Jupiter	Jupiter	Venus	Jupiter	Sun	Moon	Ketu
1	2	3	4	5	6	7	8	9	10	11	12
13	14	15	16	17	18	19	20	21	22	23	24
25	26	27	28	29	30	31	32	33	34	35	36
37	38	39	40	41	42	43	44	45	46	47	48
49	50	51	52	53	54	55	56	57	58	59	60
61	62	63	64	65	66	67	68	69	70	71	72
73	74	75	76	77	78	79	80	81	82	83	84
85	86	87	88	89	90	91	92	93	94	95	96
97	98	99	100	101	102	103	104	105	106	107	108
109	110	111	112	113	114	115	116	117	118	119	120

Note: The above are the planets of deception in the appointed age of an individual in the whole span of life.

Special Information about Wicked Planets (Saturn – Rahu – Ketu) and their Aspects

(a) Whenever an enemy planet is fully aspected by these planets (100% aspect) that planet is completely destroyed.

(b) These wicked planets strike with double the fury if there are two or more enemy planets opposite to them i.e. 100% aspect.

(c) If a friendly planet along with enemy planets is aspected by these wicked planets, the friend is also destroyed along with enemies. These wicked planets then do not discriminate between a friend & a foe and all who fall in their firing range are destroyed.

(d) Even an auspicious planet such as Jupiter, Moon or Mercury joins Saturn – Rahu or Saturn – Ketu, all the three become malefic and give worst results.

(e) When two wicked planets i.e. Saturn – Rahu or Saturn – Ketu are together in the birth chart, the results are the best but if a third planet joins them the results are the worst.

(f) Even Jupiter gives bad results when these wicked planets become malefic.

(g) When Saturn aspects Rahu, Rahu seethes with anger and jealousy and becomes all the more malefic, but when Rahu aspects Saturn, results are good.

Devastating Effect of Colliding Planets

Planets usually collide with one another and this head-on collision produces devastating results. When these planets collide against each other, they do not differentiate between a friend or a foe i.e. they hit and destroy their victims. This is because of the devastating aspect of every planet at no.8 from self. For instance, planet in no.1 hits and destroys planet in no.8, no.2 destroys no.9 and no.3 hits at no.10 and so on and so forth. Refer to the graph given below (12), which is self-explanatory.

Graph Showing Planets in Collision

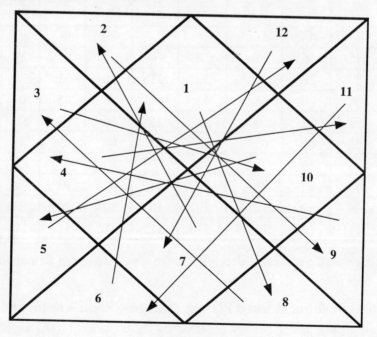

Fig. 12

(Please refer to col. no.5 in the chart showing friendship, enmity etc. at page 64)

68

Suppose Sun is in no.1 and Saturn is in no.8, Sun will strike at the very roots of Saturn and the resultant effect will be the death of spouse. Or Saturn in no.2 will hit hard Moon in no.9 (which is very exalted) and will completely destroy it or Saturn in no.8 will nullify the exalted effect of Moon in no.3.

Paying for the Sins of Forefather

Law of natural justice demands that one must pay for the sins of one's ancestors. It is indeed a negation of justice that someone else should pay for the sins committed by his ancestors, but it is a hard fact that children often become scapegoats for the misdeeds of their parents and grandparents. Even exalted planets become mute spectators when ancestral sins visit upon the children. For example: if an ancestor has killed a dog in cold blood, his children will have to atone for that sin, even though his Jupiter is exalted in the birth chart. He should adopt the remedy both for the Jupiter (parents) and Ketu (dog).

Here is the chart of sins committed by forefathers and their atonement by children

Planet	Exalted House no.	Enemy Planets	Span of Planet (after becoming major)	Kind of Sins
Jupiter	2,5,9,12	Rahu, Mercury, Venus	16 years	Sins of forefathers
Sun	5	Saturn, Rahu, Ketu, Venus	22 years	One's own misdeeds
Moon	4	Ketu	24 years	Sins perpetrated on mother i.e. treating her badly
Venus	2,7	Rahu, Sun, Moon	25 years	Wife killing or beating etc.
Mars	1,8	Mercury, Ketu	28 years	Maltreatment of brothers and relatives
Mercury	3,6	Moon	34 years	Worst behaviour towards daughters and sisters & playing fraud with them
Saturn	10,11	Sun, Mars, Moon	36 years	Homicides; killing of fellow men & animals
Rahu	3,6	Sun, Venus, Mars	42 years	Deceit, cheating, embezzlement & fraud
Ketu	9,12	Moon, Mars	48 years	Lustful conduct, misbehaviour towards son or saint or dog without any provocation

69

Planets of fate and how to find out

Four kendras are the most important in the horoscope i.e. house no. 1, 4,7 & 10 and if they are vacant i.e. without any planet, then find out the planet of fate in house no. 3, 5,9 & 11 and if they are also vacant, search for the planet of fate in house no. 2, 6,8 & 12. This search may be done both through birth and Moon charts.

If an exalted planet occupies house no. 1 or 2 or its own exalted house; in the annual charts, results will be exalted and if a weak planet is positioned in house no. 1 or in enemy's house, results are disastrous.

How to determine fate in kendras and other houses

Four kendras i.e. house no. 1,4,7 & 10 determine man's fate as indicated below:

House no. 1	Body	Profession, business regarding exalted Sun
House no. 4	Wealth	Profession, business concerning exalted Jupiter
House no. 7	Property	Profession, business concerning exalted Saturn
House no. 10	Food	Profession, business regarding exalted Mars

(1) House no. 3 (brothers and blood relations); house no. 5 (children, knowledge); house no. 9 (ancestors and parents); and house no. 11 (personal gains and income) – all these four houses will determine what one gets from blood relatives as indicated in the brackets above.

(2) House no. 2 (In-laws; temple of god); house no. 6 (colleagues, relatives of children, maternal uncles) and house no. 12 (lifeless worldly things, divine help or good luck) – will refer to the sources of income and fate from the things mentioned in brackets.

(3) House no. 6 refers to the monetary transactions; friendly planets in this house will confer good results and enemies will give bad results.

(4) Enemy planets of house no. 2, occupying house no. 1 in the annual chart gives bad results such as theft, useless expenditure, loss of wealth etc.

(5) House no. 11 is the house of income and personal gains; whereas house no. 12 is the house of expenditure and house no. 3 is the outlet of such expenditure.

(6) The planets occupying house no. 3, 5,9 & 11 indicate the position of relatives as mentioned in brackets against (2) above.

(7) Vacant kendras i.e. house no. 1, 4,7,10 signify that the person has not brought anything with him. It is just like keeping the articles in the cloakroom and not claiming it.

(8) Vacant house no. 9 means that the person receives inherited wealth.

(9) House no. 11 signifies that the person receives inherited property and also earns himself.

Income: Exalted planets in their own houses or in friends' houses or planets of fate shower all comforts, wealth and prosperity upon the individual. For example: Saturn in Aquarius in house no. 11 will confer lot of income upon the man as it is in its own sign and house of gains and personal income. Conversely, if the planet of fate or another planet is debilitated and is in the enemy's house and sign, it may lead to loss. For example: Jupiter in Capricorn in house no. 10 is the weakest and hence bad results of that house.

Two Exalted Planets and their Exalted Effect on Wealth

Two Exalted Planets	Effect on Wealth
Jupiter – Sun	Most exalted; lot of wealth and royal upbringing
Jupiter – Moon	One may get hidden wealth; lot of gold; parents like a huge Banyan tree offering shade and comforts
Jupiter – Venus	Wealth for show off and outward appearances only (but hollow from within)
Jupiter – Mars	Lot of wealth and property
Sun – Mars	Royal upbringing and legacy; landlord and administrator
Moon – Mars	Lot of wealth (especially if they are in no.3); but if these planets are in no.10 or 11, persons, though rich, will be greedy
Moon – Saturn	Lot of wealth when joined with Jupiter or in the houses whose presiding lord is Jupiter i.e. 2,5,9,12; otherwise bad for health like a black-faced monkey
Mars – Venus	Wealth controlled by wife and in-laws
Mars – Saturn	Great wealth by looting others; two dacoits becoming friends and rich
Saturn – Jupiter	Wealthy after marriage; may earn through teaching; honest

Savings and Expenditure

Moon signifies wealth and Saturn is the treasure which controls the finances. One's savings are determined by their position – good or bad – Mars and Saturn are the presiding lords over property, whereas Moon indicates possession of silver and Jupiter that of gold. House no. 11 indicates income, whereas house no. 12 refers to expenditure and house no. 9 determines savings of ancestors. House no. 2 being house of personal fate, determines personal savings & wealth and house no. 5 indicates saving from children. Naturally, the positioning of these planets in various houses will determine income, expenditure and savings – whether good or bad. If exalted, results are naturally good, otherwise bad.

Legend about Planets and Houses/Signs

In the beginning, Heavens were ruled by the Sun – the king and Moon – the queen consort. They had reserved house no. 5 and house no. 4 respectively as their mansions with an intervening door for communications. All other houses were their exclusive property and all other planets were sub-servient to them. Once it so happened that they fell out & all communications between the king and the queen were scrapped. The planets hit upon a plan to cheat upon them. Mercury, being the nearest to Sun, requested him to allot a house to him. The king acceded to his request and allotted him house no. 6 (next to house no. 5). Not content with one favour, he next approached the Moon and made a similar request. Not knowing that Mercury had already played his trick upon Sun, she allotted him house no. 3 (adjacent to house no. 4). Similarly, Venus got house no. 7 and 2; Mars got house no. 8 and 1; Jupiter got house no. 9 and 12. When Saturn came to know of this 'bounty' by king and queen, he got furious and hated his father i.e. Sun for his foolishness. He ultimately forcibly captured house no. 10 and 11. Thus, Sun and Moon remained confined to only two houses and signs i.e. no.5 (Leo) and no.4 (Cancer).

Dormant or Sleeping Houses and Planets

(a) **Dormant House:** A house without any planet or a house not aspected by any planet is called a dormant/sleeping house.

(b) **Dormant/Sleeping Planet:** (1) When a planet in the earlier house is not in direct aspect of any other planet, it is called a dormant planet, e.g. Jupiter in no.2 and no.8 vacant, or Moon in no.5 and no.9 vacant.

(2) House no. 1-6 from the Ascendent (Lagna) and house no. 7-12 are called Right (earlier) and Left (later) sides respectively. If there is no planet in the earlier houses, the planets in the later houses will be called dormant, but if the later houses are vacant, the planets in earlier houses will be regarded asleep. The dormant planets will in no way affect the later houses. A house with a planet is always awake and planets in permanent houses, such as Venus in house no. 7 and Mars in house no. 3, will be regarded as awake.

(3) When there is no planet in the earlier houses, the planet of later houses will be considered as dormant. In such a case, the planet of fate should be searched and if the later houses are vacant, the remedy should be adopted for the planet activating or arousing that particular house which is vacant. It may be remembered that activating a planet and activating a house are two different things and should not be confused with.

(4)

If there is no planet in no.10	Planet in no.2 will be dormant.
If there is no planet in no.2	Planet in no.10 will be dormant.
If there is no planet in no.2	Planet in no.9 will be dormant.

Chart indicating as to when the dormant planet will automatically become active/awake

Planet	When it will be awake	After what age	When it will give malefic effect
Jupiter	After starting one's business	16 years	6th or 22nd year
Sun	Govt./Semi-govt. job	22 years	22nd or 24th year
Moon	Education	24 years	1st or 25th year
Venus	Marriage	25 years	3rd or 28th year
Mars	Regarding wife	28 years	6th or 34th year
Mercury	Business, sister or daughter's marriage	34 years	2nd or 36th year
Saturn	Regarding house	36 years	6th or 42nd year
Rahu	Regarding in-laws	42 years	6th or 48th year
Ketu	Regarding birth of child	48 years	3rd or 51st year

Chapter No. 9

Remedies for Malefic Planets

S.No.	Name of Planet	Divine Authority	Gender	Colour	Remedy for children & other reasons	Remedies
1.	Jupiter	Lord Brahma	Male	Yellow	Vishnu worship	Daal chana (yellow lentil), saffron, gold
2.	Sun	Lord Vishnu	Male	Wheatish	Vishnu Puran	Wheat, red copper, jaggery
3.	Moon	Lord Shiva	Female	Milky white	Shiva worship	Rice, silver, milk, milky-white pearl
4.	Venus	Goddess Laxmi	Female	Curd like	Selfless service of people	Ghee, curd, camphor curd-like pearl, sand, white butter
5.	Mars	Hanuman	Male	Red hot	Gayatri paath	Masur daal (red lentil), red things, red coral
6.	Mercury	Goddess Durga	Effeminate (Vegetarian)	Green	Durga paath	Moong (green lentil), emerald
7.	Saturn	Bhairon	Effeminate (Minerals)	Black	Respect for elders	Urad (black lentil), iron, leather goods, timber, coal
8.	Rahu	Goddess Saraswati	Node (Dragon's head)	Blue	Worship of virgins	Mustard (sarson), sapphire (neelam), gomed (hessonite)
9.	Ketu	Lord Ganesha	Node (Dragon's tail)	Black & white	Donate black & white cow	Til (sesame), black & white blanket, cat's eye (Lahsunya), banana

Note: The above remedies may be adopted for 43 days consecutively and the articles mentioned against malefic planet should either be donated to the needy or the distressed or to a public place or else may be gently thrown into river.

73

Instant Remedies for Immediate Effect

(1) **Malefic Jupiter:** Put a little saffron in a drop of milk, paste it on navel, put a dot on forehead and also take it.

(2) **Malefic Sun:** Throw Jaggery (Gur) or wheat in river.

(3) **Malefic Moon:** Place a small vessel of milk under the pillow at night and water the 'keekar' tree with that milk in the morning.

(4) **Malefic Venus:** Donate white barley (jowar).

(5) **Malefic Mars:** Throw pieces of sweet bread and 'Reoris' (sweet made of jaggery and til) into river during stomach pain.

(6) **Malefic Mercury:** Put a hole in the copper coin and throw it into river.

(7) **Malefic Saturn:** Donate mustard (sarson).

(8) **Malefic Mars:** Donate sweets.

(9) **Malefic Rahu:** Donate radish (moolie) or keep barley (jau) under the pillow at night and throw it into the river in the morning or else donate it or throw coal into the river.

(10) **Malefic Ketu:** Give bread to dogs.

Note: Adopt the above remedies for 43 days without break.

Malefic Planets (according to Raashis) in the Birth Chart and their Remedies during Marriage Ceremony

(1) **Malefic Jupiter:** Take two pieces of gold of equal weight and at the time of actual marriage ceremony give one piece to the groom/bride and throw the other piece into the river. It is immaterial whether the pieces are the smallest. For a poor person, who is not in a position to afford gold, he may take two pieces of turmeric of equal weight and repeat the above procedure. It will be equally effective.

(2) **Malefic Sun:** The above remedy may be adopted instead of gold, copper pieces of equal weight may be used.

(3) **Malefic Moon:** Use milky-white pearl or silver (two pieces of equal weight) and follow the method enunciated in (1) above.

(4) **Malefic Venus:** Use two pearls (curd-like) of equal weight. Spouse should wear gold on head on auspicious occasions.

(5) **Malefic Mars:** Use two red precious stones (not very bright) and follow the method in (1) above.

(6) **Malefic Mercury:** Use diamonds or shells or cowries of equal weight and do as in (1) above.

(7) **Malefic Saturn:** Use iron or steel or black salt (two pieces of equal weight) and do as advised in (1) above.

(8) **Malefic Rahu:** The same remedy as suggested for malefic Moon at (3) above. Do not use or wear Neelam i.e. Sapphire. Give silver brick to the groom/bride which must be kept in the house or under pillow. It should never be disposed off.

(9) **Malefic Ketu:** Use black and white stones and adopt the procedure as mentioned in (1) above.

Notes: (a) Adopt the above remedies at the time of marriage ceremony and if somehow or the other one fails to do these at the time of marriage, one can perform these remedies at the time of marriage anniversary.

(b) These remedies are to be adopted in respect of malefic planets in horoscope only.

(c) These remedies are to be adopted according to Raashi (signs) as they indicate the exaltation or the debilitating signs of a particular planet. They are not to be adopted according to houses.

(d) These may be adopted during the day except Rahu (in the evening) and Saturn (at night).

(e) These may be adopted on the days and time set apart for a planet i.e. Sun – Sunday, Moon – Monday, Mars – Tuesday, Jupiter – Thursday, Ketu – Sunday, Rahu – Thursday evening, Venus – Friday, Mercury – Wednesday, Saturn – Saturday night.

ooo

Annual Chart (Varsh Phal)

Annual charts from the famous *Lal Kitab* are given and discussed in detail in the following pages.

There are many methods of working out the annual charts on the basis of ancient texts. Just like the birth chart, the annual chart is also important for predictions for a particular year, as the annual chart specifically indicates the position of planets in a year. For the in-depth knowledge of readers, four different methods are being mentioned below. Results in all the cases are the same.

Method no.1

Subtract the previous years from the year for which annual chart is to be prepared. Multiply this number by '1,007'. The figure so obtained is to be divided by '800'. The quotient is **'Days'**. Multiply the remainder with '60' and then divide it by '800'; the quotient will be **'Ghatis'**. The remainder may again be multiplied by '60' and then divided by '800'; the quotient will be **'Pals'**. Again the remainder may be multiplied by '60' and then divided by '800' to arrive at **'Vipal'**.

Example: A child was born on 17-05-1967 at 3:45 AM i.e. 4 Jeth of Samvat 2024. His 'Isht' is 55 = 30 – Wednesday – his Annual chart for the year 1982 i.e. Vikram Samvat 2039 is to be worked out.

(a)	Samvat of Birth	=	2024
(b)	Samvat of Annual chart	=	2039
(c)	Previous years (years elapsed)	=	15
(d)	Multiply 15 with 1,007	=	$15 \times 1,007$ = 15,105
(e)	Divide it by 800	=	15,105/800 = 18 Days (remainder is 705)
(f)	Multiply 705 with 60	=	705×60 = 42,300
(g)	Divide it by 800	=	42,300/800 = 52 Ghatis (remainder is 700)
(h)	Multiply 700 with 60	=	700×60 = 42,000
(i)	Divide it by 800	=	42,000/800 = 52 Pals (remainder is 400)
(j)	Multiply 400 with 60	=	400×60 = 24,000
(k)	Divide it by 800	=	24,000/800 = 30 Vipals

Thus, the number comes out to be:

	Days	Ghatis	Pals	Vipals
	18	52	52	30
Add: Isht	4	55	30	–
Total	23	48	22	30

A week comprises 7 days starting from Sunday. Divide 23 by 7, it comes to 2 i.e. Monday.

Thus, the 16th year will start from Monday – 48 Ghatis, 22 Pals and 30 Vipals i.e. 4 Jeths, 2039 (17-05-1982).

Method no.2

Previous years = 15 (1982 – 1967 = 15)

(a) Multiply 15 by 1¼ = 75/4 = 18 (Days) and 45 (Ghatis)

(b) Divide previous years by 2 = 15/2 = 7 (Ghatis) and 30 (Pals)

(c) Multiply 15 (previous years) by 1½ = 15×3/2 = 45/2 = 22 (Pals) and 30 (Vipals)

Add (a)+(b)+(c) =

	Days	Ghatis	Pals	Vipals
	18	45	-	-
	-	7	30	-
	-	-	22	30
Total	18	52	52	30

Add Birth Isht = 4 (Days) 55 (Ghatis) 30 (Pals)

Total = 23 (Days) 48 (Ghatis) 22 (Pals) 30 (Vipals)

The result is the same as worked out in example no.1.

Method no.3

Almost all the astrologers adopt this method. In all Panchangs (Ephemerides) or Jantris/Almanacs, one can find 'Varsh Sarni' (Annual Timetable) and 'Lagna Sarni' (Ascending Timetable) which contain the complete information:

Example: In an Annual Timetable (Varsh Saarni) figures under 15 in every Panchang are:

	Days	Ghatis	Pals	Vipals
	4	52	52	30
Add Lagna Isht	4	55	30	-
Total	9	48	22	30

i.e. Varsh (Annual) Isht is Monday – 48 Ghatis and 22 Pals and the 16th year will commence with above calculated day and time.

Important Note

(a) From the above Isht, annual chart may be prepared from 'Lagna sarni'.

(b) 60 Vipals = 1 Pal; 60 Pals = 1 Ghati; and 60 Ghatis = 1 Day and Night (24 hrs). If the Vipals are more than 60, divide it by 60, quotient is Pal and remainder is Vipal. If Ghatis are more than 60, quotient is Days and remainder is Ghatis. If the number of days is more than 7, divide 8 by 7 (days in a week), the remainder denotes days of the week starting from Sunday i.e. '1' means Sunday, '2' means Monday and so on. For converting the above Hindu time, refer to chapter 2.

1 Ghatis = 24 minutes; 60 Pals = 1 Ghatis; 60 Vipals = 1 Pal.

What is 'Isht': It means desire for the object. It refers to the time elapsed between the moment of birth. It is expressed in Ghatis & Pals after sunrise.

Example: A child was born at a particular station at 10:00 AM (IST) and sun rises at that station on the day of birth at 5:30 AM (IST). Then (10:00 – 5:30 = 4:30 AM). It will be the 'Isht'.

"Muntha" in the Annual Chart and its significance

Hindu Astrologers attach great importance to the placement of 'Muntha' in the annual chart, but *Lal Kitab* does not make any mention of 'Muntha'. Anyhow the following methods may be adopted in computing 'Muntha' in the annual chart.

After preparing the annual chart, add the Lagna Raashi to the previous years. Divide this number by 12. The remainder may be placed in the Raashi (Sign) of that number in the annual chart.

Example: Child is born on 27-04-1939. His previous years on 27-04-2001 will be 62. His Lagna Raashi is 11 i.e. Aquarius. Add 62 to 11 i.e. 73; divide it by 12, the remainder is one. Hence, 'Muntha' in the year 27-04-2001 to 27-04-2002 is in the Aries. Thus, the 'Muntha' is to be mentioned in the house with the Raashi Aries.

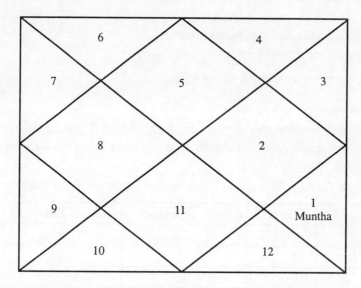

Fig. 13

Above is given the supposed Annual Chart.

Effects: (a) 'Muntha' in house no. 1,2,3,5,9,10,11 – good results.

(b) 'Muntha' in house no. 4,6,7,8,12 – bad results.

Annual Charts (Courtesy *Lal Kitab*)

For the convenience of the readers, we are giving the 'Annual Charts' for 103 years taken from *Lal Kitab*, the most famous and rare book on Astrology in Urdu. Whether one works out the Annual Charts from the methods detailed in previous pages or from *Lal Kitab*, the results are the same:

How to interpret the Annual Charts

Example No. 1: The native was born on 17-05-1967; his birth chart as prepared by the astrologers is as under:

Horoscope on 17-05-1967

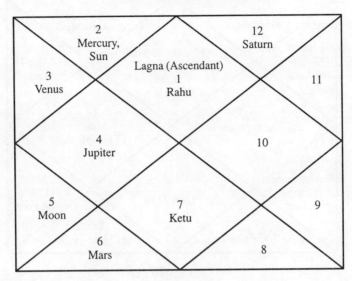

Fig. 14

The birth chart remains the same even if it is converted into one according to *Lal Kitab*, as ascendant is the same.

The boy is an engineer and an M.B.A.; got a job in a foreign country in his 24th year i.e. 1990-91 as per Annual Chart given below:

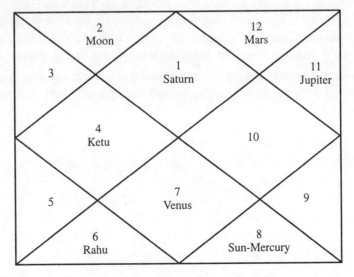

Fig. 15

"Refer to the Annual Chart fig. 15 against age 24 years".

As he was born in May (5th month), the Sun will occupy the 5th house between 17-09-1990 and 16-10-1990 i.e. 5th month from birth. Monthly chart will be as under:

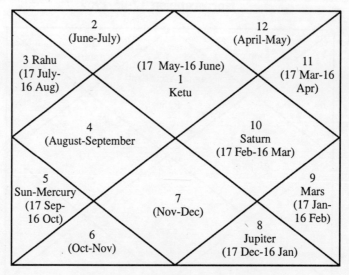

Fig. 16

In order to make predictions about the child, first refer to 'Birth chart'. All the planets are exalted except Rahu, which has eclipsed the 'House of Sun'; even Rahu no longer remains malefic, as it is aspected by Mars. Jupiter confers wealth and property; Mars makes him richer; Saturn (Shesh Nag) protects him. Venus aspects its own house (50%), although it is destroyed by Rahu (100% aspect).

Moon in the 5th house is asleep, as there is no planet in the 9th house. Thus, he is an unsuccessful traveller to foreign lands. He also met a very serious accident in his 28th year as malefic Rahu shifted to 3rd house in the Annual Chart that year, but Moon in 11th house saved him, as it aspected (50%) the 3rd house from 11th house. (See chart for clash and sudden injury, loss or accident page 64).

He went to another country later that year, but returned without any success. During the 31st and 32nd year, he suffered a lot financially and returned to India where he had to work on a meagre salary.

Annual Chart 31st year (May 1997-98)

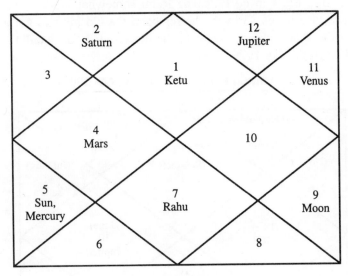

Fig. 17

He did get a better job in January 1998 in another country because of Moon in 9th house but did not accept it, although he wanted it but because of adverse aspect of Moon by Saturn from no.2 to no.9 (clash).

Annual Chart 32nd year (May 1998-99)

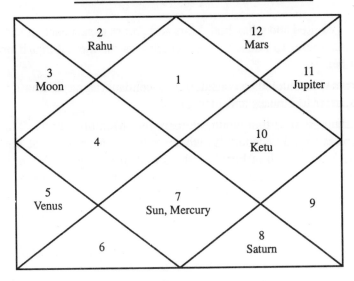

Fig. 18

Ketu in no.10 destroys Venus; Saturn in no.8 and Rahu in no.2 constitute a very malefic connection (see house no. 5 and house no. 10) for details. He did get another job in a foreign country, but could not join it because of adverse effect of Saturn on Moon – from no.8 to no.3 (clash).

He suffered financially and also had a fall. When Saturn aspects Rahu, Rahu seethes with anger and creates problem. But, Mars in no.12, made Rahu somewhat ineffective. Even Sun in no.7 created problems in service in his 33rd year, he regained the old job and got glory in the former foreign country after the solar eclipse. (Refer to the house no. 1 for details) and see the Annual Chart for 33rd year i.e., from May 1999-2000).

Annual Chart 33rd year (1999-2000)

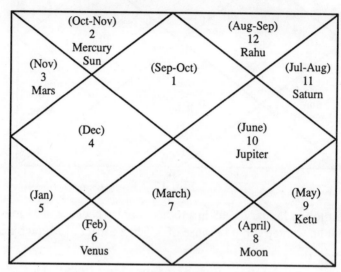

Fig. 19

Saturn in No.11 is exalted and when both Mars and Saturn aspect each other (Refer to Aspects) results are exalted. Also refer to house no. 10, where it is mentioned that if no.2 is exalted, the results are the most benefic.

Thus, birth chart may be studied by considering Ascendant (lagna) as house no. 1 and so on and so forth. For details, refer to Houses and Planets.

In order to ascertain the date in a month, prepare the 'Monthly Chart'. 'Mars' position in the monthly chart may be taken into account. In whatever house, Mars is in the Annual chart, it may be given the day no.12 and month of birth be added to it. In this case, it comes to 12 + 5 i.e. 17th day from the date of birth. The figure may be increased or decreased by adding 1 onwards or subtracting 1 for the planets ahead of Mars or behind Mars.

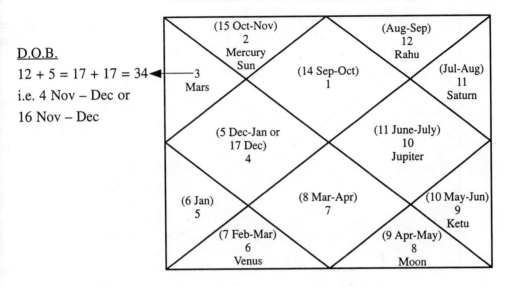

D.O.B.

12 + 5 = 17 + 17 = 34

i.e. 4 Nov – Dec or

16 Nov – Dec

Fig. 20

He got the job on 12th August 1999 – detailed predictions may be made after taking into consideration the position of planets and Aspects – favourable and unfavourable.

Example No. 2: Date of Birth: 10-03-1971. (8:15 AM), Place of Birth: New Delhi.

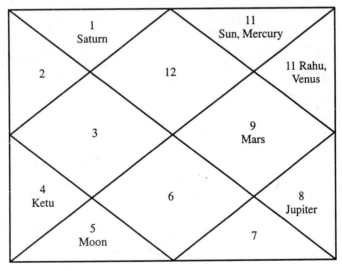

Fig. 21

She is an Engineer and an M.B.A. from a prestigious University in the States. She lives abroad, but in her 25th year, she had the shock of her life, as her engagement was broken by the boy and his parents out of greed, just a few days before the proposed date of marriage. See Rahu-Venus which *inter alia* indicated unhappy domestic life.

25th Year (Annual Chart) 10-03-1995 to 09-03-1996

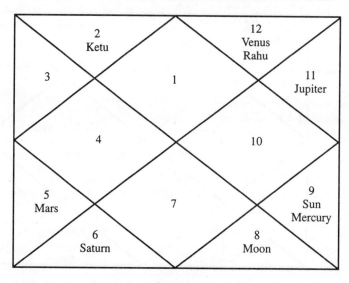

Fig. 22

Rahu-Venus combination in house no. 12 leads to separation or divorce, if Saturn is not in house no. 3 (See house no. 3). Saturn from house no. 6 destroys Ketu in house no. 2 and instigates Rahu in house no. 12. Saving grace was Mars in house no. 5. The girl, although frustrated, left for abroad to pursue her studies further. Now she heads an organization in the States and is quite well-off.

Monthly Chart (1995-1996) 25th Year

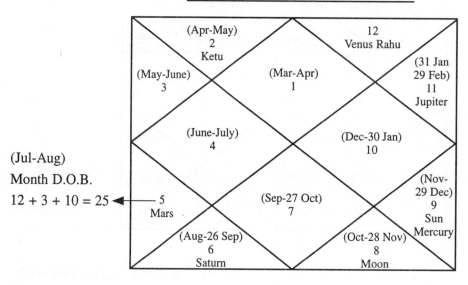

Fig. 23

Her dreams of marriage were shattered and engagement was snapped in February – March 1996 i.e. 12 + 3 (month) + 10 (D.O.B.) = 25th day of birth date was occupied by Mars in 5th house and 1st March was the day when she received the sad news. But, it was a good riddance; otherwise Rahu would have destroyed Venus. Mars was the saving planet.

Thus in order to read the Birth and Annual Charts, refer to all aspects, houses, planets and their Raashis.

Method for Calculating Monthly Effect in the Annual Chart

(1) Beginning of month is to be taken from the date and time of birth. Suppose a person is born on 31st of May, he will complete the month on 30th June.

(2) The house in which Sun is placed in the Annual chart should be assigned the month of birth and the monthly chart be computed accordingly. Example: A person born in May, his Sun will be assigned 5th house from September to October and so on and so forth (refer to the Annual chart no. 1 example).

(3) Annual Chart's results, whether good or bad, will be noticeable from the placement of Sun in a particular house. Its results will be bad regarding career etc. during 7th month when it is placed in house no. 7 in Annual charts. Whereas other planets in other houses will confer results according to their positioning in the chart.

(4) In order to find out the result of a particular planet in a year, divide the year of age of individual with the number of the permanent house in which the planet is positioned. The remainder will denote the effect of that planet in that year. For house no.1 divide the age by 12; for no.2 divide it by 11 and for no.3 divide it by 10. In the case of other houses, divide the age of the man by that particular planet in the house.

Example no. 1

Suppose a man is passing through his 31st year and Moon is in house no.3. Divide 31 by 10, the remainder is 1. Hence, Moon will give the effect of house no. 1 during his 31st year (See Moon house no. 1 for results).

Example no. 2

Suppose a man wants to know about children during 30th year. Divide 30 by 5 (No.5 is the house for children). The remainder is zero. Refer to house no. 5 for results. If house no. 5 is vacant then refer to Ketu's position in the horoscope. Similarly, one wants to have this information during 31st year; divide it by 5; the remainder is 1. Study house no. 1 in the horoscope or else house no. 5 or Ketu's position in birth chart, as enumerated above.

(5) As the Sun is the central force, its position in Hindu Astrology is of paramount importance. We have 12 houses and each house has been assigned a particular month. In the monthly chart, house no. 1 refers to 'Baisakh' (from April 13 to May 12). House no. 2 to 'Jeth' (May 13 to June 12) and so on. (Refer to Chapter 2 on division of time).

(6) When a planet occupies a house in the birth chart and if a planet occupies that house in the Annual chart, it will mean that the planet of the Annual Chart will show its effect in the month reserved for that house. Suppose Sun-Mercury is in house no. 2 in the horoscope and Jupiter

occupies house no. 2 in the Annual chart, naturally Jupiter will give its effect in Jeth (May-June) as house no. 2 is reserved for this month.

(7) Further, if some planet occupies a particular house in the Annual chart which otherwise is vacant in the Birth chart, it will give its effect in the month/house in which Sun is placed in the Annual chart. Suppose house no. 4 is vacant in the Birth chart and it is occupied by Jupiter in the Annual chart and Sun is in house no. 8 in the Annual chart, Jupiter will show its results during 8th month from birth.

Note: We have given above the position according to Hindu calendar but the results are almost the same, if predictions are made in terms of Gregorian (English) calendar. In that case, monthly chart is to be prepared and results computed by assigning the month of birth to Sun, as explained in (6) above or by assigning the month of birth to house no. 1 and so on. Before making any prediction, aspects – whether favourable or unfavourable – must be taken into cognizance. We give an example here:

Birth Chart

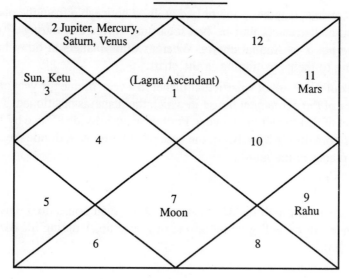

Fig. 24

86

Birth Chart according to Lal Kitab

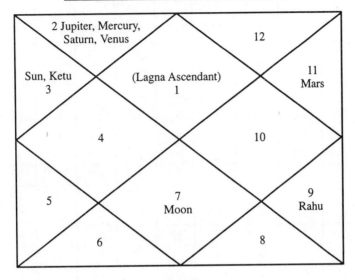

Fig. 25

Mars is exalted, but its effect is nullified and destroyed by an adverse aspect from Ketu (his enemy) from house no. 3. Hence, Mars no longer remains exalted.

We have worked out the position and effect of planets in a particular year according to English calendar i.e. dates and months, but for convenience of traditional Astrologers, who are well conversant with the 'Vikrami Samvat', another method has also been given. In both the methods, there may be a negligible difference of a few days.

Catalogue of Annual Charts (Courtesy *Lal Kitab*)

Figures 1-12 on the top against Age mean the House nos. in the horoscope and the figures under Age indicate the year.

Example: If Mars is in house no. 5 in the Birth chart, it will be in house no. 12 during the 16th year.

Herewith the Catalogue

Houses

AGE ↓	1	2	3	4	5	6	7	8	9	10	11	12
1	1	9	10	3	5	2	11	7	6	12	4	8
2	4	1	12	9	3	7	5	6	2	8	10	11
3	9	4	1	2	8	3	10	5	7	11	12	6
4	3	8	4	1	10	9	6	11	5	7	2	12
5	11	3	8	4	1	5	9	2	12	6	7	10
6	5	12	3	8	4	11	2	9	1	10	6	7

AGE	1	2	3	4	5	6	7	8	9	10	11	12
7	7	6	9	5	12	4	1	10	11	2	8	3
8	2	7	6	12	9	10	3	1	8	5	11	4
9	12	2	7	6	11	1	8	4	10	3	5	9
10	10	11	2	7	6	12	4	8	3	1	9	5
11	8	5	11	10	7	6	12	3	9	4	1	2
12	6	10	5	11	2	8	7	12	4	9	3	1
13	1	5	10	8	11	6	7	2	12	3	9	4
14	4	1	3	2	5	7	8	11	6	12	10	9
15	9	4	1	6	8	5	2	7	11	10	12	3
16	3	9	4	1	12	8	6	5	2	7	11	10
17	11	3	9	4	1	10	5	6	7	8	2	12
18	5	11	6	9	4	1	12	8	10	2	3	7
19	7	10	11	3	9	4	1	12	8	5	6	2
20	2	7	5	12	3	9	10	1	4	6	8	11
21	12	2	8	5	10	3	9	4	1	11	7	6
22	10	12	2	7	6	11	3	9	5	1	4	8
23	8	6	12	10	7	2	11	3	9	4	1	5
24	6	8	7	11	2	12	4	10	3	9	5	1
25	1	6	10	3	2	8	7	4	11	5	12	9
26	4	1	3	8	6	7	2	11	12	9	5	10
27	9	4	1	5	10	11	12	7	6	8	2	3
28	3	9	4	1	11	5	6	8	7	2	10	12
29	11	3	9	4	1	6	8	2	10	12	7	5
30	5	11	8	9	4	1	3	12	2	10	6	7
31	7	5	11	12	9	4	1	10	8	6	3	2
32	2	7	5	11	3	12	10	6	4	1	9	8
33	12	2	6	10	8	3	9	1	5	7	4	11
34	10	12	2	7	5	9	11	3	1	4	8	6
35	8	10	12	6	7	2	4	5	9	3	11	1
36	6	8	7	2	12	10	5	9	3	11	1	4
37	1	3	10	6	9	12	7	5	11	2	4	8
38	4	1	3	8	6	5	2	7	12	10	11	9
39	9	4	1	12	8	2	10	11	6	3	5	7
40	3	9	4	1	11	8	6	12	2	5	7	10
41	11	7	9	4	1	6	8	2	10	12	3	5
42	5	11	8	9	12	1	3	4	7	6	10	2

Notes: (a) Adopt the above remedies at the time of marriage ceremony and if somehow or the other one fails to do these at the time of marriage, one can perform these remedies at the time of marriage anniversary.

(b) These remedies are to be adopted in respect of malefic planets in horoscope only.

(c) These remedies are to be adopted according to Raashi (signs) as they indicate the exaltation or the debilitating signs of a particular planet. They are not to be adopted according to houses.

(d) These may be adopted during the day except Rahu (in the evening) and Saturn (at night).

(e) These may be adopted on the days and time set apart for a planet i.e. Sun – Sunday, Moon – Monday, Mars – Tuesday, Jupiter – Thursday, Ketu – Sunday, Rahu – Thursday evening, Venus – Friday, Mercury – Wednesday, Saturn – Saturday night.

ooo

Annual Chart (Varsh Phal)

Annual charts from the famous *Lal Kitab* are given and discussed in detail in the following pages.

There are many methods of working out the annual charts on the basis of ancient texts. Just like the birth chart, the annual chart is also important for predictions for a particular year, as the annual chart specifically indicates the position of planets in a year. For the in-depth knowledge of readers, four different methods are being mentioned below. Results in all the cases are the same.

Method no.1

Subtract the previous years from the year for which annual chart is to be prepared. Multiply this number by '1,007'. The figure so obtained is to be divided by '800'. The quotient is **'Days'**. Multiply the remainder with '60' and then divide it by '800'; the quotient will be **'Ghatis'**. The remainder may again be multiplied by '60' and then divided by '800'; the quotient will be **'Pals'**. Again the remainder may be multiplied by '60' and then divided by '800' to arrive at **'Vipal'**.

Example: A child was born on 17-05-1967 at 3:45 AM i.e. 4 Jeth of Samvat 2024. His 'Isht' is 55 = 30 – Wednesday – his Annual chart for the year 1982 i.e. Vikram Samvat 2039 is to be worked out.

(a) Samvat of Birth   = 2024

(b) Samvat of Annual chart   = 2039

(c) Previous years (years elapsed) = 15

(d) Multiply 15 with 1,007   = 15 × 1,007 = 15,105

(e) Divide it by 800   = 15,105/800 = 18 Days (remainder is 705)

(f) Multiply 705 with 60   = 705 × 60 = 42,300

(g) Divide it by 800   = 42,300/800 = 52 Ghatis (remainder is 700)

(h) Multiply 700 with 60   = 700 × 60 = 42,000

(i) Divide it by 800   = 42,000/800 = 52 Pals (remainder is 400)

(j) Multiply 400 with 60   = 400 × 60 = 24,000

(k) Divide it by 800   = 24,000/800 = 30 Vipals

Thus, the number comes out to be:

	Days	Ghatis	Pals	Vipals
	18	52	52	30
Add: Isht	4	55	30	–
Total	23	48	22	30

A week comprises 7 days starting from Sunday. Divide 23 by 7, it comes to 2 i.e. Monday.

Thus, the 16th year will start from Monday – 48 Ghatis, 22 Pals and 30 Vipals i.e. 4 Jeths, 2039 (17-05-1982).

Method no.2

Previous years = 15 (1982 – 1967 = 15)

(a) Multiply 15 by 1¼ = 75/4 = 18 (Days) and 45 (Ghatis)

(b) Divide previous years by 2 = 15/2 = 7 (Ghatis) and 30 (Pals)

(c) Multiply 15 (previous years) by 1½ = 15×3/2 = 45/2 = 22 (Pals) and 30 (Vipals)

Add (a)+(b)+(c) =

	Days	Ghatis	Pals	Vipals
	18	45	-	-
	-	7	30	-
	-	-	22	30
Total	18	52	52	30

Add Birth Isht = 4 (Days) 55 (Ghatis) 30 (Pals)

Total = 23 (Days) 48 (Ghatis) 22 (Pals) 30 (Vipals)

The result is the same as worked out in example no.1.

Method no.3

Almost all the astrologers adopt this method. In all Panchangs (Ephemerides) or Jantris/Almanacs, one can find 'Varsh Sarni' (Annual Timetable) and 'Lagna Sarni' (Ascending Timetable) which contain the complete information:

Example: In an Annual Timetable (Varsh Saarni) figures under 15 in every Panchang are:

	Days	Ghatis	Pals	Vipals
	4	52	52	30
Add Lagna Isht	4	55	30	-
Total	9	48	22	30

i.e. Varsh (Annual) Isht is Monday – 48 Ghatis and 22 Pals and the 16th year will commence with above calculated day and time.

Important Note

(a) From the above Isht, annual chart may be prepared from 'Lagna sarni'.

(b) 60 Vipals = 1 Pal; 60 Pals = 1 Ghati; and 60 Ghatis = 1 Day and Night (24 hrs). If the Vipals are more than 60, divide it by 60, quotient is Pal and remainder is Vipal. If Ghatis are more than 60, quotient is Days and remainder is Ghatis. If the number of days is more than 7, divide 8 by 7 (days in a week), the remainder denotes days of the week starting from Sunday i.e. '1' means Sunday, '2' means Monday and so on. For converting the above Hindu time, refer to chapter 2.

1 Ghatis = 24 minutes; 60 Pals = 1 Ghati; 60 Vipals = 1 Pal.

What is 'Isht': It means desire for the object. It refers to the time elapsed between the moment of birth. It is expressed in Ghatis & Pals after sunrise.

Example: A child was born at a particular station at 10:00 AM (IST) and sun rises at that station on the day of birth at 5:30 AM (IST). Then (10:00 – 5:30 = 4:30 AM). It will be the 'Isht'.

"Muntha" in the Annual Chart and its significance

Hindu Astrologers attach great importance to the placement of 'Muntha' in the annual chart, but *Lal Kitab* does not make any mention of 'Muntha'. Anyhow the following methods may be adopted in computing 'Muntha' in the annual chart.

After preparing the annual chart, add the Lagna Raashi to the previous years. Divide this number by 12. The remainder may be placed in the Raashi (Sign) of that number in the annual chart.

Example: Child is born on 27-04-1939. His previous years on 27-04-2001 will be 62. His Lagna Raashi is 11 i.e. Aquarius. Add 62 to 11 i.e. 73; divide it by 12, the remainder is one. Hence, 'Muntha' in the year 27-04-2001 to 27-04-2002 is in the Aries. Thus, the 'Muntha' is to be mentioned in the house with the Raashi Aries.

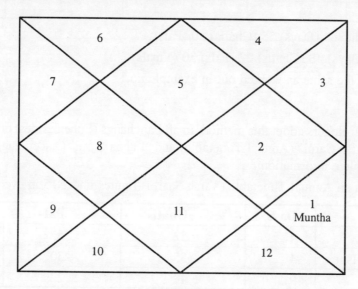

Fig. 13

Above is given the supposed Annual Chart.

Effects: (a) 'Muntha' in house no. 1,2,3,5,9,10,11 – good results.

(b) 'Muntha' in house no. 4,6,7,8,12 – bad results.

Annual Charts (Courtesy *Lal Kitab*)

For the convenience of the readers, we are giving the 'Annual Charts' for 103 years taken from *Lal Kitab*, the most famous and rare book on Astrology in Urdu. Whether one works out the Annual Charts from the methods detailed in previous pages or from *Lal Kitab*, the results are the same:

AGE	1	2	3	4	5	6	7	8	9	10	11	12
43	7	5	11	2	3	4	1	10	8	9	12	6
44	2	10	5	3	4	9	12	8	1	7	6	11
45	12	2	6	5	10	7	9	1	3	11	8	4
46	10	12	2	7	5	3	11	6	4	8	9	1
47	8	6	12	10	7	11	4	9	5	1	2	3
48	6	8	7	11	2	10	5	3	9	4	1	12
49	1	7	10	6	12	2	8	4	11	9	3	5
50	4	1	8	3	6	12	5	11	2	7	10	9
51	9	4	1	2	8	3	12	6	7	10	5	11
52	3	9	4	1	11	7	2	12	5	8	6	10
53	11	10	7	4	1	6	3	9	12	5	8	2
54	5	11	3	9	4	1	6	2	10	12	7	8
55	7	5	11	8	3	9	1	10	6	4	2	12
56	2	3	5	11	9	4	10	1	8	6	12	7
57	12	2	6	5	10	8	9	7	4	11	1	3
58	10	12	2	7	5	11	4	8	3	1	9	6
59	8	6	12	10	7	5	11	3	9	2	4	1
60	6	8	9	12	2	10	7	5	1	3	11	4
61	1	11	10	6	12	2	4	7	8	9	5	3
62	4	1	6	8	3	12	2	10	9	5	7	11
63	9	4	1	2	8	6	12	11	7	3	10	5
64	3	9	4	1	6	8	7	12	5	2	11	10
65	11	2	9	4	1	5	8	3	10	12	6	7
66	5	10	3	9	2	1	6	8	11	7	12	4
67	7	5	11	3	10	4	1	9	12	6	8	2
68	2	3	5	11	9	7	10	1	6	8	4	12
69	12	8	7	5	11	3	9	4	1	10	2	6
70	10	12	2	7	5	11	3	6	4	1	9	8
71	8	6	12	10	7	9	11	5	2	4	3	1
72	6	7	8	12	4	10	5	2	3	11	1	9
73	1	4	10	6	12	11	7	8	2	5	9	3
74	4	2	3	8	6	12	1	11	7	10	5	9
75	9	10	1	3	8	6	2	7	5	4	12	11
76	3	9	6	1	2	8	5	12	11	7	10	4
77	11	3	9	4	1	2	8	10	12	6	7	5
78	5	11	4	9	7	1	6	2	10	12	3	8

AGE ↓	1	2	3	4	5	6	7	8	9	10	11	12
79	7	5	11	2	9	4	12	6	3	1	8	10
80	2	8	5	11	4	7	10	3	1	9	6	12
81	12	1	7	5	11	10	9	4	8	3	2	6
82	10	12	2	7	5	3	4	9	6	8	11	1
83	8	6	12	10	3	5	11	1	9	2	4	7
84	6	7	8	12	10	9	3	5	4	11	1	2
85	1	3	10	6	12	2	8	6	5	4	9	7
86	4	1	8	3	6	12	11	2	7	9	10	5
87	9	4	1	7	3	8	12	5	2	6	11	10
88	3	9	4	1	8	10	2	7	12	5	6	11
89	11	10	9	4	1	6	7	12	3	8	5	2
90	5	11	6	9	4	1	3	8	10	2	7	12
91	7	5	11	2	10	4	6	9	8	3	12	1
92	2	7	5	11	9	3	10	4	1	12	8	6
93	12	8	7	5	2	11	9	1	6	10	3	4
94	10	12	2	8	11	5	4	6	9	7	1	3
95	8	6	12	10	5	7	1	3	4	11	2	9
96	6	2	3	12	7	9	5	10	11	1	4	8
97	1	9	10	6	12	2	7	5	3	4	8	11
98	4	1	6	8	10	12	11	2	9	7	3	5
99	9	4	1	2	6	8	12	11	5	3	10	7
100	3	10	8	1	5	7	6	12	2	9	11	4
101	11	3	9	4	1	6	8	10	7	5	12	2
102	5	11	3	9	4	1	2	6	8	12	7	10
103	7	5	11	3	9	4	1	8	12	10	2	6
104	2	7	5	11	3	9	10	1	6	8	4	12
105	12	2	4	5	11	3	9	4	10	6	1	8
106	10	12	2	7	8	5	3	9	4	11	6	1
107	8	6	12	10	7	11	4	3	1	2	5	9
108	6	8	7	12	2	10	5	4	11	1	9	3
109	1	9	10	6	12	2	7	11	5	3	4	8
110	4	1	6	8	10	12	3	5	7	2	11	9
111	9	4	1	2	5	8	12	10	6	7	3	11
112	3	10	8	9	11	7	4	1	2	12	6	5
113	11	3	9	4	1	6	2	7	10	5	8	12
114	5	11	3	1	4	10	6	8	12	9	7	2

Preparation of Annual Chart (when date of birth and place of birth are not known)

In the above case, the following method may be adopted:

Ask the man/woman to name the date of some fateful event in his/her life – happy or sad; or else, if he is married, he may be asked to mention the year of his marriage. Suppose he was married at the age of 25, his Venus (Lord of houe no. 7) will commence from 25th year and will end at 27th year i.e. period of three years. The chart may be prepared as under:

Jupiter 6 years	Sun 2 years	Moon 1 year	Venus 3 years	Mars 6 years	Mercury 2 years	Saturn 6 years	Rahu 6 years	Ketu 3 years
								Total = 35 years
						1 – 6	7 – 12	13 – 15
16 – 21	22 – 23	24	25 – 27	28 – 33	34 – 35	36 – 41	42 – 47	48 – 50
51 – 56	57 – 58	59	60 – 62	63 – 68	69 – 70	71 – 76	77 – 82	83 – 85
86 – 91	92 – 93	94	95 – 97	98 – 103	104 – 105	106 – 111	112 – 117	118 – 120

Note: If a person is married at the age of 31, his Venus will start from 31 to 33; then Mars from 34 to 39; then Mercury from 40 to 41; Saturn from 42 to 47 and so on and so forth. The above chart may be modified accordingly, if marriage takes place earlier or later. Also see the effect on total span of life in next paragraph.

Effect of Planets on total span of life (Ordinary Annual Chart)

Years	Effect of Planet	Years	Effect of Planet
1 to 6	Saturn	60 to 62	Venus
7 to 12	Rahu	63 to 68	Mars
13 to 15	Ketu	69 to 70	Mercury
16 to 21	Jupiter	71 to 76	Saturn
22 to 23	Sun	77 to 82	Rahu
24	Moon	83 to 85	Ketu
25 to 27	Venus	86 to 91	Jupiter
28 to 33	Mars	92 to 93	Sun
34 to 35	Mercury	94	Moon
36 to 41	Saturn	95 to 97	Venus
42 to 47	Rahu	98 to 103	Mars
48 to 50	Ketu	104 to 105	Mercury
51 to 56	Jupiter	106 to 111	Saturn
57 to 58	Sun	112 to 117	Rahu
59	Moon	118 to 120	Ketu

○○○

Moon Chart (Raashi Chart) and its importance

Astrologers also prepare Moon Chart along with nativity chart (Janam Lagna) in the horoscope. Moon Chart is prepared according to the placement of Moon in a particular sign at the time of birth. This is often called Chander Lagna or Moon Chart or Moon Raashi or radical sign of Moon. Such a chart is prepared in the following manner:

Nativity Chart

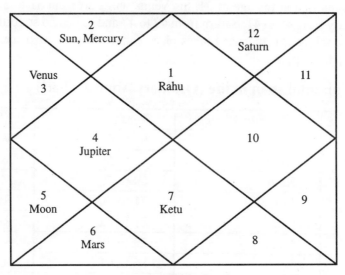

Fig. 26

Moon Chart

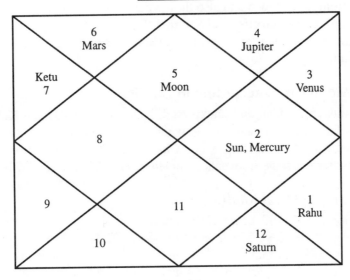

Fig. 27

Whenever a planet passes through the zodiac, its effect is counted from the Radical Moon. It can be both good and bad. Such a passage of a planet through zodiac is called Transit.

Sun bestows good results while transiting the 3rd, 6th and 10th houses from radical Moon. Moon gives good effect while transiting the 1st, 3rd, 6th, 7th, 10th and 11th houses from the Moon Raashi. Moon completes one cycle of the zodiac in 27 days i.e. two-and-a-quarter days in a sign.

Jupiter shows good effect while transiting through the 2nd, 5th, 7th, 9th and 11th houses from Moon Raashi. It stays in one sign for one year (approximately).

Venus confers good results while transiting the 1st, 2nd, 3rd, 4th, 5th, 8th, 9th, 11th and 12th houses, while Mars shows good results when it passes through the 3rd, 6th and 11th houses from the Radical Moon. Mercury bestows good results while transiting the 2nd, 4th, 6th, 8th, 10th, 11th houses from the Moon Raashi.

Now let us refer to Saturn's transit through the zodiac. It is both a great friend and the worst enemy. It confers best results when it transits the 3rd, 6th and 11th houses from the Radical Moon.

It is the deadliest of all enemies when it transits the 12th, 1st and 2nd houses from the Moon Raashi. This period extends to 7 ½ years and it is the most hateful and obnoxious. It lets loose all hell and fury on the person. Astrologers have given it the name of **"Saade-Saati"** i.e. the worst period of 7 ½ years in a person's life. People tremble at the mere mention of such a name. One must remember that life is a series of ups and downs and trials and tribulations. It is 'Dante's Purgatory' and one ultimately comes out victorious after passing through this hell. One must not lose one's patience, fortitude and courage and one must face this period with a cheerful heart as the saying goes, "if winter comes, can spring be far behind?" Ultimately, after this malefic period, dark clouds shatter and one again basks in glory and sunshine.

"Saade-Saati" has three cycles of 2 ½ years, each called an 'Adhaiya'. The first Adhaiya is bad for parents and blood relations, second cycle destroys domestic and professional life and happiness and the third Adhaiya adversely affects health and children. During Saturn's transit through 1st, 2nd, 8th and 12th houses from Natal Moon and also during the Dasha of an evil planet, the results are the worst. In order to ward off the evil effects of Saturn's "Saade-Saati" remedies for malefic Moon and Saturn may be adopted for 43 days every year. Transit results of Rahu and Ketu are almost similar to those of Saturn and Mars.

Significance of Moon Chart according to *Lal Kitab*

Raashi Chart's results are sudden and unexpected. Nativity Chart (Janam Kundali) and Annual Charts show man's fate in present and future; whereas the Moon Chart and the Annual Chart so prepared reveal spouse's nature and fate. Moon Chart gives sudden and unexpected results before one's marriage but after marriage it reveals complete results in respect of wife/husband.

Moon Chart according to *Lal Kitab*

Saturn-Moon relationship should be carefully studied, whenever Saturn aspects Moon (100% aspect) and whenever it destroys Moon (8th from Saturn). The Moon's effect is nullified and destroyed howsoever exalted it may be. (Moon in no.5, however, will act as poison for Saturn in no.10). Please refer to special aspects [page 64 and column no.5 (enmity) at page 64 and page 68 (planets which clash or collide)].

For remedy, refer to Moon-Saturn chapter no. 23 (Pages 267-269).

Moon Chart according to *Lal Kitab*

Moon Chart according to traditional astrology:

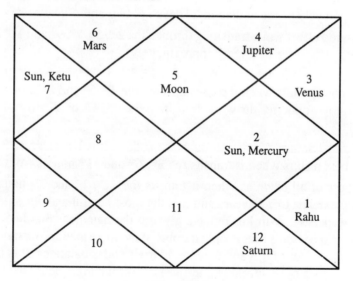

Fig. 28

Moon Chart according to *Lal Kitab*

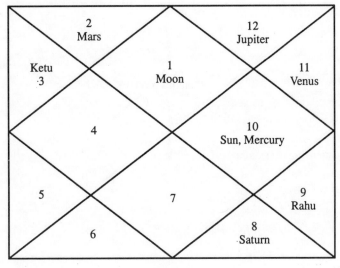

Fig. 29

How to determine Saturn's effect on Moon according to *Lal Kitab*

Whenever Moon, howsoever, exalted comes into conflict with Saturn, it spells misfortune. It destroys eyesight, brain, heart, peace of mind and mother; it happens when Moon is in direct aspect of Saturn i.e. 7th, 8th, 3rd and 10th from Saturn in the Birth chart and Annual charts. Saturn in 6th house destroys and stings house no. 2, Saturn being retrograde. Further when Moon aspects Saturn i.e. 7th and 8th aspects – Moon is afflicted. This is how Saturn's adverse effect on Moon i.e. Mind, eyesight, mother, comforts etc. is determined.

How to determine 'Saade-Saati' and its importance

According to the traditional astrologers, Saturn stays in one sign for 2 ½ years and it adversely affects not only the sign of its sojourn, but also the one earlier and one later. In other words, it affects three signs simultaneously for 2 ½ years each i.e. for a total period of 7 ½ years. All ephermerides (Panchangs) mention Saturn's entry into a particular sign of Moon. Here is an example:

Suppose a person's native Moon sign is Taurus (2nd Raashi). Saturn had entered Aries on 18-04-1998. Obviously, his 'Saade-Saati' started from 18-04-1998 and will continue for approximately 7 ½ years. Saturn entered Taurus on 07-06-2000 and will continue till 23-07-2002. That will be his second Adhaiya. The third Adhaiya will start from 23-07-2002 onwards.

This is the chart showing Saturn's Sojourn in a Moon sign.

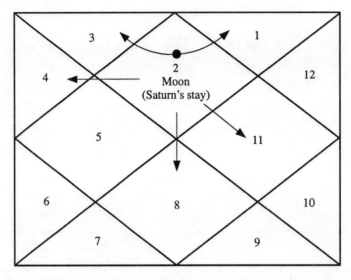

Fig. 30

Saturn aspects the 3rd and 10th house, hence it is aspecting the 4th, 8th and 11th signs. First two signs being enemies, it causes untold mental misery, but it also bestows all types of comforts such as property, vehicle etc., while aspecting its own sign i.e. 11th sign. Further, as Saturn in these days is staying in Taurus (Raashi of an intimate friend), it will ultimately confer victory over enemies. The man may suffer from depression etc. and may be surrounded by enemies, but in the end, he will be victorious, as Saturn will not harm a friend.

Sun

सूरज गुरु घर दो का इकट्ठा – असर मिला हो जुदा ही है

गुरु पिता गर सूरज का होवे – सूरज पिता खुद शनि का है ।

रुह दुनियां का गुरु जो मालिक मूर्ति दुनिया सब रवि का है

सांस इनसानी गुरु का होवे – ढांचा पर खुद रवि का है

गुरु अगर आसमान गिना तो – रास्ता रवि आसमान का है

सूरज बैठा जब एक, पांच, ग्यारह – टेवा वह बालिग होता है ।

घर एक पांच जब सूरज हो बैठा – तलवार थारी दो होता है ।

मंगल छटेया केतू पहले – ऊंच सूरज हो जाता है ।

ग्रह दुश्मन जो साथी होवे – मदद सूरज की करता है ।

सूरज नीच न खुद कभी होवे – असर साथी मंदा होता है ।

ग्रह-दोस्त अपना मरवावे – खुद ही जब वह मरता है ।

सूरज रोशनी मंगल किरणें – ग्रहण राहु केतु होता है ।

बुध आकार तो तेज गुरु का – चमक चंद्र रवि देता है ।

सूरज शनि दो इकट्ठे बैठें – झगड़ा नहीं वह कभी करते हैं ।

वजह किसी गर दोनों झगड़े – कत्ल वह शुक्र का करते हैं ।

Sun-Jupiter together confer individual results,
Jupiter is Sun's father, though Saturn is Sun's child.
Jupiter is the master of world and soul.
Sun governs Earth and its comforts.
Man's breath is Jupiter, but is Sun's infrastructure.
Jupiter is sky, Sun is the milky way.
Sun occupying house no. 1,5,11 makes the horoscope exalted.
When in 1,5 it is like a sharp sword.
Mars in 6th, Ketu in first, make Sun exalted.
Even enemies help Sun when together they sit.
Sun is never debilitating, only the
conjoined planets give malefic effect.
And makes his friend scapegoat when in trouble.
Sun is light, Mars the rays.
But is eclipsed by Rahu-Ketu – the two nodes.
Mercury confers shape; Jupiter brightens.

But Moon receives from Sun its effulgence.
When Sun-Saturn are together, never they quarrel.
But Venus they destroy when they are hostile, somehow or the other.

Miscellaneous Information

(a) **Exalted Sun:** "The glorious Sun stays in his course and plays the alchemist, turning with splendour of his precious eye, the meagre cloddy earth to glittering gold." (Shakespeare)

(b) **Malefic Sun:** "The great angry god traverses the heavens on his chariot driven by fiery steeds burning everything beneath with his fiery shaft." (Anonymous)

"Lord Vishnu" (God of Hindu trinity); King doing penance; supports and sustains life; dispels darkness and brings light and glory."

Effect of Sun on Life and Fate in Various Houses

(a) House no. 1: King like status; above the consideration of caste and creed; symbol of justice; helpful to father; king doing penance; administrator; must be a strict administrator and a polite trader for better results.

(b) House no. 2: God fearing and noble hearted; good status and position; will help relatives and friends; selfless service will confer better results.

(c) House no. 3: Bold like a lion; will have courage to fight and scare death; fond of sumptuous dishes; will do well to others but will be harsh upon liar or a hypocrite.

(d) House no. 4: Raj yoga; exalted status; himself will lead a frugal life, but will leave millions for children; though poor at birth, will have the capacity to donate pearls in later life; the more magnanimous and large-hearted he is, the better for him; illicit relations with other women will harm him.

(e) House no. 5: A thorough gentleman; upholder of sacred traditions; will serve the blood relations like a lighted and luminous lamp; best luck; very rich; the older he grows, the richer he becomes.

(f) House no. 6: Like an exiled king rejoicing at the destruction of his own empire; like king Nero, who was fiddling while Rome was burning; a Don-Quixote (Sheikh-Chilli) fighting against imaginary enemies; despite all reverses, such a man will never stoop low.

(g) House no. 7: Like the Sun which deteriorated into a meteor, shattering itself into nothingness. In short, he is like a king who has lost his crown; everything goes topsy turvy; though born a king, yet will never ascend the throne; must be a strict officer and a polite trader, for better results.

(h) House no. 8: Even though born poor, yet will occupy good position; no one can spoil his fate; but if he loses something himself, he will never be able to regain it. As long as he is not hostile to his family members, he will never suffer; Sun's chariot will conquer death, hence not the house of death, if occupied by Sun.

(i) House no. 9: Will shed his blood for family, but will never demand anything in return; man of determination who keeps his words.

(j) House no. 10: Howsoever noble and intelligent, he will be underestimated; even then full of contentment, will never bend before suppression; self respecting; a sincere friend.

(k) <u>House no. 11</u>: Noble and religious minded; but greedy; the nobler the man in his deeds and actions, the more exalted status he enjoys; should be tee-totaller, otherwise may create problems for self and children.

(l) <u>House no. 12</u>: Shortsighted king who has no worries for self and who enjoys good sleep; may face robberies; must serve cows and sadhus; of course, he will never be poor and issueless.

Effect of Sun in various houses and positions

(1) A man with an exalted Sun confers light and brightness on all; long life of 100 years; truthful in thoughts and deeds; will never be poor; will not cheat others and hit below the belt; even death, which otherwise is considered horrible, will be pleasant for him.

(2) He will earn a lot from a good govt. job, when Sun is exalted, even Moon, Mercury and Venus will confer best results.

(3) Sun, in whatever house it is placed, will give best results, if Ketu is in no.1 or Mars is in no.6.

(4) Mercury in no.6 and Sun benefic – honest and self made income will help.

(5) Sun aspecting Mercury

(a) Sun aspecting Mercury 100%	Mercury will help Sun
(b) Sun aspecting Mercury 50%	Mercury will help Sun
(c) Sun aspecting Mercury 25%	Mathematician; expert astrologer

(6) Mercury aspecting Sun (any degree) ⟹ Mercury will be exalted; good health; ideal couple.

(7) Saturn aspecting Sun

(a) Sun	Sun's effect will be destroyed but Venus will confer best results
(b) 100% aspect	Magician
(c) 50% aspect	Architect, builder
(d) 25% aspect	Mathematician

(8) Saturn in earlier house and Sun in the next ⟹ Sun's lustre will be blackened i.e. weakness of body; but will not adversely affect Mars, Jupiter and Mercury i.e. no bad effect on personal fate and wealth. Remedy: Bury a pot filled with water.

(9) Sun aspecting Saturn i.e. Sun in earlier ⟹ Spouse will be unhappy and destroyed, and Saturn in the next house but Sun's effect will not be bad.

(10) Mars, Moon, Jupiter helping Sun ⟹ Exalted status, better than father.

(11) At the time of eclipse in the birth chart (i.e. Sun – Rahu – Solar eclipse) and Moon – Ketu (Lunar eclipse, Sun's results will not be good till 45th year.)

(12) Sun may be malefic or positioned in an enemy's house, but it will never be debilitated; on the other hand, it will have bad effect on Ketu (son), short temper will destroy the man.

(13) Sun occupying house no. 1 in Annual Chart will confer good results on self, but will destroy Venus. Remedy lies in Mercury.

(14) Sun, if alone, in house no. 2,6,7,8,10 and 11 will not confer good results on the Lords of these houses; but it does not mean that it will have bad effect on them; results will be neutral.

(15) Sun associated with Venus or wicked planets such as Sun-Venus; Sun-Saturn; Sun-Rahu or Sun-Ketu will adversely affect the house in which they are placed when they occupy the same house in the Annual Chart e.g. suppose Sun-Venus are in house no. 5 and they occupy house no. 5 in Annual Chart (34th year or 25th year Venus' period), they will have adverse effect on spouse or on one's baby. Remedy lies in Mercury.

(16) If Sun's friends (Moon-Jupiter-Mars) occupy the same house in conjunction with Sun and his enemies, bad effect will be visible on friendly planets and enemies will be safe.

General Remedies for Malefic Sun:

(a) If Sun is in house no. 6 and 7, seek help from Mercury and also sprinkle a few drops of milk to extinguish fire.

(b) When Sun destroys a planet, remedy lies in Sun itself.

(c) When Sun is destroyed, adopt the remedy for the planet which is adversely affecting it.

Sun – House no. 1

Good effects

King like status; will serve his father till the end; short-tempered; long life; exalted govt. position; honesty will pay; man of integrity; will create wealth; small family, but good and obedient.

Good effects of Sun in house no. 1 and planets in other houses:

Planet	House No.	Good Effect
Moon and Saturn	No.2, No.11	Will occupy an exalted position; fortunate & wealthy
Mercury	No.7	Noble and pious
Vacant	No.7	Early marriage will be beneficial

Bad effects

If alone in this house, Sun will stop its benefic effect on Venus i.e. wife, beloved, ghee, camphor etc.; disputes concerning women, property, land and money will result in misfortune. The number of women in the family will be fewer. (Remedy lies in donating coconut or almonds or oil for 43 days).

Bad effects of Sun in house no. 1 and planets in other houses:

Planet	House No.	Bad Effect
Venus	No.7	May lose his parents in childhood; sick wife
Mars	No.5	Will lose son
Saturn	No.8	Wife will die or suffer

Sun – House no. 2

Philanthropist; architect of own fate.

Good effects

Sun in house no. 2 is exalted, if house no. 8 is vacant; upholder of traditions; even Jupiter will be sub-servient to Sun; the more liberal and generous the man, the more exalted status he enjoys; will help relatives viz. parents, in-laws, uncles, brothers, sisters, own children etc.; will have conveyance; rich, officer, having good reputation; glorious life for self and others.

Good effects of Sun in house no. 2 and planets in other houses:

Planet	House No.	Good Effect
Moon	No.6	Moon and Sun both will give exalted results.
Rahu	No.8	Technician.
Rahu	No.9	Painter.
Ketu	No.8	Truthful.
Ketu	No.9	Technician.
Mars	No.9	Fashionable.
Saturn	No.10	Intelligent, enjoys good reputation.
Saturn	No.11	Fluctuating temperament; sometimes happy and sometimes sad.
Mercury	No.8	Brave.

Bad effects

Bad effects of Sun in house no. 2 and planets in other houses:

Planet	House No.	Bad Effect
Mars	No.8	Greedy.
Moon	No.8	Bribe and corruption will destroy him; honest income will be beneficial.
Mars & Moon	No.1 & no.12	Unhappy; poor and lazy.

Sun – House no. 3

Wealthy; self-made man.

Good effects

Self-made rich; handsome; now Moon will not show bad results nor will Mars be malefic; even Venus and Mercury will confer good effect; mathematician; astrologer; will never face bad days or misfortunes.

Good effects of Sun in house no. 3 and planets in other houses:

Planet	House No.	Good Effect
Exalted Moon	Any house	Rich in old age; mother's blessing and long life.

Bad effects
Bad effects of Sun in house no. 3 and planets in other houses:

Planet	House No.	Bad Effect
Malefic Moon	Any house	Will be looted and cheated in broad daylight.
Malefic	No.9	Poor parents.
Malefic	No.11	Bad neighbourhood.
Malefic	Mercury	Bad effect on maternal uncles.

Note: Sun will give worst effect if man is lustful and of low character, but will never be cheated by fate.

Sun – House no. 4

Frugal, earns for children, leaves a rich legacy.

Good effects

Frugal and economical, but leaves millions for children; noble; generous; good-intentioned; born to rule; fountain of wealth; will serve parents; Jupiter and Moon will be the deciding factors for personal wealth.

Good effects of Sun in house no. 4 and planets in other houses:

Planet	House No.	Good Effect
Moon	No.4	Will earn through inventions and discoveries.
Mercury	No.10	Great businessman; will earn through travels.
Mars (exalted)	Any	Man of patience and contentment; good-intentioned.
Jupiter & Moon (benefic)	No.10 & any	Jupiter will give excellent results, will no longer be weak; like a pearl.
Jupiter, exalted Moon & exalted Mars	No.4 & any	Will earn through travels abroad; gold and silver business will be beneficial.
Sun in association with Moon & Venus	No.4	A noble man and noble parents.
Sun in association with Mercury	No.4	Will earn a lot through travels.

Bad effects

Thief; bad habits; will be physically and financially ruined before death.

Bad effects of Sun in house no. 4 and planets in other houses:

Planet	House No.	Bad Effect
Saturn	No.7	Night blindness.
Jupiter + Malefic Rahu & Saturn	No.10 + No.1	Malefic results of Sun; (remedy for Moon).
Jupiter	No.10	Theft of gold; loss in timber & hardware business; incidence of fire; gain through gold, silver & cloth trade.
Mars	No.10	One-eyed; but fortunate and wealthy.
Moon, Venus and Saturn	No.1 or 2 No.5 No.7	Impotent, transvestite; meddlesome.
Exalted Moon, Jupiter & Malefic Mars	No. 4, Any	Problems in marriage and children.

Sun – House no. 5

Only son; red faced monkey; bringer of good luck.

Good effects

Best luck after birth of a son; double-edged weapon i.e. if noble and pure-hearted, exalted results; but if mean, will suffer from misfortunes; but will not adversely affect job and children; will promote the interests of children and family members; long life; excellent old age.

Good effects of Sun in house no. 5 and planets in other houses:

Planet	House No.	Good Effect
Wicked planets (Saturn, Rahu, Ketu)	No.9, 11	Sympathetic; parents' blessings; Sun & Saturn will not oppose each other.
Jupiter, Moon or Venus	No.9 or 12 No.4 No.2 or 7	King like status; Phoenix (Hummah) the legendary bird will fly over his head and will make him a king.
Moon	No.4	Exalted status.
Enemy planets	No.1 or 5	Sun will help its enemies; will earn respect.
Jupiter & Mercury	No.9 or exalted in any house; No.4	Raj yoga; eminent status.
Mars, Jupiter (all exalted)	No.3, 9, 12	Best results.

Bad effects

Bad effects of Sun in house no. 5 and planets in other houses:

Planet	House No.	Bad Effect
Jupiter	No.10	More than one marriage.
Saturn	No.3	Bad children; son may die; life full of sorrows and miseries.

Sun – House no. 6

Raashi Effect – "Full of fire; no worry for wealth; wheatish colour; defect in feet".

Good effects

Now Mars (even in house no. 4) will not be malefic ('Manglik'); will have no worries about job; short-tempered; connoisseur in matters of taste & choice of women; birth in maternal uncle's house; away from ancestral house; parents must be rich at the time of birth; downfall must in life; may leave jobs many times, but will get another; best time after birth of a child.

Good effects of Sun in house no. 6 and planets in other houses:

Planet	House No.	Good Effect
Moon, Mars & Jupiter	No.2	Upholder of old traditions; Sun will be more exalted.
Ketu	No.1, No.7 in Birth chart or No.1 in Annual chart	Must be blessed with a son.

Bad effects

Sun, if alone in this house, will have adverse effect on son and his happiness. (Remedy lies in donating Sun's articles i.e. wheat, copper etc.) and those of Moon (rice or silver).

Bad effects of Sun in house no. 6 and planets in other houses:

Planet	House No.	Bad Effect
Vacant	No.2	Ill health of father during 5th, 11th, 23rd year.
Saturn	No.12	Bad for wife – death or separation.
Mars	No.10	Death of son (keep rice or silver under the pillow at night and donate to the poor in the morning); this will be the saving grace.
Mercury	No.12	Problems in job & income; bad health (blood pressure).
Saturn or Rahu	No.1	Solar eclipse; bad fate when Saturn/Rahu occupies house no. 1 in the Annual Chart. This bad patch in fate will disappear when Ketu is in house no. 1 or 7.
Rahu and Saturn	No.2, No.8	Solar eclipse on fate and health (remedy for solar eclipse).
Moon	No.12	Wife or himself will be one-eyed.
Rahu and Ketu	No.1, No.7	Birth in maternal uncle's house; away from ancestral house.

Sun – House no. 7

Debilitated Raashi Effect – Fewer family members; coward; spiritual defect.

Good effects

Will regain wealth and happiness after 34th year; no bad effect on self and family, but bad for parents and in-laws; exalted Sun in its own or friendly sign will not be bad; everything will be fine; long life of couple; will have the capacity to donate pearls and silver to poor; like the exalted Sun will have an unique personality and will face difficult times with courage; if wife is faithful to husband, life will be comfortable and happy; otherwise bad effect on wealth and domestic life.

Good effects of Sun in house no. 7 and planets in other houses:

Planet	House No.	Good Effect
Exalted planets or Mercury or Jupiter or Venus	No.2, No.3, No.5	Will have a job away from house, but will die at his ancestral place.
Saturn or Mercury or Ketu	No.2	Domestic life slightly disturbed, but not totally bad.
Jupiter or Moon or Mars	No.2	Eminent position and advisers.
Mercury or exalted Mercury	No.7	Rich, good income, but not wise.

Debilitating and worst effects

Most malefic and worst results, if alone in this house; Sun will exercise worst effect on domestic life, spouse, skin etc.; should be a strict officer and polite businessman for better results; short-tempered, peevish, selfish, prone to flattery, desire for notoriety, given to self-praise, his own enemy – all are the signs of bad days and fate.

Malefic effects of Sun in house no. 7 and planets in other houses:

Planet	House No.	Malefic Effect
All planets malefic	No.7	Dust instead of gold; suicidal inclination; but courageous to fight it out; bad domestic life for 25 years.
Venus & wicked planets	No.2	Grief-stricken wife; unfortunate in-laws; but himself lucky.
Jupiter or Venus or Mercury or wicked planets	No.1 Malefic	Large no. of deaths; bad fate; asthma, T.B.; or ill matched couple; madness; mentally unsound; selfish, suicidal tendency, incidence of fire.
Mercury	No.9	Unreliable.

Planet	House No.	Malefic Effect
Mars or Saturn and Moon	No.2, No.12, and No.1	Leucoderma (white patches on skin).
Ketu and Mercury	No.1, No.11	Officer should be strict and trader be polite, otherwise he will be destroyed.
Vacant	No.1	Sun will be dormant and asleep, it will regain its glory, when planet in no.8 occupies no.8 in Annual Chart (i.e. 13, 29, 41, 54, 64, 72, 78 years).

Remedies:

(a) Must maintain outward pomp and show; officer must be strict and trader must be polite.

(b) If Saturn is in house no. 1 or Saturn somehow destroys Sun, put out the kitchen fire by sprinkling a few drops of milk on it.

(c) Remedy also lies through Mercury i.e. donate Moong.

(d) For Son's progress, financial condition, or domestic happiness, bury 7 square copper pieces on Sunday between 8 AM and 10 AM.

(e) Take sugar or sweet or a few sips of water before doing auspicious work.

(f) Put a morsel of bread into fire before taking food for domestic happiness.

Sun – House no. 8

King doing penance; fire; Sun's chariot.

Good effects

Conqueror of death (death fears Sun in this house); power of mimicry or imitating others; promotion in service from 23rd year to 45th year; wealthy; Mars in house no. 8 will not be malefic (Mangalik).

Good effects of Sun in house no. 8 and planets in other houses:

Planet	House No.	Good Effect
Jupiter, Moon, Mars or associated with benefic Mars	No.1	Saturn and malefic Mars will show good results and Sun will also confer good results.

Bad effects

Lustful ways will destroy the man; must refrain from bad deeds; must be affectionate and respectful to his elder brothers, failing which he may face bad luck.

Bad effects of Sun in house no. 8 and planets in other houses:

Planet	House No.	Bad Effect
Saturn or malefic Jupiter or malefic Mars	No.3 No.1 or No.5 any	Short-lived, if opposes elder brothers; must respect elders.
Venus	No.1 or No.5 or No.10	Worst results regarding fate.
Malefic Jupiter	Any	May help others, but unfortunate for self.
Mercury	No.2	Loss of wealth.

Sun – House no. 9

Long life; large family; helping family members; Sun in full glory.

Good effects

Long life with honesty and integrity; children and father live long; may shed the last drops of blood for family members, but will not demand anything in return; even brothers and sisters (house no. 3) and children (house no. 5) will lead a good life. Moon will no longer be bad. Parents will be govt. employees; house no. 5 (house for children) will be exalted, even though it may be occupied by malefic planets; will spend a lot on household. In a nutshell, Sun in this house is auspicious and confers best results.

Good effects of Sun in house no. 9 and planets in other houses:

Planet	House No.	Good Effect
Mercury	No.5	Best results after 24th year.

Bad effects

Should not accept bribes, especially silver, and should not be a parasite upon others; otherwise results will be disastrous; should donate silver instead of accepting it.

Bad effects of Sun in house no. 9 and planets in other houses:

Planet	House No.	Bad Effect
Mercury	No.3, 5 or 9	Bad effect of Sun i.e. father (Keep big brass vessels in the house).
Rahu	No.1, 3 or 5	Excess of peevishness (rudeness) or politeness will give bad results; irreligious and life of luxury at others' expense; parasite.
Mercury & Saturn	No.3 or 11	Unfortunate; Mercury will befool Sun and Saturn both.

Sun – House no. 10

Lord of health, wealth and fame; superstitious.

Good effects

Will command respect; healthy; wealthy, but superstitious. White cap is auspicious, but black or blue cap or bare head is inauspicious. Moon no.4 and Sun no.10 confer good status and Sun becomes exalted.

Bad effects

In this house, Sun will exercise bad effect on his greatest enemy. Saturn will do no good to articles concerning Saturn viz. inherited property, father's happiness, timber, oil, iron, knees, thighs etc. Person residing with in-laws (Rahu) will have a bad time. Rahu will eclipse Sun; one must not crave for self-pity i.e. must not express his sorrows before others. That will usher in bad times.

Bad effects of Sun in house no. 10 and planets in other houses:

Planet	House No.	Bad Effect
Malefic Moon not helped by Mars or Jupiter	No.5, No.6, or any	Short-lived; full of sorrows and sufferings.
Moon	No.5	Age 15 days, if not helped by or associated with male planets.
Venus & malefic Saturn	No.4 or any	Father's death in his childhood.
Exalted Moon	No.2	Mother will suffer and may even die in native's 24th year.
Wicked planets	No.6 or No.7	Bad luck in every sphere till 34; thereafter good effect.
Malefic Saturn	Any	Clash between father and son; due to job problems with things connected with Saturn. 19 years of Saturn's Mahadasha will be bad for father's health and wealth. (Remedy: Install hand pumps or dig wells for public welfare).
Vacant	No.4	Even if very intelligent and competent, his superiors will not recognise his worth. (Remedy: Throw one copper coin in running water for 43 days).

Sun – House no. 11

Noble but luxurious life; red copper; religious-minded; selfish.

Good effects

A vegetarian person will be blessed with a son soon; greedy, but will have an exalted position; religious-minded, but will have a personal life of luxury; long life.

Bad effects

Sun, if alone, will adversely affect the articles concerning Saturn; liar, ungrateful; cheat; it is good if a person is a teetotaller; worst results if addicted to wine and meat; long life full of deceit and lies.

Bad effects of Sun in house no. 11 and planets in other houses:

Planet	House No.	Bad Effect
Moon, Mercury & Saturn	No.8, No.3 and Malefic in any house	Long life full of lies, deceit and treachery.
Moon	No.5	Age 12 years when not helped or associated with male planets; may be deprived of a son. (Remedy: keep carrot or turnip and almonds under the pillow at night and donate it in the morning for 43 days).

Sun – House no. 12

Sound sleep, but worried for others.

Good effects

Now Rahu will be under Sun; sound sleep at night; feelings for others; no clash between son and father; neither Venus nor Mercury will be bad; happy couple; owner of lands; pure in thoughts and actions; lively, knowledgeable, honest and man of integrity; bad luck if he deals in hardware and machines, but good luck in other trades. Connected with Mercury (i.e. business, investments etc.)

Good effects of Sun in house no. 12 and planets in other houses:

Planet	House No.	Good Effect
Saturn	No.6	Venus, even if malefic, will confer good results.
Ketu	No.2	Self-made rich after 24th year of age; happy and comfortable.
Venus and Mercury joint	Any	Will never lose job; business will make him rich, if he is not employed by govt.

Bad effects

Sun, if alone, will stop exercising its noble effect on things connected with Rahu i.e. bones of head; notoriety; sudden rise of bad thoughts in mind; conjugal relations between man and woman; bad name; problems in career; bad for employment; solar eclipse in business connected with Saturn i.e. machines, business of hardware, timber, skilled labour, brick kiln etc.; on the other hand, Mercury (trade, speculations, investments etc.) will confer good results. Worst luck, if man is involved in lustful acts, false witness, betrayal of trust, corruption, bribery and not returning loans.

Bad effects of Sun in house no. 12 and planets in other houses:

Planet	House No.	Bad Effect
Wicked planet	No.1	Sleepless nights; hand to mouth living; must act on the maxim, "Forgive and forget is the best form of revenge." This will help.
Moon	No.6	One-eyed wife or self.

110

Jupiter (Creator, Universal Guru, Lord Brahma)

पापी ग्रह या बुध मिलान – पिघला सोना गुरु होता है।

इलाज ग्रह साथी का होवे – गुरु राशिफल होता है।

पापी मंदे या केतु मंदा – गुरु भी मंदा होता है।

ग्रहण के वक्त हवा बर्फानी – असर मंदा हो जाता है।

तबाह मंगल आकाश बेल – तो बुरा शुक्र फल देता है।

दुश्मन ग्रह के जब वह अंदर – दुश्मनी खत्म कर लेता है।

एक से पांच या बारह बैठा – मदद सूर्य शनि करता है।

घर छः से ग्यारह में बैठा – सिर्फ शनि को तारता है।

गुरु जो अकेला सबको तारे – मदद न जब कोई करता है।

पर केतु को मरवा देवे – खुद ही जब वह मरता है।

When associated with sinners and Mercury,
Jupiter is like molten gold.
Remedy lies in the associated planets but Jupiter gives "Raashi"effect.
When sinners and Ketu are malefic,
Jupiter too becomes malefic.
During eclipses, there are snowstorms which lead to malefic results
When Mars debilitating is creeper (Akash Bel),
Venus also gives malefic effect.
When it enters the enemy planets,
It destroys enmity.
While in 1 to 5 or 12, it helps Saturn and Sun
And in 6 to 11, it helps Saturn alone.
Individually it helps all even when others fail to do so.
But, it destroys Ketu when it finds itself in trouble.

Exalted Jupiter: The great teacher who earns esteem and acclaim, and is blessed with supreme intelligence, wisdom and gold.

Malefic Jupiter: A cursed Sadhu who begs for alms with a begging bowl.

During the whole period of its 'Mahadasha' spanning to 16 years, Jupiter does not give bad results during first eight years. In other words, it does not harm the man during the first eight years of its 'main dasha'. Further, Jupiter must confer best results during the 1st, 2nd, 8th, 10th and 14th years of its 'Mahadasha', the remaining years i.e. 9, 11, 12, 13, 15 & 16 may give varied results according to Jupiter's position and aspect – whether friendly or not. The great guru reserves 1st year as 'Gurudakshina' (offering made by a disciple to the teacher); it gets the 2nd year from Saturn; 8th year from Rahu; 10th year is his personal year and 14th year from Ketu. Thus, 1st, 2nd, 8th, 10th, 14th years are his personal years, hence the best results. Further, during the first 8 years, it does not harm the individual. Thus, Jupiter's Mahadasha starts from the 9th year to 16th year (excluding 10th and 14th years as stated above).

Effect of Jupiter on 12 Houses

House No.	Good Effect	Bad Effect
No.1	Famous; King; scholar; scientist; researcher	A renowned Sadhu but poor.
No.2	Universal teacher; preacher; hospitable; rich, provided house no.8 is not vacant	Destroyer of one's own family.
No.3	'Durga' worship; hunter of lions i.e. very powerful and brave	Cowardly; unfortunate; accused.
No.4	Renowned; king like status (Raja Vikramaditya or Lord Indra of heaven); fountain of wealth	Sailor who sinks his own ship i.e. bad fate.
No.5	Saffron like; rich and comfortable after birth of a son; respected by all	Dead son in mother's womb.
No.6	Will get everything without efforts	Son will suffer due to poverty and troubles.
No.7	Leader of family; rich	Unhappy with brothers; even his adopted son will be unhappy; asthmatic.
No.8	Philanthropist; (like Karna of the Mahabharta or Hatim-Tai)	Like a cursed sadhu of graveyard; poor and unfortunate.
No.9	Blue-blooded; great ancestor; glittering gold	Most unfortunate.
No.10	Strict and cruel but very rich	Poor.
No.11	Even snake will bow i.e. will have lot of income	Very bad fate; even shroud and coffin will be provided by others.
No.12	Lot of wealth; divine thoughts	Will not utilise his own wealth, even though he may be rich.

Miscellaneous features of Jupiter

Planet	House No.	Effect
Jupiter	No.1 to 5 and 12	Will help Sun and Saturn.
Jupiter	No.6 to 11	Will help Saturn only.
Jupiter	In association with male planets i.e. Sun or Mars or aspected by them	Jupiter will confer best results regarding wealth.
Jupiter	In association with female planets i.e. Moon or Venus or aspected by them	Jupiter will confer best results i.e. even water will turn into milk.
Jupiter	If wicked planets i.e. Saturn, Rahu, Ketu are malefic	Jupiter will give worst results like the poisonous gases.
Jupiter (If alone)	And aspected by malefic planets	Will not give bad results.
Jupiter (Debilitated)	Mercury (good or bad)	Jupiter's effect – good or bad – will depend upon Mercury's position – good or bad.
Jupiter	Associated with wicked or enemy planets (Venus, Mercury) or aspected by them	Will give malefic results. (Remedy lies in wicked or enemy planets i.e. Saturn, Rahu or Mercury, as the case may be.)
Jupiter	If Mercury and Rahu are together in No.2, 5, 9, 11	Jupiter's results will be bad.
Jupiter	If Sun-Rahu (Solar eclipse) or Moon-Ketu (Lunar eclipse) are together in birth chart	Jupiter's effect will be disappointing.
Jupiter	If Mars-Saturn or Mars-Moon aspect Jupiter	Good results of Jupiter.

Jupiter's relationship with Saturn

Planet	House No.	Effect
Saturn and Jupiter or Jupiter and Saturn	No.1, 6 or 7	Will prosper after marriage, provided Saturn and Jupiter do not occupy malefic houses in the Annual Chart e.g. Saturn in no.1 and Jupiter in no.10 will show bad results.
Saturn aspecting Jupiter along with another planet	No. 3, 6, 9, 1	Bad effect; (Remedy: Donate almonds to ward off bad effect.)

Planet	House No.	Effect
Saturn Jupiter	No.1 No.7	Bad results.
Saturn Jupiter	No.2 No.8, 12	Bad results.
Saturn Jupiter	No.3 No.5, 9, 11	Bad results.
Saturn Jupiter	No.4 No.2, 8, 10, 11	Bad results.
Saturn Jupiter	No.10 No.2, 3, 4, 5	Bad effect.
Saturn alone	No.5 to 9, 11, 12	No bad effect on Jupiter, if alone.
Saturn	No.1 to 6	Will exercise bad effect on Jupiter.
Saturn	No.6	Saturn's effect will be suspicious (good or bad), but it will definitely exercise malefic effect on Jupiter. (Remedy: Throw coconut or almonds in running water).
Saturn and Jupiter	Earlier house and later house	Jupiter will not give its full effect.
Jupiter and Saturn	Earlier house and later house	Very rich man.
Jupiter and Saturn or Jupiter and Saturn	No.5, 9, 3 No.9 or 11	Man will be a magician.
Jupiter and Saturn or Jupiter and Saturn	No.8, 6, 2 No.12	Interested in Yoga.

Jupiter's relationship with Ketu

Planet	House No.	Effect
Ketu and Jupiter	Earlier house and later house	Jupiter's effect will be bad.
Jupiter and Ketu	Earlier house and later house	Moon's effect will be bad, instead of Jupiter's and Ketu's.

Jupiter's relationship with Mercury

Planet	House No.	Effect
Jupiter & Mercury together	In all houses except no.2 and no.4	Jupiter is destroyed.
Jupiter and Mercury	No.2 and 4	Mercury will not oppose Jupiter, but rather help it; hence good for health.

114

Mercury	No.1 to 6	Mercury's effect will be good up to 34th year of life, thereafter bad effect.
Jupiter	No.7 to 12	Jupiter's effect will be bad till 34th year of life, thereafter good effect.

Jupiter – House no. 1

Renowned king; researcher; scientist; bold like a lion.

Good effects

Will be rich and great while dealing in articles relating to Jupiter; house no.1 is king's throne and if it is occupied by exalted Jupiter, it will make the man king like rich and renowned; native's mother will bless him like Lord Shiva and she may live up to 51 years of native's age; even Moon and Sun will help Jupiter; good health; will have property, good eyesight; but short-tempered like a tiger; good-hearted; noble-natured; will easily see through other's wicked games; will be victorious in all ventures; differences in the ages of children will not be more than 8 years; scholar; research scientist; will bring glory to parents at the age of 16 & himself will be renowned person in old age.

Good effects of Jupiter in house no. 1 and planets in other houses:

Planet	House No.	Good Effect
Any & Jupiter, Not associated with enemy planet	No.7, No.1	Highly educated and very intelligent.
Mercury (exalted) & as above	Any	Highly educated; will occupy an exalted position; king like status.
Exalted Ketu	Any	Parents will be rich at native's 16th year, and will be prosperous till 75th year.
Exalted Moon	Any	The older he grows, the more exalted status he enjoys; the best old age.
Exalted and Jupiter's enemies not in	No.7 and 1,2, 5, 9, 11, 12	Will inherit great wealth and property.
Exalted Planet	No.11	Self-made rich; lot of wealth and property.
Vacant	No.7	Great rise after marriage.
Vacant	No.7	Marriage at 24th or 27th or before 28th year may be bad for father's health. (Remedy: Bury articles of Mars).
Sun or Moon or Mars	No. 1, 2, 4	Very rich; will earn from govt. job; his copper coin will turn into gold; will be very famous.
Mars	No.7	Blue blooded; royal lineage; owner of estates and lands.
Sun	No.9	Long life of self and family members.
Exalted Planets	No.2, 3, 4, 8	Long life.

Bad effects

If Jupiter gives bad results during first 35 years, it will make up for the loss and will confer good results during the next 35 years (which will commence from 49th year), provided such a man does not beg and remains contented with his lot.

Bad effects of Jupiter in house no. 1 and planets in other houses:

Planet	House No.	Bad Effect
Malefic Mercury	No.2, 5, 9, 12	Illiterate; great sadhu, but poor.
Rahu, Jupiter	No.2, 5, 9, 12	Bad fate; even gold will turn into copper and rusted iron; malefic winds will blow all over.
Malefic Jupiter with Venus or Mercury	No.2, 5, 9, 12	Even gold will turn into dust; black fate full of dust and storms.
Malefic Jupiter with wicked Saturn	No.2, 5, 9, 12	Worst results after 36th year; evil deeds, hence horrible results; urinary troubles.
Saturn	No.9	Bad health.
Malefic Saturn	Any	Unhappy himself and unhappy children.
Malefic Sun or Sun – Mercury	No.11, Malefic houses	Involvement in litigation; loss of wealth; meddling with the affairs of others; in fact, worst fate.
Rahu	No.8 or 11	Father will die of asthma or heart failure or paralysis or brain haemorrhage or drying up of body.

Jupiter – House no. 2

Spiritual teacher; lord of knowledge and education; temple of God.

Good effects

This house is the seat of Jupiter and is made exalted by Moon. This sign (Raashi no.2) can never be dominated by others. This house is, therefore, the house of respect, wealth and good name; all other houses look towards this house with respect. Wealth and respect for 27 years, provided house no.8 is not vacant; noble king like Raja Janak, who helped the poor; if there is a malefic planet, remedy lies for Jupiter and it will ward off the evil effect of malefic planet, even Rahu in this house pays homage to Jupiter, 'The Great Guru'; happy domestic life; exalted personal fate; even malefic planets will not harm Jupiter; wealth will increase manifold; noble, pious, full of milk of human kindness; will inherit from parents, and will be rich himself; full of noble thoughts and deeds.

Good effects of Jupiter in house no. 2 and planets in other houses:

Planet	House No.	Good Effect
Sun	No.10 or 12	Very Famous.
Ketu	No.6	Will have a premonition of his death.
Saturn	No.12	Exceptionally brave and famous like Napoleon Bonaparte.
Benefic planets, provided no.2 is not adversely aspected by No.8 or 10	No.2, 6, 8	Will receive legacy or property from others; may also win lottery.
Any planet, whether friend or foe of Jupiter	No.8, 9, 10, 12	Wealthy; happy family life; man of determination; full of courage and optimism.
Saturn, Mercury & Sun	No.8	Learned scholar.
Vacant and any planet among Sun, Moon, Saturn, Rahu or Mercury	No.8, 6	Will earn respect; noble man but large family.
Mars	No.8 or 9	Honest and dominating officer.
Benefic Rahu	Any	Philanthropist; good deeds; happy life; will earn respect.
Any planet	No.8, 9, 10 or 12	Happy life and good children.

Bad effects

Bad effects of Jupiter in house no. 2 and planets in other houses:

Planet	House No.	Bad Effect
Malefic (e.g. Moon-Mars combined in No.8, both are Jupiter's friend but will destroy no.8; also if malefic Mars is in no.2, this house will be destroyed	No.8, 2	Will be responsible for the destruction of his own family.
Saturn	No.2 in Annual Chart	Ill health; In-laws will suffer monetary losses.
Vacant	No.8	Jupiter's effect will be bad regarding Rahu and Ketu.
Malefic planet	No.8, 2	Accused person; causes harm wherever he goes; full of bad omen.
Saturn and malefic Venus	No.10	Wife's ill health and himself unhappy.

117

Saturn, Mercury	No.10, 8	Monetary loss; unhappy parents; may go to jail.
Mercury	No.9	Jealous.
Mercury or Venus, Rahu or Saturn as wicked planets	No.8 or 10	Worst luck.

Remedies:

(a) For Mercury or Rahu in house no.10–Remedy for Saturn.

(b) For Venus in house no.10–Remedy for Moon.

(c) For Saturn (as wicked planet) in house no.10–Remedy for Jupiter.

(d) For Mercury, Rahu, Venus or Saturn (as wicked planets). For remedy refer to house no. 8 for these planets.

(e) For malefic Jupiter–Remedy for Jupiter.

Jupiter – House no. 3

Roaring lion; rich family; teacher; happiness for relatives.

Good effects

Justice-loving; educated; intelligent; exalted govt. job; must worship minor virgins (before the age of puberty) and offer them sweet food on auspicious occasions (otherwise Jupiter in house no. 3 will give the effect of malefic Mercury in no.3 or 9); long life; happy brothers; relatives and in-laws.

Good effects of Jupiter in house no. 3 and planets in other houses:

Planet	House No.	Good Effect
Exalted Jupiter	No.3	Long life; wise, intelligent, educated; good health; prosperous & wealthy.
Exalted Saturn	No.3 or any	Very rich.
Exalted Mars or Exalted Sun, Mars, Moon or Jupiter	No.2 No.2 in Annual Chart	Brothers and sisters will be helpful; best luck after 26th year for at least 20 years; exalted status and a lot of wealth.
Friendly planet	No.5, 9, 11	Happy life; rich after the birth of a child; good position.
Saturn	No.9	Long life and lot of wealth.
Saturn	No.2	Eagle-eyed; shrewd and subtle; very clever; will recognize a man from his voice.
Mars	No.2	Will help all; have rich and happy life.
Mercury	No.7	Brave man.

Bad effects

Coward; unfortunate, bully.

Bad effects of Jupiter in house no. 3 and planets in other houses:

Planet	House No.	Bad Effect
Malefic Jupiter, surrounded by enemies (Mercury, Venus, Rahu or Saturn)	No.3	Extreme temperament – either too generous or too miser; a generous friend but a deadly foe.
Moon	No.12	Prone to flattery; may be destroyed by sycophants.
Malefic Mars	Any	Coward; chatter box; unfortunate (malefic effect of no.3 & 9); worst life; ill health; sickly; back biter.
Saturn & malefic Mercury	No.4	Will become rich after looting and cheating others; may deceive his friends; brave in battlefield, but still unfortunate.

Jupiter – House no. 4

Grand mansion, gold and wealth.

Good effects

The 'Great Guru' ruling over Moon's kingdom; royal-like; exalted; grand mansion; lands & estates; gold; goddess of wealth; best fortune; noble and good-hearted; Sun, Venus, Moon and Mars – all the four planets will confer best results like the precious pearls; will be exceptionally rich; the most eminent person in his town or family; will be owner of estates and magnificent house; will enjoy an exalted status; fountain of wealth; smiling face; man of principles; maintains best relations with all, irrespective of caste and creed; good character; will not be greedy; contented; in short, he enjoys all pleasures and comforts. He is like Indra, the chief of the gods; compassionate; goddess Laxmi (wealth) touches his feet; beautiful wife; eminent children; happiness from parents and will serve them; full of milk of human kindness; power of throne; pure like milk; faces difficulties and storms of life cheerfully and boldly like a tiger; indeed the best planet.

Good effects of Jupiter in house no. 4 and planets in other houses:

Planet	House No.	Good Effect
Venus, Rahu, Saturn (not as wicked planet)	No.2, 5, 9, 11, 12	Eminent son; occupant of King Vikramaditya's throne; i.e. seat of justice; exalted status and govt. job; very rich; his copper coin will turn into gold; grand house; education for 24 years; river of gold; like the legendary 'Eldorado'; abounding in

		gold; may receive legacy or lottery or buried treasure.
Moon – Saturn	No.1, 10	Will own all types of vehicles.
Exalted Sun or Mars	Any	Father will be an officer.
Moon	No.2	Fate will depend upon Saturn's or Rahu's position – good or bad; nevertheless he will be an eminent person; king like status; will be brother or son or relative of a person having an exalted status; may have to spend 1/4th of his income on his ill health; rich; will have flag on his car; in fact, a very exalted position.
Vacant	No.10	Jupiter will be dormant. (Remedy: Must not show his naked body to others and must keep his clothes on).
Moon	Any (except no.2)	Moon will confer good results, even though it may be malefic.
Exalted Moon	Any	Will complete his education if mother is alive.
Exalted Ketu	Any	Will complete his education, if he is of good character; will enjoy long life.
Exalted Mercury & exalted Sun	No.10	Like a pearl in a shell; will earn a lot from good job.
Saturn	No.2, 9, 11	Good reputation; helpful to all; rich; comfortable life; imposing house.
Exalted Rahu	Any	Moon's results will be exalted.
Sun Exalted Moon	No. 10 Any	Travel will bring best results; like precious pearl.

Bad effects

Bad effects of Jupiter in house no. 4 and planets in other houses:

Planet	House No.	Bad Effect
Mercury (malefic)	No.10	Will be destroyed; will also destroy his family like a sailor responsible for sinking his own boat; (will be worst when it occupies house no.4 in Annual Chart i.e. 11th, 23rd, 34th, 48th, 55th, 71st, 75th, 85th year).

Saturn (malefic)	Any	Loose character; womanizer; drunkard; drug addict; bad reputation; may lose his eyesight; even Ketu will be bad. (Remedy: Must not have illicit relationship with woman of loose character and must not take wine & drugs.
Venus, Mercury, Rahu or Saturn as wicked planets	No.10	Loss of wealth.
Malefic Rahu	Any	Bad effect on Moon i.e. mother, heart, mind etc.
Malefic Ketu	Any	May renounce the world; may kick his throne and wealth; may flee and run away instead of facing troubles and problems; a coward.

Jupiter – House no. 5

A thorough gentleman; exalted status; enjoys respect and esteem; scholar; writer; short tempered, but noble hearted; saffron.

Good effects

Rise after birth of a son; noble; religious-minded; comfortable old age; son, if born on Thursday – both son and father will be like lions i.e. will enjoy exalted status. If house no. 2, 9, 11, 12 are occupied by Jupiter's friends (i.e. Sun, Moon or Mars), they will all help Jupiter; though short-tempered yet noble-hearted; a perfect gentleman; eminent writer; will earn respect and regards from all.

Good effects of Jupiter in house no. 5 and planets in other houses:

Planet	House No.	Good Effect
Exalted Sun, Moon & exalted wicked planets	Any	Will never be childless; will occupy the throne of Lord Indra or King Vikramaditya i.e. highest seat of justice.
Exalted Mercury	Any	Prosperous and noble.
Sun or Mars or Moon	No.9	Best luck regarding wealth and sons; parents may be poor, but will be rich and enjoy exalted status.
Saturn	No.9 (in Birth Chart & Annual Chart)	Best luck for 60 years; but no gain from father or parental side.
Mercury, Venus, Rahu, Saturn (not as wicked planets)	No.2, 5, 9, 11, 12	Best results regarding wealth and happiness.
Exalted Saturn	Any	Will earn a lot of respect.

Bad effects

Bad effects of Jupiter in house no. 5 and planets in other houses:

Planet	House No.	Bad Effect
Ketu	No.11	Dead child may be born; issueless i.e. no son.
Malefic Ketu	Any	Bad son.
Mercury, Venus, Rahu or Saturn (as wicked planet)	No.2, 5, 9, 11, 12	Will be responsible for his fall; good luck after 25 (Venus), 34 (Mercury), 42 (Rahu), 45 (Ketu), 36-39 (Saturn). (Remedy: See remedy for Ketu).
Rahu	No.9	Jupiter may be quiet, but will not disappear.
Malefic Rahu	Any	Poor sadhu begging for alms.

Jupiter – House no. 6

Raashi effect: Parasitic, but good-natured; like eagle; remedy for Ketu during bad times.

Good effects

Will get everything without effort; father should be generous and if so, he will become rich; the native will live a luxurious life at the expense of others. Financial condition will depend upon Saturn's position – good or bad – maternal uncles will be prosperous, but will not help him till his 40th year.

Good effects of Jupiter in house no. 6 and planets in other houses:

Planet	House No.	Good Effect
Mercury, Venus, Rahu or Saturn (not as wicked planets) & Jupiter	No.2, 5, 9, 12 and No.6 (alone without any aspect from No.2)	Life full of respect; will have the good results of Moon no.6 and also of Mercury and Ketu, i.e., will lead a respectable life; will be parasitic but will get everything without making any effort.
Exalted Mercury	Any	Life full of luxury, but selfish.
Exalted Ketu	Any	If having good character, the person will be prosperous & rich, even maternal uncles will be rich, but not helpful.

Bad effects

Bad effects of Jupiter in house no. 6 and planets in other houses:

Planet	House No.	Bad Effect
Malefic Mercury	Any	Life full of sorrows & sufferings till 34th year; and may have to suffer the hammers of fate.
Malefic Ketu	Any	May have to beg with a begging bowl. (Remedy: Adopt remedy for Ketu).
Mars	12	Bad for father's life.

Jupiter – House no. 7

Raashi effect – Sadhu in previous life; Books; remedy for Moon.

Good effects

Takes leading part in religious affairs; rich; may buy property at other places, but will die at the place of birth; wife will be helpful and inspire in difficulties; helpful to relatives; will be blessed with a son at a later stage after 34th to 45th year; son will be bringer of good luck for him; will never be issueless; will never leave debt for children; may live away from brothers; sons will be fortunate; an eminent astrologer, luxurious life for 40 years.

Good effects of Jupiter in house no. 7 and planets in other houses:

Planet	House No.	Good Effect
Saturn	No.7 or 9	Very rich; large but fortunate family.
Exalted Ketu	Any	Religious-minded; sincere & noble, but may not be very rich.
Exalted Mercury	Any	Both Jupiter and Mercury will confer best results.
Exalted Rahu	Any	Comfortable life in youth.
Sun	No.1	Interested in astrology; worldly wise, but leads a luxurious and easy-going life; may not be very rich.
Sun, Moon, Mars (Jupiter's friends)	No.1, 2, 5, 9, 12	Rich and royal ancestors, but himself may not be rich; noble-hearted and good doer.

Bad effects

Asthma; poor vagabond sadhu; Jupiter will never be malefic in a girl's horoscope; but that is not the case with boy's horoscope.

Bad effects of Jupiter in house no. 7 and planets in other houses:

Planet	House No.	Bad Effect
Associated with malefic Mars or malefic Mercury	No.7 or any	Poor vagabond sadhu; unfortunate; will earn his living even though may be rich; may not care for his children during youth; hence, will be unfortunate in old age.
Malefic Jupiter	No.7	Neither brothers will be helpful nor he will have any exalted position.
Mercury, Venus, Rahu, Saturn as wicked planets	No.1, 2, 5, 9, 12	Unlucky children when Venus is malefic; father may die of asthma; worst fate.
Mercury or Saturn	No.2, 6, 12	Will yearn for a male child; may have a son at the age of 45, but will then be ruined; even adopted son will be unhappy.
Malefic Mercury or Saturn	No.9 or 11	May stammer; bad for life, fate and monetary position.

123

Remedies:

(a) Adopt remedy for Moon.

(b) Keep yellow cloth or gold in yellow cloth at home or seven 'Rattis' in a yellow cloth.

Jupiter – House no. 8

God's blessing in distress; blessings of ancestors; voice of the people.

Good effects

Whether rich or not, he will have all the comforts of life; God will help him in time of distress; as long as he keeps gold on body, he will never be unhappy; and will never have bad health; will glitter like gold in his career; will never be a poor sadhu; grandfather will die either before his death or in the 8th year after his birth and if he lives thereafter he will live up to 80 or more; will have long life and father will also live long; he will not see death in his family in his presence.

Good effects of Jupiter in house no. 8 and planets in other houses:

Planet	House No.	Good Effect
Exalted	No.2 and No.4	Will be like a rising star; will extract gold and wealth even from sand; happy life and family.
Exalted Moon and benefic planets in	Any No.2, 5, 9, 12	Fabulously rich; long life.
Venus	No.2, 6, 8	Will have sons; comfortable long life.
Mercury not in	No.9	Long life.
Benefic Mars or aspecting no.2 in a friendly manner	Any	Philanthropist like 'Karna' of Mahabharata; will bring back even dying man to life; good doer; noble actions and thoughts.

Bad effects

Sadhu living in the cremation ground, whose head is besmeared with ash i.e. poor and God forsaken.

Bad effects of Jupiter in house no. 8 and planets in other houses:

Planet	House No.	Bad Effect
Saturn or Mars	No.4 or 7	Will be financially and physically ruined.
Malefic Jupiter or surrounded by enemies	No.8 or any	Notorious lover; lustful conduct.
Malefic Mars	No.8 or any	Always under debt; even though may earn enough; worst luck; an ill fated sadhu; unhappy, cowardly and lazy.
Malefic Mercury or malefic Ketu	No.8 or any	Cowardly, lazy, indolent, sickly and diseased.

Vacant	No.2	Financial and health problems.
Malefic Sun	No.8 or any	Bad fate
Malefic Rahu	No.8 or any	Not a good life; will be just like a "fill in the blanks".
Saturn	No.2	Full of determination; freedom loving.

Remedy: During difficult times donate things connected with Jupiter or Venus.

Jupiter – House no. 9

Good effects

Royal blood; Yogi who does not hanker after wealth; rising fortune; rich legacy; man of words; as he grows older, he gets interested in spiritualism; may live up to 75 years; very rich ancestors having lot of wealth; noble and royal blood; happiness from parents; good character; an expert jeweller; upholder of family traditions.

Good effects of Jupiter in house no. 9 and planets in other houses:

Planet	House No.	Good Effect
Vacant	No.3 & 5	Self-made rich.
Mercury, Venus, Rahu or Saturn (not as wicked planet)	No.2, 5, 9, 11	Rich; noble and religious-minded.
Mercury	No.4 or 5	King among 'yogis'.
Exalted Sun	Any	Good health; prosperity; happiness; great rise in life even though Jupiter may be weak.
Jupiter aspected by Male planets	From No.3 and 5	Jupiter will be three times exalted; best results.
Saturn	No.5	For wealth, refer to Saturn's age 16 ½ to 19; or 33 to 39 years; rich but unlucky in respect of son.
Aspected by Moon and Venus	From No.3 or 5	Sometimes very rich and sometimes very poor; sudden rise and fall.

Bad effects

Bad effects of Jupiter in house no. 9 and planets in other houses:

Planet	House No.	Bad Effect
Jupiter adversely affected	By enemies	Poor; may convert to another religion.
Mercury, Venus or wicked planets	No.5	Bad children, especially son; irreligious; ill health; heart patient.
Vacant	No. 3 or 5	Will have to struggle for promotion in life.
Malefic Mercury	No.9 or any	Short-lived; unfortunate; bad effect of malefic Mars.

Jupiter – House no. 10

Worst results; loss of wealth; disruption in studies; lifeless and dry 'Peepal' tree; Sadhu yearning for food and clothes.

Good effects

Must work hard for good results; the more noble and good doer he is, the worse the fate; conversely, the more clever and subtle, the better for him; but, should not indulge in lustful acts; may have less wealth, but will be intelligent; may get less than what he deserves.

Good effects of Jupiter in house no. 10 and planets in other houses:

Planet	House No.	Good Effect
Exalted Saturn or Exalted Sun or Moon	Any Any No.2 or 6	Lucky; even iron will be converted into gold i.e. must deal in things connected with Saturn (i.e. iron etc.); comfortable life and long life of parents.
Venus or Mars	No.4	Rich, provided he does not indulge in lustful act with other women.
Sun	No.4	Now Jupiter will not be debilitated, but will become exalted and will confer riches.
Mars	No.8	Must keep good relations with brothers for better results.
Saturn	No.2	Best luck.
Sun And Saturn	No.3 or 5 No.9	Best if he is a jeweller, worst if he deals in articles concerning Saturn.
Sun or Moon	No.2	Will earn a lot through travels or official duty.
Exalted Mercury, not aspecting or disturbing Jupiter	Any	Will have sons and be prosperous and rich.

Bad effects

Though noble and religious-minded, yet will be deprived of wealth; everything will go topsy-turvy; father will not help him while alive and will not leave any property after his death; hence most debilitated planet.

Bad effects of Jupiter in house no. 10 and planets in other houses:

Planet	House No.	Bad Effect
Malefic Saturn	Any	Ignorant, fanatic, spendthrift; bad luck.
Saturn or Moon	No.1, 4, 10 No.4	Must not help a person out of way; otherwise the same man will hit back and create problems for him.
Malefic Ketu	Any	Worst luck; even gold will turn into ash. (Remedy: Adopt remedy for Jupiter or Ketu).
Saturn and Ketu	No.1, 4, 10 No.2	Very poor; worst fate; may even starve; will be kicked by all.
Vacant	No.2, 4, 5, 6	Ill fated; poor; unhappy, but will struggle hard and succeed.
Sun	No.5	Wife may die or may leave him or run away.
Mercury	No.4, 9, or 10	Father may die an untimely and unnatural death through blood poisoning; worst till 34th year; like a hollow drum. (Remedy: Pierce the nose or keep the nose clean).

Remedies:

(a) Put a yellow dot of saffron on forehead.

(b) Blow out the nose and keep it clean.

(c) Throw copper coin for 43 days in running water for better luck; otherwise he may not get his dues.

Jupiter – House no. 11

Rule of Saturn; devoid of piety or dharma; lonely like a palm tree; gilted gold; but bringer of good luck.

Good effects

If religious-minded, noble and helpful to others; good luck; as long as he lives in a joint family, he will be fortunate; when alone he is like a palm tree, Jupiter will be zero and weak; during father's life all will be fine, but after his death, he may suffer and even though multimillionaire, his father may not leave much property for him; for best results, must be noble and religious-minded and a good-doer; must keep his word.

Good effects of Jupiter in house no. 11 and planets in other houses:

Planet	House No.	Good Effect
Vacant	No.3	Jupiter will be dormant and asleep; Saturn will decide his fate which will be good.
Sun, Moon or Mars	No.3	Comfortable life till 33rd year; thereafter darkness all around. (Remedy: Keep gold on body or saffron in pocket).
Sun, Moon or Mars	No.5	Business with brother will do well for 12 years, thereafter not so good.
Sun	No.1, 4, 5	Will earn a lot through govt. job; bad results, if any, will be on grandfather and not on father.
Rahu	No.9	Jupiter will be quiet, but will not disappear.
Exalted Mercury	Especially No.6	Self-made multimillionaire.
Exalted Saturn	Any	Though father may not help him, he will have a comfortable life; even Mars will help him.
Jupiter and Saturn together	No.11	Both the planets i.e. Jupiter and Saturn will confer results.

Bad effects

Sister will be ungrateful, but himself will be good; will be spineless or cowardly after father's death; person of loose character will confront worst fate; at his death, someone else will offer shroud and coffin to him.

Bad effects of Jupiter in house no. 11 and planets in other houses:

Planet	House No.	Bad Effect
Mercury And Moon	No.6 and No.2	Bad old age; bad eyesight.
Mars	No.3	Unhappy on account of deaths in the family but good for in-laws.
Mercury	No.3	Deprived of father's love; will be under debt, though having considerable income.
Exalted Venus	Any	Unhappy life.
Malefic Mercury and Vacant	No.3	Irreligious; selfish, but rich. If tall and soft spoken, liberal and noble, then 'unfortunate'.
Malefic Moon	Any	Mars, Saturn, Jupiter – all will be malefic.

Remedy: Must help relatives and condole their death.

Jupiter – House no. 12

Forgiveness – the best form of revenge – will help even enemies; yogi; scholar; green Peepal tree; air and breath.

Good effects

If noble and religious-minded, best results; will not care for money; Venus will confer best results; must be liberal; the more he donates the more he gets; foundation of wealth; a good-doer will never be poor; will have divine powers; lot of expenditure, but will spend on household affairs; best results, if he is honest, truthful and noble.

Good effects of Jupiter in house no. 12 and planets in other houses:

Planet	House No.	Good Effect
Saturn or in conjunction with Jupiter	No.9	Will earn a lot through machines and cars (Saturn's trade); will not care for money.
Rahu	No.6	Will have the best of both the worlds.
Ketu (Exalted)	Any	Multimillionaire; noble children.

Bad effects

Bad effects of Jupiter in house no. 12 and planets in other houses:

Planet	House No.	Bad Effect
Wicked planets (except Ketu in no.9 or 12)	No.2, 5, 9, 12	Bad till 45th year.
Malefic Mercury	Any	Ketu's (son) effect will be bad till 34th year. (Remedy: as for Jupiter).
Malefic Rahu	No.9, 12	Irreligious; lot of useless expenditure.

129

Moon

चंद्र पक्का घर चौथा गिनते – ग्रह सबका पेट माता है ।

हर घर में यह राशिफल का – घर उसका धरती माता है ।

खाली पड़ा है घर जो चंद्र का चौथा – असर उमदा और नेक दे देता है ।

चंद्र घर से बाहर हो बेशक ख़राब – घर खाली ही दूध पिला देता है ।

जहां चंद्र पानी – वहां असर सूरज भी आ जाता है ।

ग्रह लड़ते बाहु में आ बैठे चंद्र – तो दोस्त वह उनको बना जाता है ।

चंद्र बैठा पहले या दुश्मन को देखे – असर नेक बंद अपना कर देता है ।

ग्रह दुश्मन पापी जब बैठे हों पहले – असर चंद्र मंदा ही हो जाता है ।

दुश्मन हो साथी तो दोनों ही मंदे – खड़ा पाप दुनिया में हो जाता है ।

पड़ा पाप ख़ुद अपने चंद्र के घर जब – शनि बुध भी नेकी पे हो जाता है ।

चावल चंद्र का जितना पुराना – कीमत बुढ़ापे बढ़ती है ।

नज़र चंद्र में गुरु जो बैठा – दौलत ज़्यादा जो मिलती है ।

Lord of 4th House refers to mother's womb;
In every house it confers Raashi effect. And dwells in Mother Earth.
Vacant fourth house means all is well;
Even if it is malefic outside its permanent House,
It does even then offer abundance of milk.
Where there is moon and water pure;
There sun also confers its effect pure.
Amongst mutually destructive planets when Moon resides
It makes them shed enmity and shake hands.
Moon in earlier House or aspecting the foe;
It shuts up its good effect and becomes ineffective so.
Enemy planets and sinners occupying earlier houses;
Moon's effect does become malefic,
When in conjunction with enemies, both are malefic.
It multiplies in the world sin & evil.
Sinners (Rahu-Ketu) in moon's House,
Make even Saturn & Mercury become benefic & shun evil.
The older the rice of Moon in the house,
the greater the price and respect;
When aspecting Jupiter it brings lot of wealth.

Exalted Moon

"Queen moon is on her throne, surrounded by her starry feys." (Keats)

Malefic Moon

"Whom the gods destroy, they first make mad." (Euripides)

(1) Moon and its attributes:

Lord Shiva, the most compassionate and merciful; mother earth showering all her blessings; ocean of milk; boat of life i.e. saviour from death, theft and destruction; Pegasus (the Greek flying horse). In house no. 3, it is Lord Protector and in house no. 7, it is goddess of wealth (Laxmi); mind, memory etc.

(2) Miscellaneous information about Moon:

(a) When Jupiter occupies the earlier house and Ketu the latter; Moon's effect will be bad; but as long as Mercury is exalted, Moon cannot be malefic.

(b) Venus aspecting Moon: women will oppose each other.

(c) Moon aspecting Venus: A great fakir or sadhu and ringleader of drug addicts.

(d) If Sun throws its reflection on Moon i.e. if it is aspected by Sun; Moon will not be malefic.

(e) A single planet occupying Moon's house will not give bad results; but house no. 4, if vacant, will confer good results.

Remedy: Seek elder's blessings.

(3) Moon in relation to Mercury:

(a) When Moon occupies the earlier house than Mercury, Moon will dominate Mercury.

(b) If Mercury is in the earlier house than Moon, Mercury will dominate Moon.

(c) (i) If Moon and Mercury aspect each other (100%); results are very bad.

    (ii) If it is 50% aspect, results are bad.

    (iii) If it is 25% aspect, results are slightly bad.

In all the above cases, man will not lose wealth, but will have a weak heart; may even commit suicide. For example, Moon in no.7 and Mercury in no.4 will confer best results, but if they are together in no.4 or 7, results will not be good.

(4) Moon in relation to Saturn:

(a) Moon aspecting Saturn: Moon's results will be benefic, but Saturn's malefic; hence very bad.

(b) Saturn aspecting Moon: Moon's effect will be the worst; but Saturn's effect will not be bad.

(c) When Sun-Mars are together in the Birth chart, Moon is not good.

(d) If Moon aspects Jupiter and house no. 2, 5, 9, 12 (Jupiter's house) are occupied by Mercury or Venus, or Rahu-Ketu or Saturn, Moon's effect will be bad.

(e) Wicked planets will always poison Moon's milk or water; (Remedy for Moon).

(f) Even if Moon is malefic, it does help others. Such a person should deal in things connected with Moon i.e. milk, jewels etc. and not those of Venus i.e. mud and earth.

Moon's Effect on Education

Moon in House No.	Effect
No.1	Money spent on education will bear fruit; will get job according to qualifications; like pure water in a pitcher.
No.2	Mother's blessings; will receive inherited property, wealth and full education; exalted Moon (purest fountain).
No.3	The better the education, the worse will be father's financial position; education will give good returns provided Moon is not destroyed by Ketu. Such a man will suffer demotion etc. if he joins education department; like water in a desert.
No.4	Like a sweet water of fountain; best and exalted results of education; mother's patronage.
No.5	Money spent on education may not give full results; like camel providing water to selfish urbanites; may be highly qualified; will not receive any help from those whom he helps.
No.6	Will complete his education; like a deep well or a hand pump.
No.7	Will complete his education before marriage; beneficial education; incarnation of 'Laxmi' (the goddess of wealth); like a river irrigating precious and fertile land.
No.8	If educated, will inspire his children; if illiterate, his children will be uneducated or semi-literate; like divine 'amrita', the nectar of gods or poison.
No.9	Will provide comforts to all through knowledge; life full of comforts and luxuries like Indra – the chief god of heaven; like an ocean of knowledge.
No.10	Obstacles in education; totally disinterested; may, however have knowledge of medicines; if no.8 is malefic, results are bad; but exalted no.2 confers best results.
No.11	Will receive full education; may be illiterate but intelligent; like the gutter full of rain water.
No.12	Benefic Sun or Jupiter will confer best results regarding education; if wicked planets are in malefic houses, results will be bad; in short, such a person, even if illiterate, will be the father of highly educated children; like rain, hailstorm and snow.

Moon – House no. 1

Mother's blessings; heart like pure milk; wealthy.

Good effects

Will inherit all virtues from benign mother; successful life; long life (approximately 90 years); best luck like pure milk; success in service; happiness for full 27 years; happiness from children; his

132

brothers and sisters might have died before his birth; parents may not be rich at the time of his birth; must not marry before 28th year; marriage at the age of 24 will destroy mother's love and patronage; must take milk in silver tumbler; must not accept bribes or gifts of silver articles; should offer milk to the needy; in order to have comfortable sleep, must fix copper nails to the four legs of the cot on which he sleeps; offer water to Banyan tree off and on; will have wealth during mother's life, especially 24th to 38th year; learned scholar; as long as he respects his mother and seeks her blessings, he will progress a lot, otherwise benefic life will be full of sorrows. Moon in 1st house in Annual Chart will give best results during 13, 25, 37, 49, 61, 73 years. (Remedy lies in burying sugar or Masur daal (red lentil) in the earth, if Moon in house no.1 is weak and bad).

Good effects of Moon in house no. 1 and planets in other houses:

Planet	House No.	Good Effect
Sun, Mars or Jupiter	No.4 or 10	May earn a lot through overseas travel, if Moon is benefic.
Exalted Planet	No.7 or 8	Even dust will turn into gold.
Exalted Moon	No.1	Will receive legacy of immovable property and money.
Jupiter & Saturn	No.4 No.10	Pleasures of conveyance; lot of wealth; comfortable life.
Venus	No.7	Cordial relations between mother-in-law and daughter-in-law; keep a dog for the benefit of children.
Venus-Mercury or Mars-Mercury	No.7	Dust will turn into gold; comfortable life; but if no.8 is malefic, worst results.
Mercury	No.7 or 11	Wealthy, but foolish; may travel abroad on govt. job; the same results as in Moon no.5.

Bad effects

Must not deal in business concerning wicked planets and Moon's enemies, such as Rahu, Ketu, Saturn, Mercury and Venus, should not be a parasite; must not sell milk. Venus may be exalted, but wife will suffer till mother's life.

Bad effects of Moon in house no. 1 and planets in other houses:

Planet	House No.	Bad Effect
Saturn & Sun	No.6	Poverty.
Jupiter	No.11	Bad results, if marries at the age of 24 or 28 and also if he leads a lustful life.
Malefic Mars or Mercury or Malefic no.8	No.8	Life full of sorrows and sufferings.

Remedy lies in keeping things concerning Moon i.e. silver, rice, white pearls etc.; must also seek elders' blessings. Bury sugar or masur daal in the earth for better results.

Moon – House no. 2

Self-made rich; bringer of luck; mother, milk, rice.

Good effects

Best childhood and old age; ordinarily may not have sisters but must have brothers; rich, eminent position; happiness from parents and children (if Jupiter is exalted); victorious; even Jupiter will lend its exalted result of house no. 4; best luck when Moon occupies house no. 1 in the Annual chart i.e. 2, 14, 26, 38, 50, 62, 81 etc.; will definitely receive legacy; will have a son even though other planets may be malefic for children; even Mercury in house no. 9 will not be bad.

Good effects of Moon in house no. 2 and planets in other houses:

Planet	House No.	Good Effect
Saturn	No.4	Father's blessings; ancestral property.
Mercury	No.4	Mother's blessings, but bad eyesight.
Sun, Saturn	No.1, 11	Exalted status; very wealthy and lucky.
Rahu, Ketu or Saturn (not as wicked planets)	No.4, 6, 8, 9, 10, 12	Long life of mother; may live for 48 years or even beyond the nature's age.
Exalted Moon	No.2	Rich in-laws and himself also.
Exalted Venus	No.7	Moon will exercise best results; successful lover.

Remedy: (Keep articles concerning Moon i.e. silver, white pearls and rice for the best results); must bury silver and milk in the foundation of the house; mother's blessings.

Bad effects

Chances of being issueless; Ketu in 12 which is exalted will adversely affect Moon in no.2 which otherwise is also exalted. In other words, one of the two will confer good results and the other bad. If Moon shows good results regarding education etc., results for Ketu i.e. son will not be good and vice-versa.

Bad effects of Moon in house no. 2 and planets in other houses:

Planet	House No.	Bad Effect
Malefic	No.1, 2, 7, 10,11	Bad results of Moon, Jupiter and Venus.
Sun	No.1	Bad results between 25 and 34 and 50 and 75 years of age.
Saturn	No.10	Bad old age.
Jupiter	No.11	Bad old age.
Mercury or Venus, Rahu-Ketu and wicked planets	No.1, 9, 10, 12	Bad for mother's life, mother may die at 9th, 18th, 36th year of native's life.
Mercury and Jupiter	No.3, 9	Problems in business, though he may be prosperous. (Remedy: Donate green cloth to a poor virgin for 43 days.)

Moon – House no. 3

Saviour of life; conqueror of death; lord Shiva – the compassionate – saves from loss and theft.

Good effects

Fountain of goodness; full of piety and purity; peace-loving; yogi; sage or sadhu having communion with god; a householder must be very wealthy; long-life; respect for women; all-round progress.

If Venus in no.3 is the incarnation of Laxmi (goddess of wealth, prosperity and domestic happiness), Moon in no.3 is very exalted; even if born poor, nature helps him; saves him from calamities, losses and even death; Moon in no.3 is the angel of life who conquers in war, disputes etc, if Moon is benefic.

Good effects of Moon in house no. 3 and planets in other houses:

Planet	House No.	Good Effect
Vacant	No.9 or 11	Venus will be exalted, even Mars will not be malefic. (Mangalik).
Moon in Annual chart or Mercury or Malefic Mercury	No.1 No.11 Any	Moon and Mercury, both will shower exalted results (3rd, 15th, 27th, 39th, 51st, 63rd, 75th, 87th years of life). Moon will exercise benefic effect as women will be worshipped in such a house.
Sun Saturn Mercury Jupiter exalted	No.1 No.11 No.5 No.9 or No.4	Rajyoga; long and prosperous life of parents, peace-loving and rich.
Benefic Rahu-Ketu	Any	Business concerning milk, mud i.e. farming and dairy etc. will be benefic.
Mars	No.4	Inventor or discoverer; very rich; intelligent, good-intentioned; courageous, victorious.
Mercury	No.11	Will live up to 80 years.
Mars	No.10	Best results; may get divine help when in trouble.

Bad effects

Bad effects of Moon in house no. 3, and planets in other houses:

Planet	House No.	Bad Effect
Malefic planet	No.8	Loss of wealth; worst results on Moon no.3.
Saturn or Rahu/Ketu	No.8	Moon no.3 will be destroyed; will result in loss of wealth, if not theft.

Remedies:

(a) Donate rice or silver or milk at daughter's birth for wealth and prosperity.

(b) Donate wheat or copper or jaggery at son's birth.

(c) Offer milk or water to the thirsty traveller.

Moon – House no. 4

Ocean of income; fountain of wealth.

Good effects

Moon's effect will depend upon Saturn's position in no.8 or 10 or 11; age 85/96 years; advantage of vehicle; if Mars is exalted, relatives viz. brothers and uncles will be rich; will bring good luck to parents and members of family; Moon will be like the ocean of milk; such a person should donate milk while doing some auspicious work. Now wicked planets and even enemies, such as Venus and Mercury will not do any harm; even Rahu-Ketu will swear by the Mother to shun evil ways; malefic Mars and malefic Saturn will no longer be bad; in other words, wicked planets will give up their evil designs and deeds; even no.2 and 8 will not be debilitated, and the planets in kendras i.e. house no. 1, 4, 7, 10 will exercise good results; long life and old age will never be bad; if a person is born in 'Shukla Paksha' i.e. when the Moon is just rising – good old age; otherwise good childhood.

Good effects of Moon in house no. 4 and planets in other houses:

Planet	House No.	Good Effect
Moon (alone)	No.4	The more he spends, the more he earns; mother's blessings – whether real or stepmother – business concerning Moon i.e. cloth etc. will be beneficial, provided he respects his mother.
Jupiter	No.6	Ancestral business beneficial; may receive legacy or property from others.
4 planets including Moon	No.4	Four times wealthy; children will be helpful.
Saturn	No.9 or 11	Good and noble; parents are also noble.
Sun or Jupiter	No.5	Eminent position after son's birth.
Jupiter or Sun or Venus or Mars or Mercury	No.2, 5, 9 No. 5 No.10	Rajyoga; rich; king-like status; may visit abroad on govt. expense and earn a lot.
Venus and Moon alone in no.4	No.7	Exalted position; best govt. job, if of good character, honest and noble.
Venus	No.10	Best relations between mother-in-law and daughter-in-law.
Mars	No.10	Domineering govt. job; boss dominating over others; wealthy.

Bad effects

Bad effects of Moon in house no. 4 and planets in other houses:

Planet	House No.	Bad Effect
Rahu	No.10	May break head; bad for things associated with Mercury.
Two or more planets along with Moon i.e. three planets	No.4	Every planet will give bad results.
Jupiter	No.10	Person whom he helps will be thankless and create problems for him.
Jupiter or Ketu	No.2	Visit to a religious place jointly by grandson and grand-father will help.

Remedy: Must donate milk and keep his cool.

Moon – House no. 5

Purity of mother's milk; spiritual; beautiful like a bird; heavenly canal.

Good effects

Truthful; justice-loving; fountain of pure milk i.e. spiritually pure and noble; like a diamond among colleagues; will stick to truth; may die, but will not bow before tyranny and cruelty; long life; exalted status; age about 100 years; now Rahu will be ineffective and will not hit; compassionate; merciful; whichever side he joins, will be victorious, but will earn name and fame, wealth and respect in his profession; a noble soul who may convert a desert into a flourishing and blooming garden; may travel abroad; soft-spoken and polite; must be a good-doer; full of milk of human kindness; will help others. Sun brightens Moon in this house.

Good effects of Moon in house no. 5 and planets in other houses:

Planet	House No.	Good Effect
Friendly planets (Sun, Mercury)	No.2, 3	Good results.
Wicked planets or enemy planets or Mercury, Venus	No.9, 11	Good results.
Mercury	No.7 or 11	Moon will be precious like a pearl; exalted results even if no.3 and 8 are malefic.
Exalted Ketu	Any	Best for sons.
Vacant	No.9	Now Moon will be dormant and asleep. (Remedy: Take some sweets, sugar or sweet food etc. before leaving home for work).
Rahu	Any	Will now be ineffective.

Bad effects

Moon will be malefic, even if no.10 and 12 are occupied by benefic planets; no.10 will not be destroyed; but house no. 10 will completely destroy Moon in no.5, Planet in no.12 may be destroyed, but will not be able to destroy Moon in no.5; such a person may be very intelligent but short tempered and use of foul language will ruin him and also his aunts, sisters, daughter etc. (i.e. Mercury); such a person beats his own trumpet; indulges in self praise; and can not keep a secret – this defect in his character may lead to his downfall; greed and selfishness will destroy him; must think hundred times before harming others; though a traveller of seas, jungles and hills, yet unsuccessful; bad for business.

Bad effects of Moon in house no. 5 and planets in other houses:

Planet	House No.	Bad Effect
Malefic Moon	No.5	Will be like the knight of chess; moving 2 1/2 houses; hence bad for house no. 3, 8, 10 and 12.
Moon no.5	Any planet in No.10 (whether friend or foe)	Moon will be destroyed.
Moon no.5	Planet in No.12	Planet in no.12 will be destroyed.
Enemies (wicked planets Venus, Mercury) or Friends (Sun, Mercury)	No.2 or 3 or 9 or 11	Moon will be destroyed by lightning or Lord Yama – the Lord of death.
Sun	No.10	Age: 12 days.
Sun (when male planets are not helping)	No.11	Age: 11 years; short-lived.
Jupiter, Mercury	No.9, 3	Bad results.

Bad effect will be visible on articles concerning Mercury (i.e. use of foul language); will be an unsuccessful traveller to jungles (Mercury) and hills (Saturn).

Moon – House no. 6 (Raashi Effects)

Complete lunar eclipse; mother of deception; bitter water.

Good effects

Tit for tat; good and helpful to friends and bad for enemies; as you sow, so shall you reap; age 80 years.

(a) For respect and fame–See house no. 2, if good, honour and fame.

(b) For wealth and prosperity–See house no. 4, if good, wealthy.

(c) For age–See house no. 8, if good, long life.

(d) For domestic happiness–See house no. 12, if good, best, conjugal life.

Good effects of Moon in house no. 6 and planets in other houses:

Planet	House No.	Good Effect
Jupiter	No.2	Moon will not be bad; for mother's health, serve your father i.e. offer milk and donate milk, rice, silver etc. to the needy and poor.

Bad effects

When Moon is destroyed or adversely aspected by Ketu, bad results for parents and on their life; loss of wealth and health. (Remedy: Do not take milk at night).

Bad effects of Moon in house no. 6 and planets in other houses:

Planet	House No.	Bad Effect
Malefic	No.2, 4, 8, 12	Venus and Ketu will also be malefic; bad for parents and maternal uncles till 34th year.
Mercury	No.2 or 12	May commit suicide when Mercury occupies no.1 in the Annual chart.
Sun	No.12	One-eyed wife or self.
Mars Mercury	No.4 or 8 No.6	Early death of mother or enmity with her.
Mars Mercury	No.6 or 12 No.8	Early death; enmity with mother.
Malefic Venus	Any	In-laws will be financially ruined.
Malefic Ketu	Any	Father's family will be destroyed.
Malefic Mercury	Any	Maternal side will be destroyed.

Remedies: Donate articles concerning Sun, (i.e. wheat, jaggery, copper etc.), Mars (i.e. sugar, masur daal etc.) and Jupiter (gold, saffron, chana daal etc.) to the needy and the poor. Never take milk at night.

Moon – House no. 7 (Raashi Effects)

Incarnation of 'Laxmi'; very rich. Even if man is born poor (Saturn no.3 and Jupiter no.7), he becomes rich; Moon may destroy Mercury, but will confer wealth and prosperity on man, as long as it is not afflicted by Rahu or Ketu; may have less of inherited property, but will have a lot of wealth and gold; will die at his native place; must shun lustful ways; pure like milk; will earn respect in service; expert astrologer; mathematician; will have his latent faculties awake i.e. sixth sense; noble wife; happy life; will have all comforts such as conveyance, noble children, benign mother and good govt. job; age 80 years; provided, not afflicted by Rahu-Ketu or Saturn; in that case, will be critically ill for 15 years.

Good effects

Good effects of Moon in house no. 7 and planets in other houses:

Planet	House No.	Good Effect
Benefic Mercury and vacant	Any No.8	Inclined towards spiritualism; interested in occult; god-fearing; very intelligent.
Exalted Mercury	Any	Though born poor, yet will be self-made rich.
Exalted Venus	Any	Happy domestic life and wealthy; good job.

Bad effects

Must not invite the wrath of old mother; must not sell milk and water; must not marry at 24th/25th year; must keep things connected with Moon at home i.e. silver, milk, rice etc.; if afflicted by wicked planets, will be critically ill for 15 years.

Bad effects of Moon in house no. 7 and planets in other houses:

Planet	House No.	Bad Effect
Jupiter or associated with wicked planet and Mercury	No.7 No.2 or 8	Unhappy childhood; Mars will be debilitated; bad for business or investments etc. (Mercury).
Malefic Moon	No.7	Venus' results will be bad; but, exalted for self.
Venus with wicked planets	Any	May lose child early. (Give silver to daughter at the time of marriage and groom's house must also keep silver in the house. This will help the child).
Venus	No.1	Clash between mother and wife.
Mercury	No.1	Drug addict; drunkard.
Saturn	No.7	Death with a weapon.
Malefic Venus	Any	Unhappy domestic life, but wealthy.

Moon – House no. 8

Dead mother; burnt milk; epilepsy; weak heart.

Good effects

Though malefic, it is the bringer of good luck; person will never be issueless and will definitely be blessed with a son.

Good effects of Moon in house no. 8 and planets in other houses:

Planet	House No.	Good Effect
Jupiter and Saturn	No.2	Rahu will not exercise evil effect; Mars will also not be malefic, now Moon will not be debilitated.
Exalted Mercury	Any	Long life of self and mother, approximately 80 years.
Exalted Sun or Venus	Any	Will make the man wealthy.
Mercury and Jupiter	No.4 No. 9 or 12	Long life of parents; Moon's effect will be exalted.

Bad effects

Most malefic; ill health for 6 years; if Mars is malefic, mother may die; his ancestral property and lands will be of no use to him; worst luck; will see many ups and downs in life; worst fate if there is a tank near his ancestral house. In combination with Saturn, it is a dirty drain.

Bad effects of Moon in house no. 8 and planets in other houses:

Planet	House No.	Bad Effect
Malefic Mars or malefic Mercury or debilitated Saturn; Rahu or Ketu	Any	Should not indulge in lustful acts with other women. Relatives, in-laws and children will be unhappy; Illicit relations will destroy him.
Wicked planets or Mercury or Venus and Vacant or Wicked planets	No.11 No. 3, 1	Bad concerning Moon i.e. mother, mind, heart etc.
Three debilitated planets	No.3 or 4	Bad for parents, children; and loss of ancestral property.
Malefic Venus or malefic Mercury	Any	Worst luck like poisoned sugar; illicit relations with a prostitute will completely destroy him.
Mercury or Saturn – Rahu	No.4 or 12	Bad eyesight; bad for children. (Remedy: pierce the nose).
Malefic Sun or Jupiter	Any	Bad luck in service; and defect in body.
Enemy Planets	No.1	Bad life till 34th year; loss of wealth.
Malefic or Rahu-Jupiter or Mercury-Jupiter or Mercury	No.2, 2, 2, 2	Bad effect on Venus or Moon because of one's own folly.
Venus	No.4	Touch the feet of elders for long life.

Remedies:

(a) For the welfare of children, donate milk in the memory of ancestors or keep water from the well of a cremation ground.

(b) Donate sugar, milk or rice or silver.

(c) Jewellery business will be the worst.

(d) Avoid illicit relations with other women/men.

(e) Seek the blessings of elders.

(f) Must keep silver, rice, milk etc. in the house.

(g) Loss of sensation will indicate the worst times ahead – adopt the above remedies.

Moon – House no. 9

Ancestral property, precious pearl, full of kindness.

Good effects

A perfect gentleman/lady; honest, humane, full of kindness, a noble man always doing good to others; polite; provides succour and comfort to the needy and poor; travels for 20 years; exceptionally good; a noble soul in fact; incarnation of goddess Moon. House no. 5 (for children) will automatically become bright, even if no.3 is occupied by enemy planets or Moon is associated with wicked planets. In order to find out the results regarding children, Moon may be considered at no.5 and planets in no.9 may be considered at no.5. In short, such a man will definitely be blessed with son. It gives the same exalted effect after 24 as is the case with Moon-Jupiter; Moon-Sun; Moon-Jupiter-Venus or Moon-Sun-Venus combinations; age at least 75 years; a good mathematician.

Good effects of Moon in house no. 9 and planets in other houses:

Planet	House No.	Good Effect
Exalted Moon	No.9	Patron of the needy and the poor; humane; compassionate; like a big precious pearl (nine times more beautiful) i.e. a perfect gentleman/lady.
Sun-Jupiter-Mars (all friends of Moon)	No.3	Wealthy.
Sun-Jupiter-Mars (Friends)	No.5	Noble; religious-minded; noble children; even though hemmed between wicked planets.
Any planet	No.4	Best luck; blessings of parents; wealthy; noble and religious-minded.
In association with or aspected by Jupiter i.e. Jupiter or Moon-Jupiter	No.1, 3, 5, 9	Will have power over air and ocean; though born poor, will be very wealthy; all planets in no.3 and 5 will be under Moon; Moon will be like a big ocean full of milk; will be the master of big ships and industries i.e. a business tycoon.

142

Bad effects

The enemy planets like Saturn, Rahu, Ketu, Venus or Mercury in house no. 3 or 5 may not harm. Moon and articles associated with her, even then there will be sandy ocean (Mercury), dust stones (Venus), dangerous rocks (Saturn) and tempests or sea stones (Ketu) in the ocean of her life i.e. there may be ups and downs in her life.

Bad effects of Moon in house no. 9 and planets in other houses:

Planet	House No.	Bad Effect
Ketu and Mercury	No.2, 5	Good luck only after 34 or 48 years of age; (Moon's milk may be drunk by Mercury (34 years' life-span) and Ketu (48 years' life-span), but not necessarily bad before that.
Venus	No.3	Bad eyesight of mother between 24th and 25th years.

Moon – House no. 10

Poisonous water and milk; night time milk of swallow-wart (oak tree).

Good effects

Long life, not less than 90 years; wicked planets will not adversely affect house no. 5; should be religious-minded and having good luck; must shun lustful ways; and should not have illicit relations with other women/men.

Good effects of Moon in house no. 10 and planets in other houses:

Planet	House No.	Good Effect
Vacant and Male planet	No.2, 4	Will earn a lot as a surgeon though Moon may be malefic.
Saturn or Venus	No.4, 1	Happiness from parents, but illicit relations with other women will destroy him.
Sun or Jupiter or Mars	No.4	Best luck; exalted results of Moon; wealthy and full of comforts.

Bad effects

Poisonous water or milk; may be a great physician or surgeon, but will be unsuccessful; must not treat or operate upon his patients at night; houses (Saturn) and in-laws (Rahu) will be destroyed; Moon in no.10 is like a female snake who will eat up her own children; malefic Mars makes such a person a cheat and thug; if Moon and Saturn are in no.1, it will lead to bad times, such as ill health; enmity with mother; and bad name. Such a person may, however, live till 90 years and may earn for 42 years.

Bad effects of Moon in house no. 10 and planets in other houses:

Planet	House No.	Bad Effect
Any planet	No.5 or No.6	Bad luck if he accepts silver or things connected with Moon as bribes or gifts.
Saturn	No.1 or 4	Best luck if he deals in things connected with Saturn i.e. iron, houses, building material; will be exceedingly rich by looting and fleecing others; but, will lose a lot, if he indulges in sinful acts with dirty women.
Saturn	No.3	Thief and dacoit, hard life.
Sun	No.7	Will die by drowning in broad daylight.
Venus and wicked planets	No.7, 4	Children will die; mother's life doubtful.
Wicked planet	No.2 or 3	Malefic Moon; mother will suffer.
Malefic planet or Moon's enemies.	No.3	Everything will turn topsy-turvy i.e. to man's disadvantage.
Wicked planets or Venus-Mercury	No.5 or 8	If corrupt and dishonest, Moon's effect will be disastrous.
Moon, Mercury and Saturn together	No.10	All the three will be bad; inauspicious; wet blanket; accursed fellow.
Ketu, Jupiter, Rahu, Sun and Mercury	No.4, 5, 2 or 10, 6, 8	The whole family will suffer.
Mars and Sun	No.7, House next to Saturn	Loss of limbs; handicapped.
Malefic Mars	Any	Thief, cheat, swindler, dacoit.
Vacant	No.3	May suffer from diseases of lungs, asthma, respiratory trouble.

Remedies:

(a) Must not take milk at night.

(b) Keep river water for 10 years to revive good luck.

(c) Take help from planet in no.2 and if it is vacant, remedy lies in the house occupied by Jupiter.

Moon – House no. 11

Zero; bloody tank; flying clouds.

Good effects

Good effects of Moon in house no. 11 and planets in other houses:

Planet	House No.	Good Effect
Exalted Saturn	Any	By donating milk, person and his children will enjoy all worldly comforts.
Exalted Jupiter	No.4 or any	Wealthy & prosperous.
Sun (exalted) or Mercury exalted	No.4	Good income; peace-loving and full of contentment.
Moon	No.1 & 2 in Annual chart	Best results; lot of wealth. (17th, 27th, 42nd, 55th, 69th, 81st year – Moon in no.2) and (23rd, 36th, 48th, 57th, 72nd, 84th year – Moon in no.1)
Mercury	No.5	Good results for both the houses.

Bad effects

Moon will be just zero i.e. nothing; life sometimes full of storms and sometimes completely; Ketu's result will be bad i.e. bad for son.

Bad effects of Moon in house no. 11 and planets in other houses:

Planet	House No.	Bad Effect
Saturn	No.3	Bad for mother's health and life.
Malefic	No.3	Unhappy childhood and bad for: (a) Saturn (house building or business concerning Saturn). (b) Mercury (business concerning Mercury i.e. investments etc.). (c) Venus (marriage on Friday). (d) Must not take gifts or donations. (e) Must not deal in gold during Thursday evening (Jupiter). **Remedy:** Grandmother of the newly born child should not see the child for 43 days.
Ketu	No.3	Loss in sea voyages; may be cheated by others; bad for mother's life. **Remedy:** Throw 11 'pedas' (made of milk/khoya & sugarless) in river for 43 days – if Ketu is in no.3 and Moon is in no.11 – for mother's well being.
Mercury	No.3	Bad for brothers and inherited property.

Additional Remedies:

(a) Mother should wash her hair and eyes with milk.

(b) Dip a thin needle of gold in milk or water 11 times and take that milk or water for virility and manhood.

(c) If Moon and Jupiter are together in no.11, keep gold for better results.

Moon – House no. 12

Flood and tempest destroying property and wealth; flattery; white cat. Remedy lies in bathing with rain water.

Good effects

House no. 4 (Moon's house, which is ocean) will be flooded; when Moon is in no.12, the results of houses occupied by Mars, Ketu and Mercury will be as per table given below. In this case, Moon will poison its own permanent house i.e. no.4 which is otherwise malefic will cool down; Ketu will be like a barking or groaning dog who has fallen in a well, hence malefic. Mercury in no.4 (when Moon is in no.12) will be very bad for mother and her family.

Good effects of Moon in house no. 12 and planets in other houses:

House No.	This house occupied by Mars	This house occupied by Ketu	This house occupied by Mercury
No.1	Will get honey i.e. best luck.	Very bad; may receive warrant for arrest.	Bad for service matters.
No.2	Will get wealth from in-laws.	Bad luck while visiting in-laws.	In-laws will be destroyed.
No.3	Relatives i.e. brothers will be rich.	Bad luck for self and brothers.	Amputated limbs of brothers.
No.4	Happy brothers & relatives.	Duffer sons.	Bad for mother's family.
No.5	Children will have lot of property.	Rude sons.	Bad children; bad eye-sights; and weak heart.
No.6	Relatives will be rich.	Unhappy relatives.	Married daughter's relatives will suffer.
No.7	Best domestic life.	Sons will be rude and may destroy him.	Bad and uncomfortable domestic life.
No.8	Will not die of an accident or burns.	Son will suddenly disappear or die.	Lot of expenditure on disease.
No.9	Lot of ancestral property, but may leave home.	Bad luck for maternal uncle.	Will cry over loss of ancestral property.

No.10	Will never be unhappy even though may face difficulties.	House will be destroyed in a storm.	Grand houses will be suddenly destroyed.
No.11	Will be exonerated by the court even though he may be culprit.	Loose character, will run after women; corrupt.	Though innocent, will suffer ignominy and bad name.
No.12	Life full of honey; peaceful and contented life.	May earn a lot; but will lose everything.	Friends will deceive him at the time of need.

(a) Rain water will help.

(b) Silence will ruin him.

(c) Man of scholarship and learning.

(d) (1) House no. 1 – will determine personal fate.

    (2) House no. 5 – will determine children.

    (3) House no. 6 – will determine age, residence and earthly blessings.

    (4) House no. 9 – will determine past, religious inclinations and inheritance.

(e) Sun-Mercury no.3 – will help the family i.e. good for family.

(f) Exalted Jupiter & Sun – moon's results will be exalted; lot of wealth & happiness.

Bad effects

Moon will be like a flood or storm which will destroy property, especially inherited from parents, but his self-made property will remain intact. Moon in no.12 floods everything; sleepless nights; bad for mother and things associated with moon.

Bad effects of Moon in house no. 12 and planets in other houses:

Planet	House No.	Bad Effect
Moon	No.12 in Annual chart	Destroy his own and in-law's property (4th, 17th, 28th, 48th, 55th, 68th, 80th, 90th year).
Moon	No.1 in Annual chart	Will destroy his lands, money and property (12th, 24th, 35th, 46th, 59th, 71st year).
Mercury or Venus or wicked planets	No.2 or 6 or 12	Ancestral wealth and property will be lost or destroyed.
Mars or Sun	No.1 or 2	Indolent, lazy and poor; will be afraid of drowning till 45th/48th year; thereafter, condition will improve.
Sun	No.6	One-eyed wife or self or both.

Such a person is like a dirty drain; he fondly and foolishly remembers his ancestral glory and greatness and sheds tears over his misfortunes.

○○○

Mars

दो रंगी अच्छी नहीं एक रंग हो जा – सरासर तू हो मोम या पत्थर हो जा ।

दान, करम, भलाई दुनिया में – मंगल नेक खुद ही होता है ।

तुख़्म बदी का बदला खूनी – मंगल बद हमेशा लेता है ।

मौत नागहानी रास्ता तीजे – नेक मंगल ही रोकता है ।

मौत का घर आठवें दुनिया लेते – जहां मंगल बद बैठा हो ।

चंद्र-सूरज की मदद जो पाता – मंगल बद नहीं रहता है ।

माता चंद्र से बेशक डरता – मंगलीक वही घर माता हो ।

पापी कोई हो या दुश्मन साथी – मंगल मंदा नहीं होता है ।

नेक कुलों की दूर लावलदी बेड़ा गरक वह करता है ।

राहू बना है हाथी इसका – केतु से हरदम लड़ता है ।

नेक रहे तो दयालु शिवजी – टुकड़े बदी वह करता है ।

खून शनि का मंगल बंद हो – शुक्र पर भी जुल्म करता है ।

गुरु पिंदर है दोनों जहां का – सूरज पिता है शनि का ।

शनि का ऐसा चौथा दर्ज़ा – बद मंगलीक है कयामत का ।

शनि चारों तरफ ही चलता – घर चौथा चंद्र का ।

उमर का मालिक तीन, आठ, चंद्र – मारता यह मंगलीक को है ।

It is not good to be a double-edged weapon;
Either be straight and soft or hard like stone.
Do good; be kind and shun evil;
And become Mars auspicious.
Evil in genes; belief in bloody tit for tat;
is malefic Mars evil trait.
Sudden accidental death through the 3rd House's road.
But is only checked by Mars auspicious 8th House.
Mar's own house is the house of death.
If helped by Moon and Sun death is averted.
Though afraid of Mother Moon yet she becomes debilitating herself in Mars House.
When associated with two enemy or sinful planets, Mars is no longer diabolical.
It destroys progeny of good and noble families when out to do evil,

148

Rahu is his elephant; but inimical.
If auspicious and kind God Shiva decimates the evil in it.
Mars malefic evil in its blood destroys Venus even.
Jupiter is the father of both the worlds,
Sun, the father of Saturn devil.
Saturn moves in all four corners.
Moon's house is No.4 – four yugas is Satyug, Treta, Duapar and Kalyug,
where Mars malefic works havoc on Doom's day.
Life's lord Moon in no. three and eight destroys Mar's evil effects.

Exalted Mars

"The commander of the army is full of patriotic fervour and valour and exclaims with joy, 'it is a famous victory.'" (Anonymous)

Malefic Mars

"The man turns into a butcher, a terrorist and a man-eater." (Anonymous)

Mars (Lord Hanuman)

Man-in-arms; red in colour; patriotic fighting for the country; if malefic – butcher and beast; lord Shiva – the god of death and destruction.

1. Relationship with Saturn

(a) **Saturn:** Rahu and Ketu, the Nodes controlling evil and good are Saturn's agents. Naturally Saturn can both be benefic or malefic. It is the Lord of eyesight also. Saturn does not oppose Mars; it is Mars who opposes Saturn; hence, Saturn in house no.3 (whose Lord is Mars) is poor and unfortunate.

(b) **Mars:** Mars, if exalted, helps all and is a good-doer; if debilitated, it is all evil and dances the dance of death and destruction. In Saturn's house i.e. no.10, it is like king and enjoys an exalted status, provided it is all alone and without aspect.

(c) **Saturn & Mars mutually aspecting each other:** Very bad luck; thief; cheat; and a fraud. Results will be those of Saturn no.1 and Mars no.4.

(d) **Mars aspecting Saturn:** Bad for professions concerning Mars; may be deprived of a son; but exalted results regarding profession connected with Saturn.

(e) **Saturn aspecting Mars:** Two dacoits shaking hands to become friends; hence, both will confer exalted benefits.

(f) **Mars and Rahu:** (i) Mars aspecting Rahu: Rahu will not exercise bad results. (ii) Rahu aspecting Mars: one may suffer from diseases of arms, stomach & blood; may give lot of troubles on the right side of the body. (Remedy lies in Moon.)

(g) **Mars and Ketu:** When both of them aspect each other, both give adverse results; it is a case of a fight between a tiger and a dog in matters of fate. (Remedy: Refer to chapter on Mars Ketu).

2. Miscellaneous Points about Mars

(a) If Sun and Mercury are together in the horoscope, Mars will not be malefic.

(b) If Saturn and Sun are together in the Birth chart, Mars will be malefic.

(c) Strife, quarrels, diseases and grief etc. will be up to 28 years (Mars period).

(d) Navel (the middle of the body) is considered as the seat of Mars and also that of the rays of the Sun. That is why house no. 4 (the navel of the horoscope) tells us of the good and bad effects of Mars. In other words, the planet in no.4 will indicate the blood of Mars. A benefic Mars, if alone, is like a tiger; whereas a malefic Mars will destroy everything. Its speed is always the same – whether that of a tiger (exalted Mars) or a cowardly deer (malefic Mars).

3. Malefic Mars (Manglik)

(a) Evil ingrained in the marrow of bone i.e. devil incarnate.

(b) Believes in the philosophy of "Eye for an eye" or "Tit for tat."

(c) When Venus (ghee) and Mars (honey) are of equal strength, it will be all poisonous i.e. malefic Mars. In other words, firstly, Venus will confer bad results and then Sun i.e. both Venus and Sun will be malefic in turn. If they receive help from Sun or Moon, then Mars will no longer be malefic.

(d) If two wicked planets (Saturn-Rahu or Sturn-Ketu) or two mutually opposite planets (Mercury-Ketu or Sun-Venus) are in conjunction with Mars, it will not be malefic.

(e) When malefic Mars is out to harm anyone, it will destroy the whole family, not to speak of one individual.

(f) When Mercury is malefic, malefic Mars becomes all the more malefic and debilitated. It will then behave like a timid domesticated lion in a zoo, instead of the king of the jungle.

Characteristics of Mars in 12 houses

House No.	Characteristics of Mars
1	Sword of justice in the battlefield; or else a falling star.
2	Supporter of brothers; or else a snake up the sleeve.
3	A tiger chained in a zoo oblivious of its strength; or else a cheat and a fraud.
4	Worst effect on brother's wife, wealth, mother, mother-in-law, and may even cause their death; full of satanic tendencies.
5	Father and grandfather of rich children; if debilitated, may destroy everything, or else naughty.
6	Like a contented sadhu; or else a rioter.
7	Will help relatives; sweet pudding; or else accursed and unfortunate.
8	Trap of death, noose around the neck.
9	Throne of king emperor; must obey and serve elder brother's wife for better results; or else an atheist.
10	King like status, if alone; or else will sell his gold.
11	May follow Mercury and Saturn in virtues; beehive over brimming with honey; or else worst fate.
12	Traditionalist; man of word and principles; Rahu becomes zero; or else foolish spendthrift and unhappy married life.

150

Mars – House no. 1

Sword of justice in the battlefield; if debilitated – like a falling star and if exalted – eminent status; otherwise worse than faeces or stale food or dirt.

Good effects

Will not be the only brother – whether younger or elder; 32 teeth; will be rich after 28th year; a thorough gentleman who never forgets the good thing done to him; truthful; a brave fighter, wielding the sword of justice; exalted status; good health; good effect in Saturn's business i.e. iron, timber, machines, house building etc.; such a business in partnership with nephews or uncles etc. of equal age may flourish; will earn a lot for at least 28 years or more; nature will help him against enemy attacks; after Saturn's (36th) or Rahu's (42nd) period will occupy an exalted position in a govt. department; will help his brothers; noble, truthful and truth-loving.

Good effects of Mars in house no. 1 and planets in other houses:

Planet	House No.	Good Effect
Mercury & Vacant	No.3, 2	Sister, if any, will be like queen; but brothers will face ups and downs in life i.e. sometimes very rich and sometimes poor.
Mars (without any aspect)	No.1	Will have the strength to face enemies boldly.

Bad effects

Unfortunate; may lose everything; must shun evil ways, otherwise, will be completely ruined and reduced to nothingness; he will be like a falling star or meteor which shatters itself and shows worst results within 40-43 days; malefic Mars will show its curse on brothers just after his birth; will be an ungrateful wretch; bad luck for brothers and self.

Bad effects of Mars in house no. 1 and planets in other houses:

Planet	House No.	Bad Effect
Mercury & Vacant	No.3 No. 7, 9, 11	For no.7, adopt remedy for Venus; for no.9, 11, adopt remedy for Jupiter; otherwise, ill health and bad fate. Good after 39 years.
Sun or Moon or Jupiter along with Mercury or wicked planets	No.7	A fighter; but bad results for parents till 28th year.
Sun and Moon Sun or Moon	No.12, 22 No.12	Worst luck if corrupt and parasitic; lazy, poor and unfortunate; bad for parents who may die early.

Mars – House no. 2

A good man helping and protecting brothers, a sort of sheet anchor for them; if malefic – a snake up the sleeve.

Good effects

Must be eldest brother from birth, otherwise may have to become eldest; supporter of family; will be like a sheet anchor for them; if he helps his brothers, he will never starve or become poor, otherwise, he may have to face criminal troubles.

Good effects of Mars in house no. 2 and planets in other houses:

Planet	House No.	Good Effect
Mars (not aspected or associated with Mercury or Ketu)	No.2	May earn a lot through in-laws; if of firm decision, may receive legacy from in-laws; will have a son; even in-laws will prosper.
Mars no.2 aspected by Jupiter, Sun, or Mercury (except Mercury in no.2)	No.8, 9, 10, 12	May earn a lot but self-made rich; well dressed; takes sumptuous food; healthy and prosperous. If Mercury is in no.2, bad results; if Ketu is associated, man will enjoy an exalted status and will be prosperous.

Bad effects

Debilitated Mars in house no. 2 will be most malefic; worst results; such a man is like a snake up the sleeve; may sting others and die either in a battlefield or in a scuffle or fight.

Remedy: Adopt the same remedies as mentioned under Mars no.4.

Mars – House no. 3

For others, a grove of trees laden with fruits, but for self, bad in respect of money and peace; stomach, lips, chest problems; if debilitated – a lion chained in a zoo – keep ivory for good results.

Good effects

Will have brothers; for others, he is like a grove of fruit-laden tree; otherwise, a captive lion in a zoo who does not know about his strength; but if he becomes a man-eater, he works havoc everywhere. If exalted, Mars is like Lord Shiva blessing everyone with his benedictions, expert in martial arts; if polite, prosperous; age 90 years; man of determination; good eyesight; like a lion may tear bad men into pieces; but a great friend of others; rich in-laws and may get legacy from them; justice-loving.

Good effects of Mars in house no. 3 and planets in other houses:

Planet	House No.	Good Effect
Jupiter, Sun or Moon	No.7, 9, 11	Rahu will not exercise bad effect; happy domestic life.
Jupiter	No.9	Rich in-laws and will leave wealth for him.
Saturn	No.9	Exalted Saturn; good health; house and a lot of wealth; in fact, very happy.

Bad effects

Such a person is a cheat and fraud; unreliable; he believes in the philosophy of 'eat, drink and make merry'; outward show; poor but luxurious life at the other's expense; age 90 years; ill fated; hated by all; if hot headed and obstinate, he will suffer from bad debts; ill health and troubles; may not have a son.

Bad effects of Mars in house no. 3 and planets in other houses:

Planet	House No.	Bad Effect
Jupiter	No.11	Will be unhappy on account of deaths in the family, but good for self.
Jupiter, Sun or Moon	No.7, 9, 11	Meddlesome and will unnecessarily interfere in the affairs of others and face difficulties and problems; ill fated but may help in-laws.
Mercury or Saturn	No.3, 9, 11	Very bad results; money problems but will help his family members.
Mercury and Saturn combined	No.3, 7	Same as above.
Saturn	No.9, 11	Will not witness any death in the family.

Remedy: Keep ivory for better results.

Mars – House no. 4 (Worst Raashi Results)

Most debilitating Raashi effect – remedy lies in Moon. All fire; ringleader of evil; satanic tendencies; most malefic and debilitating – sword, diseases between throat and navel; red pepper; fire that engulfs all and destroys happiness and wealth.

Mars will not be debilitated (Mangalik) under the following conditions. In all such cases, person will be brave and will have the courage to fight against his enemies. If he supports his family, he will be noble and truthful.

(A) Mars – Not malefic :

(1) Two wicked planets together (Rahu-Saturn) or (Saturn-Ketu).

(2) Two opponents together (Mercury-Ketu).

(3) Moon or Venus alone or together in no.3, 4 or 8.

(4) When Moon is not in kendras i.e. no.1, 4, 7, 10 and is being destroyed in some or other house or Sun is in no.6 or Sun or Moon or Jupiter is in no.3, 4, 8, 9 i.e. they are helping Mars in no.4.

(B) In the following situations, Sun will not help Mars :

(1) When Sun is not in no.1 and no.8 along with Mars, or

(2) Sun is alone in no.7, 10, and 12, or

(3) Ketu is with Sun in no.5, 9, or

(4) Rahu is with Sun in no.6, 12, or

(5) Saturn is with Sun in no.10, or

(6) Mercury is with Sun in no.12.

If Mars in no.4 is exalted, man is wealthy; there will be no bad effect on elder brothers and their children.

Bad effects

Worst results; will destroy everything; such a person is obstinate, foul-mouthed; bitter in speech; shortsighted; foolish; will like to serve and not rule; will believe in "Physician, heal thyself first"; will call a spade a spade i.e. outspoken in rude sense; ill fated; will be full of fire which will engulf and destroy everything; bad for mother, mother-in-law and wife; will also be bad for brothers till 28th year i.e. if elder brothers are alive, they will be worse than dead i.e. sickly and poor.

If Moon, Jupiter and Sun are not in no.3, 4, 8 or these friendly planets are not helping Mars, Mars will be most debilitated and show worst results. Even if friendly planets are helping Mars, but if it is joined with malefic Saturn or Ketu, Mars will be utterly malefic (Mangalik). Such a malefic Mars will destroy everything – house, wealth and religion of man.

When Mars is alone and it is in one of the houses viz. 3, 4, 8 and in other two – Mercury and Ketu – even then Mars will be debilitated.

Debilitated Mars in no.4 (Mangalik) destroys not only wealth and family, but also spreads fire and destruction all around in one's own family or in wife's family; even there may be separation or divorce of couple. Malefic Mars in no.4 (except no.8, 12) will cause trouble to his elder brothers till 28th year. If they survive after that, they will be sick with problems in blood and arms. The man with Mars in no.8 will be bad for his elder brothers till 28th year. Such a person with malefic Mars in no.4 will be bad for his family till 70th year; may become blind and die unhappy in the end.

Bad effects of malefic Mars in house no. 4 and planets in other houses:

Planet	House No.	Bad Effect
Mercury-Ketu	No.8	His own aunts will destroy him.
Either Venus or Mars	No.4 or 8	Uncle will be the cause of destruction. (**Remedy:** for above two – must receive the blessings from the widow aunt or widower uncle by touching feet.
Mercury or Moon	No.6	Bad till mother's death; or in childhood.
Mars-Saturn	No.4	Diseases of tongues, but ringleader of thieves.
Wicked planets	No.9	Bad for family.
Mercury	No.12	Unhappy; foolish and full of grief.
Jupiter	No.8	Cowardly and lazy.
Saturn	No.1	Thief; cheat; fraud; worst fate.

Remedies:

(a) Clean your teeth with water in the morning.

(b) Adopt remedy for Moon.

(c) Take mud from under the root of 'Banyan' tree; put a dot of it in sugared milk and paste a dot on the navel and forehead for all the diseases of the stomach.

(d) Bury an earthen pot filled with honey in a deserted place or cremation ground.

(e) Bury a silver square piece in the foundation of house.

(f) Keep and donate copper or jaggery or wheat (Sun); silver, rice (Moon); gold, saffron, chana daal (Jupiter) and also serve the ancestors for best results.

(g) Feed birds with sweet bread.

(h) Ivory will be auspicious, keep it, and also skin of deer.

Mars – House no. 5

If benefic, father of wealthy children; 'Neem' tree; if malefic – naughty and deprived of sons.

Good effects

Planets in no.3, 5, 9 (whether enemies or friends) will help each other; even Venus and Moon will confer exalted results; if benefic, it is five times exalted and if malefic, it is five times worse; man is like a 'Neem' tree – the older he grows, the richer he is; justice-loving in worldly affairs; man of letters; scholarship and great learning; will have eminent sons; will be happy in respect of wife and children.

Good effects of benefic Mars in house no. 5 and planets in other houses:

Planet	House No.	Good Effect
A planet or elder brother alive and vacant	No.9, 10	Ancestor of rich sons and grandsons.
Moon	No.8	Will adversely affect no.9 i.e. parents.

Bad effects

Fear of fire; unhappiness from children; child may suffer during 8th day or 8th year or 18th year; deaths among paternal uncles or nephews; his paramour or beloved will cause his downfall.

Bad effects of malefic Mars in house no. 5 and planets in other houses:

Planet	House No.	Bad Effect
Enemy planets (Mercury-Ketu)	No.9	Sleepless nights. (Remedy: Must keep water under pillow side – it will save him from enemies).

Mars – House no. 6 (Raashi Effect)

Saint and sadhu full of contentment; navel; if malefic – rioter and instigator. Remedy as for Saturn.

Good effects

Full of courage and fortitude; supporter of family; exalted status; justice-loving; a saintly figure full of contentment; noble and religious-minded; Sun will now give exalted results; fond of music; writing and manual work; his pen will be mightier than sword; good character; now Rahu in no.12 will be ineffective and zero, but Ketu's effect will be bad.

If Mars is exalted in no.6, the native will rise in life and along with him his brother will also rise i.e. the more prosperous he is, the better luck for brothers also; must worship virgins (who have not attained puberty) for better results and help brothers.

Good effects of Mars in house no. 6 and planets in other houses:

Planet	House No.	Good Effect
Exalted Venus or Saturn, Mercury, Ketu or Benefic planets	Any (especially no.7)	Will die after seeing his three grandsons i.e. long life and prosperous children and grand-children.
Exalted Jupiter, Sun or Mercury	Any	Will be blessed with eminent children; even though Ketu may be in no.8 and Saturn in no.5.

Bad effects

His brothers will earn less than him; if somehow they earn more, they will suffer heavy losses. They should, therefore, help him off & on; will be bad for maternal uncles, sisters and in-laws; rioter and instigator.

Bad effects of malefic Mars in house no. 6 and planets in other houses:

Planet	House No.	Bad Effect
Malefic Jupiter, Sun or Mercury	Any	Will have only one son.
Malefic Ketu	Any	Child born before 34th year will survive; first son may not survive. (Remedy: Distribute salty things instead of sweets at the birth of child; let the child not wear gold, it will be inauspicious.)
Mercury	No.12	Brothers and sisters create problems; they will be like 'Yama', the god of death.
Mercury & Mars not getting any help from Sun or Moon	No.4	Mother may die in childhood.
Mercury	No.4	May die in childhood; thereafter mother may die.

Remedies:

(a) Remedy as for Saturn for domestic problems.

(b) 'Virgin' worship for the welfare of brothers, daughters etc.

(c) Remedy as for Moon, for the welfare of son.

(d) Must have good character, it will enable him to fight against heavy odds.

Mars – House no. 7

Sweet pudding; red-coloured fruit tree; red lentils (Masur daal); first child will be a son; supporter of family like Lord Vishnu. If debilitated – unfortunate and accursed.

Good effects

He will either be exceedingly rich or poor; must eat sweet pudding or sweet bread for better results; if Mars is exalted, it will be 'Macch Rekha' i.e. abundance of wealth and property; happy married life; himself a reliable adviser; a competent minister; religious-minded; noble; jovial; may console others in distress; supporter of all like Vishnu; justice-loving, but will be known by the company he keeps – good or bad; nevertheless exalted status; efficient minister; lot of wealth and estates; mathematician.

Good effects of exalted Mars in house no. 7 and planets in other houses:

Planet	House No.	Good Effect
Jupiter or Venus	No.1	One will get the things of his desire; wealthy; lot of landed property; perfect yoga for eminence.

Bad effects

Mars in house no. 7 confers property, wealth and children, but everything becomes topsy-turvy and is destroyed when it is associated with Mercury.

Bad effects of malefic Mars in house no. 7 and planets in other houses:

Planet	House No.	Bad Effect
Malefic Mars and Mercury or Malefic Mercury	No.1, 7, 8 Any	Unlucky; accursed; worst fate; especially when a widowed sister or sister-in-law or aunt or niece or granddaughter lives with him; lustful; pale body; anaemic; impure blood.
Mercury or Saturn or Jupiter or Sun or Moon or Mercury or Sun-Mercury	No.6, 7 No.1, 7 No.1 No.7	Will poke his nose into the affairs of others and suffer; but supporter of family and will in turn be helped by others and family members.

Remedies:

(a) Take yoghurt.

(b) Adopt remedy for Saturn.

(c) Offer sweets to widow sister etc. every morning before doing any work.

(d) Keep silver in the house.

Mars – House no. 8

Gallows; noose of death around the neck; mortality of life; body without arms.

Good effects

(1) Hard working; will have the courage of facing enemies; justice-loving.

(2) Mars will be exalted if no.2 is vacant or no.2 is occupied by Jupiter or Moon or Sun (friends of Mars).

(3) Mars will not be debilitated (Mangalik), if Moon is in no.1, 3, 4, 8 or 9.

(4) If Mercury is in no.8, both Mars and Mercury will confer best results, provided there is a dark room in the ancestral house.

Bad effects

Difference in ages of the native and his younger brother will ordinarily be 4-8 years; sometimes it may be 13-15 years, but thereafter no younger brother. It has also been observed that sometimes such a 'Mangalik' elder brother destroys the younger one i.e. younger brother is either not born at all or he dies soon; if there is a brother born 8 years earlier or 8 years later than his younger brother, he will confer worst results for all.

Malefic Mars in no.8 will not exercise bad results on the native himself when Mars is not helped by Moon or Sun or Jupiter, but it adversely affects the elder brother, elder uncle or elder maternal uncle after his birth or since his presence in the womb, but will not be bad for mother who will be rich, healthy and long-lived. He will also be rich and long-lived but will be bad for others.

Remedy: Get the blessings of widowed relatives; do not maltreat them; give sweet tandoori bread to a dog or birds for 43 days. When iron plate (tawa) is hot, sprinkle a few drops of water on it and then bake the chapatis.

Bad effects of malefic Mars in house no. 8 and planets in other houses:

Planet	House No.	Bad Effect
Mercury-Ketu	No.2	If the younger brother remains alive, his arms will be injured.
Not vacant (hence malefic Mars). Malefic Mars (i.e. Sun or Jupiter or Moon is not in no.1, or 3, or 4, or 8).	No.2 No.8	Mars, if alone, will be like a death trap or gallows till 28th year; worst for life and breath. **(Remedy:** Wear a pure silver chain around neck; and also feed dog with tandoori sweet bread for 43 days.) Ill-fated and unhappy.
Mercury	No.6	Mother may die in his childhood.
Exalted Mercury	Any (except in No.6 & 8)	The more exalted the Mercury, the more malefic the Mars (worst results).

Remedy: Please refer to remedies for Mars no.4, besides the above remedies.

Mars – House no. 9

Royal upbringing; exalted status; king's throne; like a precious ruby; if malefic – atheist and notorious.

Good effects

If brothers live together and amicably, the results will be exalted; Mars in this house confers king like status. After his birth and especially during 13th/14th year of his life, parents become rich and enjoy all the pleasures of the world. He himself gets an exalted position in his 28th year; justice-loving; will have as many brothers as elder uncles and younger uncles (father's brothers).

Venus and Moon will also confer best results (if associated with or aspected by Venus or Moon). Even Sun, wherever it may be, confers best results; even no.3 and no.5 will also be benefic.

Mars, if alone, will confer wealth, happiness and life; brothers will be helpful; will have a comfortable living; will be like a tiger in bearing; upbringing and status; will amass great wealth and be an administrator.

Bad effects

When Mars is malefic, person is atheist, notorious and a beggar begging for food.

Planet	House No.	Bad Effect
Malefic Mercury	Any	Unhappy and poor parents till 28th year.

Mars – House no. 10

God visiting a poor man's hut; king-like status; sweet honey; most exalted planet.

Such a person is like a god visiting and blessing a poor man's cottage i.e. he may be born poor but brings good luck not only to the parents but also to family and himself; will enjoy an eminent position and be extraordinarily rich; will be like king since birth; will earn a lot; will never be issueless; as long as elder brothers are alive, he will continue to rise.

Saturn, howsoever good or bad, will guide Mars. Mars, if alone, without any adverse aspect, will be noble and gentle like a deer or bold like a tiger; but in no case, it will be a man-eater. Mars in Saturn's house (no.10 or 11) is the most exalted; and confers king-like status, provided no.2 is not occupied by a female planet: brothers will be helpful; 96 years of age; rich; good health; domestic happiness; bold and full of determination.

Good effects

Good effects of Mars in house no. 10 and planets in other houses:

Planet	House No.	Good Effect
Moon	No.4	Good status; sweet and comfortable life like honey mixed in milk; good for family.
In conjunction with or aspected by Saturn	No.4	More notorious and clever than a leopard.
Saturn	No.3	May have lot of land and many houses, but less of ready cash.
Vacant	No.5	Best results.
Mars (alone without any aspect)	No.10	Like a king; most comfortable and best life.

Bad effects

Will sell his gold and then will be destroyed; will be bad for children.

Bad effects of malefic Mars in house no. 10 and planets in other houses:

Planet	House No.	Good Effect
Malefic Mars & enemy planets	No.10	Bad relations with brothers; may indulge in black magic/tantra/black occult, which may destroy him.
Venus or Moon or wicked planets	No.2	Late birth of son. (Remedy: Serve an issueless person or a black one-eyed man).
Moon or Sun or Jupiter and malefic Mars	No.3, 6 No.10	Mercury will be malefic; bad results; Jupiter, Sun will be destroyed; loss of wealth and gold; unhappy parents; bad for children.
Sun or Moon	No.4, 6	One-eyed man, when he lives with maternal uncles.
Saturn	No.4	May languish in jail, although innocent.
Any planet	No.5	Bad for others; but good for self.
Sun	No.6	Sons may die.

Mars – House no. 11

Beehive over-brimming with honey; vermilion (Sindur); precious red ruby; a tiger chained by Jupiter (in good sense); if malefic – unhappy and bad monetary conditions.

Good effects

Such a person is like a beehive over-brimming with honey, provided Mercury is benefic; even if Mercury is not benefic, bees (i.e. Saturn) will bring the honey and fill the beehives to the brim i.e. very rich man, having all the pleasures at his feet; such a person is like a tiger fed on milk i.e. he is not like a man-eater; his parents lead a comfortable life when he is 13 years old.

He will be like a king at his 28th year (provided Mars is exalted; he is a tiger whose chains are in the hands of Jupiter i.e. he will be noble and pious like Jupiter, the great guru. After 13 years, Mars will give the exalted effect of Mars no.9.

Good effects of Mars in house no. 11 and planets in other houses:

Planet	House No.	Good Effect
Mercury & Saturn (exalted)	Any	Will have a lot of wealth till 24th to 28th year.

Bad effects

'Kaag – Rekha' – worst fate; accursed; ill fated; always under debt despite good income.

Bad effects of Mars in house no. 11 and planets in other houses:

Planet	House No.	Bad Effect
Vacant or bad	3	Will squander ancestral wealth.

When Mars is debilitated in this house, not only children but also brothers and uncles will be unhappy; he will also be not happy.

Remedy: Keep a dog.

Mars – House no. 12

Traditionalist; man of words and principles; Rahu becomes zero; mahout riding and controlling an elephant.

If malefic – spendthrift; unhappy married life; bad eyesight and loss of wealth.

Good effects

Rahu will become ineffective and be reduced to zero; even Mercury in no.1 will not be bad; Ketu in no.1 will be benefic; such a person is short-tempered, freedom-loving, man of his own actions and thoughts; given to self praise.

He is like a roaring lion; pure-blooded; noble family; respectful to teachers and elders; will have all comforts, though may be born in a poor family; will be like a mahout riding an elephant i.e. comforts of vehicles; justice-loving; now Mercury will not be malefic (except in no.3, 8, 9, 12); all planets will be benefic and planets in no.1, 3, 8, 11 will no longer be malefic, but Ketu (groaning and barking dog) and Mercury (goat) will not give up their habit of acting as spoil sport (except in no.1, 3, 8, 11 – where both of them will be quiet). When a son or brother is born at the age of 24/28, he will have all the pleasures.

Good effects of Mars in house no. 12 and planets in other houses:

Planet	House No.	Good Effect
Ketu Jupiter Jupiter-Venus or Ketu	No.3 No.4 No.1,3,8,11	Best results; if rich, he will occupy an exalted and king-like status; if poor, he will become rich; it confers prosperity; he will have helpful attitude; all enemies will shed enmity.
Sun	3, 11	Will be saved from death and disease as long as the planet in no.11 is not the enemy of planet in no.8

Bad effects (Mangalik)

May suffer from respiratory problems; unhappy domestic life; loss of wealth; unhappy in respect of son; conspiring enemies; unnecessary expenditures; diseases; bad trade etc.; in fact, a bad placement in horoscope. He may act foolishly or may spend on foolish acts; marital discord; bad eyesight (may become one-eyed or even blind) or suffer from night-blindness; if Ketu is malefic, should be the eldest brother or else may have two elder brothers (not applicable in case of a girl); his elder brothers should offer him milk and keep silver, rice etc. (Moon's articles) with them. Should take sweet bread, pudding etc. for wealth and long life; must offer sweet water to Sun (Argh) in the morning and also offer sweet bread to dog for better results.

Bad effects of Mars in house no. 12 and planets in other houses:

Planet	House No.	Bad Effect
Mercury	3, 8, 9, 12	Malefic Mercury; Mars will not mitigate its bad effect.
Malefic Sun	Any	Worst effect of Mars; even Sun will give bad effect on no.3, thereafter no.1 and later on no.11.
Mercury (but not aspected by Sun or Moon)	4, 8	May die at an early age; later mother may also die.

Remedies:

(a) Must offer sweet milk (with honey or sugar) to others.

(b) Must take sweet bread.

(c) Must offer sweet bread to dog.

(d) Must offer sweet water (Argh) to Sun in the morning.

(e) If Saturn is in no.2 with malefic Mars in no.12, there will be problems in arms; donate 'batashas' (made of sugar) for 43 days.

Venus

शुक्र आंख है शनि की पाई – चार तरफ जो देखता है ।

शनि यदि कहीं जावे मारा – बली वह अपनी देता है ।

साथ मंगल के चंद्र बनता – बुध केतु जिसमें न हों ।

शुक्र अकेला बुरा न करता – बैठा खा किसी ही घर हो ।

घर सातवें जब अपने बैठा – असर, नज़र रुह अपनी को ।

दे देता ग्रह उसी को है यह – बैठा जो घर सातवें हो ।

चंद्र भला या बुध हो अच्छा – बुरा शुक्र नहीं होता है ।

घर तीजे में जब आ बैठा – शुक्र मर्द हो जाता है ।

नौवें मंगल बद है यह होता – छठे में खुद मंदा है ।

काण रेखा है तख़्त पे होता – चौथे औरत दो होता है ।

बारह-दूसरे सबसे बढ़िया – दसवें शनि खुद बनता है ।

घर पांचवें में पक्की मिट्टी – ग्यारह लट्टू बन घूमता है ।

घर आठवें ग्रह सब ही मंदे – शुक्र भी मंदा होता है ।

भवसागर से बेड़ा पार है करता – शुक्र कामधेनु गऊ होता है ।

Venus gets its eye from Saturn;
Hence sees all around in all the four corners.
But when Saturn finds itself in trouble,
Venus becomes the scapegoat & meets adverse fate.
With Mars it becomes Moon provided,
Mercury and Saturn are not together.
It is never malefic when alone, though occupying any House.
But when it occupies its own House i.e. Seventh,
It confers all benefits on sight and soul of self.
When in conjunction with another planet,
It is ruled by the associated planet.
When in 3rd House it shuns feminiety,
And behaves boldly like a man.
In 9th it is all the more malefic.
And in 6th it becomes most debilitating.
'Crow's line' it becomes when in lagna;
In 4th one may have two women.

163

In 12th and second it is the most exalted.
In 10th it becomes Saturn the exalted.
In 5th it is pucca mud full of children,
In 11th it spins like a top, full of wealth.
In 8th all planets become malefic.
So is Venus, it too becomes malefic.
It gives all wealth glory and delight,
When it acts like a blessed 'Kam Dhenu' cow.

Exalted Venus

1. "Venus, thy eternal sway; all the race of men obey." (Euripides)
2. "Love conquers all; let us too yield to love." (Virgil)

Malefic Venus

"Heaven has no rage like love to hatred turn'd; nor hell a fury like a woman scorn'd." (Congreve).

Venus: Goddess Laxmi (wealth); curd-like; domestic happiness; loved and adored by man; heavenly cow (Kamdhenu) showering love and abundance of everything.

(a) **Miscellaneous Features:** "In the beginning," said a Persian poet, "Allah took a rose, a lily, a dove, a serpent, a little honey, a dead sea apple, and a handful of clay. When He looked at the amalgam – it was a woman." (William Sharp)

Thus, the woman is both the goddess of love (if exalted) and demon of hatred and lust (if malefic). It is the Ruling Planet of domestic happiness, prosperity and upbringing of children; Venus in man's Birth chart means wife and vice-versa. If alone, it will never show bad results; one-eyed, hence can shower happiness (if benefic) and misery and suffering (if malefic).

(b) **Relationship with Mercury:**

 (i) If Mercury is in earlier houses, then Venus's result will be benefic.

 (ii) If Venus is in earlier houses, Rahu's effect will be bad.

(iii) If Venus and Mercury aspect each other (100%), both the planets show malefic results.

　　(1) Venus no.2 – Mercury no.8

　　(2) Venus no.3 – Mercury no.9

　　(3) Venus no.6 – Mercury no.12

　　(4) Venus no.8 – Mercury no.12

The above condition is not applicable to the Kendras (1, 4, 7, and 10 houses).

(iv) If Venus is in no.12 and Mercury is in no.6, best results of both the planets as well as Ketu.

(c) **Relationship with Enemy Planets:** Sun and Saturn are both enemies. If they are together in the birth chart, it will not have bad effect on the native. Sun is light (plus sign) and Saturn is darkness (minus sign) and the result will be neutral. But when Saturn and Venus are together, the planet aspecting them is destroyed by Saturn. Whenever there is a clash between Sun and Saturn, it is the Venus that suffers. If Sun aspects Saturn, it is the Venus that is destroyed instead of Saturn. (Example: Sun no.6 and Saturn no.12 – spouse dies). If Saturn aspects Sun, Venus will confer good results.

(d) **Venus's relationship with Rahu:**

(i) Venus is cow and Rahu is elephant.

(ii) When they aspect each other, Venus is destroyed; wife and wealth will be destroyed; even life will be in danger.

(iii) If Venus is in an enemy's house and Rahu occupies the adjacent house, Venus will be destroyed.

(iv) If Venus aspects the enemy house in the Birth chart and whenever Venus becomes malefic in the Annual chart, then the enemy planet which was being aspected by Venus in the Birth chart will destroy Venus which will be more malefic and destructive.

(e) **Venus – a double-edged weapon:**

(i) It is both a blessing (if exalted) and a curse (if debilitated).

(ii) Venus in house no.1 to 7: It is completely involved in the affairs of love or lust like Casanova or Don-Juan in his youth.

(iii) Venus in house no.8 to 12: It is just like a person preaching in old age i.e. sinner in youth and becoming a preacher in old age.

(f) **Venus in various houses and Raashis:**

Venus in House No.	Effect
No.1	Both benefic and malefic; man of extreme temperament e.g. Razia Sultan – queen of India – fell in love with Yaqut (a Negro slave) forgetting all traditions and her status.
No.2	Comfortable and happy domestic life; loved by all; but being proud of her beauty, may not be liked by some.
No.3	Legend of Satyavan-Savitri; when the dutiful wife saved her husband from the jaws of death; wife inspires and encourages the husband; so attractive that she will be like a perennial flower for her husband.
No.4	Two women or two men at the same place opposed to each other.
No.5	House full of children who may not serve their father.
No.6	Good-for-nothing woman; impotent man and infertile woman.
No.7	Affect of the associated planet in this house; "As you are, so am I."
No.8	Malefic Venus; ungrateful; if exalted, best results.
No.9	Loss of wealth due to woman's ill health; but will have all comforts and items of luxury.
No.10	Woman will dominate the man; but man may have relations with another woman.
No.11	Woman/man spinning like a top i.e. not constant in his/her affections; but will have gentle appearance.
No.12	Heavenly cow (Kamdhenu cow); goddess of wealth; wife providing all pleasures and comforts, but herself may suffer.

Venus – House no. 1

Life of a crow (long, but miserable) or life of a fish (exalted); upper portion of cheeks; love of another woman or man.

(a) **What is life of a crow (Kaag Rekha):** Crow has a long life, but it is all miserable. When Venus is in house no.1 and Saturn is malefic or no.7 or no.10 is occupied by any planet except Rahu-Ketu or Saturn (wicked planets or Mercury), that means 'Kaag Rekha' or life of a crow.

(b) **What is life of a fish (Machh Rekha):** It means happiness, prosperity and all types of comforts i.e. fish is gliding in warm waters without any interruption. If Saturn is exalted or no.7 or no.10 are vacant or are occupied by Rahu-Ketu or Saturn or Mercury – that constitutes 'Machh Rekha' i.e. life of a fish.

Good effects

(a) Such a person will not bother for caste or creed while in love; may be irreligious, but will have a comfortable life. Venus, if exalted, will sacrifice its all for the sake of a lover; but if malefic, will destroy its enemy out of sheer hatred. If exalted, it constitutes 'exalted life of a fish'; for children; happiness and wealth; but if malefic, it means 'life of a crow' i.e. loss of health and wealth; such a person will, of course, have the comfort of a conveyance.

(b) Such a person will woo or court another woman and may lose his heart and soul to her; he will be like a moth beating its wings around a lighted candle; will be like a water-melon split into many parts; wife's health may be bad; but himself will be rich and enjoy good position.

Good effects of Venus in house no. 1 and planets in other houses:

Planet	House No.	Good Effect
Exalted Saturn	No.10, 11 (i.e. its own house)	May marry before his own job or livelihood; she will be the 'master' of the house.
Mars	No.6, 7, 12	Long life of 100 years.
Exalted Saturn or vacant (If no.7, 10 are occupied by Rahu, Ketu or Mercury or Saturn, they will be regarded as vacant) & if Mercury is not in no.6 to 12, it will be 'crow's life' even though no.7, 10 are vacant).	Any No.7, 10	Rich (life of a fish); will help others, provided there is no beautiful maidservant in the house.
Exalted Mercury	No.3, 6	Will be victorious in litigation; even Moon will not give bad results.

Bad effects

(a) If Saturn and Venus are together in no.1, it will constitute 'crow's life' i.e. all round destruction and suffering.

(b) If Venus is malefic, mother may die in his childhood or she may lead a life worse than death, but Sun's effect will be good.

Bad effects of Venus in house no. 1 and planets in other houses:

Planet	House No.	Bad Effect
Not vacant	No.7, 10	'Crow's life', marriage at 25th year may lead to separation or death of spouse and also loss of health.
Rahu	No.7	Mad wife; bad health; unhappy married life; may even lead to divorce.
Malefic Mercury	Any	Bad sons.
Malefic Sun	Any	Unhappy domestic life.
Malefic Saturn	Any	Unhelpful relatives and friends; Venus will give the effect of no.10; his wife will be like ever blooming flower for him & he will himself lead a luxurious life.
Malefic Mercury, Saturn and Sun (all three)	Any	Worst life; may encounter deaths in family.
Rahu, Moon, Sun	No.1, 7	Lover may suffer from asthma or lung problem.

Remedies:

(a) Must keep control over his heart and senses and seek advice from elders and friends.

(b) Donate 7 cereals or barley for 43 days.

(c) Must keep silver brick or give one to daughter at the time of marriage. This silver brick must not be sold at any cost.

Venus – House no. 2

Happy married life; will have God's bounty; ghee; mica; camphor.

Good effects

(a) Such a person will always have God's bounty and plenty without making efforts; will have large number of children; will earn a lot till 60 years.

(b) Raashi no.2 (Taurus) will never be debilitated; Venus, the Lord of Taurus will always be goddess of wealth and happiness; domestic happiness, exalted personal fate; will be a preacher to others after leading a luxurious life in youth; must have good character; will be victorious over enemies.

(c) Jupiter, Ketu and Mercury will confer good results; even Saturn will be benefic; will enjoy king-like status; lot of wealth, may have three houses.

Good effects of Venus in house no. 2 and planets in other houses:

Planet	House No.	Good Effect
Saturn	No.2, 9	Venus and Saturn both will be exalted; if Saturn is in no.9, Venus will be doubly exalted; will earn for 60 years from the date of first job.
Jupiter	No.6, 12	Will have a large number of brothers & all will offer mutual help to each other.
Jupiter and Mars	No.2	A successful lover.
Vacant	No.8	Laxmi yoga; rich; marital happiness.

Bad effects

Malefic Venus in no.2 (provided no.8 is vacant) makes the man incapable of producing children; and in the case of a woman, she is infertile; Sun-Rahu (solar eclipse) or Moon-Rahu (Lunar eclipse) and malefic Venus in no.2, fate is somewhat destroyed.

Bad effects of Venus in house no. 2 and planets in other houses:

Planet	House No.	Bad Effect
Malefic	No.9 or 12	Wife will be a shrew; will torture the spouse, howsoever rich he may be.
Rahu-Ketu	No.2, 5, 9, 12	Prostitutes and women of loose character will be the cause of downfall.
Jupiter	No.8, 9, 10	Bad in respect of household affairs and sons; must remain faithful to husband/wife.

<u>Remedy:</u> Such a person will suffer from anaemia; urinary troubles and sexual debility. Adopt remedy for Mars.

Venus – House no. 3

Faithful and loving wife; legend of Satyavan and Savitri (Satyavan died in the prime of his life. As Yama, the Lord of the nether world was carrying his soul. His wife, Savitri, followed Yama and won a boon from him. Thus, she revived her dead husband back to life through devotion, prayer, courage and fidelity).

Good effects

Woman adores the man with Venus in no.3, but his own wife is more like 'that of a bull rather than a cow'; she is like tigress in temperament, but cowardly; even a bad woman will be of great help to him; such a person would like to court every woman, but for best results, must respect and love his wife, who will not only inspire him, but will stand by him like a rock in the hour of distress. If he goes wrong, wife will dominate him; hence, there is need for remaining loyal to his wife.

Good effects of Venus in house no. 3 and planets in other houses:

Planet	House No.	Good Effect
Exalted Ketu	Any	Women will be respected; faithful wife; no theft.
Saturn	No.9	Happiness from parents; long life.
Mercury, Saturn, Ketu or Mars	No.2 or 7	Very faithful and devoted wife; even Moon will confer best results, comfortable life.
Exalted Mercury	Any	May travel abroad happily for 20 years; happy and long life of parents.
Exalted Moon & not malefic	Any no.8	Jupiter, Sun, Mercury, Ketu will not be bad, may conquer death even if no.8 is malefic.

Bad effects

Bad effects of Venus in house no. 3 and planets in other houses:

Planet	House No.	Bad Effect
Jupiter	No.9	Marital discord; ill health; unhappy
Mercury	No.11	Venus will be destroyed till 34th year; may have bright and imposing buildings, but sleepless nights; may go on losing wealth.
Any planet	No.9, 11	These planets will not be destroyed; Venus herself will be destroyed, if planets in no.9, 11 are its enemies.
Venus and malefic Mars together	Any (especially no.3)	Even though multi-millionaire, he will have to earn his living.
Malefic Mercury, Mars	Any	Bad effect on wealth; wife will misbehave; even daughter and wife will face bad fate; daughters and brothers may squander his gold and wealth; ancestral property will be of no use to him; instead of gold, he may receive books and articles of entertainment from father.

Venus – House no. 4 (Raashi effect)

Good effects

Will gain through travels on land; life will be fine and comfortable for 4 years after marriage; thereafter clash with mother (Moon) and wife (Venus). It is Moon that opposes Venus. Bad for maternal uncles and children (Remedy lies in Moon and also throw articles concerning Jupiter i.e. saffron, Chana daal etc. into the well for 43 days).

Good effects of Venus in house no. 4 and planets in other houses:

Planet	House No.	Good Effect
Venus alone and vacant	No.4 No.2,7	Two women in the house – young and old. Younger one will be fashionable and foppish, but may be issueless.

Bad effects

Lustful conduct and illicit relations with women of loose character and prostitutes will bring disaster; it will be just like termites (white ants) eating up and destroying the whole building.

Bad effects of Venus in house no. 4 and planets in other houses:

Planet	House No.	Bad Effect
Malefic Venus and malefic Moon	Any (especially no.4)	Bad results for both Moon & Venus. [Remedy: Fill up the kernel of apricot with surma (black lead) and bury it in grass in a deserted place]. Marriage at 22nd, 24th, 29th, 32nd, 39th, 47th, 51st, 60th year will be possible.
Venus and Saturn together	No.4	Drug addict, drunkard; hence worst results; even Mercury and Ketu will be malefic.
Venus and Moon together	No.4	Utter poverty, but will have God's blessing.
Malefic Saturn	No.4 or any	Lustful conduct will bring his downfall; dearth of sons.
Jupiter	No.1	Clash between mother-in-law and daughter-in-law.
Malefic Mercury or malefic Moon	Any (especially no.4)	Unhappy married life; bad for daughter.
Mars, Mercury or any wicked planet helpful to Venus	No.1 in Annual chart in their second round	Will give good results as regards children.

Venus – House no. 5

Home full of children.

Good effects

(a) Home full of happy children; will never lose his job, as long as his wife is alive.

(b) Patriot full of love for family, land of birth and community. If noble and pious, best results and if lustful, will be ruined.

Good effects of Venus in house no. 5 and planets in other houses:

Planet	House No.	Good Effect
Exalted Mercury, Saturn, Ketu	Any	Noble, religious-minded, teetotaller; very wealthy wife – goddess of wealth.
Benefic male planets or associated with	No.5	Wealthy and prosperous; lover of family, country and community.
Mercury or wicked planets	No.1 or 7	Good results for planets in no.1 or 9 (except Sun in no.1 and Jupiter in no.9).
Sun and Mars	No.1, 10	Very auspicious; best luck.

Bad effects

Bad effects of Venus in house no. 5 and planets in other houses:

Planet	House No.	Bad Effect
Malefic Venus	No.5	Worst luck if of loose character; but no bad effect on children, but may adversely affect planets in no.1 & 7 (except Sun in No.1 & Jupiter in no.9); may also adversely affect in-laws and elder brothers.
Sun, Moon, Rahu	No.1 or 7	H.no.12 will be destroyed, even though no.3 or 8 may be benefic; but no bad effect on the native; such a man will be lustful.
Malefic Venus (without any aspect – neither aspecting nor being aspected)	No.5	Thief; stolen money will never be regained; will be like Dr. Jeckyl and Mr. Hyde i.e. noble during day time and lustful and dacoit during night; if he marries without the consent of parents, children will not serve him.
Malefic Moon	Any	Venus will be destroyed. (Remedy: Adopt remedy for Moon i.e. donate rice, milk or silver).
Venus & enemy planets together	No.5	The enemy planets will not have any adverse effect on Venus.

Remedies:

(a) Serve your mother and remain noble and of good character – this will make him prosperous.

(b) Wash your private organs i.e. penis or vagina etc. with milk and not with water.

Venus – House no. 6

Woman is honoured, loved and adored, prosperous & wealthy; otherwise destined to lose all; a woman scorned and insulted is more furious than a wounded tigress; most malefic; sparrow; eunuch; transvestite.

171

General characteristics: Such a man wants to be leader among colleagues; may accuse, insult and let down his relatives; irreligious; indulge in flattering and praising women and singing hymns about their beauty; good health and good eyesight; insult his friends many times; unlucky in domestic matters; wife of such a person (Venus no.6) is like a perennial flower and he is himself prone to luxury (same is the case with woman with Venus no.6). (Remedy: Spouse should not walk barefooted.)

He may be short-tempered and asthmatic. (Remedy as for Moon). It becomes the most malefic, when it occupies house no.1 in the Annual chart. He may act foolishly, but nature is kind to him and helps him. He is an ungrateful man.

When Venus is in no.6, it is the most debilitated; such a person donates his all belongings to the poor; will act like a fool; will be deprived of the love of wife and hence unhappy, but will have comfortable old age. (Remedy as for Moon).

Good effects

God is kind to such a person, who does many things against his wit and intelligence; must maintain decorum and good conduct for better results and must also donate articles concerning Moon i.e. milk, rice and silver; comfortable old age; bad conjugal relations; malefic in respect of Sun.

Good effects of Venus in house no. 6 and planets in other houses:

Planet	House No.	Good Effect
Sun, Moon, Rahu or Malefic planets	No.2 or 8	Venus will show good results (Venus no.12); may be a bit unlucky in service matters.
Exalted Moon	Any	Venus will not be malefic.
Venus, Mars together	No.6	Best life, but Venus's effect will depend upon Rahu-Ketu.
Sun or Jupiter and any planet	No.2 or 6 No.12	"Fish's life" i.e. rich and prosperous – either himself or father.
Sun or Jupiter or both and Venus	No.2 or 6 No.6	Very rich; Venus is like a precious diamond, but children will be duffer and stupid.

Notes: Venus in house no.6 will be debilitated, when such a man or woman is the only child. Mercury, Saturn and Ketu will become malefic first.

or

Sun, Jupiter, Moon, Rahu will also start showing bad results in respect of houses; machines etc. (Saturn) or daughter, sister (Mercury) or son, spinal cord, ears, joints etc. (Ketu).

Bad effects

Bad effects of Venus in house no. 6 and planets in other houses:

Planet	House No.	Bad Effect
Any planet except Mars or Jupiter	No.6 or 7	Venus and the associated planets will give bad results. (Remedy: Keep silver in the house).
Vacant or Sun and Mercury	No.2, 6	Bad in respect of children; parents may die in his childhood; wife and children will confer good results after 28th year.
Malefic Mercury	No.5	Planets in no.3, 4, 7, 9 will give bad results; but planets in no.1 will help or when Mercury occupies house no.1 in the Annual chart, everything will be revived.
In association with Ketu and Jupiter	No.6, 12	All these planets will be malefic, despite help rendered by Sun, Moon and Jupiter.
Rahu	No.2	Death of first wife/husband; trouble from enemies till 42nd year i.e. Rahu's span of life.
Malefic Mercury (except in no.5)	No.9 No.3 No.4 No.6 No.7 No.10 No.11	Bad for ancestors, brothers mother maternal uncles spouse father's life income. (Remedy lies in planet occupying house no.11. When Mercury occupies house no.1 in the Annual chart, everything will be retrieved).
Mercury	No.8	Malefic effect of Venus; may not have son.
Malefic Saturn	Any	Loss of wealth.
Malefic Ketu	Any (especially no.6)	Like a dirty drain; man like an eunuch and woman barren; no son; will have daughters only; may be shortsighted and duffer, but will have lot of wealth; wife will be shrew and peevish and cause his downfall.
Malefic Venus without any aspect	No.6	Guardian of family will spell doom for all, especially when he behaves like Casanova, who falsely praised women.
Jupiter or Sun	No.7 to 12 No.6	Loss of wealth; worst effect of Venus.
Enemy Planets (Sun, Moon, Jupiter)	No.7	Bad effect for all.

Remedies:

(a) Spouse should not walk barefooted.

(b) Wash private parts with some antiseptic, especially potassium permanganate (red colour). Or wash your private parts with 'Saunf' (fennel) mixed with water.

(c) Wife should wear gold on her hair.

(d) Must respect the spouse. The more she/he is adored and loved, the better for both; otherwise she/he will be ruined. (loss of wealth and domestic discord).

Venus – House no. 7

Venus, if alone, most exalted; white cow; brass utensils; love between husband & wife; fortunate.

Good effects

Venus will confer exalted status, provided it is alone in this house and sign; otherwise, will give the effect of the associated planet. May live away from house; life will be comfortable.

It will all depend upon planet in house no. 1 or when Venus occupies house no. 1 in Annual chart (31st year); everything will be fine regarding spouse and domestic happiness for 25 years (Venus's life span); wife will be noble, good-looking in fact, best in every respect, provided she is neither exceedingly fair nor exceedingly black-complexioned.

Good effects of Venus in house no. 7 and planets in other houses:

Planet	House No.	Good Effect
Exalted Venus	No.7	Happy couple; happy domestic life; spouse's parents rich; age 80-90 years.
Jupiter (Dormant)	Any, especially No.7	Will not die in foreign land; death at his native place.
Sun, Moon, Rahu (Venus's enemies)	No.1, 7, 9, 11	Rich and devoted wife.
Saturn, Mercury, Ketu (Venus's friend)	No.1, 7, 9, 11	Result of Venus will be the same as per any of the friendly planets.
Saturn	No.9, 11	Philanthropy and social service will confer better results.
Benefic Mercury	No.2, 4, 6	Best results after marriage for 37 years.
Venus and Moon	No.7 (alone) No.4 (alone)	Will not be lustful and lecherous; in fact, a good man.

Notes:

(a) Ketu will determine children.

(b) Rahu will determine income.

(c) Saturn will determine domestic happiness.

(d) Mercury will determine family.

174

Bad effects

Lustful conduct and illicit relations with other women will destroy his property and wealth; should not be a shareholder in business with in-laws.

Bad effects of Venus in house no. 7 and planets in other houses:

Planet	House No.	Bad Effect
Malefic Jupiter	Any	Bad for business and children.
Moon, Rahu (Venus's enemies)	No.1 in Annual chart & no.3 malefic	Theft, loss of wealth during 4th, 16th, 28th, 40th, 52nd, 64th, 76th, 88th year.
Moon	No.1	Bad results regarding marriage and father.
Sun, Moon, Saturn	No.4, 1, 7	Like a castrated bull; impotent; transvestite; eunuch (whether a man or woman).
Sun or Mercury	No.8	Bad for spouse. (Remedy: Must wear black and blue clothes).
In association with Rahu or malefic Rahu	No.7	Bad effect of Venus; will be destroyed, if lustful.
Vacant	No.1	Venus will not be malefic; must not have illicit relations with other women.
Malefic or Sun-Moon-Rahu	No.4	Worst effect of Venus; selfishness will cause his doom.
Jupiter & Mars (Combust)	No.2	Will be deprived of son.
Saturn and Moon	No.6	Wife suffers from some disease of vagina & also from heart disease. (Remedy: Throw Saturn's articles, such as alcohol, wine, mustard oil etc. in running water).

Venus – House no. 8

Carrot; graveyard; shrew; short-tempered woman.

A shrew, termagant, nagging wife; short-tempered woman; dominating; will have her say; husband must not oppose her for better domestic life; must not accept bribes and gifts; must pray in place of worship.

Good effects

Good effects of Venus in house no. 8 and planets in other houses:

Planet	House No.	Good Effect
Any planet	No.2	Venus will give the same effect as that of planet no.2.

175

Bad effects

Venus will not always be bad; whenever Venus no.8 occupies house no. 12 in the Annual chart, it will confer bad results. <u>Must not marry before 25 years of age.</u> (Remedy: Must throw copper coin or flower in a dirty drain to ward off its evil effect).

Bad effects of Venus in house no. 8 and planets in other houses:

Planet	House No.	Bad Effect
Vacant	No.2	Bad health of wife; bad for in-laws and male child. (Remedy: Donate barley for 43 days or bury it in the earth).
Sun, Moon, Rahu (enemy planets)	No.8	May suffer from venereal diseases, if of loose character. (Remedy: Donate cow and must not stand surety for others).

Venus -- House no. 9

Black duststorm (malefic Mars); cruel; relentless; barren land; earth destroyed by salinity.

Good effects

Ancestors will be rich, but bad in respect of children, especially son; beneficial travels; intelligent, wise, a good adviser or minister may have to work hard for his living. (Remedy for monetary position: Bury silver square pieces under *Neem* tree). Such a person meddles in the affairs of others; troubleshooter.

Good effects of Venus in house no. 9 and planets in other houses:

Planet	House No.	Good Effect
Venus in conjuction with Moon or Mars	No.9	For spouse's health, peace of mind, wealth, etc. bury silver dipped in honey in the foundation of house.

Bad effects

Fate full of bad duststorm, i.e. very bad till 25 years (Venus's span) and malefic Mars for monetary conditions and in respect of children.

Bad effects of Venus in house no. 9 and planets in other houses:

Planet	House No.	Bad Effect
Malefic planets or Sun, Moon, Rahu (Venus's enemies)	No.4	Loss of wealth; when planets of no.4 occupy house no.1 in the Annual chart, i.e., 4th, 16th, 28th, 40th, 52nd, 64th, 76th, 88th year.
Moon or Malefic Moon	No.7, any	Unhappy domestic life regarding wealth and sons.
Vacant	No.1	May suffer from anaemia.
Malefic Jupiter	Any	Loss in business; problems in respect of sons.

Remedies:

(a) Make a hole in a *Neem* tree, put 9 silver square pieces in the hole and cover it with the wood of the *Neem* tree.

(b) Bury a silver square piece in the root of the *Neem* tree, if the remedy no. 1 is not possible.

Venus – House no. 10

Dreams of beautiful women; if Saturn is exalted – good and noble; mud, cotton; heir to Saturn.

Good effects

One will have many opportunities to court and woo many women; may dream of women of exceptional beauty. The results of Moon and Mars will be bad.

Good effects of Venus in house no. 10 and planets in other houses:

Planet	House No.	Good Effect
Saturn or in association with Venus	No.1, 10	Religious-minded; Saturn's effect will be exalted; but clever and subtle like a snake; must refrain from taking wine and meat.
Vacant	No.4	Venus will now be as exalted as Saturn; husband lean and thin; wife fat and full of sexual desires.
Exalted Saturn or Saturn, but not associated with enemy planet	Any, no.9 or 11	Mercury will give good results, will never meet with an accident; good health of wife; imposing house; both husband and wife noble and religious-minded.
Any planet (whether enemy or friend)	No.1 or 5	Comfortable life; especially luxurious life in youth.
Moon (alone)	No.2, 4 or 7	Even dust will turn into gold; prosperous and rich, having cars etc.

Bad effects

Spouse must wash her private parts with curd in order to have best results in respect of birth of a son; otherwise unfortunate in respect of sons and wife is likely to lead a sinful and lustful life; may suffer from urinary troubles or some skin problem. During bad health, donate Kapila cow i.e. cow having silver with black strips or black and white cow. It will result in recovery of health; may have illicit relations with another woman for 12 years which may adversely affect son (Ketu), brothers (Mars), and wealth (Moon); such a man is a lover of women in youth and preacher in old age.

Bad effects of Venus in house no. 10 and planets in other houses:

Planet	House No.	Bad Effect
Venus or	No.1 in Annual chart	10th, 22nd, 32nd, 47th, 58th, 70th, 79th, 97th year. or
Venus or Saturn	No.7 in Annual chart In the same house in Annual chart	4th, 16th, 33rd, 44th, 50th, 66th, 76th, 94th year. In all these cases, results will be very good, provided man does not indulge in vices associated with Saturn i.e. drinking, cheating, conspiring etc.

Malefic Saturn Saturn	Any No.5	Bad effect of Venus; wife may become blind. Clash between Venus (cow) and Saturn (snake); may affect eyesight of spouse. (Remedy: Keep or feed a goat).

Venus – House no. 11

Beautiful woman or handsome man; running after wealth or spinning wealth like a top; pearl (curd-like).

Good effects

Such a person runs after wealth and rich beautiful woman (or man); lot of wealth; otherwise impotent and effeminate and suffering from skin disease; may forget his sexual urges, being busy in quest of money.

Good effects of Venus in house no. 11 and planets in other houses:

Planet	House No.	Good Effect
Mercury or Moon – exalted	Any	May change colour like a chameleon; unreliable but rich; will earn a lot of wealth for 12 years; otherwise, eunuch.
Rahu	No.12	Will earn a lot after the birth of daughters, who will be many in number.

Bad effects

Secretive in nature; outwardly simple and naïve, but inwardly very clever and subtle like a snake; changes colours like a chameleon i.e. wavering mind; may be assassinated; wife should not have the purse strings in her hands. (Remedy: Donate black and white cow).

Bad effects of Venus in house no. 11 and planets in other houses:

Planet	House No.	Bad Effect
Mercury or Venus – Mercury	No.3, 11	No dearth of wealth, but daughter will destroy the property; even spouse will be unreliable i.e. may give wealth to husband's relatives instead of her daughters; will not act against her husband's wishes.
Vacant	No.3	May suffer from urinary troubles; woman may cause downfall, though she may appear lucky for family. (Remedy: Donate oil).

Venus – House no. 12

Heavenly cow; most exalted; woman helping her husband in distress; in fact, goddess of happiness and comfort.

Good effects

Faithful and devoted wife; like the heavenly cow (Kamdhenu cow) providing all pleasures and comforts; bringer of good luck; must enjoy all conjugal pleasures; good fortune after marriage; even Moon and male planets will also confer best results i.e. threefold better; Venus will give the best result of no.2; exalted status; happy married life at least for 37 years; poet; interested in music; wife provides all comforts but not vice-versa; wealth during the whole life; victorious over enemies; thus, Venus in Pisces is indeed very exalted.

Good effects of Venus in house no. 12 and planets in other houses:

Planet	House No.	Good Effect
Jupiter, Saturn or Jupiter, Saturn and Venus	No.7 No.12	Very wealthy (fish's life); unhappy spouse, but children and relatives will get all comforts.
Benefic Mercury	No.2 or 6	Long life of 96 years; poet; musician; wealthy; exalted results.

Bad effects

In distress first wife will face problem and then husband. Donate cow or other cereals for spouse's health and even wealth; wife inspires him.

Bad effects of Venus in house no. 12 and planets in other houses:

Planet	House No.	Bad Effect
Vacant or malefic	No.2 or any	Bad effect of Venus.
Malefic Mercury	Any	Very bad results of Venus; foul-mouthed.

Remedies:

(a) Bury a blue flower in a deserted place in the evening for spouse's health.

(b) Bury articles regarding Venus's enemies (Rahu, Sun, Moon) i.e. rice, wheat and mustard seeds in a deserted place. It will offset the bad effect of malefic Venus no.12.

○○○

Saturn

शनि सांप का सांस गो मंदा – इच्छाधारी पर होते हैं ।

मदद पे जिसकी हों बैठे – तारते एकदम दोनों हैं ।

दुश्मन ग्रह जब बढ़ते जावें – ज़हर रंग शनि बढ़ते हैं ।

शुक्र बच्चा वह कभी न मारे – सांप दो बच्चे वह मारते हैं ।

गुरु के घर वह कभी बुरा न करता – न ही पाप खुद करता है ।

पाप किया जो राहु-केतु – फैसला, धर्म से वह करता है ।

तीन गुणा घर पहले मंदा – दो गुणा मंदा तीसरे है ।

एक गुणा घर छठे में मंदा – पर मंदा नहीं हमेशा ही है ।

घर चौथे में सांप-पानी का – पांचवें बच्चे खाता है ।

दूसरे घर में ख़िदमत गुरु की – तो आठवें हेडक्वार्टर है ।

नौ-सातवें घर बारह बैठा – तकदीर का कातिब होता है ।

ख़ाली कागज़ हों घर दसवें का – छठे स्याही होता है ।

घर ग्यारह में लिखे अपनी तकदीर – जन्म बच्चे का होता है ।

किस्मत का हो हरदम रखवाला – स्याही पाप की धोता है ।

Saturn, the black snake stings and breathes poison,
But is also 'Ichchha Dhari' to confer beneficence.
When it is out to help; it outrightly helps and brightens life.
When enemy planets are on prowl, Saturn becomes the most diabolical.
It never destroys Venus and child, pregnant women.
Though two snakes – real and artificial – destroy children.
In Jupiter's house it is never malefic.
Nor does it commit sin itself?
Even the sins of Rahu-Ketu
Are judiciously adjudged by it.
Three times malefic it is in no. one,
And twofold bad in no. three,
And just malefic in no. six,
But is not bad always.
In fourth it is water-snake,
And in fifth it eats its own offspring,
In second it bows before Jupiter,

And in eighth it resides in its own headquarter.
In nine, seven and twelve it is the pen of fate.
In tenth it is an empty paper writing its own fate.
And in sixth it is all black ink.
In eleventh it writes its own destiny – architect of fate.
The moment the child takes birth,
It's the watchman which protects and watches fate,
And washes off sin's black stains.

Exalted Saturn: A snake with a glittering sapphire on its hood; filling the coffers with power and wealth; a prolific fish.

Malefic Saturn: Black cobra that stings and brings death; Lord Yama (the Hindu God of death); crocodile which devours its victims.

Characteristics of Saturn in various houses:

House No.	Characteristics
No.1	It is three times malefic.
No.2	It pays its respect to Jupiter, the great teacher; hence noble and exalted.
No.3	It is two times malefic.
No.4	It is like water-snake.
No.5	It feeds on its own offsprings.
No.6	Retrograde; it destroys house no.2, whether friend or foe, but it is not always bad.
No.7	It writes its own destiny; hence exalted.
No.8	It is in its own headquarter.
No.9	Exalted; in Jupiter's house and Raashi i.e. in no.2, 9, 12, it is exalted.
No.10	It is blank paper and writes its own destiny, whether good or bad.
No.11	It is the architect of fate and blesses the man with son.
No.12	Benefic, being in Jupiter's house.

Miscellaneous characteristics of Saturn:

(i) Dishonesty, addiction to wine, thanklessness, cheating etc. are the various attributes of malefic Saturn and they are the root cause of one's destruction.

(ii) Rahu is the hood of snake and Ketu is the tail. If Ketu is in the earlier houses and Saturn in the latter, then Saturn confers best results. If Rahu is in earlier houses, snake becomes malefic.

(iii) Its period of life is 36 years i.e. such a person earns wealth and property through subtle and clever means for 36 years.

(iv) In Jupiter's house i.e. no.2, 9, 12, Saturn will never give malefic results.

(v) If exalted, it will confer good effects during the 10th, 19th, and 37th years of one's life.

(vi) If Jupiter and Moon are benefic, Saturn will give best results on Jupiter's house i.e. no.2, 9, 12.

181

(vii) Snake, howsoever dangerous, will never sting a pregnant woman or the only son in the family; it will rather become blind.

(viii) If Venus is in earlier houses and it aspects Saturn, his relations will squander his wealth and property.

(ix) When debilitated, Saturn is all black from inside-out, it will be a snake which is out to sting and spread venom; such a person does not feel ashamed of looting even a sadhu, not to speak of giving alms. Despite that he will be poor; lustful conduct, dishonesty and womanizing will be his undoing; there will be incidents of fire and in the end, such a person meets dirty death.

(x) Malefic Saturn will always have bad effect on black things; if Rahu-Ketu also aspect it, Saturn will become more sinful and wicked. Obviously, when malefic Saturn occupies the malefic houses, results will be disastrous during the 9th, 27th, 36th years of life. Moon-Rahu combined or alone in no.12, Saturn will be poisonous, howsoever benefic it may be in the Birth chart.

(xi) If two or more than two male planets (Sun, Mars, Jupiter) are with Saturn or are in direct aspect, it will not be malefic, but if three enemy planets (Sun, Moon, Mars) aspect it, Saturn will become all the more malefic.

(xii) Saturn-Ketu together give good results, but if any third planet joins them, results will be bad.

(xiii) When two planets (male and female) or more combine with or are in direct aspect of Saturn, results will be bad.

(xiv) Saturn alone with Sun or in Sun's house will give the effect of Mercury i.e. it will be partly bright and partly dark. But if Jupiter and Sun are together with Saturn, both Sun and Jupiter will be destroyed.

(xv) Saturn in Jupiter's house i.e. no.2, 9, 12 will never be malefic, but Jupiter in Saturn's house i.e. no.10 will be the most debilitated.

(xvi) Mars in no.10 (Saturn's house) will be like a king, but Saturn in no.3 (Mars' permanent house) will be like a poor watchman who will watch and protect the treasure, but cannot enjoy.

(xvii) Sun in no.11 will be exalted and noble.

(xviii) In house no.4 (Moon's house), Saturn is a water-snake which may cure paralysis, but Moon in no.8 (Mars' house of death) will be the most debilitated.

(xix) Saturn in no.7 (Venus' house) is the most exalted.

(xx) Rahu is the devil or Satan; but Satan in no.12 will help all.

(xxi) Ketu is the angel of goodness; but Saturn in no.6 (Ketu's house) is often a poisonous snake, but off and on it does serve the master like a bad son or a counterfeit coin.

(xxii) If Saturn aspects Rahu, Rahu will fly into rage and will give very bad results, but if Rahu aspects Saturn, the results are the best i.e. iron (Saturn) will be converted into copper (Sun).

(xxiii) Saturn is the son and Sun is the father; son is opposed to father and not vice-versa.

If Rahu-Ketu are on either side of malefic Saturn, the house where Rahu-Ketu are placed, will give bad results as mentioned below:

House No. with malefic Saturn	House No. with Rahu-Ketu	Bad effect on House No.
No.1	No.12	No.2
No.2	No.1	No.3
No.3	No.2	No.4
No.4	No.3	No.5
No.5	No.4	No.6
No.6	No.5	No.7
No.7	No.6	No.8
No.8	No.7	No.9
No.9	No.8	No.10
No.10	No.9	No.11
No.11	No.10	No.12
No.12	No.11	No.1

Further, if Saturn aspects or is aspected by female planets along with an enemy planet, Saturn will spare the female planet, but will destroy the enemy planet.

Malefic Saturn in house no.1	Will poison & destroy Sun and Mars
Malefic Saturn in house no.3	Will poison & destroy Mars
Malefic Saturn in house no.4	Will poison & destroy Moon
Malefic Saturn in house no.5	Will poison & destroy Sun
Malefic Saturn in house no.8	Will poison & destroy Mars

Remedy: Donate almonds or iron tong or iron plate or iron hearth off and on to sadhus and the poor at public places.

Saturn – House no. 1

If benefic, exalted conferring all pleasures.

If malefic, three times bad effect; most debilitated; worst fate; dirty insect; 'Kaag Rekha' (crow's life – long but bad).

Good effects

Saturn will now be the Lord of one eye i.e. if benefic, man may become rich and if malevolent, man will be reduced to utter poverty. Saturn-Venus no.1 can both be good as well as bad i.e. 'Machh Rekha' (fish's life of abundance) or 'Kaag Rekha' (crow's long life of dearth and poverty); if Rahu-Ketu are in no. 4-10 or Mercury or Venus in no.1 and Saturn in no.7, Venus in no.7 or Saturn in no.1 and both the houses i.e. no.1 & 7 will be considered vacant. Further, if Mars is in no.6

to 12, it will constitute 'fish's life of abundance and prosperity' and will be good for wealth, prosperity and career.

Good effects of Saturn in house no. 1 and planets in other houses:

Planet	House No.	Good Effect
Mercury	No.7	Now Mercury will give the effect of Ketu no.7; lot of wealth if Moon is exalted.

Bad effects

If a person has large growth of hair on body, it is indicative of poverty and bad days. With the birth of such a son with Saturn and Venus in no.1, everything is auctioned till 18th year. If he is addicted to wine and is given to lustful conduct, all will be over between 36 and 39 years or may be before 42 to 48 years. Everything, including house, land and wealth, will be destroyed. He will be like a log of wood which has been eaten up by white ants. Saturn-Venus in no.1 will nullify the effect of other planets and man is reduced to utter poverty and starves in the end. Life will be long but absolutely wretched. There will be disruption in studies as well.

Bad effects of Saturn in house no. 1 and planets in other houses:

Planet	House No.	Good Effect
Malefic Rahu-Ketu or any planet	No.7	Saturn will be three times malefic; bad for education, wealth; sickly wife; wife and mother unhappy.
Malefic Mercury	Any	Crow's life i.e. worst fate, but long life; everything will be destroyed; all planets poisonous and malefic.
Sun, Moon, Mars (Saturn's enemies) or Sun, Moon, Rahu (Venus's enemies) except Sun-Jupiter together.	No.4	Worst results; bad for father; ancestral property will be destroyed; Rahu, Ketu and Saturn will give worst results; a thief, cheat and dishonest.
Sun	No.7	Bad for career; liar; ungrateful; but Sun (father) will help Saturn (son).
Sun	No.10, 11	Unhappy married life; unfortunate and ill fated.
Malefic Mars (Mangalik)	Any	Cheat; dishonest; thief; quarrelsome; bad eye-sight; unhappy regarding children; ill-fated; loss of wealth.

Remedies:

(a) Get help from Sun for monetary gains i.e. donate wheat, copper or jaggery for 43 days.

(b) Bury 'surma' for 43 days for good health and progressive career.

(c) Take a pinch of mud from the root of 'Banyan' tree, mix it with sugared milk and put a dot on forehead for health and to save oneself from diseases and troubles.

(d) Donate black lentils (urad daal) or almonds or iron tong or iron plate off and on to sadhus and the poor.

Note: Saturn in Aries (Raashi no.1) loses its sting and poisonous effect, if Mars is in Capricorn (Raashi no.10) as both the enemies occupy each other's house and have to perforce become friends.

Saturn – House no. 2

At the feet of Jupiter – the great teacher; black pepper; black lentils (urad daal).

Good effects

Healthy; does not believe in visiting places of worship; outwardly naïve and stupid but very intelligent; happy life; competent advisor; compassionate; merciful; justice-loving; will not tease and trouble others; master of lands and property.

As long as he is alive, he continues to be the leader among men with independent thinking, good position and good living.

House no. 7 refers to wealth; no.6 to male members; no.8 to longevity of life and no.2 to big houses and mansions.

Good effects of Saturn in house no. 2 and planets in other houses:

Planet	House No.	Good Effect
Exalted Moon	Any	Mother's blessings and her long life, but Jupiter (father) may be weak.
Jupiter	No.4	Very intelligent; divine blessings; can read future; most fortunate; though outwardly simple, yet very wise & shrewd.
Jupiter	No.10	Religious preacher; economical; rich but miser.

Bad effects

Just after engagement or marriage, malefic Saturn will start destroying the in-laws' house i.e. the more machines, houses or cars etc. (Saturn's articles) they purchase or bring, the more they suffer.

Bad effects of Saturn in house no. 2 and planets in other houses:

Planet	House No.	Bad Effect
Rahu (Saturn working against Rahu-Ketu)	No.8, 12	In-laws (Rahu) will be completely destroyed; the native will also suffer and will face problems from the day of engagement; but Jupiter (father) will help.
Jupiter	No.11	Notorious; prone to self-praise; weak-hearted; a broken man.

185

Sun	No.12	Notorious; superstitious; a famous jeweller but hand-to-mouth living.
Malefic Mars (Mangalik)	Any	Sick from 28 to 39 years.
Rahu	No.8	Superstitious.
Rahu	No.9	A loner; does not like company.
Mars	No.9	Chicken-hearted.
Mercury	No.9	Full of bad, imaginary thoughts.
Mercury	No.12	A daughter born before 34th year and given to in-laws will bring luck; otherwise bad for both the native and in-laws.

Remedy: Visit the place of worship barefooted and feed the snake on Lord Shiva's phallus (Shiv Linga).

Saturn – House no. 3 (Raashi Effect)

If malefic, twice bad (remedy for Ketu for loss of wealth and remedy for Saturn for loss of property); wood (Keekar tree).

Good effects

Three-eyed angel of death; long life, if not addicted to drugs.

Good effects of Saturn in house no. 3 and planets in other houses:

Planet	House No.	Good Effect
Ketu	No.3 or 10	A mason; will build houses; will earn money; eye specialist; profit in dealing in things connected with Saturn (machines, houses, timber, iron etc.).

Bad effects

Saturn will be debilitated; relatives will cause harm; will lose wealth; will be malefic like the three-eyed 'god of death'; will have better eyesight, if he gives medicines free to the needy; a dark room at the end of the house will be auspicious for wealth.

Bad effects of Saturn in house no. 3 and planets in other houses:

Planet	House No.	Bad Effect
Malefic Mars (Mangalik)	Any	Others will help him; will create problems for others, but himself will be comfortable.
Saturn	No.1, 3, 5	Bad for sons; Saturn's effect will be bad.
Moon	No.10	May die by drowning; thief but poor.
Saturn together with enemies	No.3	Theft; loss of wealth; may face problems.

186

Remedy: Remedy lies in Ketu; if Ketu is in no.10, there is no need of any remedy; but still remedy for malefic Saturn may be adopted on and off.

Saturn – House no. 4

Water-snake; black insect; sprinkle a drop of milk.

Good effects

Such a person will have all the facets of love present in him i.e. love for parents, wife, God; four-eyed man; Saturn will never exercise bad effect on the native; doctor; snake's sting will never kill him, but may cure him of even paralysis; things connected with Saturn will be helpful; will deal with medicines or surgery and other professions of Saturn. If parents or uncles are doctors, the natives will also adopt the same profession; he must not be a drug addict, otherwise will lose his eyesight.

Good effects of Saturn in house no. 4 and planets in other houses:

Planet	House No.	Good Effect
Moon	No.2, 3	Best for parents and self regarding money and comforts; long life and domestic happiness.
Jupiter	No.3	Will be rich after looting others.

Bad effects

The moment he lays the foundation stone of his house; snake may sting mother and maternal uncle, may suffer till 36th year (Saturn's period); Saturn will now be a water-snake i.e. Saturn will now have no ill-effect upon the native; but Venus will be bad if the spouse is not faithful.

Bad effects of Saturn in house no. 4 and planets in other houses:

Planet	House No.	Bad Effect
Moon	No.4, 10	Moon no.10 will be bad for mother; full of tension and depression; may die by drowning; property and wealth will be destroyed; will spend all on widows or beloveds.

Remedies:

(a) Do not take milk at night.

(b) During ill health, donate things connected with Saturn i.e. iron articles, almonds, mustard oil or throw a few drops of mustard oil and wine.

(c) Feed the snake on Lord Shiva's phallus with milk.

(d) Help a poor person, especially labourer.

(e) Throw a few drops of milk into the well for monetary well being.

Saturn – House no. 5

Snake feeding on its own offspring; black lead; naïve and simple son.

Good effects

Self-respecting; Ketu will determine children and Rahu acquisition of house; but will never be issueless; simple and innocent like Lord Shiva, but very intelligent; will have a comfortable life; he must keep articles concerning Jupiter and Mars in the ancestral house in order to preserve and protect the ancestral property.

Good effects of Saturn in house no. 5 and planets in other houses:

Planet	House No.	Good Effect
Exalted Ketu	Any	Will weigh all pros and cons before taking a decision; very good life.
Exalted Rahu	Any	Will acquire and build houses.
Venus or Sun or Moon	No.7, 12 No.5, 9,10	Saturn will not have any adverse effect on the birth of children, no need of remedy.
Mars or Jupiter	No.10	Son may steal gold or money from father's house and will sell it cheap.
Vacant	No.11	Saturn will be noble and good; religious-minded.
Jupiter	No.9	Best luck during 5th, 17th, 29th, 41st, 53rd, 65th, 77th, 89th year; but worse for male child.
Ketu	No.4	No adverse effect on male child.

Bad effects

If there is a large growth of hair on the body, native will be unfortunate though he may be a thief or a cheat. Man of letters but poor; may be involved in litigations; ill health and troubles.

Bad effects of Saturn in house no. 5 and planets in other houses:

Planet	House No.	Bad Effect
Mars-Mercury together or aspect each other	Any	Saturn will exercise malefic effect; very bad during 9th, 18th, 36th year (Saturn's period); relatives in respect of planet no.2 may be stung by a snake.
Vacant	No.10	A blind snake feeding on its own children; may have many marriages, but will have only one son till 48th year; if he constructs a new house or purchases one, it will be bad for children.
Sun or Saturn	No.1 in Annual chart	May appear innocent or simple, but very shrewd.
Malefic Saturn	Any especially no.5	Bad life like that of a slave.
Sun or Moon or Mars	No.7 in Annual chart	Bad health.

Remedies:

(a) Take a few almonds to a place of worship, donate half at the place of worship and bring back the other half and keep them in your house. Adopt the process for 43 days, after that donate them also to the poor and the distressed at the place of worship after the 43rd day. This should be done whenever Saturn occupies house no.5 in the Annual chart.

(b) Keep articles concerning Sun (wheat, copper etc.); Mars (sugar, honey, red coral, saunf etc.) and Moon (rice, silver, natural water from spring etc.) in the western part of your ancestral home.

(c) Distribute salty things instead of sweets at the birth of a child.

Saturn – House no. 6 (Raashi effect)

Writing on the wall; crow; one time malefic; retrograde; striking at the very roots of house no. 2. (Remedy as for Rahu for illness and troubles; as for Mercury for wealth; goat auspicious).

Good effects

Saturn in no.6 is always retrograde; it adversely aspects the planets in no.2 and destroys them; even Venus in no.2 (a great friend of Saturn) is not spared and is completely destroyed by the poisonous stings of snake. Night blindness; when Rahu is in no.8, Saturn will be all the more poisonous for no.2, but will not harm the planets in no.10; when Saturn occupies benefic houses, it will confer good results; even Mercury will not be malefic; will be blessed with children; must not marry before 28th year; marriage after 28th year will be auspicious for children, parents, wealth, intelligence and wisdom etc.

Good effects of Saturn in house no. 6 and planets in other houses:

Planet	House No.	Good Effect
Exalted Rahu	No.3 or 6 in Annual chart or Birth chart	Bad period upto 42 years; even if Sun is in no.12, Saturn in no.6 will bring good effect after 42nd year; even a counterfeit coin or a prodigal son sometimes helps. So is the case with Saturn no.6.
Exalted Ketu	Any or No.10	Best results; will be blessed with a son; earning through travels; famous sportsman; abundance of wealth and long life.
Sun	No.12	Venus will not suffer; wife will be happy.

Bad effects

Malefic Saturn in no.6 will show its adverse effect in the form of loss of shoes or purse or machinery. Such a theft or loss is indicative of bad days ahead. When Saturn is in no.6 or malefic, Saturn of Birth chart occupies no.6 in the Annual chart, bad time will start with the loss of shoes; purse or machinery. One must not buy new shoes etc. immediately thereafter; otherwise, he may have to face litigation, police cases or demotion in career etc.; such a Saturn is malefic only once; it is not always bad. Throw coconut or almonds in the river. It will help. Marriage

189

before 28th year will spell doom and destruction; should build house after 36-39th year, it will be auspicious.

Bad effects of Saturn in house no. 6 and planets in other houses:

Planet	House No.	Bad Effect
Mars	No.2	May affect eyesight of elder brother or elder uncle; If Rahu is in no.1, maternal uncle will be blind at the age of 21.
Moon, Venus or Rahu or Mercury combined with Sun, Moon, Mars	No.4 / No.2	Will be beheaded or assassinated; ill-fated and worst luck.
Venus or Moon	No.2	Saturn will destroy not only the spouse, but also the mother; especially when Rahu is in no.8 or malefic.

Remedies:

(a) In order to ward off the poisonous effect of Saturn no.6, bury an earthen pot filled with mustard oil in the earth under the river water in a dark night, when Moon is not visible.

(b) Saturn in no.6 with no.2 vacant is blind at night; hence, purchases regarding articles of Saturn should be made at night.

(c) Throw coconut or 6 almonds in a river or donate them at a place of worship when one loses shoes, purse, machinery i.e articles concerning Saturn.

(d) Keep or feed a black dog for child's welfare or donate mustard oil.

(e) Feed the snake on Shiva's phallus (Shiv Linga) with milk.

Saturn – House no. 7

Most exalted; God's pen writing about exalted status; animals; black cow; white lead (surma); eyesight; black lentil or cereals.

Good effects

Will be very rich; may be poor at birth, but will become very rich by 36th year; will be seven times richer; but should not marry before 22nd year; will be an administrator; will receive a lot of wealth from in-laws; if noble and humane, he will earn a lot. Saturn in house no. 7 is as exalted as Jupiter and will make the man fabulously rich; long life; may travel a lot; will be an expert engineer or a doctor.

Good effects of Saturn in house no. 7 and planets in other houses:

Planet	House No.	Good Effect
Exalted Mars	Any	Ancestral property may not be more; but monthly income will be in lakhs.
Mercury, Venus, Rahu (friends)	No.3, 5, 7, 11	Saturn, Venus, Mercury, Rahu will all be exalted; all relatives will help him.
Mercury	No.11	A rich landlord.
Mars, Venus and Saturn together	No.7 or any	Best fate regarding sons, wealth and status.
Mars-Jupiter or Mars-Venus aspecting	Saturn in no.7	Very rich.

Bad effects

If such a person is infatuated to another woman (i.e. having illicit relations), he and his family plus wealth will be ruined; it will however be retrieved, if the ancestral property is still maintained. If drug or wine addict, Saturn will spell doom; may have to face imprisonment.

Bad effects of Saturn in house no. 7 and planets in other houses:

Planet	House No.	Bad Effect
Mars, Moon, Venus – all malefic	Any	Life full of sorrows and sufferings.
Malefic Jupiter	Any	Jealous, mean but will outwardly maintain pomp and show.
Mars-Mercury together or Jupiter-Venus together	Any	Fear of weapons till 27th year; bad health till 29th year; quarrelsome and ill-fated.
Malefic Moon	Any	Disease of head and brain; loss of wealth.
Mercury or enemies of Saturn i.e. Sun, Moon, Mars	No.3, 5, 7, 10	Bad for ancestral wealth and property, own life; father's life and wealth.
Vacant and together with Venus i.e. Saturn-Venus together	No.1, 7	Lustful and dirty lover; sick wife. (Remedy: Keep a pot full of honey for better results regarding wealth and happiness).
Mercury	No.1	Will be assassinated.
Mercury	No.7 in Annual Chart	Eye ailment.
Sun	No.4	Impotent; good for nothing fellow; suffering from nightblindness.
Malefic Mars (Mangalik)	Any	Malefic results of Saturn no.1; danger to life from weapons till 27th year.

191

Remedy: Fill a black flute with sugar and bury it in a deserted place or bury an earthen pot filled with honey in a deserted place.

Saturn – House no. 8

Saturn headquarter; house of death; scorpion; most delicate part of head.

Good effects

Snake or thief, even if dead, frightens and scares the onlooker; Saturn in no.8 is holed up in its own burrow; and no one knows how it will behave. In this house, Saturn alone has the power and authority to hit and sting. Now Saturn will act according to the wishes and designs of its agents – Rahu and Ketu; but Saturn alone in this house will not cause death. If alone, Saturn changes colours; it may not be bad, but it is not sure whether it will give good results.

Remedy: Keep square pieces of silver with you. It will reveal Saturn's true nature and worth.

Bad effects

Avoid wine and drugs to ward off the evil effects of Saturn; a large growth of hair on chest will indicate slavery throughout the life. The number of associated planets with Saturn no.8 will indicate the number of deaths in the family before his birth.

Planet	House No.	Bad Effect
Sun, Mars, Moon (enemies) and Saturn	No.8	Most debilitated Saturn; death in the family; bad eyesight in old age.
Vacant	No.12	Worst fate till the end; bad for relatives; loss of eyesight in old age.

Saturn is the snake; Rahu is its hood, and Ketu is its tail. If Ketu (tail) is in earlier houses, Saturn will confer exalted results. If Saturn aspects Rahu, Rahu will seethe with rage and jealousy and will destroy that house, but if Rahu aspects Saturn, results are good.

Remedy: When Saturn no.8 is malefic, keep a piece of pure silver with you. Sit on a stone and take your bath with milk and water. Let not your feet touch the earth while bathing.

Saturn – House no. 9 (Raashi effect)

Most exalted; benign hand of fate (houses and life); black and seasoned wood; (Remedy as for Jupiter, if malefic).

Good effects

Before leaving this world, he will own three houses. He is like a fresh whiff of fragrant breeze – educated, compassionate; merciful and large-hearted; owner of lands; always happy; long life; blessings from parents. Saturn will be exalted for at least 60 years with the condition that the person should be humane and noble. After the death of parents he must adopt remedy as for Jupiter, otherwise his enemies will oppose him and may sting him like a snake.

When Saturn is exalted, Venus will automatically be exalted in whatever house it may be placed; if Venus is in no.2, Saturn will be 9 times exalted. In that case, Moon will be malefic.

Good effects of Saturn in house no. 9 and planets in other houses:

Planet	House No.	Good Effect
Mercury or Venus and Saturn	No.6 No.7 No.9, 11	Now all the three planets i.e. Saturn, Mercury, Venus will be exalted. In-laws will be rich.
Sun, Moon, Mars (enemies)	No.3	Not bad, provided the dark room in the house is provided with ventilation.
Vacant	No.2	Cunning and depraved; although rich, will loot others.
Jupiter Mars or Sun, Moon or Mars	No.5 No.3	Nature will be kind and he will not meet with any mishap or will not encounter any suffering.
Moon	No.4	Parents will be rich and noble.
Sun and Saturn	No.5, 9 or 11	No clash between Sun and Saturn; compassionate and sympathetic; good relations with parents.
Jupiter	No.12	Very rich, but spendthrift.
Ketu	No.5	No bad effect upon children; large family.

Bad effects

Such a person will be unsympathetic towards poor; father may die, if the house is constructed while child is in the womb; very slow promotions like a snail.

Bad effects of Saturn in house no. 9 and planets in other houses:

Planet	House No.	Bad Effect
Mars	No.4	Saturn in no.9 will be destroyed; worst fate regarding wealth and health; like a rat spreading plague.
Jupiter	No.10	Believes in tit for tat; revengeful; incidence of fire; profit from business concerning Jupiter and Moon i.e. gold, cloth; but loss from business concerning Saturn i.e. iron, leather, machines, house building etc.

Remedy: During bad days, adopt remedy as for Jupiter.

Saturn – House no. 10

Saturn's own house; bringer of best luck; benign snake. If malefic: crocodile, blank paper of fate.

Good effects

Such a person is rich and will have a lot of property and wealth, but if he is good and noble, he will fall like a broken tree at the fag end of his career. If he is cunning and cruel like a snake, he will be better off; otherwise, bad fate and heart-rending death. As an employee, he should prefer office duties; in that case, he will rise in his profession, but if he performs field duties, he will be like a dead snake being trampled over by all i.e. worst results regarding fate and health.

Saturn within this house will be twice benefic, if it helps planet in no.1; otherwise, it will destroy planet in no.1. Father will live at least till son is 48 years old. Saturn will bestow wealth, respect and comforts every 7th year i.e. 3rd, 9th, 15th, 21st, 27th, 33rd, 39th, 45th, 51st, 57th, 63rd, 69th, 75th, 81st year etc. Now Saturn and Jupiter both will be benefic. Saturn, if alone, will be beneficial every third year.

Ketu may be malefic, but Rahu and Saturn will never give bad results; father will have a long life – at least from 39 to 48 years of the native's age; will enjoy respect of colleagues and officers; interested in magic. He must not take wine; and must not construct house before 48th year; otherwise, he will lose his wealth.

Good effects of Saturn in house no. 10 and planets in other houses:

Planet	House No.	Good Effect
Moon, Jupiter	No.1, 4	Luxurious life; will own vehicle.
Mercury	No.7 in Annual Chart	Rich in-laws.
Vacant	No.2	Saturn though dormant and asleep, will give good results.

Bad effects

If malefic, Saturn will be like a bloody snake. Such a horoscope will be a blind horoscope. The native will be ill-fated, accursed and unfortunate. All other planets howsoever exalted, will also become blind i.e. they will give worst results. If he is intelligent and shrewd, all will be well, but if he is just dull and duffer, he will meet a heart-rending death.

Bad effects of Saturn in house no. 10 and planets in other houses:

Planet	House No.	Bad Effect
Malefic Sun, Moon, Mars (enemies)	No.4	Very bad. (Remedy: Adopt the remedy for Jupiter).

Saturn – House no. 11

God writes his destiny; hence exalted; architect of his own fate; must have a son, engineer dealing with machines.

Good effects

Saturn's effect – whether good or bad – will depend upon the position of Rahu and Ketu; rich. Saturn, if exalted, will reward the man with honours and wealth and if malefic, will financially ruin the man. Such a man will write his own destiny; he will never be issueless; he is a man of vision and determination; will inherit wealth from parents; nevertheless, he will be noble and religious-minded. Saturn in no.11 will help all the good and auspicious planets, provided Mercury is not in no.3. Saturn in no.11 becomes the 'Planet of Fate' (good or bad), whenever it occupies the 1st house in the Annual chart i.e. 11th, 23rd, 36th, 48th, 57th, 72nd, 84th year.

Good effects of Saturn no. 11 and planets in other houses:

Planet	House No.	Good Effect
Sun, Mars and Moon	No.10 No.6	Best results regarding health, wealth and children.
Sun and Moon	No.1 No.6	Exalted status; will have a lot of property.
Venus	No.7	Philanthropist and humane.

Bad effects

Even malefic, Saturn gives good effect from the day it occupies house no. 1 i.e. 11st, 23rd, 36th, 48th, 57th, 72nd, 84th year. If drug or wine addict, Saturn gives worst effect. Such a person must not take wine and deal in Mercury's things, such as investments, speculations etc. Corruption and dishonesty will ruin him.

Bad effects of Saturn in house no. 11 and planets in other houses:

Planet	House No.	Bad Effect
Mercury Jupiter or Sun	No.3 No.9 No.9	Bad results of all the three.
Malefic Mercury	Any	Saturn will be malefic.

Remedy:

(a) Keep an earthen pitcher full of water as 'Kumbh', while doing auspicious work, whether Saturn is good or bad. It will always confer best results.

(b) Throw a few drops of wine or spirit or mustard oil on the ground at sunrise for health, wealth and marital happiness, if Saturn is malefic.

(c) When Jupiter is malefic, remedy lies in Jupiter.

(d) Must worship Moon i.e. must keep a brick of silver for wealth.

(e) If Rahu-Ketu are malefic, remedy lies in Mars.

(f) Avoid wine etc. at all costs.

Saturn – House no. 12

All comforts; man of destiny; fish; bedsheet on a couch; almonds; falling of hair. (Remedy: Bury red flower when Sun is in no.6 and Saturn is in no.12).

Good effects

Bold; full of courage during adversity; comfortable life; very rich, if bald-headed; Rahu-Ketu and Mercury will not exercise bad results; may construct a new house every 6 to 12 years; must not be dissuaded from constructing a house. Bury 12 almonds in the foundation of house and Saturn will offer all protection and blessings to such a man. Exalted status and exalted business; though rich, yet will care a fig for wealth; victorious over enemies.

Good effects of Saturn in house no. 12 and planets in other houses:

Planet	House No.	Good Effect
Rahu & Ketu	No.3, 6, 9, 12	Very rich; comfortable life. ('Machh Rekha' i.e. happy life).
Rahu	No.12	Saturn will now be helpful and bringer of best luck; it will be a benevolent snake.
Sun, Moon, Mars	Not in no.2	Comfortable life; architect of his own fate.

Bad effects

Lustful conduct; wine and drug addiction; comfort and dishonest dealings will nullify the good effect of Saturn. Saturn's malefic effect will start after one suffers from eye ailments.

Bad effects of Saturn in house no. 12 and planets in other houses:

Planet	House No.	Bad Effect
Moon & Rahu	No.12	Moon will now lie dormant or asleep; bad for mother and wife and women of family.
Sun	No.6	Wife may die, especially when ventilation is constructed in the well built house; death or separation from spouse. (Remedy: Bury a red flower in the earth).
Mercury	No.12	Bad results of Mercury.
Jupiter & Rahu	No.12	Bad for men of the family; Jupiter will lie low.
Sun	No.12	Short-tempered; henpecked and one who flirts with women. Bad results in service matters.

Chapter No. 18

Mercury

बुध अकेला आसमान का चक्र – इंसाफ़ पसंद निर्लेप होता है।

घर दो, चार, या छह में बैठा – राजयोगी भी होता है।

घर तीजे से आठवें होवे – मदद सूरज को देता है।

नौ से बारह या दूसरे पहले – शनि को ताकत वह देता है।

सातवें घर में पारस होवे – ग्रह साथी को तारता है।

नौ, बारह, आठ, तीन में बैठा – कोढ़ी थूकता होता है।

घर पहले, नौंवे घूमता राजा – औलाद, दौलत पांच देता है।

शनि, बृहस्पति ग्यारह राशि बुध से दोनों चलते हैं।

बुध दबा या हो मंदा, दोनों के फल खत्म हो जाते हैं।

जिधर देखता हूं उधर तू ही तू है।

कि हर शह में जलवा तेरा कू व कू है।

Mercury alone is sky's dome, neutral and eunuch;
In 2, 4, & 6, it is called Raj Yogi.
In 3 to 8, it helps Sun;
In 9 to 12, it strengthens Saturn;
In 7, like the philosophers' stone,
It helps the planet associated.
In 9, 12, & 8, 3 it is a leper, who must be shunned by all.
In 1 & 9, it is a wandering king,
And confers in 5 wealth and children.
Saturn, Jupiter, Raashi 11 are propelled by Mercury.
When asleep or malefic, it makes both Saturn and Jupiter ineffective.

"Wherever I see I find you everywhere,
Your manifestation pervades everywhere."

Exalted Mercury
Goddess of green vegetation, blessing the man with abundance of wealth and prosperous business.

Malefic Mercury
Man is reduced to an unfortunate wretch; a bat hanging by a rock.

197

Mercury

Lord of green vegetation; all powerful goddess Durga; lord of speech; precious diamond; parrot. If malefic: bat hanging upside down; leper; eunuch.

Miscellaneous features of Mercury

(a) Mercury in no.2, 4 or 6 is exalted and confers king-like status.

(b) Mercury in no.7 is like a philosopher's stone – changing base metals into gold i.e. benefiting the associated planets.

(c) Mercury in no.1 confers benefic results, but such a person is selfish. In a girl's horoscope, it is the most exalted.

(d) If poisonous Mercury occupies no.3, 8, 9, 11 or 12, it is to be avoided like a leper; its bad results are as follows:

 (i) In no.3, it will be bad for family.

 (ii) In no.8, it will have adverse effect on life.

 (iii) In no.9, it will have bad effect on self.

 (iv) In no.11, it will create problems for income.

 (v) In no.12, it is very bad for service matters or business and will destroy sleep.

(e) It may be remembered that malefic or poisonous Mercury will not adversely affect no.1 to 4 (except no.3, which will be like an infectious leper spitting at others); in no.5 to 10, it may scare or frighten others; in no.11, 12 it will be a mad dog, whomsoever it bites, will also become mad.

(f) Ordinarily, Mercury in no.1, 2, 9 to 12 will help Saturn (i.e. poison negating the effect of another poison); in no.3 to 8, it will help Sun in respect of wealth (although it may create problems when in no.3 and 8).

(g) Exalted Mercury confers wealth through business, writing and intelligence till 34th year (Mercury's span of life).

(h) Poisonous Mercury in no.1 to 4 (except no.3, where it is like a leper) will never show bad results; whereas malefic Mercury in no.11 and 12 is like a mad dog biting and infecting others with madness.

(i) Mercury is destroyed when there is a dispute between Moon and Rahu.

(j) If Mercury is associated with a benefic planet, it will make it all the more benefic and if it is associated with a malefic planet, it increases its malefic power twofold.

(k) Malefic Mercury is like a bat hanging upside-down; its first sign of maleficence appears when the stairs of a newly constructed house are demolished and then reconstructed.

(l) For a person with malefic Mercury, *piercing of nose, cleaning of teeth with alum, worship of Virgin girls (who have not attained puberty); wearing of yellow thread round the neck; and avoidance of green-coloured clothes is advised* in order to offset the bad results of malefic Mercury. If a person stammers or stutters, Mercury's bad effect is confined to stammering or stuttering only. If Mercury is still giving worst results, donate a ripe, yellow pumpkin off and on.

(m) Mercury in no.4 confers Raj Yoga, as it is here Rahu-Ketu take an oath to shun evil.

(n) Mercury gives help even to malefic Venus, but if Venus also occupies the same house where Mercury is regarded as malefic, Venus is destroyed.

(o) Mercury, if alone, is powerless and good for nothing; but it gives the effect of the permanent house it occupies e.g. Mercury in no.1 will give the effect of Sun, but if it has to give bad effect, it will affect Mars whose Raashi is 1 (Aries). Here is the list of houses which are beneficially or adversely affected by Mercury (if alone).

House No. in which Mercury (alone) is placed	Planet whose effect Mercury will give	Planet which will be destroyed by Mercury, especially planet in no.9 at that time
No.1	Sun	Mars
No.2	Jupiter	Venus
No.3	Mars	Venus
No.4	Moon	Moon
No.5	Jupiter	Sun
No.6	Ketu	Ketu-Mercury
No.7	Venus-Mercury	Venus
No.8	Mars-Saturn	Mars
No.9	Jupiter	Jupiter
No.10	Saturn	Saturn
No.11	Jupiter	Saturn
No.12	Rahu	Rahu-Jupiter

Malefic Mercury in no.3, 8, 9, 11, 12 is like a foolish leprous sailor who sinks his own boat at the time of danger.

1. Relationship with Rahu

When both Rahu and Mercury are together or separately placed in malefic houses (Mercury will be bad in no.3, 8, 9, 12 and Rahu will be bad in no.1, 5, 7, 8,11). Such a person may suffer from hospitalization or admission in a mental hospital, or ejection from property, imprisonment, though he may be innocent. He may also be given to unnecessary worries and expenditures. (Remedy: Wear a pure steel ring without any joint of another metal). Both the planets will give adverse results in respect of sisters, aunts (Mercury) or in-laws, or business in electrical goods (Rahu).

2. Relationship with Ketu

When both of them aspect each other, Ketu's effect will be bad. When they are together (Raashi effect), man may face problems and blows of fate, if not death. Both will be malefic – the dog and the tail.

3. Relationship with Venus

When both of them are together, they are auspicious; house no. 7 is their permanent house; but if they are separately placed opposite to each other at 180 degrees i.e. 100% aspect; their results will be malefic.

4. Secret of Mercury

When the Birth chart has been prepared and it is converted into the Birth chart according to the ancient text of *Lal Kitab*, find out Mercury's secret. Here is the Birth chart:

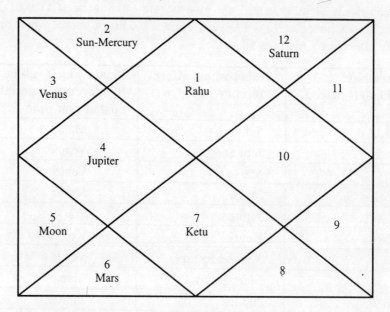

1.	Name of planet	Jupiter	Sun	Moon	Venus	Mars	Mercury	Saturn	Rahu	Ketu	Total
2.	House in which planet exists	4	2	5	3	6	2	12	1	7	
3.	Power of Planet	6/9	9/9	8/9	7/9	5/9	4/9	3/9	2/9	1/9	= 45/9 i.e. 5
4.	Multiply no.2 & 3 above	24/9	18/9	40/9	21/9	30/9	8/9	36/9	2/9	7/9	= 186/9 i.e. 20 6/9

Total comes to 20 6/9; ignore the main digit and concentrate on the remainder i.e. 6/9 which has the power of Jupiter. In other words, Mercury, which is in no.2 (Jupiter's house), will give the effect of Jupiter. Thus, during Mercury's period, both will confer good results, as here Mercury is in Jupiter's permanent house. For Mercury in no.3 or 9, keep a red ball; but if Mercury is good, keep a glass ball or marble without colour of the associated planet; for Mercury in no.12, keep a black and white dog.

5. Mercury alone

Mercury will give exalted results if it is alone in Jupiter's permanent house no. 2 or in its own exalted sign in house no. 6, but it should be without any aspect i.e. no.8, 9, 12 should be vacant and Mercury should be alone in all respects.

Relationship with other planets

Name of Planet	Sun	Moon & Venus	Jupiter	Mars	Rahu	Ketu	Saturn
Relationship with Mercury & effect	Mercury (Para in Hindi)	Water in curd	Ash	Tiger's teeth	Elephant's trunk	Dog's tail	Tin plating

Mercury, if associated with or in aspect of a planet, will increase the power of that planet, but if a third planet joins, Mercury's effect will be bad.

Mercury's effect in relation to Sun and Moon

Mercury's effect will be zero i.e. Mercury will remain quiet for half of its period i.e. 17 ½ years, if associated with Sun or exalted Mars, but will secretly play its notorious role. Exalted Mars is the one which sides with Sun and Mercury becomes silent with Sun.

Mercury – House no. 1

King; administrator, but selfish and notorious; tongue; exalted in girl's horoscope.

Good effects

Mercury may destroy Mars, but will give added strength to Sun; mercurial temperament; unreliable like a spinning top; happy; exalted position; will confer best results on the house where Sun is placed; may earn from govt. job; will never lose wealth; not only Saturn but all wicked planets i.e. even Rahu-Ketu will be under the influence of Mercury.

Good effects of Mercury in house no. 1 and planets in other houses:

Planet	House No.	Good Effect
Venus or Saturn or any other planet	No.7	Bold and courageous, provided he is black-complexioned i.e. not very fair.
Associated with Sun	No.1	Wife will be from a rich family; noble and good.

Bad effects

Malefic Mercury may confer exalted results on a woman, but she may have to face humiliation and charge of character assassination in her youth. Mars' effect will be bad, but not that of Sun. Person will be naughty and notorious. If Mars is in no.12, Mercury in no.1 will never be malefic. If malefic, may adversely affect things related to Mercury (must not take egg), but will be rich after the middle age. Even Rahu (in-laws) and Ketu (sons) will not be good, if he takes wine and is a drug addict; may live abroad, but will be greedy; best young age; foul-mouthed without a loud voice.

Bad effects of Mercury in house no. 1 and planets in other houses:

Planet	House No.	Bad Effect
Mercury alone and Vacant	1,7	Mercury's own effect will be bad; but 'Raj Yoga'; will help others – a throne without legs.
Moon	7	Ringleader of drug-addicts. Worst results.

Mercury – House no. 2

King among yogis; man of letters; standing egg; manly girl; green lentils (Moong); sister-in-law; beak of a bird; selfish.

Good effects

Intelligent; best personal fate; fortunate but selfish; narcissus (lover of self); yogi raja; rich but effect of Venus; victorious over his enemies; good for in-laws; good orator; witty; man of letters; author; full of determination; rich but zero for son; self-made rich; good status; though bad for father, yet mother and he himself may live up to 80 years; will serve the family; good life indeed.

Good effects of Mercury in house no. 2 and planet in other houses:

Planet	House No.	Good Effect
Mercury alone	2	Yogi raja; helpful to all.
Vacant	6 or 8	Will never face worries and mental problems.
Moon helped by no.8	12 / 8	Father's long life, provided Moon is not malefic – in that case, bad for father and wealth.
Jupiter	9,12	Mother will have long life; will command respect.
Mars (alone) or Mars-Jupiter	6	Now Mercury in no.2 will not have bad effect on Jupiter i.e. father; may adversely affect Mars, but not necessarily.
Saturn	6	Very smart like a flying eagle (in good sense).

Bad effects

Malefic Mercury is like an ash which may spoil the taste of mouth and tongue; Ketu's effect will be bad i.e. unhappy from son, but will not be issueless i.e. must have a son who may live away from father; bad investment; bad for trade, speculations and gambling; father may be a multimillionaire, but will leave nothing for him; father may die between 16 and 31 or at the most 34 and 36 years of age; father's wealth will be destroyed; sisters, aunts, daughters etc. will not behave well. (Remedy: Pierce the nose; it will help).

Bad effects of Mercury in house no. 2 and planets in other houses:

Planet	House No.	Bad Effect
Sun	8	Inventor; discoverer; scientist, having full confidence in his intelligence; but proud; though intellectual and physically healthy, yet monetarily unwell.
Saturn	6	Like a weather cock; unreliable.
Jupiter	8	Mercury will have adverse effect on grandfather instead of father.
Moon or Saturn	12	Father's wealth will be destroyed between 17 and 36 years. (Remedy: Donate articles concerning Moon).

Remedy: Adopt remedy as for Jupiter and Moon.

Mercury – House no. 3

Most malefic; leper to be avoided; niece; termite; bat hanging upside-down.

Good effects

Good for self; but like a leper for others; i.e. very bad; will never lose wealth; age 80 years.

Good effects of Mercury in house no. 3 and planets in other houses:

Planet	House No.	Good Effect
Mars	1	Mercury will bring good luck; increase in wealth; and good for things related to Mercury.
Sun	11	Good for sons and maternal uncles (Ketu); will be a doctor treating patients of asthma; long life.
Vacant	9, 11	Mercury will be exalted.

Bad effects

Most debilitated; it destroys not only no.9 and 11, but also no.4 and 5. If a person stammers or stutters, Mercury's malevolence will be confined to that house only; otherwise, it will work havoc not only on house no. 3, but also house no. 9, 11, 4 and 5 as mentioned above. Mercury is like the cruel maid who is out to destroy everything.

Remedy: It lies in Ketu and avoid taking green lentils (moong) and green colours.

Bad effects of Mercury in house no. 3 and planets in other houses:

Planet	House No.	Bad Effect
Benefic Venus	3 or any	Moon's effect will not be bad; will be a good writer.
Enemy planets (Moon)	8 & 6 not occupied by friends	Venus's effect will be malefic; even Saturn and Rahu will be destroyed.

Wicked Planets	6, 7	Maternal uncles will be destroyed.
Moon, Jupiter	5, 9	Bad results of these houses.
Malefic Mars	5, 11	Both the houses will be destroyed.
Moon	11	Worst results for no.3 (brothers) and no.11 (income).
Debilitated Venus without aspect	Any	Bad for mother; may have a stepmother.
Sun, Saturn	9, 11	Both the planets will be destroyed; worst life.
Saturn	7	Bad for father's life and business.

Remedies:

(a) Clean your teeth with alum.

(b) Avoid taking Moong (green pulses) and also avoid green colour.

(c) Wash moong at night and feed sparrows and animals in the morning for 43 days.

(d) Wash leaves of 'Palash' or Dhak trees with milk and then bury them in a pit in a deserted place; cover them with a black stone and mud. Do not bring back home the pot containing milk.

(e) Stone buried in the house may be washed with milk.

(f) In order to get rid of the malefic effect of Mercury in no.3, take 3 yellow-coloured cowries, burn them and throw the ash into river or jungle or deserted place. Person will be saved from destruction.

Mercury – House no. 4

Rajayog; exalted status; specialist; parrot; tin-plating; precious diamonds; very wealthy.

Good effects

Mercury in cancer or friendly signs, if alone, is exalted. Such a person is like a philosopher's stone for others; Moon's effect will also be exalted in respect of wealth and career, but will always be restless and under tension; happy couple leading a life of bliss, like that of the legendary 'tota-maina' (the story of the parrot and its spouse).

Good effects of Mercury in house no. 4 and planets in other houses:

Planet	House No.	Good Effect
Benefic male or female planets	Any	Contented, but helpful to others.
Moon	2	Exalted position in service; Rajayog; very wealthy, Mercury and Moon or Mercury and Venus will also be benefic; will bring good luck to the family.
Sun or Moon and Jupiter	3, 5, 11 11	Will rise high in life; rich; wicked planets will be ineffective.

Moon and vacant	3, 6 2	Happy and long life of planets.
Exalted Jupiter	Any	Rajayog; will earn a lot; will enjoy exalted status with all perks in his career.

Bad effects

At his birth, people will congratulate his parents, but his mother will shed tears because of the death of her mother. She is, of course, like a swan who has given birth to a precious jewel. Mother's health will deteriorate. ·

Bad effects of Mercury in house no. 4 and planets in other houses:

Planet	House No.	Bad Effect
Malefic Rahu	In malefic houses	Bad for male members.
Malefic Ketu	In malefic houses	Bad for travels and bad results, if one is advised by others.
Malefic Moon	6	May commit suicide.

Remedy: As for Sun and Jupiter.

Mercury – House no. 5

Prosperous; a soothsayer; word of God; granddaughter.

Good effects

Man of knowledge and learning; a soothsayer who can predict future; prosperous and wealthy; Sun, Jupiter and Moon will confer best results; even Saturn will be benefic; Mercury will help Sun.

Good effects of Mercury in house no. 5 and planets in other houses:

Planet	House No.	Good Effect
Mercury (and no aspect)	5	Humanitarian; good man; happy family life.
Sun, Moon & Jupiter	3 or 9	Lucky and fortunate after 24th year.
Moon & Jupiter	3, 9	Best results.
Moon, Venus & Sun	Any	All will be helpful; bad for father; but it will not have any bad effect on children.

Bad effects

Bad effects of Mercury in house no. 5 and planets in other houses:

Planet	House No.	Bad Effect
Moon or Malefic Moon	1, 2, 4 6 or 12	Mercury will destroy planets in no.4, 6, 7, 8, 9.
Malefic Mercury, but if Moon or Jupiter	5 3, 9	No.3, 4, 5, 7, or 9 will be destroyed. All the above will become benefic and give good results.

Malefic Moon or Jupiter	Mercury in earlier houses than Moon & Jupiter	Worst results because of one's own short-temper and foul language.

Mercury – House no. 6

Large-hearted; unknown and unrecognized Yogi; most exalted; flower; daughter; domestic happiness for 27 years.

Good effects

Most exalted; Mercury will be like a faithful dog wagging its tail and following the master; will serve the master like a loyal maidservant; will have power of speech till the last moment; self-made rich; life like a beautiful flower; unrecognized yogi; large-hearted; Mercury will give the effect of all benefic planets; will confer best results, if Venus is exalted; best results if contented; may travel abroad; sisters, aunts (Mercury) will confer happiness; will prosper in business; matters concerning intelligence and authorship and lands; will be victorious over his enemies; honesty will pay; all exalted planets become more exalted, if Mercury in no.6 is exalted.

Good effects of Mercury in house no. 6 and planets in other houses:

Planet	House No.	Good Effect
Mercury alone without aspect	6	Moon will be benefic; will earn through printing press and paper business.
Saturn	9 or 11	In-laws will be rich.
Sun or Jupiter or Saturn	1	Rajayog; rich; religious-minded; traditionalist; landlord.
Exalted Jupiter	Any	Rajayog; if he is honest, he will prosper; business in printing and paper will be auspicious.

Bad effects

Malefic Mercury will now be an ungrateful wretch who will decamp with the property of the master; in fact, worst results; if he is a dishonest and greedy doctor, he will never prosper and flourish; malefic Mercury in no.6 will be as debilitated as malefic Mars, which will adversely affect mother's life and health during 34th year. First issue will be a daughter. He must shun corruption and must not accept bribe.

Bad effects of Mercury in house no. 6 and planets in other houses:

Planet	House No.	Bad Effect
Malefic Venus	Any	Bury a pot of milk in a deserted place; if Mercury in no.6 is malefic. For Moon's help, bury a bottle filled with 'Ganga Jal' (water of the Ganga) inside the earth.
Mars	4 or 8	Mother may die in his childhood; bad for household.

Venus & Malefic Ketu	4 any	Son after 34th year; wife should wear silver ring in left hand.
Moon or Jupiter or Jupiter and Moon	2 11 2	Weak eyesight; Saturn's effect will be bad; bad old age; in fact, whole life will be bad.

Remedy: Worship virgin girls (who have not attained puberty) or flowers while doing auspicious work.

Mercury – House no. 7

Philosophers' stone for others; in boy's horoscope he will help others; in girl's horoscope Mercury will never be malefic; green grass; goat.

Good effects

Mercury will now be like a philosophers' stone for others i.e. will help others; but not the native; man of letters; writer; will help even an ordinary acquaintance; best old age; a good businessman; will be victorious in litigations; his pen will be mightier than his sword; may not be worldly wise, but rich.

Good effects of Mercury in house no. 7 and planets in other houses:

Planet	House No.	Good Effect
Exalted Mercury & vacant	7 1	Like a precious diamond for the whole family.
Moon	1	Benefits from sea travelling.
Saturn	3	Very rich in-laws.
Any planet – whether friend or foe	1 or 10	These planets will not give bad results.

Bad effects

His sisters, sister-in-law, aunt, and even daughter will be unhappy; his notorious sister will conspire with his brothers and destroy his domestic happiness i.e. Venus will be destroyed i.e. malefic Mercury will poison both Mars and Venus.

(a) Ketu no.1 or 8—Bad for business.

(b) No aspect from no.1—Unhappy childhood; but good old age; bad for Venus till 34th year.

(c) Jupiter no.9—Bad domestic life; problems in marriage.

Mercury – House no. 8

Illness; bad fate; notorious; accursed; cause of destruction; loser of wealth; leper; dying or withering flower; termite, sister, disease of teeth & veins – in fact, most malefic.

Good effects

In association with male planet:

(a) Mercury no.8 will never be malefic; it will confer the same benefic effect as that of the associated male planet.

(b) Sun, Moon or no.4 exalted – Mercury will not be poisonous after 34th year; even Ketu will be benefic; best results in respect of mother & Moon.

(c) Mars no.12 – Mercury in no.8 will no longer be malefic.

(d) In association with Mars in no.8 – Both will confer good results, although if alone, both give best results.

Bad effects

Malefic Mercury in no.8 causes tooth decay; disease of the veins; in fact, it is a leper whom everybody avoids; will entail loss in income; will destroy things connected with Mercury i.e. sister, aunts etc. Whenever the staircases of newly-built house are demolished, Mercury's malefic effect is visible.

(a) Mercury (alone) in no.8 – Will give bad results.

(b) No.2 vacant (in the horoscope or Annual chart) – Worst results till 34th year; every malefic planet becomes all the more malefic, such as Saturn in no.1; Ketu in no.3 & 6; Mars in no.4; Sun in no.7; Moon in no.8; Rahu in no.9, 12; Jupiter in no 10.

(c) Jupiter in no.2 or another planet – Father's life and wealth in danger from 16th to 21st year.

(d) Moon in no.2 – To counteract the malefic effect of Mercury, donate things concerning the planet in no.2 in Annual chart e.g. Moon in no.2, Mercury in no.8 – Donate rice or milk; Sun in no.2 – Donate wheat or jaggery etc.

(e) Malefic in no.6 – All planets (except Jupiter) will be bad.

(f) Male planet in no.6, Mercury in no.8 or 12 – Mother will die early; otherwise, both mother and son may face trouble.

(g) No.12 vacant – Diseases of shoulders, ribs, thighs etc.

Remedies:

(a) Pierce the girl's nose, let her wear silver nose pin.

(b) The daughter should not wear red-coloured clothes.

(c) Keep rain water or milk on the roof.

(d) Whenever Mercury in no.8 occupies the 8th house in the Annual chart, bury a small earthen pot filled with honey or sugar in a deserted place a few days before the birthday and also after it.

(e) Fill up the copper pot with 'Moong' and throw it gently into running water as in (d) above.

Mercury – House no. 9

King but leprous; ill-fated; shortlived; a shadowless imaginary ghost; bat hanging upside-down; green colour; stuttering/stammering; green vegetation and a jungle full of green trees; debilitating.

Good effects

May be penniless, but will help other family members; if no.11 is vacant, Mercury will be like a shameless girl, guilty of incest i.e. its effect will be the most malefic.

Moon, Ketu, Jupiter in no. 1, 3, 6, 7, 9, 11 – Mercury will never be malefic; very rich; comforts & happiness all around.

Bad effects

Mercury will be absolutely bad & without base and foundation; if a person stutters, it will not be malefic; like a bat hanging upside-down signifying malevolent fate.

(a) Mars or Sun or both in no.9 – Bad & slippery fate; which may deceive. Worst fate (1st, 4th, 13th, 15th, 17th, 28th, 34th year) i.e. Mars's & Mercury's period.

(b) Moon no. 3, 5, 8, 9 – One will be saved from the onslaught of malefic Mercury.

(c) Malefic Mercury – Planets in no.9 being destroyed:

1. No.6 — Mercury, Ketu
2. No.1, 8 — Mars
3. No.2, 7 — Venus
4. No.3, 6 — Mercury
5. No.1, 10 — Saturn
6. No.9 — Jupiter
7. No.12 — Rahu
8. No.4 — Moon
9. No.5 — Sun

Any of these planets in no.9 will be destroyed as per Mercury's position as explained from 1 to 9.

(d) Moon, Ketu no.11 – Ungrateful; cheat; will not keep his promise.

(e) Jupiter (alone) in no.6, 8, 10, 11 – Shortlived; ($8 \times 8 = 64$ years), howsoever exalted Moon may be, otherwise bad in respect of children and wife.

(f) Moon or Jupiter or both in no.3, 6, 7 – Long life but problems in respect of marriage & children.

(g) Mercury in no.9 of horoscope occupying no.11 in Annual chart – Very bad results; <u>must not receive amulet from a sadhu</u>; otherwise, it will spread poison between 17 and 34 years (Mercury's period); besides, it will also have adverse effect in 7th, 15th, 25th, 37th, 49th, 66th, 76th, 96th year.

Remedies:

(a) Pierce the nose; wear nosepin (for a girl).

(b) Wear new clothes – white & yellow – after sprinkling a few drops of river water or washing them.

(c) Bury a piece of silver beneath the foundation of the house.

(d) Donate mushrooms for good career.

(e) Keep a red iron ball.

(f) Keep silver, saffron (*kesar*) or gold with you.

(g) Do not receive any amulet from a *sadhu*. (if Mercury in no.11 occupies Mercury no.11 in Annual chart).

(h) Avoid green colour.

Mercury – House no. 10 (Raashi effect)

Comfortable life; sycophant & flatterer; – if malefic – addiction to drugs; atheist; subtle like a snake; like a dry grass. Remedy as for Saturn.

Good effects

Such a man is naughty but ungrateful, selfish; subtle like a snake; flatterer.

(a) Moon no.1, 3, 4, 5, Good for business & male members, but inauspicious for women and children.

(b) No.2 vacant – Will earn a lot from foreign travels.

(c) Exalted Saturn – Exalted result of Mercury & Saturn; best for Ketu (son).

(d) Exalted no.2 – Mercury will be doubly exalted; man will be exceedingly rich.

Bad effects

If drug addict, Saturn's effect will be poisonous; must not be of loose tongue, otherwise, all will be destroyed like a house of cards or lac.

(a) Malefic Saturn – Very bad results; may lose eyesight and father may also die.

(b) Malefic no.8 – Mercury will be twofold malefic; man will be completely destroyed and reduced to poverty.

Mercury – House no. 11

Very rich; inauspicious like an owl; like a precious diamond after 34th year; pitcher; parrot; alum; diamond.

Good effects

Mercury's nature, whether bad or good, will depend on Jupiter's position; will get prosperity & comfort after 34th year; Mercury will then be like a precious diamond and confer wealth upon the native; when it occupies 1st house in the Annual chart, man will become very rich (11th, 23rd, 36th, 48th, 57th, 72nd, 84th, 94th year) even though no.3 may be malefic.

Bad effects

Now Mercury will be inauspicious or ill omened like an owl; idiot; worst results till 34th year; thereafter prosperous & well to do.

Remedies:

(a) During bad days, get help from the Sun, i.e., wear a copper coin or copper piece around the neck. It will save the man from Mercury's idiotic and foolish acts.

(b) When Mercury in no.9 of the horoscope occupies no.11 in the Annual chart, do not accept any amulet from a *sadhu,* otherwise it will spell disaster.

Mercury – House no. 12 (Raashi Effect)

Noble, long life, comfortable life; if malefic, may face onslaughts of malevolent fate; worst results; most debilitated; mad dog; sleepless nights; always suffering. Remedy as for Ketu.

Good effects

Only Sun or Saturn in no.12 will be able to save themselves from the poisonous arrows of Mercury in no.12; Sun is monkey and Saturn is snake and they have the power to protect themselves from Mercury's poison. But every planet including Sun or Saturn is destroyed when Mercury in no.12 adversely aspects and destroys planets in no.6. In that case, one should play one's cards cleverly (Saturn) and intelligently (Mercury) to protect himself.

(a) Jupiter or Saturn no.2, 12 or 3 – Wealthy; will earn a lot.

(b) Jupiter no. 2, 12 – Name, fame, power, exalted position, but may spend lavishly and his money may be stolen.

(c) Saturn, Jupiter no.7 (Machh Rekha) – Mercury will give good effect, if Jupiter and Saturn are together in any house, but not with Mercury. In that case, daughter, sister etc. will be unhappy in his home, but will be comfortable with in-laws.

Bad effects

Such a person is like a man who hunts with the hound and runs with the hare; short-tempered; loose tongue; unreliable; may flee away from home; will stoop to any length to fulfil his intentions, whether bad or good, without thinking of the consequences; must not take wine, otherwise he will suffer; worst fate awaits a man, but in a woman's horoscope, it is not poisonous. If Mercury is positioned in no.12 in man's as well as wife's house, the results are disastrous for both, but exalted Ketu (in Birth or Annual chart) saves from the poisonous arrows of Mercury.

Mercury and Ketu are two parts of Venus. Mercury in no.12 will be malefic, but will also destroy no.6 (i.e. Ketu even). In other words, man will be deprived of son; such a man loses in speculation investments and may suffer because of sharp tongue and bad writings; must not marry before 25th year. May suffer from the disease of tongue, teeth, veins, nose and throat. If aspected by or associated with Ketu, one may suffer from humiliation, bad name, loss of wealth on account of dishonesty, criminal cases, imprisonment, fraud, cheating, embezzlement (whether actually committed or concocted by enemies).

(a) Sun or Mars no.6 – Mother & maternal uncles unhappy; mother may die in childhood, otherwise both unhappy.

(b) Jupiter no.6 – Father's wealth and life may be destroyed.

(c) Mars no.6 – Brothers will be destroyed, if they create problems.

(d) Rahu/Ketu no.6 – In-laws (Rahu); son (Ketu) will be unhappy.

(e) No.2 vacant – Foolish; doing things in hurry; must visit place of worship.

(f) Rahu no. 8 or 12 – Will suffer humiliation through imprisonment or may be sent to mental hospital for no fault or disease; must not bow before the sanctum-sanctorum of a temple.

(g) Moon no.6 – Unhappy mother; may commit suicide.

(h) Saturn no.6 – Bad for uncles and profession connected with Saturn; unreliable; may destroy property, if lustful.

(i) Malefic Mars no.4 – Mother's death during childhood; both unhappy.

(j) Sun no.6 – Worst fate regarding career & wealth.

(k) Venus no.6 – Very bad for both Venus and Mercury.

(l) Moon no.5, Saturn no.9, Mercury & Rahu no. 12 – If Mercury is in no.12 or Mercury-Rahu are in no.12 – one must not buy a new motor car of green colour; if he travels by such a green-coloured car, he may meet with an accident.

(m) Rahu no.2 – Bad for in-laws; they meet death or mishaps.

Remedies:

(a) Wear yellow thread or gold chain around your neck.

(b) Women must pierce her nose and wear a nosering of gold and silver.

(c) Wear a pure steel ring without any joint of another alloy; do not get it free.

(d) Put a dot of saffron on forehead.

(e) Put an unused pitcher in flowing water and let it float.

(f) Keep silver and saffron with you.

(g) Avoid green colour.

(h) Keep your temper under control; do not lose your temper and must always fulfil your promise.

Notes:

(a) Please adopt remedy as for Ketu.

(b) If Saturn is in no.12, Mercury will never be malefic. If Jupiter-Saturn are together in a horoscope, there is no need of any remedy for Ketu.

212

Rahu

राहु मालिक है लहर दिमाग़ी – बिजली कड़क भी होता है ।
रंग स्याम या नीला इसका – काम चमक के करता है ।
शनि मंगल का हाथी होवे – पदम नीलम भी बनता है ।
चंद्र को यह मध्यम करे तो – ग्रहण सूरज का होता है ।
गुरु के साथ धुआं हो तकिया – बुध को ख़त्म करता है ।
रहे शुक्र का दुश्मन हरदम – सरदार केतु होकर चलता है ।
भूचाल आग जिस दम होवे – ख़ून अचानक करता है ।
गर्मी सूरज से और भी बढ़ती, ठंडा चंद्र से होता है
श्मशान (आठ) बैठे आसमान (बारह) है डरता – ऊंच छह में होता है ।
मंगल बैठे कुंडली बारह – ख़त्म राहु हो जाता है ।
असल बैठक गुरु मंदिर (दो) होवे – दस गुरु को मारता है ।
सूरज को घर पांचवें तारे – कसम पाप चौथे करता है ।
शनि नज़र जब राहु पे करता – लोहा, तांबा सूरज बनता है ।
राहु मगर हो उलट जो चलता – हसद तबाही करता है ।

Rahu is the master of brain waves and the thundering, lightning;
This blue-coloured node works like a shaft of lightning.
It is an elephant whose mahouts are Mars and Saturn;
It becomes Padam and sapphire on Saturn's hood.
It bedims Moon and eclipses Sun;
With Jupiter its smoke is pillow, which makes Mercury disappear.
Always it is Venus's enemy;
But is Ketu's master.
When it is like a fiery volcano and earthquake;
It spills blood and destroys all.
It becomes more fiery with Sun,
But cools down under Moon.
It refers to bones, back and chest and else hand's nails.
When in cremation (8) ground even sky (12) trembles.
But is the most exalted in the nether world.
Mars in 12 makes Rahu a cypher world.
In 10, it completely destroys Jupiter.

213

It helps Sun in 5 and vows not to sin in 4.
If aspected by Saturn, it destroys Sun (copper) into iron dust.
If it resorts to evil, it seethes with jealousy and destroys all.

Exalted Rahu

"The elephant precious in life and more so after death conferring power and wealth on its master." (Anonymous).

Malefic Rahu

Mad elephant that tramples over the Master and works havoc all around.

Rahu

The guide & friend of the strangers and the downtrodden; elephant; lord of sky and ocean; snake's hood with sapphire which raises the man to great heights, tramples over enemies; if malefic, throws the man into gutter with its trunk and makes life miserable; lord of thefts and fever.

Good effects

(a) Rahu is the lord of sky and ocean; if exalted, it confers power & prestige i.e. it raises the man to the zenith of the sky; vanquishes his enemies and rules over all that he surveys.

(b) If associated with Mars or in its direct aspect, Rahu gives the effect of Ketu i.e. Rahu is the elephant controlled and commended by its mahout i.e Mars, provided one does not have sign or dot of 'Lahsun' on his body. It also becomes exalted, if house no. 4 is exalted or Moon is exalted or Mars is in no.2 or 3; Sun-Mercury are in no.2 and Rahu is alone in no.4. Rahu will then help the native the most.

(c) If Mars is in no.12, Rahu becomes ineffective and is reduced to zero.

(d) If Rahu is in a later house than Saturn, it will be at the command of Saturn; and if it is in earlier houses, it will command and order Saturn to do its bidding.

(e) Rahu bedims Moon, but its tremors are stopped by Moon only i.e. Moon cools down Rahu; Sun is completely destroyed & eclipsed, if it is associated with or aspected by Rahu. It afflicts Jupiter with asthma and skin diseases; but will give great strength to Mercury and Saturn or Mercury-Saturn or Mercury-Rahu combination. It is a deadly enemy of Venus; Ketu is always at the beck and call of Rahu.

(f) It is also the sapphire (precious stone – Neelam) on snake's hood which bestows all power, prestige and exalted status on man; and in conjunction with Mars, it is the elephant that hunts the tigers.

Bad effects

(a) Rahu's malefic period continues till 42nd year; thereafter everything (wealth, power and health) is revived. It is like a fatal flash of lightning, earthquake, and volcanic lava; agent of Saturn or devil and has the power of creating problems, even death. It is the ringleader of thugs, dacoits, thieves and cheats. It strikes at once without warning.

(b) When Sun & Venus are together in the Birth chart, Rahu becomes all the more malefic. Further, if Sun & Saturn are together, Rahu will be malefic; even Mars will be debilitated i.e. Mangalik.

(c) If Ketu is in earlier houses in the Birth chart and Rahu in later houses, Ketu will be zero and Rahu's effect will be bad.

214

(d) If Rahu is in conjunction with Sun or Mars, Venus aspects Ketu, it will have bad effect on Ketu i.e. on son's birth and other things associated with Ketu.

(e) If Rahu & Sun are together or if Rahu aspects Sun, Rahu will not only adversely affect that house, but also the adjoining one.

Remedies:

For malefic Rahu creating problems by enemies; in service matters, health and wealth; adopt the following remedies:

(a) Keep a silver square piece; donate rice and milk for peace of mind.

(b) Donate 'Massur' daal (red lentil) or give some monetary help to the poor off and on.

(c) Throw jau (barley) in the running water.

(d) Keep jau (barley) under the pillow at night and donate it to the poor in the morning.

(e) For respite from problems in business or service career, throw coal into flowing water.

(f) Wash barley with cow-urine; wrap it in a red-coloured cloth & keep it.

Rahu's effect in 12 houses

(a) House no. 1 – It eclipses the Sun and causes tremors in Sun's throne.

(b) House no. 2 – It obeys Jupiter and vows to give up evil ways.

(c) House no. 3 – Most exalted; confers power and prestige.

(d) House no. 4 – Such a horoscope is noble and religious and Ketu swears by Moon (mother) not to do bad things.

(e) House no. 5 – It helps Sun rather than oppose it.

(f) House no. 6 – It is exalted in this house.

(g) House no. 7 – It destroys Venus.

(h) House no. 8 – It brings death and disaster.

(i) House no. 9 – It destroys Jupiter and is malefic.

(j) House no. 10 – Its role is doubtful.

(k) House no. 11 – It destroys Jupiter.

(l) House no. 12 – It entails a lot of unnecessary expenditure and is debilitating; if Mars is in no.12, Rahu is reduced to zero.

Rahu – House no. 1 (Raashi effect)

Sign of richness; elephant raising the man to great heights; solar eclipse for 2 years; chin; maternal grandparents. Remedy as for Sun.

Good effects

Elephant raising the man to great heights; if Mars is in no.12, Rahu will lose sting; such a man spends a lot on self and household; symbol of richness. If Venus or Mercury or both are exalted, man will be saved from the evil designs of Rahu, but still there will be artificial darkness. The house, in which Sun is placed, becomes dark. In the Birth chart during solar eclipse or lunar eclipse, Rahu will not exercise malefic effects. There may be darkness on one half of the hemisphere; the other half will still be bright. In other words, one may lose one job; but the other job will be immediately available. When the period of eclipse is over, which may extend from 1 to 2 years, one gets back the same glory and livelihood. Rahu from no.1 to 6 will be like elephant's trunk i.e. Mercury; in the Birth or Annual chart from no.7 to 12 it will be like Ketu (the lower portion of the body).

(a) Venus no.7 – Very rich man; bad for wife's life and health.

(b) Mars no.12 – Rahu will be zero.

Remedy: Keep cat's placenta (*jeir* in Hindi) in a copper-coloured cloth for better effect. Or else donate wheat, copper and jaggery.

Bad effects

Such a man may see many changes, but promotion will be limited; will be bad for father during 11th, 21st and 42nd year. Rahu's malefic period will last ordinarily for two years and according to Annual chart, for one year. During the whole span of life or during the first 42 years (Rahu's span), Rahu's mahadasha period will be of 18 years. Whenever a person faces problems during the solar/lunar eclipse, he himself is responsible for such problems; may also suffer from a sort of insanity (talking at random without any substance).

(a) Sun No. 9 – Irreligious.

(b) Sun No.7 – Sun will be eclipsed by Rahu; loss of wealth; bad for career and business; unnecessary expenditure due to one's own folly.

Remedy: Lies in Moon i.e. donate rice or silver or milk and also keep silver with you.

Rahu in no.1 and its effect on Sun in twelve houses:

Sun in House No.	Effect
1	Man will himself be responsible for the bad luck; unfounded, superstitions and loss of income etc.
2	Irreligious and having contempt for house of worship.
3	Relatives will face problems.
4	Will create obstacles for maternal uncles and own income.
5	Rahu will now help Sun; he will be blessed with a son.
6	Humiliation and insulting attitude of relatives of sons and daughters.
7	Litigation and bad domestic life.
8	Unnecessary and useless expenditure.
9	Careless about religion.
10	Unreliable and ungrateful.
11	His ego will destroy him, though he may be just and justice-loving.
12	Sleepless nights.

Rahu – House no. 2

King will pay homage to Jupiter; clouds full of rain; fate will swing like pendulum; mud under the elephant's feet; mustard (sarson); in-laws. (Remedy as for Moon i.e. keep silver when Rahu opposes or destroys Venus).

Good effects

One's financial condition, whether good or bad, will depend on Jupiter; but Rahu will confer a lot of wealth, when Saturn occupies no.1 and Jupiter is also exalted. If Saturn is malefic, Rahu will be like a snake that suffocates the man and destroys him financially and physically.

Rahu will be like king in this house, but will always obey Jupiter; will be an administrator or will enjoy an exalted status; if a saint or sadhu, he will have the capacity to feed thousands; fate will swing like a pendulum – sometimes taking the man to great heights and sometimes throwing him down.

Venus will have its exalted effect for 25 years and will confer wealth and happiness on man for 25 years. He will never be arrested, whether he is involved in criminal/civil case or he may abscond; will definitely be charged with embezzlement of public money or fraudulent dealings. People often donate things to ward off evils, but man with malefic Rahu in no.2 does steal public money; Rahu will help the native even if Jupiter, Venus, Moon, Mars, Saturn and Ketu are malefic.

Bad effects

Bad fate; like that of a pendulum – rise and fall – rich and poor both; may lose money on account of embezzlement and theft; may even be involved in police cases regarding betrayal of trust and misappropriation of public money; will never donate, even if he enjoys free hospitality of others; will be responsible for his own downfall; old age may be full of sorrows and troubles; good luck till 25th year and thereafter worst fate befalls the man. Both Rahu and Ketu will be the most malefic; only Moon (mother) will control the tremors of Rahu; someone may steal his purse in broad daylight.

Malefic Saturn – Worst fate, full of poison.

Remedy: Always keep solid silver ball (Moon) and gold, saffron and yellow things (Jupiter) on your person or with you. This will ward off the evil effect of Rahu, as mentioned above.

Rahu – House no. 3

Most exalted; Lord of life and wealth; multimillionaire; guard protecting the man with a loaded gun; roaring voice like that of a tiger; barley; ivory; inauspicious.

Good effects

Rahu will protect and raise the man to great heights; multimillionaire and owner of landed property. Rahu, if alone, will protect the native from all troubles; protector of life and property like a guard with a loaded gun; bold and fearless; the native is a magnanimous enemy; will foretell events and dreams will come out true; will vanquish all enemies; will never be issueless. Promotion is certain; happy life; Sun will be doubly exalted; enemies will tremble.

(a) Mars no.3 – King-like status.

(b) In association with Mars, Venus or Sun (all enemies) – Enemies will not harm; wife, children will confer happiness and will be rich.

(c) Sun-Mercury in no.3 along with Rahu – Govt. will confer title upon him; will have all comforts, power and prestige; but may have a widowed sister.

Bad effects

Relatives will deceive him and will squander his wealth; they will never return his money.

Any planet in no.12 or associated with Rahu in no.3 (except Mars) – Mercury and Ketu will be malefic till 34th year.

Remedies:

(a) Seek blessings of Moon (mother) and donate silver, milk and rice; keep silver with you.

(b) Never keep ivory with you.

Rahu – House no. 4

Religious and noble, but worried about health; dreams, coriander, Moon will be dim, but will have qualities of Moon.

Good effects

Very rich; religious and noble; but Moon will be dim i.e. full of tension, but will have the qualities of Moon; will spend on household and good things; now Ketu and Saturn will refuse to collaborate with Rahu in evil deeds; Rahu will now bow before mother; after Rahu's period, Moon which has been bedimmed, will regain its glory.

(a) Exalted moon or in no.1 – Very rich; multimillionaire.

(b) Moon no.1; Mercury no.11 – Will fill the coffers of relatives, related to Mercury i.e. sisters, aunts, daughters etc.

(c) Exalted Venus – In-laws will become rich after his marriage and help him financially.

(d) Sun or Mars or both in no.2 – Benefic effect of Rahu; Now Sun and Mars will also be helpful.

(e) Exalted Ketu – Parents will gain after child's birth.

Malefic effects

Bad for Moon's articles till 48th year; but himself will be noble and religious-minded; after 45th year, both Rahu and Ketu will confer exalted results; will be worried about wealth.

(a) Malefic Moon – Bad for wealth.

(b) Moon or Sun, Mars, Jupiter in no.10; or Moon in no.4 – All planets will give bad results; but after Moon's period is over, everything will be revived.

Rahu – House no. 5

Naughty and notorious; bad for son, but will help Sun.

Good effects

Will have wealth, intelligence and honour; will be witty and intellectual; good health. Rahu will help Sun i.e. will have exalted position in service. If mother is alive, the native will have all comforts and pleasures; wealth and sons; and if Jupiter-Venus are in no.7, it will confer the most exalted results regarding sons, wealth, comforts, position and prestige.

(a) Moon in no.5 or Sun in no.1, 5, 11 – God's man or worshipper; teetotaller; man of divine thoughts; Rahu will help Sun and Moon or both; mother may die or separate from native, but as long as she is alive his life will be full of pleasures and comforts.

(b) Sun, Moon, Mars no.4, 6 or Saturn-Mars in no.5 – Must be blessed with Sun; king like status.

Bad effects

Will have to spend a lot on illness and health problems; will be deprived of son; Saturn in no.5 kills son and Saturn in no.9 creates obstacles in the birth of male child; and in these two conditions, Rahu will be the most malefic for a male child. Children may either die in the womb or during infancy; If grandfather is alive, chances of grandson's survival are dim; usually issueless; the first wife/ husband may not see the male child.

Jupiter in conjunction with Rahu or adversely aspected – Child's health will be bad till 12th year; bad for father's fate till 12th year.

Remedy: Keep elephant made of silver to ward off the evil effects of Rahu.

To nullify Rahu's poison, perform the marriage ceremony once again with the same wife/ husband.

Rahu – House no. 6

Exalted; black dog will bring luck; beneficial elephant conferring power and wealth; if malefic – a mad elephant and notorious thief.

Good effects

Will spend a lot on personal luxuries and household; if alone in no.6, the native is like a powerful elephant which has the strength to vanquish the enemies; Rahu protects him; Rahu will refrain from evil deeds; native will be very intelligent; promotion is always assured; self-respecting and proud.

Bad effects

A mad elephant trampling over its own master; a notorious thief not afraid of sentence; if he sheds brother's blood, he will be completely destroyed.

(a) Mercury or Ketu (malefic) – Loss of wealth.

(b) Mars no.12 – If he quarrels with elder brother or sister, he and his children will be destroyed.

(c) Fate like a rainbow, but usually bad. Not only no.6 but no.2 and 7 will also be destroyed.

Remedies:

(a) Keep black marble or small lead ball for better results.

(b) Keep a black dog even if Rahu is exalted or malefic.

Rahu – House no. 7 (Raashi effect)

Ill-fated; wretched; destroyer of Venus; marital discord; broker. (Remedy lies in donating coconut as for Saturn).

Good effect

Very rich, but bad and unhappy domestic life; in-laws i.e. Rahu may be malefic, but Sun will never be debilitating; will have an exalted status; Mercury and Saturn will help him and he will be victorious over enemies.

Mercury, Venus in no.2, 11 – Rich man.

Bad effects

In girl's horoscope, it gives most malefic effect if she is married before 21st year. In that case, either she will die or may be divorced or may become a widow; may earn bad name for her lustful conduct; the same effect will be visible in man's horoscope; ill-fated, accursed; worst married life. If he adopts Rahu's profession i.e. jail deptt. or police, everything will be malefic.

(a) Mercury, Saturn, Ketu no.11 – Relatives and business pertaining to these planets will destroy the native.

(b) Venus no.1 – Wife physically and mentally sick.

Remedies:

(a) With Rahu in no.7 in the horoscope, give a piece of silver at the time of marriage ceremony as 'Kanya Daan' and the girl/boy should keep it with her/him. It should never be sold or given to others.

(b) Throw coconut in a river or running water.

(c) Whenever Rahu no.7 of horoscope occupies no.7 in the Annual chart, keep a silver brick in the house and also take a glass or pot of silver fitted with a silver lid, fill it with water and put a piece of silver in it and keep it in the house. Do not let the water dry; change it when necessary.

(d) If the marriage of such a person takes place before 21st year, he/she should put a piece of silver in a small silver glass or pot and fill it with water of river, especially of the sacred Ganga. One such glass should be donated to a place of worship and the other be kept.

Rahu – House no. 8

Harsh voice of death; drum proclaiming the advent of death; black and stifling smoke; mad man talking irrelevantly and incoherently.

Good effects

Life full of ups and downs; fate will sometimes smile and sometimes frown upon the man.

(a) Exalted Mars no.12 – Rahu will no longer be malefic.

(b) Exalted Mars or Mars in no.1, 8 or exalted Saturn or Saturn in no.8 – When Mars (28 years) is exalted or is in no.1 or 8 (in Annual or Birth chart) or Saturn is benefic or is in no.8 (in Annual chart) – fate will be revived and he will regain his lost wealth.

Remedy:
Keep silver square pieces with you for 43 days to assess the secrets of Rahu.

Bad effects

Dishonesty and corruption will destroy his wealth eight times; will be like bitter smoke; a hypocrite; life full of ups and downs; fate will depend on Saturn's position; Rahu will work against Saturn and its result will be the most malefic; life full of litigation; strife and struggle, quarrels and lot of expenditure; in such circumstances, one should not lose one's courage; sudden accident, illness, problems and loss of life, especially when Rahu is the hood of snake and Ketu the tail and it poisons the Moon; everything including health and wealth will be destroyed. If the eldest member of the family is black in complexion, fat or issueless, Rahu's malefic effect will be nullified.

(a) Saturn no.2 or 3 – Rahu may cause death or ill health (especially Saturn no.6 and Rahu no.8).

(b) Malefic Mars (malefic Mars or malefic Mercury) in any house except Mars no.12 – Worst fate.

Remedies:
(a) Keep silver square pieces.

(b) Throw a copper coin off and on in the hearth of a person selling popcorns etc.

(c) Counterfeit coins or lead pieces may be thrown into running water; eight coins or lead pieces or one coin or lead pieces for 43 days.

(d) When Rahu in no.8 of the Birth chart occupies no.8 in Annual chart, one may suffer losses in health and wealth. In the 8th month after the birth date, take 8 almonds to the temple daily and donate 4 at the temple & bring the remaining back home. Continue this process till the next birthday i.e. for five months continuously. The almonds so brought back to home may be donated on next birthday. Do not use them.

Rahu – House no. 9

Most malefic; threshold; blue colour; solar eclipse (for career and business); absolutely bad fate; partial lunar eclipse; disease above the throat; psychiatrist attending and curing the mad persons, but dishonest.

Good effects

Jupiter no.9, 11 – A competent doctor who treats mad men; but dishonest. Jupiter will now be silent, but will not disappear.

Bad effects

Rahu will be nine times malefic: it will bedim Moon and will adversely affect no.5 (children) and no.11 (income). Whenever a planet in no.4 occupies no.1 i.e. 6th, 16th, 28th, 40th, 52nd, 64th, 76th, 88th, 100th year, Rahu will exercise its malefic effect on no.1 i.e. may lead to worst fate.

Saturn no.5 – May not be blessed with a son.

<u>**Remedies:**</u>

(a) Keep gold, saffron on your body; donate chana daal.

(b) Feed a dog.

(c) Should live in a joint family and should maintain cordial relations with in-laws.

Rahu – House no. 10

If exalted – like a precious sapphire on snake's hood.

If malefic – stinging poisonous snake causing immediate death, pond full of dirty, stagnant water; dirty drain.

Good effects

Good for father; noble-hearted; will be respected by all; Rahu's effect – good or bad – will depend upon Saturn's position; if exalted, best results; if malefic, bad results; rich man; Rahu will be like the most precious sapphire on snake's hood.

Exalted Saturn – Very rich and bold like a tiger; long life, an eminent businessman or industrialist.

Bad effects

Good for father, but bad for mother (Moon and connected relatives and things); bad health; Rahu's effect will depend upon Saturn's position – good or bad; lot of expenditure on good things of life; if Saturn is malefic, will suffer losses in money and will be responsible for destruction of ancestral property. Rahu will be like the snake's poisonous fang which will cause immediate death; miserly, mean and jealous of others.

(a) Malefic Saturn – Danger to life and eyesight.

(b) Malefic Mars (Mangalik) – Poor; life full of troubles.

(c) Blind horoscope i.e. Sun, Venus and Mars together (enemy planets) in no.1 – Rahu will be like a mad elephant which will destroy its own master i.e. worst fate.

(d) Exalted Mars – Rahu will no longer be bad.

(e) Moon alone in no.4 – Full of depression and tension; verging on madness; may break his head or lose eyesight; even loss of wealth (Remedy as for Mars).

(f) If not associated with or aspected by Mars – Must wear cap etc. over his head for better results.

Rahu – House no. 11

Sapphire; posthumous child; bad for father.

Good effects

Though bad for father's life, yet Rahu's effect on wealth will be the best till father's death. After his death, one must keep gold or sapphire with him for better results. Better if he wears gold chain or yellow clothes.

(a) Saturn no.3, 5 – Rahu will no longer adversely affect father's life.

(b) Saturn or Ketu no.1, 3 – Self-respecting; architect of his own fate; will not claim wealth from parents; will not be sinful, nor deceive others i.e. sincere to all; self-made rich.

222

Bad effects

Person with Rahu no.11 will be born at a time when his parents may be leading a comfortable life, but after his birth they may suffer losses, unnecessary expenditure, incidence of fire, sickness in family or quarrel with neighbours etc. Planet no.2 will adversely affect Rahu (in-laws) no.11; may suffer a lot till 36th year when he will be almost zero; may be a posthumous child; or father may die after his birth (especially 11 months, 11 years or at the most 21 years); or may lose his business; malefic effect on Jupiter indeed.

(a) Mars no.3 – Brother will suffer disability; eldest uncle may be issueless or lame.

(b) Ketu no.5 – Bad for son; may suffer from disease of ears, legs, spinal cord; urinary troubles, arthritis of the knees and thighs, spraining or fracture of feet etc.

Remedies:

(a) Keep gold or saffron on your body; wear gold chain or yellow thread.

(b) Donate to the temple or poor man off and on.

(c) Take water or milk etc. in a silver glass.

Note: Jupiter means boy's father or girl's father-in-law.

Rahu – House no. 12

Most malefic; Don Quixote fighting imaginary wars; foolish person imagining big things; dreamer; coal; mad elephant; upper part of head.

Good effects

Rahu's effect – good or bad – is dependent upon Mercury in the horoscope. Such a person is like 'Don Quixote' who imagines big things but everything comes to naught in the end; will have to spend a lot which will of no use to him; may have to spend unnecessarily on sisters, aunts and their relatives; rich in-laws; comfortable life; protection from enemies.

(a) If associated with Mars – Good job; comfortable life.

(b) Exalted Saturn – Best results.

(c) Saturn no.10, 11 – Rahu will depend upon Mercury and Jupiter for good results; will never be short of money.

Bad effects

Such a person may be involved in criminal cases, theft, embezzlement etc.; will have to spend a lot on family members; will be full of imaginary but malefic ideas; hard-working but will have sleepless nights; may even think of suicide; unnecessary expenditure and sleepless nights.

(a) Malefic Saturn – Rahu's personal effect will be the most malefic; may earn bad name and humiliation.

(b) In association with Venus and Sun – Rahu will destroy both Sun and Venus.

Remedies:

(a) Keep a bag of sugar or saunf (fennel) in the bedroom.

(b) Must take meals in the kitchen.

Ketu

केतु छलावा है चलो चली का – पापी बुरा ही होता है।

सूरज को गर वह मध्यम करे – तो ग्रहण वह चंद्र को करता है।

केतु मिला जब शनि या मंगल से – ऐसा बुरा नहीं होता है।

साथी मगर जब तीसरा होवे – फल तीनों का ही मंदा है।

गुरु मिले तो सबसे बढ़िया – माता मिले तो खुद मंदा है।

बुध मिले खुद शैतान कहलावे – मदद शुक्र की करता है।

पाताल पक्का घर छठा होवे – नीच वहां यह होता है।

घर बारह आसमान पे चढ़ कर – दुनियां से ऊंचा होता है।

पहले घरों में केतु जो होवे – गुरु मंदा हो जाता है।

चंद्र अगर बद मंगल रोके – केतु बद मंगल करता है।

बुध-केतु दो वाह्य लड़ते – बद मंगल भी डरता है।

राहु पाप गर ख़ुफ़िया होवे – केतु ज़ाहिरा ही चलता है।

शारायाम दोनों ही मिलते – मार दो तरफी करता है।

सफेद-काला दो रंग-बिरंगा – लाल मिला बुध होता है।

केतु तख़्त से सूरज हो ऊंचा – छठे मंगल केतु मरता है।

बच्चा अगर कभी एक ही होवे – नसल कायम हो जाती है।

केतु-राहु से मुख़ातिब :

सरे तसलीम ख़म है जो मज़ाजे यार में आए।

हम तो सिर्फ खिदमत करने तेरे दरबार में आए।

और

सपुर्दम बुत्तो माया ख़वेशरा
तू दानी हिसाब कमोवेशरा (कम और ज़्यादा)

Ketu is a deceptive node and spreads evil when malefic.
It bedims Sun but destroys Moon.
When associated with Saturn or Mars,
It is not so bad.
But when another one joins,
All become malefic.

Associated with Jupiter, it is most exalted.
But with Moon it is most malefic.
With Mercury it is most diabolical;
But helps Venus the most.
It's most debilitating in its own House no. 6, the nether world,
But over the sky-House no. 12, it governs the earth from above.
Ketu in earlier houses makes Ketu asleep.
If Moon obstructs Mars, malefic Ketu makes it more malefic.
When Mercury and Ketu both quarrel,
Even Mars malefic trembles.
Rahu works secretly, Ketu does it openly.
They meet on the thoroughfare and destroy both ways.
It is white and black in colour;
But when Red (Mars) joins it becomes Mercury.
Ketu in Lagna makes Sun exalted and Mars in 6th destroys Ketu;
Even one pup of a bitch perpetuates progeny.

It addresses Rahu:

"I obey thee, and your will my lord & master,
I have come to your durbar to ask for your will."

and

"You are the master, I have offered myself at your service,
You keep the accounts, I am thy slave who unflinchingly obey thy will."

Ketu (Son)

Exalted Ketu

(a) "A wise son maketh a glad father." (Old Testament)

(b) "O Lord, my boy, my Arthur, my son! My life, my joy, my food; my all the world!"
(Shakespeare)

Malefic Ketu

"A roguish bad son is like a whining and groaning dog that does not augur well for the family."
(Anonymous)

Ketu (Lord Ganesha)

'Dervish' (Muslim religious man vowed to piety and austerity); man of god; future generation; a saint; far-sighted; bringer of good fortune; son; pig; faithful dog guiding the passerby to Dargah (house of God or resting place of a saint); soothsayer.

Ketu's position in 12 houses

Ketu in House No.	Effect
1	Must bless the man with a son; but he is full of imaginary fears.
2	Beneficial travels; promotion and exalted status.
3	Debilitating; may face ups and downs in life; unhappy with relatives; will be worried for brothers; may settle away from kith and kin; will remember the good and forget the injury done to him.
4	Late birth of son; barking dog that frightens children.
5	Noble sons; watchman of Jupiter.
6	Debilitating; lunar eclipse i.e. Moon completely destroyed; but victorious over enemies; ferocious dog.
7	Bold like a tiger.
8	Loses his children and fills the grave with them; groaning dog crying for children.
9	Brings good luck to father; dog at the command of master.
10	Depends upon Saturn for exalted or malefic results; opportunist.
11	May lose eyesight; depends upon Saturn for good or bad results.
12	Very exalted; makes man very rich.

Ketu's relationship with other planets

With Jupiter	Eminent; noble thoughts.
With Sun	Storms; bad for son and maternal uncles; Sun is bedimmed.
With Moon	Sweat of a dog; both malefic; lunar eclipse.
With Venus	Lustful; calf of a cow.
With Mars	Ferocious and bold like a tiger.
With Mercury	Dog's tail; if one is good, the other is bad.
With Saturn	Snake's ears missing; depends upon Saturn.
With Rahu	Totally at the command of Rahu, who is the master and Ketu, the slave.

Miscellaneous Features of Ketu

(a) Ketu with Moon causes complete Lunar eclipse (Moon is destroyed) and with Sun it is partial solar eclipse (Sun becomes dim but not completely destroyed).

(b) With Saturn, it gives best results, but if a third planet joins them, the results of all the three become malefic.

(c) With Jupiter, it gives best results.

(d) With Venus, it is good as it helps Venus, but with Mercury, it is malefic.

(e) If Ketu is in earlier houses, Jupiter is malefic; if it is in later houses, Moon becomes malefic.

(f) Ketu blesses the native with a son who perpetuates his memory.

(g) Ketu is the angel of goodness; lord of travels and helpful till the end, if exalted.

(h) When Jupiter or Sun or both are destroyed by enemy planet, Ketu's effect will be bad.

Remedies:

(a) For malefic Ketu (son), remedy lies in Jupiter (donate saffron, chana daal or yellow things).

(b) For bad health due to malefic Ketu, remedy lies in Moon (donate silver, milk or rice).

(c) If son goes astray or creates problems, donate black and white blanket.

(d) During urinary troubles or problems in feet, spinal cord, arthritis, gout, backache, pain in knees, legs, joints, tie a white silky thread or silver ring on the toes of the feet.

(e) When Ketu is malefic (if Moon-Venus are together or aspect each other in the birth chart) and the child's body starts drying up; apply mud paste on his body for 40-43 days before taking bath.

Ketu – House no. 1

Worried about children; will be blessed with a son; maternal grandfather's house; malefic wind; disease below navel.

Good effects

One may receive order for transfer or travel or may be ready for travel with bag and baggage, but he may not travel at all, provided house no.7 is vacant in the Annual chart; will be worried about children and job; if he loses his one job, the other job will be readily available; even Sun's effect will be exalted, howsoever debilitated it may be, even in no.6 or no.7. Whenever Ketu is in no.1 in Annual chart, he/she will be blessed with a son or grandson and a nephew. Howsoever malefic Ketu may be, Jupiter's effect will be exalted. Such a person must serve saints, teachers and, above all, father.

(a) Mars no.12 – Ketu will never be malefic in no.1.

(b) Sun no.6 or 7 – Now Sun's effect will never be bad.

Bad effects

If Mars is in no.12, Ketu's effect will never be malefic in no.1; Ketu often creates imaginary fears; it may adversely affect planets in no.6 or 7, but never on Sun; Whenever Ketu gives bad effect after marriage, Saturn helps a lot; Remedy lies in Saturn, otherwise Ketu will destroy even Jupiter i.e. father; such a person is born away from his home (in a hospital or maternal grandfather's house); such a place of birth will either be destroyed or be alien to him. Bad days will commence with malefic Mercury (business), then Venus (domestic life), then Mars (impure blood), and in the end, Jupiter (father).

(a) No.2 or no.7 vacant – Bad for Mercury (business) and Venus (domestic life).

(b) Sun no.7 – Bad health at the time of birth of a grandson.

Ketu – House no. 2

Prosperous, administrator; beneficial travels; exalted status; tamarind; sesame (til); mole.

Good effects

Every new travel will lead him to new directions i.e. from east to west and north to south; will travel a lot on land and be prosperous; promotion and transfer will be together, provided no.8 is not malefic; Venus' result will be exalted, but Moon's effect will be dim; may earn titles from the govt., may even earn millions, but will not save much; generous; may not be beneficial for mother, but will have a lovely and caring wife.

(a) No.8 vacant and Ketu alone in Annual chart – Promotion and transfer are certain; will have to travel.

(b) Sun no.12 – Self-made rich after 24th year.

Bad effects

Should not have illicit relations with others; no son will help him in the old age.

Moon or Mars (Ketu's enemies) besides Rahu in no.8 – Ill health; may even have short life.

Ketu – House no. 3

Whining dog; but noble ascetic (fakir); spinal cord; banana; boils, cuts and wounds; life away from kith and kin; unhappy with relatives, but worried for brothers.

Good effects

Such a person is a noble ascetic who never forgets the good done to him; believes that 'forgiveness is the best form of revenge'; will help his relatives unasked for; will live away from kith and kin; may be opposed by relatives, but will be helpful to them; will always be worried for brothers who will not let him down.

Mars no.12 – Best luck after 24th year or after birth of first child.

Bad effects

Unnecessarily complaining and worried; but noble like a sadhu; usually unhappy with brothers and may live abroad; this planet may not be so good; may lose wealth in litigation; children will not give him any happiness.

Moon or Mars in no.3, 4 – Very poor.

Remedies: If suffering from diseases of lungs, ears, spinal cord, knees, arthritis, feet, backache, waist etc. or financial losses, adopt remedy as for Jupiter, i.e.:

(a) Throw chana daal (yellow lentil) in running water for 43 days.

(b) Put dot of saffron on your forehead.

(c) Wear golden chain or keep saffron, gold etc. on your body.

(d) Throw sesame (til) in water or donate an image made of silver with black strips i.e. 'kapila' cow.

(e) To avoid harmful travels, throw rice, wheat or jaggery into flowing water.

Ketu – House no. 4 (Raashi Effect)

Barking dog frightening the children; oceanic tides; tempest; hearing; lunar eclipse.

Good effects

Good & auspicious for father; adds lustre and strength to Jupiter (i.e. father & teacher); late birth of a son (especially when Jupiter is exalted either in Birth chart or Annual chart), the son will have a long life, may be 100 years; bad for mother, but will be rich and long-lived; hard-working and man of courage and determination; Ketu or Rahu in no.4 makes the man noble, pious and religious-minded; wise and resourceful.

Moon or Mars in no.3 or 4 – Daughters more in number, but intelligent, wise & rich; but bad for Ketu (son) and Moon (mother).

Bad effects

Barking dog scaring and frightening children; trouble for 6 years; complete lunar eclipse; bad health; diabetic; bad for mother and son; tempest in the ocean; oceanic tides (rise and fall of waves); late birth of son; full of wild thoughts; loss of wealth.

Moon or Mars in no.3 or 4 – Both Moon and Ketu will be malefic; mother and son will be unhappy.

Remedy: Donate gold or saffron or chana daal (yellow lentil) or yellow things to the poor at the place of worship.

Ketu – House no. 5

Faithful and loyal dog i.e. watchman of Jupiter.

Good effects

If the person is noble and of good character in his youth, he will be blessed with sons and Ketu's results will be exalted; may depend upon father till 24th year, thereafter he will earn for himself.

(a) Jupiter, Sun or Moon in no.4, 6, 12 – Good financial condition; will be blessed with sons.

(b) Saturn no.9 & Venus no.4 – Saturn will not have bad effect in the birth of son, nor there will be marital discord; 'Machh Rekha' i.e. good results regarding children.

Bad effects

Such a person is handsome, but if he is of bad character and indulges in extramarital relations; his youth and beauty will be ruined. If Jupiter is malefic, such a person gets son late in life (may be 45th year) and the child may suffer from asthma.

(a) Mercury, Venus, Rahu or Saturn as wicked planets in no.2, 5, 9, 12 – Bad domestic life; family will be complete with two sons; they will confer happiness.

(b) Moon or Mars no.3, 4 – Ketu's effect bad; poor; full of wild thoughts; worst fate. (Remedy: Donate things concerning Moon and Mars).

(c) Saturn no.5, 9 – Will be blessed with a male child after death of 2-3 male children; especially when Moon or Mars are in no.3 or 4.

Ketu – House no. 6

Most debilitating; tiger like dog; complete lunar eclipse; foreign lands; male sparrow; wear gold ring in left hand finger.

Good effects

Ketu's effect – whether good or bad, depends upon Jupiter's position; Ketu is compared to a son or a dog or a pig. If son or dog somehow goes wayward or becomes good for nothing, even then he will be helpful to the father or master at the time of need, In other words, Ketu no.6 helps Jupiter (father) in whatever home Jupiter is situated. Ketu is the Lord of house no. 6, but how strange it is debilitated in its own house. One must wear gold ring in left hand. Such a person gets out of the enemy's trap by virtue of his shrewdness and intelligence. If Jupiter and Ketu are exalted in this house, the native may live long (80 years), happy maternal uncles; affectionate sons; wealthy and comfortable life away from native land, may visit even abroad.

(a) Mercury No.6 – Both Mercury and Ketu will give exalted results.

(b) Jupiter (exalted) – Good sons; very clever and shrewd; will come out of enemy's trap.

(c) Exalted Venus – Venus will help the native.

(d) Jupiter or Mars not in no.6 and no.12 along with Mercury – Ketu will confer best results provided the man is not an egoist and given to false sense of praise.

Bad effects

Ketu is Mercury's enemy and friend of Venus; but strangely in this house, Ketu becomes Mercury's friend and opposes Venus; such a person is unreliable, cowardly and is treated as a non-entity or worthless everywhere.

(a) Adverse aspect from no.2 – Bad for Ketu and things concerning it (wear gold ring in left hand).

(b) Malefic Jupiter – Large no. of enemies and futile travels.

(c) Moon no.2 – Bad for mother and her relatives; even old age will be bad.

(d) Venus no.6 – Bad results for both Ketu and Venus.

(e) Mercury no. 12 – Ketu will be destroyed.

Remedy: Wear gold ring in left hand, if Ketu is malefic.

Ketu – House no. 7

Domesticated dog kept by a shepherd; ferocious and bold like a tiger; protector and watchman of herd i.e. companion of children; second son; if malefic – donkey, pig.

Good effects

Will earn a lot of wealth in youth; it will be like shepherd's dog, more ferocious and braver than even tiger; protector and playmate of children i.e. very lovable.

Helped by Mercury, Venus and Jupiter – good results; Venus, Saturn will be benefic; if enemy planets (Moon-Mars) will not have adverse effect, they themselves will be destroyed. But he should fulfil his promise; otherwise he will be destroyed.

Bad effects

Such a person, if egoist or with a false sense of pride, will be destroyed; even if Ketu is malefic, or when the son becomes major, it will give the best results when it occupies house no. 1 in Annual chart; must not be foul-mouthed or short-tempered, marital life will be unhappy.

(a) Malefic Mercury – Worst results if he does not keep his word; (story of Mehmood and Firdausi).

(b) Mercury No.7 – Best luck after 34th year.

Remedy: Must keep his word for best results.

Ketu – House no. 8

Groaning and crying dog lamenting the loss of children; premonition of death; ears; illusion; ghost.

Good effects

If Mars is in no.12, Ketu cannot be malefic; if Venus and Mercury are exalted, Ketu will not exercise bad results. In other words, Ketu's effect, good or bad, depends on no.12; long life – more than 70 years; will have a premonition of death; 34th year is the deciding age for the birth of a male child; if Mercury is in no.1 to 6 in Birth chart, male children born till 34th year will live long and if Mercury is in no.7 to 12 in the Birth chart, the male children born after 34th year will live long; Ketu is the Lord of house no. 6 and here Ketu is debilitated; naturally if Mercury is in no.6, male children born before and after 34th year will survive.

(a) Exalted Mars and Jupiter in no.1, 2 or Moon in no.2 – Ketu now will be benefic; no remedy is required, if Moon is malefic, remedy for Moon is recommended.

(b) Jupiter and Mars not in no.6 or 12 – Ketu will not be malefic.

Bad effects

When Ketu is in no.8, Mercury and Venus are usually in bad houses; his loose character or lustful conduct will be responsible for wife's ill health; like a crying dog lamenting the loss of his children; may suffer from the disease connected with Ketu i.e. urinary troubles etc.; Ketu may give good effect till 25th year, thereafter Saturn, Rahu/Ketu will be malefic; there may be domestic discord.

(a) No.2 vacant (Rahu in no.2 will not be counted) – Remedy for Jupiter for malefic children; pierce the nose; may suffer from Ketu's disease such as urinary troubles, boils, wounds, arthritis, pain in feet, knees or backache etc.

(b) In association with Ketu in no.8 – Ketu will be malefic; ups and downs in life.

(c) Malefic Jupiter – Ketu and Mars will be malefic; even Mercury, Venus will give disappointing results; male child late in life.

(d) Jupiter or Mars in no.6 or 12, Mangalik (malefic Mars) no.4 – Very bad results regarding Ketu and Mars i.e. regarding male child and wealth.

(e) Saturn or Mars no.7 – Very bad results regarding property, wealth, male children and domestic problems.

(f) Mars no.12, Saturn no.1 – May lose his brother before his birth.

Remedies:

(a) Adopt remedy as for Jupiter as mentioned in Ketu no.4.

(b) Pierce the nose.

(c) Bury a piece of black & white blanket along with the articles concerning the associated planets in a cremation ground or a deserted place.

(d) If Ketu is alone in no.8, donate a new black & white blanket to the poor or an orphanage or a house of charity or a place of worship.

Ketu – House no. 9

Most exalted; faithful dog who understands master's command; obedient son; mascot (bringer of best luck) for father, but not for maternal uncles; lives abroad; soothsayer.

Good effects

Promotion or prosperity is certain; but not transfer or travel; will earn through hard work; faithful (like a dog & bold like a pig); even children will also be bold and sincere; Ketu's personal effect – good or bad – depends upon Jupiter's position in the Birth chart; limited number of children; will live abroad for most of the period; Venus, Saturn & Jupiter will give exalted results. Planets in no.2 (even Moon) will be benefic; keep a gold brick in the house; the more the gold, the richer he will be; keep gold on body for relief from disease connected with Ketu i.e. urinary trouble, spinal cord; arthritis; backache, pain in legs, feet and ear troubles. Son will be the best adviser; loyal son who will always be grateful to parents; a soothsayer; will bring best luck for father til 12th, 24th & 48th year; father will become prosperous; will have at least two to three sons, who will be prosperous.

(a) Exalted Moon or in a benefic house – Good for mother and her relatives.

(b) Exalted Jupiter or Rahu or exalted no.2 – Eminent position; will bring good luck to parents.

Bad effects

If malefic, it is bad for mother and her relatives; (even though Moon may be benefic or malefic, Ketu is with Moon in no.9).

(a) Moon or Mars (enemies) in no.3 – Death of son.

(b) Malefic Saturn – Thief, dacoit, miserable life.

Remedies:

(a) Keep gold on body; keep gold brick in your house or under pillow.

(b) Refer to page 227 (Remedies for Ketu).

Ketu – House no. 10 (Raashi Effect)

Walking alone quietly; a loner; opportunist; rat; Saturn will finally decide its effect; remedy for Mars.

Good effects

Forgiving nature; will forgive his errant brothers; his motto is "forgiveness is the best form of revenge"; this attitude will help him; will never lose money; final verdict lies with Saturn, rich; if of loose character having illicit relations with another woman, he will be completely destroyed.

(a) Exalted Saturn or in benefic houses – Wealthy and happy regarding sons; Jupiter will be exalted, even mud will turn into gold.

(b) Saturn no.6 – Famous sports person.

Bad effects

Very bad effect on Ketu (son etc.) till 48th year, especially when Saturn is malefic; must be of good character; if he is of loose character and a womanizer, his sons will be destroyed.

Saturn no. 4 – Very bad for children.

Remedies:

(a) For the welfare of sons, bury a silver vessel with honey in a deserted place before 48th year.

(b) After 48th year, keep dog.

(c) Adopt remedy as mentioned for Ketu no.8.

(d) If Ketu and Mars are together in no.10 and both are malefic or Saturn is malefic, then the man will be womanizer and everything including wealth, domestic comforts will be destroyed. Remedy as for Moon or bury honey and milk in the foundation of the house.

(e) If Saturn is malefic, offer water and milk to Sun in the morning (Argh of milk and water).

Ketu – House no. 11

Jackal like dog; precious stone (cat's eye or white & black stone); black dog will bring good luck.

Good effects

The native may not have large tract of land, but will earn lot of wealth and property; Rajayog, provided Mercury is not in house no.3; will rise very high; Jupiter's seat i.e. learned and intelligent; dog having the habit and temperament of a jackal.

(a) Saturn no.3 – Eleven times richer than parents; exalted status; lot of wealth.

(b) Mercury not in no.3 – Rajayog; eminent position.

Bad effects

Moon's result will be bad till Ketu's period i.e. 48 years; but children will be noble; in girl's horoscope it will just be the reverse i.e. everything will be fine and auspicious.

(a) Mercury no.3 – Moon's results will be the worst during 8th, 11th, 23rd, 36th, 48th year of age when Ketu occupies 1st house in the Annual chart.

(b) Malefic Saturn – Worst results regarding wealth and property; but Ketu will not be malefic in girl's horoscope, even if Saturn is malefic.

Remedy:

First male child may be born dead; keep white radish under the wife's pillow at night and donate it in the morning to a place of worship; it will save the woman and next year she will be blessed with a male child; nevertheless, first child may not survive.

233

Ketu – House no. 12

Exalted; life of luxury; legacy; ancestral property; best luck; fish.

Good effects

Promotion is certain, but not transfer; it will give the exalted effect of no.2; after the birth of son or after his son attains 24th year, he will be blessed with all comforts, prestige and wealth; will also lead a life of luxury; Venus, Saturn, Jupiter will confer exalted results, but Mars (i.e. elder brother, uncles) will not be helpful; only his children will help him; promotion is assured; will earn from travels and property; will be helpful to his family; will be blessed with sons who will be healthy and rich (even though Ketu in no.12 is associated with an enemy planet), provided he keeps or feeds a dog; Mars (elder brother, uncles) and Rahu (in-laws) will feel jealous and will not help him; only his children will be of great help to him; will have sons only; sucking of thumb dipped in milk or simply keeping it in mouth is auspicious.

No.6 vacant (except Rahu alone) – Very rich children and family; will inherit ancestral property; domestic happiness; everything, including sons, fine and exalted, as long as he lives a luxurious life.

Bad effects

Ketu's effect will never be malefic on the native, but Ketu (son) will itself be malefic or destroyed. When Rahu in no.6 is associated with certain planets Ketu (son) may not be born till the age mentioned against each:

Rahu in no.6 with Mars	Bad for birth of a son till 28th year.
Rahu in no.6 with Moon	Bad for birth of a son till 24th year.
Rahu in no.6 with Sun	Bad for birth of a son till 22nd year.
Rahu in no.6 with Venus	Bad for birth of a son till 25th year.

But if he leads a luxurious life, son will be born at the right age and Ketu will not be malefic.

(a) Rahu & Mercury no.6 – Ketu will not be bad although Mercury is Ketu's enemy.

(b) Rahu and enemy planets (Sun, Mars, Venus) & Rahu's friends in no.6 or Moon, Mars or Venus in no.2 – Ketu will be meaningless and will not be exalted.

Remedies:

(a) Dip the thumb in milk and then suck it or simply suck it. It will be good for sons & wealth.

(b) Feed a dog.

(c) Remedy as for Rahu will also help.

Two Planets in a House

While considering the effect of two or more than two planets in a house, the following facts may be taken into account:

(a) Their individual effect – whether good or bad – should not be lost sight of. Usually, they give their individual effect, but sometimes they blend into each other like sugar in milk (if friend & exalted) or like poison in milk (if enemies & malefic).

(b) When two or more planets occupy the same house, the planets mutually opposed to each other give up their enmity, but those which are friendly, will continue to be friends.

(c) Female planets (Moon or Venus or both with Mercury) with male planets will give good results.

The following combination of planets is detailed below:

1. Jupiter-Sun Combined (Royal Wealth)

General

Sun-Jupiter effect will be in the ratio of 3 : 2; Jupiter will confer its results in the beginning and Sun later on. When both of them are combined together, they, in fact, become 'Full Moon' (exalted). Such a person's fate will have the strength and speed of light and brightness of gold. Jupiter alone means grandfather or father or teacher, but when both of them are together, Jupiter signifies native's father and Sun means son (i.e. the native). In short, there is a harmonious blending of fates of father and son and they will help each other. Individually, both these planets may not be good, but in combination, they will confer good results for both the father and son till the following years.

House No.	Years
1	38
2	39
3	40
4	41
5	42
6	43
7	44
8	45

9	46
10	47
11	48
12	49

Jupiter-Sun & their effect in various houses

House no. 1	King-like status; an eminent administrator; long life; all comforts of life; happy married life; (even though illiterate & stupid) – sudden death.
House no. 2	Owner of great mansions; grand life; bold like a tiger but cruel.
House no. 3	Prosperous and rich if not greedy; otherwise wealth will be destroyed.
House no. 4	Will extract milk even from stones i.e. earn through business concerning Saturn; splendid life; exalted position, provided not aspected by Saturn from house no. 10.
House no. 5 and Moon in no.4	Eminent position; noble and wealthy children; victory over enemies; even wicked planets like Rahu-Ketu and Saturn occupying this house will not harm Sun-Jupiter. However, if Mercury occupies this house, Jupiter will be dormant or asleep.
House no. 6, 7, 10 & 11	Individual effect of each planet (whether good or bad); but will give combined effect in old age. In other words, both father and son will be prosperous till 70 years.

Good effects

Such a person is learned; intellectual, wise and enjoys an eminent status; he has the blessings of Lord Brahma (the creator i.e. Jupiter) and Lord Vishnu (the protector i.e. Sun) and has the power to fight even against his malevolent fate. He is the symbol of justice, long life and exalted status.

Sun & Jupiter in relation to other planets

(a) Venus in later houses – Eminent and noble children; prosperous, honour, fame and good status.

(b) Exalted Sun – Good health; name and fame; prosperous; bright future.

(c) Both aspect Moon – Exalted Moon; exalted status or job; promotion; bright future; someone will help and patronize him. Now Moon will give best results, even if it is afflicted and destroyed by enemies.

(d) Exalted Moon and both aspect each other – Will earn a lot; will travel at govt. expense; prosperous.

(e) Together with or aspected by Mars – Very rich.

(f) Together with or aspected by Sun – Writer; successful businessman and may help others.

(g) In house no. 8 – Conqueror of death.

(h) In house no. 9 & 12 – Best effect on self and family; prosperous and wealthy.

236

Bad effects

(a) Venus in earlier houses – Both will give worst results; will be a loser; muddy and poor fate; unfortunate.

(b) Both aspected by Saturn or both in no.4 & Saturn in no.10 – Both the planets are dormant and asleep; Ketu's Mahadasha of 7 years will be the worst; loss of wealth; bad for maternal uncles; worst fate; Saturn, if exalted, may be the saving grace i.e. may help.

(c) Houses in which sun's effect is bad – Will face troubles; unsuccessful life; life like a 'fill in the blanks' i.e. just living without any happiness.

Remedy: Do not take bribes and also do not accept gifts and donations; keep gold or saffron in the house.

2. Jupiter-Moon Combined

Rich legacy; inherited wealth; banyan tree providing shade to all; law department.

General

When Moon in no.2 is exalted, Jupiter's effect will be the best and when Jupiter in no.4 is exalted, Moon's effect will be the best. When combined together, Jupiter-Moon effect will be in the ratio of 2:1. When both of them are together, Jupiter's effect will commence from 16th year, but will be alone after 28th year, when it may be adversely affected by enemy planets.

If Mercury, Venus, Rahu are in no.2, 5, 9, 12, then both son and father will meet the same adverse fate ('Pitri-Rin'); if wicked planets occupy no.4, mother's adverse effect will recoil upon Venus (spouse) and Mercury (daughter) 'Matri-Rin'. Mercury in house no. 2 is bad for father and Mercury in no.4 is bad for mother, though very rich, yet will have to face lot of problems.

Good effects

Exalted fate; like a banyan tree providing shade to all; Moon's effect will be exalted; he may suffer from loss of memory in old age, but as he grows, he becomes more prosperous and is blessed with all comforts, he may be infirm (weak) in old age, but will be very rich; will inherit lot of wealth and property from mother and father; may even get divine help; will have additional income; highly educated (till 24th year); travels for 20 years; comfortable old age.

(a) Exalted Moon – Lot of wealth, comfortable past and future.

(b) Both in earlier houses than Mercury – Everything exalted and fine; like divine 'Amrita'.

(c) Both in good and benefic houses – Parents will bless him like the banyan tree providing shade and comfort: Moon and Sun laden with benefic rains. (Keep a plate of silver in the house for best results).

(d) Both in no.1 to 6 and friendly planets in no.7 to 12 – Jupiter and Moon will confer exalted results individually; friendly planets may not help.

(e) Both in no.7 to 12 and friendly planets in no.1 to 6 – Friendly planets will receive help from both – whether they aspect them or not – i.e. Sun, Mars, Mercury (friends) will be helped by Jupiter-Moon.

(f) Together with or aspected by Mars – Very rich.

237

(g) Together with or aspected by Sun – Successful businessman; can be a good writer.

(h) Both in no.7 to 12 and friendly planets in no.1 to 6 and exalted Saturn – Best results regardin both Moon and Jupiter; intelligent, wise and wealthy.

(i) Together with or aspected by Venus – Loss of wealth after marriage.

(j) Together with or aspected by Saturn – Others may gain through friendship; like a philosopher stone for friends.

(k) Together with or aspected by Mercury – Now Mercury will no longer be enemy; it will rathe be helpful.

(l) Both aspecting (100% – just opposite) Mars-Venus; Venus-Saturn; Mars-Saturn – Good Result

Jupiter-Moon in Various Houses (Good effects)

House No.	Good Effect
1	Exalted results, just like those of Jupiter-Moon in no.2; must not marry or build a house before 28th year. (Otherwise, worst results). Bury articles concerning Mars in the earth for good results.
2	Most exalted results; Jupiter will confer the best results of no.4 i.e. fountain of wealth; like a banyan tree providing cool refreshing wind and shade to all; additional income; divine help; lot of wealth and property; but association with Rahu and Mercury (sister-in-law) will be poisonous and malefic.
3	Prosperous; very lucky; royal status; helpful to others (especially brothers); association with Mercury will not be good.
4	Most exalted combination; fountain of wealth gushing out since childhood; parents like the huge banyan tree providing him shade and refreshing breeze; his small boat will be like a ship; peace of mind; best results regarding Jupiter & Moon; in fact, the most exalted fate.
5	Even Sun will confer best results; a rich merchant; a renowned and successful writer; will help others also.
6	The effect of Mercury and Ketu in the Birth chart (good or bad) will be reflected on these two planets. Remedy lies in providing water etc. to the hospital & cremation ground or doing deeds of philanthropy by providing comforts to patients.
7	Both lose their power in this house; whenever their enemy occupies the 1st house in Annual chart, bad effect on parents but profit through investment, brokerage and speculations etc.
8	Long life; brothers will aspire for his wealth; they will both be friends and enemies i.e. some will help him and others may oppose him; but will never lose his wealth.
9	Exalted fate; man is like a tree watered with milk; benign influence of parents who will protect him like a banyan tree; may get rich legacy

	when they occupy house no. 9 in the Annual chart, i.e., best results in respect of Moon and Jupiter; travel for 20 years; peace of mind; mother's blessings.
10	Will behave like 'true man', though may not be rich; rude to others, even to his own father; will be shortsighted; foolish, having false sense of ego and pride. (Remedy: Throw copper coins in the river).
11	Must do self service to others; humanitarian deeds will help; if no.3 is vacant, both these planets in no.11 will be meaningless and dormant, even no.5 will not help. (Remedy: Worship virgins and help them and get their blessings).
12	May have royal blood (i.e. son of a rich man), but will be like a sadhu or ascetic like Raja Janaka of the Ramayana; loss of wealth after marriage or birth of a daughter, but good position after birth of a son. (Remedy: Bury a silver cup in the foundation of the house).

Bad effects

House no. 1:

(a) Both in later house than Mercury – Mercury's individual effect will be bad.

(b) Both in malefic houses – Most unfortunate; loser, however courageous and bold.

(c) Both aspect each other (100%) being in different houses – Whenever things concerning enemies i.e. Saturn (construction of house), Venus (musical instrument) are brought or bought, they will have adverse effect on parents. {Remedy: Bury articles concerning Ketu or wear black & white stone (cat's eye) around neck or body.}

(d) Debilitating or malefic Saturn – Full of false hope and wishful thinking; atheist.

House no. 2:

(a) If associated with or aspected by Rahu or Mercury – Worst results; both Jupiter and Moon will act like poison; must not keep sister-in-law (wife's sister) in the house.

(b) Mercury no.6 – Bad eyesight; Saturn's effect will be bad; bad old age.

House no. 3 (Associated with Mercury) – Worst results of all the three. (See malefic Mercury no.3). Moon-Jupiter will also give bad results.

House no. 6 – Must not dig well on agricultural land; it will bring bad results.

House no. 7 – Ill health in childhood; unhappy parents during 6th, 12th & 24th year; loss of wealth after marriage and birth of daughter.

House no. 8 – For the sake of wealth, he may oppose and destroy his brothers. Things associated with Saturn, Mars will ruin him.

House no. 9 – Both will act as poison and destroy him if he sells his daughter or takes money from her.

House no. 10 – Parents may be rich, but such a man will get nothing; he is like a bubble of water that bursts; bad fate.

(**Remedy:** Throw copper coins).

House no. 11 – When Mercury, Venus or Rahu are in no.3 – Both will be useless and ruined; parents will be unhappy at 12th or 16th year. {Remedy: Help Mercury (sister, aunts etc.), Venus (wife); Rahu (grandmother, sweeper) off and on by giving them something}.

House no. 12 – Loss of wealth and property after marriage and birth of daughter. (Remedy: Bury a silver pot in the foundation of house).

2. Jupiter-Venus

General

When both Jupiter-Venus are combined; Jupiter confers its effect first and then Venus (good or bad); both will be regarded in conjunction with each other till 33rd year. If Jupiter's effect is one, then Venus' effect will be 3 ¾ times. As regards speed of effect, if Venus travels two times, Jupiter's speed will be just half.

Good effects

Jupiter's effect will be dim, but Venus' effect will be exalted. Such a person is a successful lover. Women will always help him; if both of them are exalted and in their own Raashi (sign) and free from adverse aspect or are in a Kendra, such a person courts a beautiful damsel and is rich and master of vehicles.

House No.	Good Effect
1	Unfortunate sadhu getting respect only in wilderness or jungle; will be lucky only after the death of father or wife.
2	Gold will turn into dust but that dust will be more precious than gold. Benefits from dealing in land.
3	Prosperous, wealthy and fortunate; will financially help brothers; wife will be bold and courageous and help him.
4	Wife may leave the husband or die after the birth of a son; Jupiter in no.4 will confer exalted results, provided he is not lustful and does not deal in women trafficking.
5	Will earn a lot through knowledge and education; will rise through children who will be noble.
6	Wife must wear gold pin or clip on her hair for the protection and welfare of sons.
7	Fortunate if he deals in business associated with Mercury i.e. investments etc.; even if he loses, he will not have a miserable life i.e. he will not live from hand to mouth and will become wealthy again; adopted child will enjoy his wealth.
8	For Venus' effect refer to house no. 10 i.e. bad for wealth, but good for all other things; as regards wealth the results are the same as mentioned in no.2 i.e. will earn through lands. In short, different and opposing effects of both Jupiter and Venus.

9	Individual effect of both the planets, but good; all comforts, beneficial travels for 20 years.
10	Personal wealth will not be destroyed; but ancestral wealth will be completely destroyed, especially when he is lustful and of bad character.
11	Individual effect of both the planets; Jupiter in no.2 is good, but it is bad in no.11 (gold will turn into dust).
12	Happy married life, full of comforts.

Bad effects

General: Lustful conduct and illicit relations with women of doubtful character will destroy him physically and financially; may develop physical defects because of bad character; may even be issueless. (Remedy: Must be of good character).

House No.	Bad Effect
1	Worst fate; like a poor fakir; unhappy married life.
2	Problems in the birth of a son; business in gold will ruin him.
3	Flatterers will deceive him.
4	Wife will deliver one child and will die after that.
5	Will lose his wealth through a married paramour i.e. illicit relations with another married woman.
6	Problems regarding sons, bad luck if he hates or insults his wife.
7	Family members will enjoy at his expense and will himself be unhappy because of womanizing and lustful conduct; will be like a moth hovering around a candle i.e. beautiful woman. Problems in the birth of a son; will lose his wealth i.e. his gold will turn into dust.When Mars is in no.4 – will be like a castrated bull i.e. will not be able to produce children; even adopted child will cause unhappiness. Mercury in no.7 – Mercury will be helpful; will never starve.
9	Bad in respect of wife i.e. bad domestic life.
10	Will be ruined because of his illicit relations with other women; may have physical defects; will fondly remember "the good days that are no more".
11	Bad fate; the same bad effect as mentioned in Venus no.11 if no.3 is vacant; will suffer from impotence (Pandu of Mahabharata). (Remedy: Refer to Venus no.11, donate oil during bad times).
12	Bad for speculation business.

3. Jupiter-Mars

General

When Mars is exalted, it indicates exalted status of the family; both the planets will be together till 72 years and Mars's benefic effect will be in the ratio of 1 : 2.

Good effects

If Mars is exalted, the person will be just and bold and will not tolerate injustice; royal position; administrator. Leader among men; noble; good-doer; learned and intellectual; will have divine blessings.

Mars-Jupiter aspecting Saturn – Will be a terror for enemies; will be victorious over them; very rich; long life.

House No.	Good Effect
1	Very rich; eminent and royal status; even Rahu-Ketu will confer good results.
2	Rich and loving in-laws; they will help him; best domestic life; if Mercury is in no.6, he will be self-made rich because of his intelligence and wisdom.
3	Noble man always praying to God; religious-minded person; will preserve and protect ancestral property and wealth.
4	No dearth of men folk; but may not be rich.
5	Fountain of wealth i.e. very rich for 28 years after the birth of a son; charity and deeds of charity will make him richer; if he accepts bribes or presents, he will be destroyed.
6	Will be the eldest brother; Mercury in no.2 will now give good results which will not adversely affect Jupiter in no.6.
8	Individual effect of both.
9	Best results in respect of domestic happiness, wealth and children.
10	Fate will be decided by planets in no.4 and 6; if both these houses are vacant, life will be like the artificial gold i.e. good-for-nothing; will however become rich by looting and cheating others.
11	Will be rich during father's and brother's life. (Remedy for Jupiter and Mars).
12	Best fate regarding children and wealth and domestic life; will be free from tension and bless others.

Bad effects

If Mars is malefic, he will be unfortunate and ill fated; relatives may suffer till 31st year and may bear losses for 5 years; during Saturn's malefic period, Jupiter will be the deciding planet and vice-versa.

House No.	Bad Effect
2	Worst results if Mars is malefic.
5	Should not accept bribe, gifts and charity; otherwise he will be destroyed.
6	Bad results regarding business and things associated with mercury and Ketu (son).
7	Will be under debt, even though having good income.
8	Whenever both the planets give bad effect, it will adversely affect his family members.
11	Must do business in respect of things connected with Jupiter and Mars for better results; otherwise adverse effect.

4. Jupiter-Mercury

General

Jupiter's and Mercury's effect will be in the ratio of 1 : 2; when both are together, there will be loss of wealth from 8th to 25th year; and parents will be unhappy from 17th to 25th year.

When both of them are together or when Mercury aspects Jupiter, Jupiter (father) will be destroyed provided:

(a) Jupiter in no.1 to 6 and Mercury in no.7 to 12 – Jupiter will confer good results till 34th year and Mercury will give bad results after 35th year.

(b) Mercury in no.1 to 6 and Jupiter in no.7 to 12 – Mercury will confer good results till 34th year and thereafter bad; but Jupiter will be bad till 34th year and thereafter it will be good.

When both of them are together, Jupiter's effect will be bad i.e. Mercury will crush Jupiter in its fatal embrace. This will, however, be set right under following conditions:

(a) When Jupiter occupies house no. 10 or 11 (Saturn's house) or house no.5 (Sun's house) in the Annual Chart; or

(b) Sun or Saturn occupies house no. 2, 5, 9 12 (Jupiter's house) in the Annual chart; or

(c) Saturn occupies house no.5 (Sun's house) and Sun in no.2, 5, 9, 12 (Jupiter's house).

In terms of the above conditions, if Sun or Moon or Saturn (any of these three) is exalted or benefic, Jupiter may give some good results i.e. there is hope of earning some wealth; otherwise, it will be a mere show off and Jupiter will be totally destroyed. He will be like Don Quixote, fighting against imaginary enemies and indulging in wishful thinking. Further, if Mercury is alone in no.2 and 4 or both Jupiter and Mercury are combined in these houses, Mercury will no longer oppose Jupiter and financially man will not be a loser. If both of them aspect each other 100% or 50%, results will be bad.

In short, when both of them are exalted, they confer exalted status and if both of them fully aspect Moon (100%), travels will be harmful.

Good effects

Will earn through business; but will be rich and poor alternatively i.e. may face ups and downs of life; will earn through intelligence.

House No.	Good Effect
1	King like; rich, administrator.
2	Learned scholar and preacher.
3	Full of contentment and patience; bold.
4	If exalted, Rajayog.
5	Prosperous & lucky, provided son is born on Thursday and daughter is not born on Wednesday.
6	Noble soul busy in prayers and meditation.
7	Ups and downs in life; learned. In daughter's horoscope, Mercury in no.7 will be good; but not in the case of son.
8	Mercury will never be bad, if house no. 2 is vacant.
10	Prosperous and wealthy.
11	Will become rich when both of them occupy house no.1 in the Annual chart i.e. 11th, 23rd, 36th year; learned scholar; noble soul and comfortable domestic life.
12	Good for self; long and comfortable life; will be an ordinary businessman.

Bad effects

Father or grandfather or father-in-law may suffer from asthma; will suffer from speech problem or may feel shy while talking; will not have blessings of parents i.e. may be orphan or parents may die; parental money will be ruined; may have to support family members; loss of wealth and gold; humiliation; problems and false hopes; may suffer because of his own folly in youth.

House No.	Bad Effect
1	Poor, foolish sadhu.
3	Malefic Venus i.e. bad for domestic life.
4	Coward; good for nothing; may commit suicide by doing sinful acts.
6	Lustful and given to life of luxury.
7	Bad effect of Mercury in son's horoscope; such a son will be unlucky and face ups and downs of life.
8	Always sick; everything goes topsy-turvy; life full of malefic storms and cyclones. (Remedy: Wear a silver wire in the nose for 96 hours, it will save from death; also bury a pot filled with sugar in a deserted place).
9 (When Mercury in no.9 is malefic)	Worst results for marriage, children and domestic life; ill fated and short-lived.

5. Jupiter-Saturn

General

The Hindus begin their auspicious work by uttering the sacred hymn. "Ohm Ganeshay-Namah" – (i.e. I bow to Lord Ganesh and seek his blessings); the Muslims utter the sacred name of God – "Bismillah-er-Rahman-er-Rahim" – (i.e. I begin with the name of Allah, who is the most compassionate and merciful). In other words, it is a sacred place worthy of worship; or is like a Dervish's or Fakir's bag which is unfathomable i.e. its beginning and end cannot be measured.

Fate – good or bad – depends upon planets in house no. 11 and if house no. 11 is vacant, Saturn's individual effect will be good. Both the planets will be considered together till 34th year for father's life and till 43rd year for wealth and prosperity. Jupiter and Saturn's effect will be in the ratio of 4 : 3.

It means that man may suffer from grief for 14 years; losses for 15 years and wealth for 12 years; both of them will give individual effects i.e. Saturn's effect will be bad but Jupiter will be helpful in saving.

Mutual Relationship between Jupiter and Saturn

When both Jupiter-Saturn are together in any house or Saturn in no.9, such a horoscope will be noble – all other planets will also become noble. Saturn in Jupiter's house and signs (Raashis – i.e. 2, 9, 12) will never be bad; but Jupiter in Saturn's house and Raashis (signs) i.e. 10 and 11 will be meaningless and zero, although Jupiter is the lord of both the worlds.

Jupiter-Saturn combined	Results
Jupiter in exalted house and Saturn in malefic house.	Like a philosophers' stone; will help and enrich others, but bad for self.
Saturn in exalted house and Jupiter in malefic house.	Like a sword; will overcome all obstacles.
Both exalted and Sun in no.1	Best results; most fortunate.
Both malefic and Sun in no.1	May lose wealth and a part of body.
Saturn exalted, but Jupiter is malefic and Sun in no.1	Loss of money only and not part of body.
Jupiter exalted, but Saturn malefic and Sun in no.1	Loss of part of body and not wealth.

Further, the planets aspecting Jupiter-Saturn (combined) will brighten them and their effect will start from the period or year assigned to that planet such as:

Sun – 20 to 22 years; Moon – 24 years; Mars – 28 years; Venus – 25 years; Mercury – 34 years; Rahu – 42 years and Ketu – 48 years. (Both Rahu-Ketu – 45 years).

Good effects

When the person is content with his lot, both the planets will confer good reslts; even though Saturn may be in no.1 where it is debilitating; debilitating Jupiter may be in no.10; in such a case, Saturn obeys Jupiter – the great guru.

When both are aspected by Venus, such a person's wealth will be like a mound of mud i.e. will show off but worthless; his ancestral wealth will be enjoyed by the spouse; but there will be an increase of wealth after marriage.

House No.	Good Effect
1	Sadhu or teacher but poor.
2	A great scholar; man of letters – which will depend upon Saturn's position – good or bad – both the planets will confer best results like the cool breeze; will be a true lover.
3	Rich, but average living; comfortable life in old age.
4	Very famous; snake will be beneficial; if stung by a snake, even paralysis will be cured and a diseased body will become strong.
5	Ordinary luck, but may earn name and fame; Sun's effect will not be good; problems in matters concerning Jupiter; problems in official life, involvement in civil cases, but will be victorious, provided he is not cunning like a snake and does not indulge in wine and women.
6	(When Saturn is exalted and Jupiter is quiet i.e. Rahu-Ketu in no.2) Happy married life.
7	Gains through articles concerning Saturn (i.e. construction of new house or buying property etc.); the more he spends on them, the greater the gain. Such a man will be noble and thorough gentleman and will be kind to all. (a) When Moon or Venus or both are benefic – Lot of wealth; the poor will become rich and rich will have royal status; will have a large family; Saturn's effect will be exalted. (b) Benefic Venus – Rise after marriage, but will have independent judgment. (c) Benefic Moon – Mother's blessings; brothers and sisters will help him; Moon's effect will be long lived; and when Mars is exalted (especially when it is exalted/benefic in house no. 6 to 12), both Moon and Venus will confer good results. Rich, but after looting and cheating people. In short, it will be the exalted effect of Saturn-Jupiter no.9.
8	Average income, but long life; now house no. 8 will not be the house of death; no mishap or death will take place in his family in his presence.
9	Most exalted effect; large but rich family; will have lot of property and wealth; will help others. Will be intelligent and shrewd like Saturn; people may call him cruel, but he will be very fortunate and rich; will be independent and work under none, even under his father; he will be a worshipper of Mammon, the god of wealth; he will earn by hook or crook; just as bigger fish eats the smaller one, so is the case with such a man; he will destroy all his opponents and have long life.
10	Best for self; will be respected by all.
11	Fate will be decided by planets in no.3 and no.5 will not affect it; if no.3 is vacant, it will have the effect of Saturn no.11; his friends will gain a lot.

	from him, though he may be poor, yet will be a sincere friend and a true lover; will be like a philosopher's stone.
12	Noble; good-hearted and fortunate; Rahu-Ketu will not be bad; Saturn and Jupiter will confer individual results of house no. 1, 2; rise in income after marriage. If Mars, Moon, Venus are benefic, the good results will be those mentioned in Jupiter-Saturn no.7; but good fortune will be for a short period. (Remedy lies in Moon).

Bad effects

If the man is a drunkard, the exalted effect of Jupiter and Saturn will be destroyed; must not take bribe or gifts; bad and infirm old age; if Ketu aspects both of them, bad effect on sons.

House No.	Bad Effect
1	If Saturn is malefic, worst fate.
2	Sickness; whenever both of them occupy house no. 2 in the Annual chart (i.e. 9th, 21st, 33rd, 45th, 57th, 65th, 74th, 96th year) bad for health and for father's life. (Remedy lies through Saturn i.e. donate almonds coconut or iron articles etc.)
3	May lose father or his wealth during 9th, 18th, 36th year.
6	Unhappy family life (i.e. spouse may die or may be sick), if Saturn is exalted, but Jupiter is malefic. Though adverse aspect from no.2 and unhappy married life and wife from a poor family, if Jupiter is benefic and Saturn is malefic because of adverse effect from no.2.
7	Loss of wealth (Mercury) after daughter's birth but Mercury will not have adverse effect on Saturn; problems during childhood. (a) Both in no.7 or 12 and Moon, Venus and Mars malefic – Whenever malefic planets i.e. Moon, Venus and Mars will occupy house no. 1, Mother (Moon), Venus (wife) and Mars (elder brother or eldest uncle) will be destroyed and there may be enmity. It is also probable that such a person is lustful and womanizer, which may cause mother's death after marriage and father's death in 34th year. (b) Both in no.7 or 12 and Sun in no.1 – Very bad plight during Saturn's period i.e. 9th, 18th, 36th year.
10 (And Sun in no.4)	Saturn will destroy both Jupiter and Sun; Sun may be destroyed, but Sun being in house no. 4 will convert all those destroyed by Saturn into precious stones i.e. all other planets except Jupiter destroyed by Saturn will be benefited. Lustful conduct and corruption will ruin the man.
11	If Mercury is malefic, one may face financial problems; and if Mercury is benefic, man may be bold and enterprising and may become rich even from a scratch.

Remedy: For malefic planets and their bad effect, adopt the remedy for that planet according to its sign (Raashi).

6. Jupiter (Tiger)-Rahu (Elephant)

Fight between tiger and elephant; fate like life-giving oxygen and curls of suffocating smoke alternatively; Jupiter walks straight, whereas elephant's gait is never straight.

General

Jupiter walks straight and fast like a tiger, whereas elephant's gait is never straight; obviously one's life is like that of 'rainbow' of different colours; sometimes fate ia as bright as gold or saffron (Jupiter) and sometimes like the dark blue rays of poverty (Rahu). In other words, such a person sees many ups and downs in life; the resultant effect is that such a person, if born in a royal family, may be reduced to poverty and a poor man may become rich, but bad days will be over when he is blessed with a son.

Jupiter-Rahu combined means artificial Mercury which will give useless reputation i.e. Mercury will be meaningless and zero; Rahu will be malefic and bad, but Jupiter may be dormant or asleep but will maintain its entity and never disappear.

Jupiter is the master of both the worlds – earthly and spiritual, but if Rahu is in earlier houses, Jupiter will be earthly and if Jupiter is in earlier houses, it will be the lord of spiritual as well as mundane worlds; if both are together or separate and malefic, it will be just like Mercury giving useless reputation. As long as Sun, Moon and Mars are benefic and Rahu is exalted, Jupiter like the great guru, will dominate both the worlds. Rahu in combination with Jupiter or in Jupiter's house will be malefic, but Jupiter, though quiet and silent, will never disappear. In other words, Jupiter associated with Rahu will be like gold which has turned into copper. If Jupiter gets Moon's help, it will overpower enemies. In a nutshell, when both Jupiter-Rahu are together in house no.1 to 6, Jupiter will be the lord of both the worlds; but if they are in house no. 7 to 12, Jupiter will be the master of worldly affairs only. When both of them give bad results, remedy lies in Ketu; if Ketu (worthless son) is also bad, remedy lies in Moon.

Remedy: Barley may be washed in milk and thrown into the river for 43 days to remove the black smoke and ill effect of Rahu; or

Take a two-coloured (black and white cat's eye) stone (i.e. Ketu) and wash it daily with used water of cow and donate sugar or masur daal (red lentil) for 43 days.

Good effects

Such a person will not have to work hard to earn living; he will get everything effortlessly.

House No.	Good Effect
1	Generous and large-hearted, whether rich or poor; will never starve, howsoever bad the fate may be.
2	Rahu will pay obeisance to Jupiter i.e. Rahu will now work at the behest of Jupiter; good doer; will help the poor.

3	Bold and shrewd; after Rahu's period (i.e. $10\frac{1}{2}$th, 21st, 42nd year), both Jupiter and Rahu will give the effect of house no. 3; during bad period, remedy lies through Ketu and then through Jupiter-Rahu as suggested earlier.
4	Full effect of exalted Moon; Jupiter will be silent, but it will secretly confer good effects.
5	Administrator, leader; exalted position.
7	Will have comfortable life in youth; either father or father-in-law will be alive and either of them may suffer from asthma.
12	Now Rahu & Jupiter will not oppose each other; skilful; intelligent and wise, but may not gain much from mechanical works.
6, 9, 10, 11	Individual effect of each house.

Bad effects

Except house no. 2 and 12, in other houses from 8th to 12th year of age, gold will turn into copper; fate full of stifling smoke and mishaps; father may suffer from asthma and partial paralysis between 16th and 21st years.

During 42nd year, incidents of theft of gold may occur or bad effect on business (associated with Jupiter and Rahu).

Both Jupiter-Rahu together will give the malefic effect of Mercury (i.e. sister, aunt etc.). Their effect is bad in respect of father's life and wealth as mentioned in Rahu no.11; as regards personal income, it will be good and bad alternatively i.e. one may rise like a king and fall like a poor sadhu; in other words, one will see rise and fall alternatively.

House No.	Bad Effect
2	If no.8 is occupied by enemies of Rahu and Jupiter or otherwise malefic planets, there will be problems in the birth of a son.
3	The effect of Mercury and Ketu will be bad till 34th year.
5	Effect of Rahu no.5 regarding birth of a son.
7	Either father or father-in-law will be alive, otherwise either of them may suffer from asthma.
8	Life is dull, insipid and bad; overcast with dark clouds of hopelessness and misery. (Remedy as for Jupiter in house no. 8).

Remedies:

(a) Remedy through Ketu.

(b) Keep gold on person.

(c) If Ketu (son) is malefic, remedy lies through Moon.

(d) Wash the ring made of black and white stone (Ketu) everyday with cow's used water and then donate sugar or masur daal (red lentil) for 43 days.

(e) Wash barley (jau in Hindi) with milk and then keep a few grains of the washed barley with yourself and thereafter throw the remaining grains of barley into the river for 43 days.

7. Jupiter-Ketu

Yellow lemon; sacred seat of great guru.

General

When both of them are together, they will give exalted results; Ketu will be the successor to the sacred seat of the great guru (Jupiter) and will confer wealth and prosperity. Jupiter is the great teacher and Ketu is his disciple; if Jupiter is the lord of sacred prayer and meditation; Ketu is the sacred seat where the great guru sits. Jupiter is like the free and unfettered air but Ketu (if malefic) is like a deceiving spirit or benefic elf (if exalted).

Good effects

Ketu (son) will be exalted; Jupiter's personal effect will not be bad.

House No.	Good Effect
1	A noble king; auspicious for all; comfortable life.
2	Exalted position; merciful; provided house no. 8 is vacant, if there are friendly planets in no.8, such a person is a wealthy administrator.
4	Noble planets; rich and happy family; intelligent, learned scholar; dame fortune (Laxmi) smiles upon him. When Jupiter is exalted (even if Ketu is bad), one will be blessed with a son.
6	If aspected by friendly planets from no.2 or no.2 is vacant, good fortune and happy life; may have premonition of his death.
7	Poor, starving sadhu praying to God.
8	Indolent and lazy.
12	Very wealthy and prosperous.
3, 5, 9, 10, 11	Individual effect.

Bad effects

Enemies will trouble him if Moon-Mars are in house no. 6 (Ketu's house) and Venus, Mercury or Rahu in house no. 9 or 12 (Jupiter's house). (Remedy: Donate yellow lemon).

If either of the two gives bad effect, both the planets will confer good results on the native, but bad results regarding living things in respect of Ketu (son) and Jupiter (father).

House No.	Bad Effect
2	If aspected by planets from house no. 8, the man is selfish and unfortunate.
4	Late birth of a son.
6	(a) If Ketu is malefic and Jupiter is benefic, according to aspect from no.2, one may lose the first child. (b) If Ketu is benefic and Jupiter is malefic according to aspect from no.2, one will be a slave to others.
7	Poor, famished fakir.
8	Indolent, lazy, poor and chicken-hearted fellow. (Remedy: Donate yellow lemon).

OOO

Chapter No. 22

Sun & Others

1. Sun–Moon

Pure milk of banyan tree; sweet and juicy fruit; tonga (carriage).

General

Both the planets will be considered together till 40 years and their effect will be Sun 4 and Moon 3 i.e. in the ratio of 4 : 3, but Sun will be the most exalted.

Good effects

Comfortable old age; lot of ancestral property; from no.1-6 Moon is exalted but from no.7-12 it is not so. Happy and peaceful domestic life; good govt. job (may be a doctor); if Sun aspects Moon, fountain of wealth will sprout up.

House No.	Good Effect
1	King-like status; exalted position; will rule over others.
2	Both will confer exalted results; prosperity and promotion in Govt. job, provided he is not pitted against women and women are not his competitors.
3	Good for self, but selfish towards others.
4	King-like status, like a pearl in a shell; very wealthy; all comforts of life; owner of all sorts of vehicles, provided no.10 is vacant.
5	Comfortable life throughout; fortunate, birth of a son.
6	Individual effect of both, provided they are not associated with wicked planets (i.e. Rahu-Ketu and Saturn); if house no. 2 is vacant, will get nothing from parents or they will be meaningless for him. (Remedy: As for Mars i.e. donate sugar or masur daal etc.)
9	Mother's blessings; travel for 20 years; exalted results.
12	Individual but Sun's results will be the best; provided no.2 is not occupied by enemy planets.

Bad effects

Must not oppose women; if no.4, 5 are occupied by enemies i.e. Venus, Rahu/Ketu and Saturn, he will have a disturbed and unhappy life; sleepless nights; may face problems; though very rich, yet full of tension, unnecessary expenditure and meaningless travels.

House No.	Bad Effect
1	Sudden death.
2	If opposed to women, will suffer losses; may hate women, but he will be the loser.
4	Sudden death. If Saturn is in no.10, he may die by drowning during the day time.
6	Doubtful long life (not necessarily short life), if Rahu-Ketu or Saturn are in no.2.
11	Bad effect of both; life 9 years only; if he gives up meat eating (non-vegetarianism), he may live up to 100 years.

2. Sun–Venus

Whenever Sun is associated with Venus or any enemy planet, it gives bad effect on the planet occupying that house. These enemy planets will give bad effect between 22nd and 25th year. (Remedy lies for Mercury); if Jupiter, Mars or Moon are also together with these enemy planets, bad effect will be visible on these friends of Sun (i.e. Jupiter, Mars and Moon); enemy planets will not be harmed; Rahu will give malefic effect in such a horoscope.

Both Sun and Venus will be considered combined till 45th year; their effect will be in the ratio of 4 : 3. Venus will now be malefic; and out of their union will issue forth Mercury i.e. flower without fruit at a time.

One will confer good results and the other bad. If Sun's result is exalted, one may get good job, name and fame; but will have unhappy married life; if married life is comfortable, his official life will be full of problems.

Both these planets will have nothing to do with Jupiter's articles i.e. gold, but when both of them are together, Jupiter will be almost meaningless.

Good effects

There will be no physical defect; but either of the two will always give exalted results.

House No.	Good Effect
1	Good for self and service; but bad for wife.
7	Best results for self, like Sun in no.9; beneficial travels for 20 years; but worst for wife.
9	Rich and poor alternatively i.e. sometimes very rich and sometimes too poor; beneficial travels for 20 years; but bad for wife.
10	Worst fate; like a beggar with begging bowl, if house no. 4 does not help. (Remedy – Give milk to snake on Shiva's idol; if no.4 is vacant, remedy lies with Moon).
2, 3, 4, 5, 6, 8, 11, 12	Individual results.

Bad effects

Father may not live long; will get a son quite late i.e. between 36 and 39 years (Saturn's period) or after 47th year, otherwise no happiness from wife and her relatives.

Wife will be sick, she may suffer from chronic disease such as T.B. etc. and family life will be destroyed; wife may have dirty spots or freckles on her cheeks; such a man is credulous, selfish henpecked, rude, short-tempered and a philanderer (fond of women) and the results are indeed very bad. One must not marry before 25th year, otherwise his self and family life will be destroyed.

House No.	Bad Effect
1	Mentally and physically sick or mad wife; bad for service matters; may suffer incarceration for lustful conduct, illicit relations with other women; selfishness.
7	Quarrel with wife; bad health of wife; even her life is doubtful; foundation of the ancestral house should not be of red colour.
9	Worst family life; rich and poor alternately.
10	Bad and unsuccessful official life; even Saturn will be malefic; Although born rich, will be reduced to utter poverty; may have to beg with a begging bowl; planets in no.4 will be helpful; if no.4 is vacant, remedy lies through Moon; must not have illicit relations with other women; may suffer from skin disease; impurities in blood; bad domestic life. (Remedy lies in: (a) Giving milk to snake on Shiva's idol. (b) Donating articles concerning Moon. (c) Donating cow.
All other Houses	Individual effects.

Remedies for malefic Sun-Venus:

(a) Wife should wear gold bangle on right hand.

(b) Donate barley (jwar in Hindi) equal to the weight of wife, if she does not keep good health.

(c) Must not take jaggery (gur) after marriage.

3. Sun–Mars

(Ancestral wealth and property)

Both the planets will give combined effect till the 48th year in the ratio of 1 : 2 (Sun one and Mars two). Sun will be exalted; when Mars is exalted, Sun will confer the best results, but bad in respect of the Moon, i.e., mother, treasury and articles concerning Moon. In other words, mother of such a person will remain ill and sad after his birth. Without Sun, Mars is malefic, but when both of them combine, Mars is no longer bad and debilitated; Sun is light and Mars is its rays, and the resultant effect is good in every respect.

Good effects

Best results regarding things, relatives, own children and employment concerning Mars; four-cornered house confers exalted results; such a person and his elder brother will be rich and landlords; best fate since birth; victorious over enemies; age 100 years; noble-hearted, pious and fortunate; the more he grows up, the better status he enjoys.

House No.	Good Effect
1 & 2	Exalted results like the rising Sun; noble-hearted; age 100 years; always victorious over enemies.
9 & 10	Exalted status; rich and fortunate if Saturn is in no.11 and Moon in no.4.
3, 4, 5, 6, 7, 8, 11, 12	Individual effect; but Sun's effect will be the best.

Bad effects

When Mars is debilitating (Mangalik), one must not reside in a three or twelve-cornered house, it will give worst results. He may have to face stiff opposition and deception in employment and worldly affairs, but not death; will see deaths of close relatives; may suffer from bad eyesight.

House No.	Bad Effect
1 & 2	If Mangalik (debilitating Mars) one may die in a battlefield or in a scuffle.
9 & 10	Problems and clash with relatives over money matters if Mangalik (malefic Mars).
3, 4, 5, 6, 7, 8, 11, 12	Individual effect.

4. Sun–Mercury

(Govt. job; bureaucrat; red alum; white glass)

Both the planets will give combined effect till 39th year; their effect will be in the ratio of 2:1 i.e. Sun two parts and Mercury one part; but Sun will confer exalted results, when Sun-Mercury are combined; Mercury may be malefic and destroyed. In other words, houses in which Sun is debilitating, Mercury will give bad effect and when Mercury is malefic, Sun may have a small dark patch but Mercury and things associated with it will help Sun. If Sun is the soul, Mercury is the pen with which God writes the fate of man and if Sun is the monkey, Mercury is the tail which will help the master; Mercury will not give its individual effect till 17th year (half of Mercury's span of 34 years). When both of them are combined, it is the effect of benefic Mars; he will have the courage of conviction and will believe in his own power and talent. When both of them are aspected by Saturn, one may gain through Saturn's business till 37th year, but govt. job may not be beneficial. If Moon and Jupiter aspect them, results may not be good.

Good effects

Will have a govt. job which will be beneficial; long life; good education; man of letters; a good writer.

255

House No.	Good Effect
1	A competent minister; best luck; exalted status; mathematician; expert in yoga; rich; exalted govt. job; will be victorious in all official problems, provided it is not associated with Saturn i.e. Saturn should not be in no.6 & 7 and all will be benefic, if friends are in no.6 & 7.
2	Best effect on mind and body i.e. healthy and noble; effect of no.1 will also be visible.
3	Rahu will not exercise bad effect; best results, if having a true lover and sincere friend.
4 & 5	Individual but good effect of both planets; in no.4, it is Rajayog i.e. exalted status; may earn a lot through business of silk and cloth. When both of them are in no.5, there will be no adverse effect on parents and children; age at least 90 years; but sudden death.
6	Good results regarding fate and children when both of them are benefic and no.2 is vacant; even if Sun is benefic and Mercury is malefic because of adverse aspect from no.2, good results regarding fate.
7	The good or bad effect of wife will depend upon the positioning of Venus in the horoscope; if exalted, wife will be from a rich family and will be pure and chaste like the rays of the Sun; in fact, best and most comfortable domestic life. If Venus is exalted, the native will have a steady flow of income and a fountain of wealth will gush out; during bad days, he will have the courage to cross over the river of sorrows and will be victorious; comfortable old age. Interested in astrology and mathematics. Ketu and Mercury will give best results after 34th year.
8	Individual effect of both the planets; Mercury will confer good results provided no.2 is vacant; otherwise, it will adversely aspect and destroy the planet in no.2; but long life. (Remedy: Bury a small bottle of glass filled with jaggery in the cremation ground; only then both the planets will give individual effect.)
9	Good effect of both the planets regarding education and service after 24th year; will have steady rise and promotion after 34th year; daughter will be auspicious.
10	Rich but notorius; planets in no.1 and 2 will exercise their effect (whether good or bad) on Sun-Mercury in no.10; if no.1 & 2 are vacant, best results for both Sun & Mercury, but Saturn's effect (good or bad) will depend upon its position in the horoscope.
11	The good or bad effect of both the planets will depend upon the good or evil ways of his family members; if they are noble, good results, otherwise bad.
12	Individual effect of both the planets; Mercury will not adversely affect Sun i.e. service and employment, provided such a person keeps gold on body. Mercury will destroy the planet in no.6. (Remedy: Wear gold ring or keep gold on the body or wear yellow thread around the neck, also refer to Mercury no.11).

Bad effects

Venus will give bad effect for 25 years; troubles in childhood; problems in service, but decision will be in his favour; when Sun is aspected by or associated with enemies, Mercury's effect will be bad. When Moon is malefic, man may suffer from mental disease; when both of them are aspected by Saturn, one will lose in litigation.

House No.	Bad Effect
1	One may have quarrels and disputes with his superiors in service, but when these are aspected by Saturn, according to Annual chart one may lose his case.
2	Financially not sound or may lose his money.
3	If lustful, bad effect of both Rahu and Venus; will be notorious and selfish; unfaithful lover; will suffer losses during 17 or 34 years of Mercury's period.
5	Sudden death.
6	If Mercury is benefic and Sun is destroyed through aspect from no.2, results of both the planets will be bad i.e. ill fated, unlucky; may face humiliation; even long life is doubtful.
7	If Venus is debilitating, wife, children and in-laws will be destroyed. If house no. 9 is occupied by enemies of Mercury (i.e. Moon, Mars, Jupiter), Mercury will not help Sun till 34th year (Mercury's period), but will create humiliation for him; may also lessen or mitigate the effect of Sun. One may suffer humiliation in service temporarily.
8	If Mars is malefic, the planets in no.2 will be destroyed; Mercury (i.e. sister, aunt etc. and business connected with Mercury) will be destroyed; will be quarrelsome, cruel and of bad character; may die in a scuffle or in a battlefield.
9	When Mercury is malefic, everything will be bad during 17 to 27 years. Son will be born after 34th year. Remedy lies in Sun i.e. donation of wheat, copper or jaggery or Mars (i.e. donation of masur daal – red lentil or sugar). If a daughter is born on Sunday or Thursday, there will be no need of these remedies.
10	Saturn's malefic effect will also be visible; notorious; will himself be responsible for his own downfall.
11	If a person residing in his ancestral house starts doing malefic and bad acts, he himself will be destroyed.
12	Worst effects of Mercury i.e. unnecessary expenses and problems; physical and mental disease such as hysteria, epilepsy, depression, fits etc. Mercury will destroy the planets in no.6. (Remedy: Wear gold rings or gold chain or yellow thread; also keep saffron).

5. Sun–Saturn

General

Saturn is Sun's enemy, though Sun is the father and Saturn is the son. Sun is all light and brightness. Saturn is all darkness. Sun confers wealth; Saturn is the lord of theft and evil. Sun confers long life, but Saturn in association with malefic Mars, lays the death trap. Sun is all light and noble, but Saturn is black in its exterior as well as interior. When Saturn strikes, it gives heart-rending death; whereas Sun, if malefic, may give peaceful death.

When Sun, in conjunction with Saturn (or wicked planets), occupies any house, the associated enemy planets will give bad effect on that house; the bad results will be visible from 22nd year to 45th year. Remedy lies through Mercury; if Sun's friends i.e. Moon, Mars, Jupiter are also there, the bad effect will be visible on friends and enemies will be saved.

Sun-Saturn relationship can best be summed up in the parable of a monkey and a weaver bird where the weaver bird was sitting quite comfortably in its nest. Out of pity, the bird advised the monkey to build his house or nest before the setting in of winter, but the monkey instead of appreciating the advice, got angry, destroyed weaver bird's nest and proved to be a spoilsport. Similar is the fate of a man who is stung by a venomous snake, if he tries to help it. This, in fact, sums up the Sun-Saturn relationship and its malefic effect. In their fight, it is the nest i.e. Venus is destroyed. Astrologers refer to their enmity to that of the fight between monkey and snake; in this fight, both of them are bruised and injured. In their enmity, it is the Venus (i.e. spouse) who suffers and is destroyed; but children do not suffer. In their fight, no one gains i.e. Sun (+ sign) and Saturn (– sign), the result is neutral in the matter of fate. Saturn will never sting a pregnant woman i.e. it will not harm the son; rather it will become blind while confronting a pregnant woman.

For wealth, both will give joint effect till 46 and Saturn's effect will be 2/3rd and for father's life, both will give combined effect till 40 years and Saturn's effect will be half. Both the planets for worldly comforts will be considered together till 24th year and Saturn's effect will be 1/3rd.

When both of them are together, one of them will give bad effect; even Rahu will be like malefic Mars till 36th year. Lustful conduct and corruption will destroy Venus. Such a person is like a spinning top i.e. unreliable, when both of them are not together. If Sun is in the earlier houses and Saturn in later houses, Sun's effect will be good i.e. will have good health and cheerful face; and if Saturn is in earlier houses, one will have a weak body and gloomy look.

Good effects

When both of them are in Mars' house i.e. no.1 or are aspected by Mars, both will confer best results; business in gold and silver will be beneficial.

Note: Weaver birds ('Baiya' in Hindi) are the most community-minded birds in the bird kingdom. They build straw thatched-roof-like apartment blocks, high on the branches of trees. More than 100 to 200 pairs of birds join hands to build these colonies and teach us the lesson of unity.

House No.	Good Effect
1	Learned, man of God.
5	Man of determination, bold.
6	If both Mercury and Moon are benefic, Sun's effect will be good; happy domestic life; but Saturn's effect will be malefic. (Remedy: Keep or feed a black dog.)
7	Rich but selfish.
12	Both will confer best results; even spouse (Venus) will also be benefic.
2, 3, 4, 8	Individual effects.

Bad effects

Such a man is like a person who gleefully watches his house burning i.e. he is like "Nero. Saturn's effect will be worst like black ink. Two headed snake i.e. effect of malefic Mars and debilitating Rahu; 'Keekar' tree will signal bad days; ill health, problems in youth and loss of hard earned money are the worst hall marks of the combination; unreliable friend wavering like a chameleon.

When both of them are in a house, where one is malefic, Rahu will be debilitating like malefic Mars (whether Mars is exalted and Rahu is benefic) till 22nd year (Sun's age) or 29-36 years (Saturn's age). Further if Sun is powerful and Saturn weak, man will have physical strength but thin and lean body.

Remedy: Throw coconut, almonds etc. (Saturn's articles) in running water at the time of solar eclipse. This will help when both Sun-Saturn are together; Venus is destroyed.

Further, keep copper (Sun); gold (Jupiter) and red coral but not very bright (Mars – red stone) in any shape except triangular on woman's hair.

House No.	Bad Effect
1	'Machh Rekha' & 'Kaag Rekha' combined i.e. rich and poor alternatively; cheat like a crow; Rahu-Ketu will be malefic; son will squander father's wealth; Sun or things and business related to Sun give good results; conversely Saturn's result (regarding its business and things) will be absolutely bad; wife will also suffer.
	Jupiter or Moon in no.12 and Venus + Mercury in no.2 – A rogue or cheat; problems in employment, whenever Sun-Saturn (combined) occupies a house in Annual chart; where Sun's effect is malefic, person may be imprisoned or sent to a mental hospital.

Example	Birth Chart	Annual Chart	Effect
31st year	Sun-Saturn in no.1, Jupiter-Moon-Venus in no.12, Mercury no.2	Sun-Saturn in no.7, Venus-Jupiter-Moon in no.2, Mercury in no.5.	Imprisonment or mental hospital.

5	If Saturn is malefic and when it occupies no.5 in Annual chart, worst results for 9 years.
6	Bad plight; Mercury is malefic; even Moon gives bad results. If Mercury & Moon are benefic, Ketu's effect will be bad. Saturn's effect on Ketu (i.e. Sun and things associated with Ketu) will be adverse; utter poverty; gold will turn into dust. If a son suffers from ill health and bad eyesight, everything will be revived (good luck) after he attains 18 years of age. (Remedy: Keep or feed black dog). If Sun is malefic and Saturn is benefic, according to an aspect from house no. 2 — bad plight like that of a rootless traveller i.e. unhappy domestic life. (Remedy lies in having flowerpot full of green plants and blooming flowers or domesticating singing birds). (Remedy for domestic happiness: Bury blue flower or blue marbles in a crossing at a deserted place in the evening.)
7	May be imprisoned, if Mercury is in no.5 and Moon is in earlier houses.
8	When Rahu is in no.11 and Jupiter is in no.12, Saturn will be like a poisonous snake till 36th year of life. (Remedy lies in burying Saturn's idol i.e. black idol in the walls of the house equal to the weight of the native). For example, during the 37th year, Sun-Saturn will occupy house no. 5 in the Annual chart and if the native deals in Saturn's business i.e. housing or hardware etc. he suffers losses after losses. (Remedy: While placing the above black idol in the wall, make a small hole in the wall to allow a whiff of air to the idol. This will help.)
9	If aspected by Mercury from house no. 3, or is associated with malefic Mars, the planets in no.3 and no.9 will be destroyed.
10	Will be ruined on account of humiliation, defamation and character assassination (if Mercury is also in no.10); and whenever Mercury occupies no.8, one may suffer imprisonment.
11	The same effect as in no.9, but bad.
2, 3, 4, 12	Individual effects.

6. Sun–Rahu

Complete solar eclipse; fate completely blackened; Jupiter's effect will be that of a thief rather than a master, if one is corrupt. Just as the Sun regains its brightness after the solar eclipse, so is the case with man's fate i.e. when Rahu's adverse effect is over, one regains the lost glory and position. In such a horoscope, Mars usually dominates Rahu. During the bad effect of Sun-Rahu, if Mercury and Venus are together or if they aspect each other, there will be no solar eclipse (bad effect); one will receive monetary help in service. Sun will confer its brightness from 39 to 78 years. Solar eclipse usually lasts for two years and total period may be up to 22 years.

Good effects

House no. 5	Will be an advisor or president of an organization till Rahu's period; will not be an ordinary clerk.

260

Bad effects

Solar eclipse will be at its peak when Sun-Rahu are in no.9 or no.12. If Rahu is an earthquake, Sun is all fire. When both of them are together in a particular house, they will destroy not only that house, but also the adjoining house (the house being aspected by Rahu). For example, if both of them are in house no. 6, Rahu will adversely affect not only house no. 12 but also the adjoining house of no.7. If Rahu is in no.6 and Sun is in no.2, it will destroy not only Sun (no.2) but also no.12 and no.7.

Bad effect will be on children for 21 years (Rahu's full period or half); if Mars, somehow does not dominate Rahu, or if Mars is malefic, or the Rahu-Sun are in a house from where Rahu destroys or adversely aspects Mars, such a person will suffer from ill health and longevity of life may be doubtful. His fate will be black and dark like the solar eclipse.

Such a person may face problems in service (except house no. 5) because of his own folly; may even suffer losses and spend a lot foolishly. There may be dark-white spots and patches on the body. He is prone to allergy such as itching, eczema, dermatitis, etc. Rahu is also the lord of theft, fire and fever. If Moon also joins the Sun-Rahu, Rahu's bad effect will be limited to that house only, i.e., it will ruin that house only and will not have an adverse effect on the opposite and adjoining houses.

Remedies:

(a) In order to save oneself, from theft or losses, keep barley under some weight in a dark corner.

(b) During fever, donate barley and jaggery or wash barley in milk or cow's urine and throw into the river for 43 days.

(c) In order to revive the brightness of the Sun, donate articles concerning Venus-Mercury (combined) or those of Venus or Mercury alone.

(d) At the time of solar eclipse, throw coconut, almonds, mustard, sesame (til) and curd (Sun's enemies) into the river.

Whenever Rahu destroys Sun and man faces problems, he should burn a copper coin throughout the night (at least for 12 hours) or just burn it and let it cool and throw it into a river or jungle or a deserted place. Here is a note of warning that no child should confront or see this, otherwise it will have a bad effect upon him.

House No.	Bad Effect
1	Blind at birth when Saturn or Mars or both are in no.5 or 9.
2	Mercury & Ketu will give bad effect till the 24th year.
5	Till Rahu's period, a person will not be an ordinary clerk, but an advisor or head of an organization; bad for children till the 21st year, but good for self and career. If Moon is in no.4 – Poor in-laws and maternal uncles till the life span of Rahu, i.e., 21 or 42 years, they will have hand-to-mouth living; Moon will be destroyed.
9	Complete solar eclipse.
10, 11	Age 22 years only when no.8 is occupied by the life-destroying planets and Sun-Rahu in no.10 and malefic Saturn along with female planets is positioned in no.2, or Sun-Rahu in no.11, and Saturn is debilitating and

	occupying house of death. All the above become meaningless if Sun-Rahu in no.10, 11 are helped by or associated with male planets, such as Jupiter & Mars. In that case, one will have long life.
12	Complete solar eclipse.
All other houses	Individual effects.

7. Sun–Ketu

Sun will become dim (but not eclipsed); maternal uncles and Ketu (children) will be meaningless; whenever Sun is combined with enemy planets (i.e. Ketu, Rahu, Saturn & Venus) in any house, the results will be bad on the things connected with that house between 22 to 45 years. Remedy lies through Mercury; even if Sun's friends (i.e. Jupiter, Moon or Mars) are also together, results will be bad on these planets, but enemies will not be adversely affected.

One may have to undertake travels which may not be beneficial; may suffer if he takes advice from others; prone to allergy such as eczema, itching and dermatitis; will be responsible for his own downfall.

Fate will be dim, but not completely blackened as in the case of Sun-Rahu; it will be partial solar eclipse and the black clouds ultimately disappear.

Bad effects

Sun will become dim; loss in travels; must not act upon advice from others; prone to allergy of feet; Ketu & Venus are friends, but they are Sun's enemies. It means that his daughter-in-law will be fat, foul-mouthed and outspoken; she will bark like a bitch and will destroy his son's marital happiness; son may also destroy his wealth. The first indication of coming bad days appears when the dog cries and groans towards the Sun; will not have happiness from children; may not live to see grand-children; there will be no harm to him, but Sun will be dim.

House no. 2	Dark storm; son (Ketu) and maternal uncles will be destroyed; may suffer from urinary troubles.

Remedy: Throw coconut, almonds, sarson (mustard), til (sesame) and curd in a river/stream at the time of solar eclipse.

262

Moon – Venus

Both the planets will confer combined effect till 37 years in the ratio of 2 : 1 (Venus two and Moon one), fate will be like that of milk full of mud i.e. bad fate. (Wear silver around the neck).

The effect on houses pertaining to both the planets (i.e. no.2 & 7 for Venus and no. 4 for Moon) will be bad; in other words, Venus (daughter-in-law + natives' in-law); Moon (mother) and mother-in-law will give bad effect. There will be clash of ego between mother-in-law & daughter-in-law. It is the Moon (mother) who opposes Venus (wife). If Moon is malefic, mother-in-law will harass the daughter-in-law & if Venus is malefic, reverse will be the case. If both of them are exalted, the game i.e. battle ends in a draw. Agricultural land can be compared to Venus & the foundation of the house to Moon. Moon is all white; whereas Venus is white like curd. White cotton is associated with Venus & milky white silken clothes to Moon.

Good effects

Both will confer good results secretly; man will neither be rich nor poor i.e. may lead an ordinary life. If Moon is wealth, landed property; Venus is a beautiful woman conferring happiness & comforts (like Laxmi). The only difference is that if Moon is silver & wealth, Venus (wife etc.) is essential for domestic happiness i.e. she will be goddess Laxmi spreading happiness all around.

House no. 2	Business in medicine will be beneficial i.e. a successful pharmacist, a successful lover.
House no. 4	An eminent ascetic or fakir, parents are gentle & noble; himself a good man, when not aspected by any planet. (1) Saturn in no.10 – Will have mother's blessings. (2) Sun in no.3 – Will have father's blessings. (3) Sun in no.5 – Bashful like a girl but will not be foolish. (4) Moon in no.4 & Venus in no.7 and not aspected by any planet from no.10, will be noble & good.
House no. 7	Teetotaller; man of God; generous; if he uses his wealth for noble cause, it will have exalted effect & will be the owner of hounds & stables; if he is addicted to bad & lustful ways, he will be destroyed. Sun no.1 – Will have father's blessings.
House no. 8	For benefic results, he must serve his old mother & cow.
Other houses	Individual effects.

Bad effects

Clash between mother-in-law & daughter-in-law from the first day of marriage; both the planets will give bad results regarding worldly affairs. Mother may not be alive; if alive, she may be blind or one of them, i.e. wife or mother, will be dead.

Remedy: When Moon destroys Venus, take the help of Mercury i.e. if water is to be taken out of curd, put cloth (Moon) over the curd (Venus) and sprinkle a little ash. Now Mercury (ash) will act as a sponge over water & the effect of Venus will no longer be bad & if Moon is being destroyed by Venus, then take the help of Mars i.e. donate sugar or Masur daal.

House no. 1	Ill health of wife; she may be even mad & suffer from memory lapses.
House no. 2	Worst fate like mud in milk instead of sugar; even Jupiter will not give good effect; lustful conduct or wife's illicit relationship with other man will ruin him.
House no. 4	If malefic, he will be drug addict, lazy, and always tipsy.
House no. 7	Bad eyesight of mother; loss of wealth after marriage.
House no. 8	Impotent, coward; will squander his wealth & destroy his family's peace and domestic happiness & health through evil & lustful ways. Remedy lies in serving old mother & cow.
House no. 3, 5, 6, 9, 10, 11 & 12	Individual effect.

Moon–Mars

(Lot of wealth)

When both of them are in the houses where Moon is exalted, both will give combined effect till 52 years. When both of them are in the houses where Mars is exalted, they will be considered combined till 38 years & when Mars is malefic (Mangalik), the combined effect will be till 33 years. They will be of equal & benefic power; but when Moon is exalted, Mars's effect will be half, but when Mars is exalted, Moon's effect will be two-fold. In the case of malefic Mars, $1/3^{rd}$ effect will be bad.

When both are in no.3, 4, 8, Mars will never be malefic (Mangalik). The following aspects should be taken into consideration before making any prediction:

Aspect	Effect
(1) When both aspect Jupiter or both are aspected by Jupiter.	Very wealthy; friends will help him.
(2) Aspected by Sun or Sun being aspected by them.	'Rajayog'; eminent & exalted position; Sun's effect will be exalted.
(3) Aspected by Venus or Venus being aspected by them.	Problems regarding children; may not utilise his wealth i.e. will not enjoy his wealth.

(4) Aspected by Mercury or Mercury being aspected by them.	Businessman; learned scholar; very wise; intellectual (but may not be very rich); people may help him.
(5) Aspected by Saturn or Saturn being aspected by them (except Saturn in no.10 or 11).	Saturn's worst & most poisonous effect; danger to life from poisonous animals; may even die of snake's bite; stubborn & foolish; in short, may die by taking poison or may be killed with a weapon.
(6) Aspected by Ketu or Ketu being aspected by them.	Nearest relative (sons or nephew) may join a govt. job, but will not be helpful financially.

Good effects

Both will confer best results; life will be very sweet, comfortable & full of all pleasures like the harmonious blending of honey in milk. In short, best domestic life & worldly happiness.

House no. 2	Rich man.
House no. 3	Wise, resourceful, eminent & exalted position; may get accelerated promotions; respected by all; comfortable life; fabulously rich, but will be haughty & proud.
House no. 4	Will spend a lot (outlet for wealth), provided Mercury & Saturn are not in no.4 & 10.
House no. 7	Very rich; may die in an accident.
House no. 9	Rich but haughty, proud & cruel; rich sons; may die of a shock.
House no. 10	Good effect will depend upon Saturn's position; if Mercury & Mars are good, man is very rich, provided it is not adversely aspected by enemy planets from no.4 (in that case, everything will be destroyed).
House no. 11	Saturn will decide about wealth; if Saturn is exalted, lot of wealth, otherwise poor.
House no. 12	Most comfortable life, like honey in milk.
All other houses	Individual effect of the planets.

Bad effects

House no. 7	Greedy; may die in an accident.
House no. 9	May die of a shock.
House no. 10	Heart-rending death in an accident.
House no. 11	Superstitious & greedy. If Mars is malefic (Mangalik), man is an unsuccessful & meaningless lover.

Moon–Mercury

(Mother-daughter; sandy river water; parrot; swan; well with descending stairs)

Both the planets will be considered combined till 29 or 58 years. If Moon is exalted, Mercury's effect will be bad up to 50%. Mercury's good effect (business etc.) and Moon's good effect (travel abroad etc.) will be after 34th year.

Mercury will give worst results in its houses i.e. no.3, 6, 7 & Moon in its own house i.e. no.4 (one may commit suicide), provided they are not aspected by any planets.

Good effects

(a) When both of them occupy a house where Mercury is benefic, Moon will confer good & noble effect.

(b) When both of them occupy a house where either of the two may be malefic, both will confer good results.

(c) When both of them are not in their own houses (i.e. no.4 for Moon & no.7 for Mercury) & are not aspected by any other planet, one will be fortunate & wealthy and may have an exalted position; but will be a great coward.

When both of them combined are aspected by Jupiter or Sun or Saturn, they will confer good results.

House no. 2	Father will live long; his wealth will not be ruined; Mercury will be helpful.
House no. 4	Precious diamond; very rich; comfortable life. If malefic, refer to house no. 4 under bad effects.
House no. 6	If exalted, will have the blessings of parents; will earn as a cloth merchant, but will be a man of extreme temperament. If malefic, refer to house no. 6 under 'bad effects'.
House no. 10	Will earn a lot through travels abroad; will have the good effect of Jupiter no.3.
House no. 11	Rich; like a pearl in a shell; best results after his or her daughter's marriage.
House no. 1, 3, 5, 7, 9, 12	Individual effects.

Bad effects

(a) When both of them occupy a house when Mercury's effect is malefic, even Moon will give bad effect. Lustful conduct will ruin the man; even Saturn will be malefic.

(b) If they are associated with wicked planets (i.e. Saturn, Rahu-Ketu), results will be bad.

(c) When both are aspected by malefic Mars, Ketu's effect will be bad; but no harm to his life; may suffer from fits and swoons.

Remedy: In order to ward off the malefic effect of Mercury; take help from Rahu or malefic Mars i.e. donate articles concerning Rahu (mustard or fennel) or Mars (sugar or Masur daal).

266

House no. 3	Saturn & Rahu will be destroyed; Venus' effect will also be bad, especially when no.6 is not occupied by Mercury's friends i.e. Sun or Venus or Rahu.
House no. 4	Worst results regarding worldly affairs; both Moon-Mercury (combined) will give bad effect of malefic Saturn; will create problems for himself by meddling in the affairs of others; may also have imaginary fears & superstitions, which may lead to 'suicide' – i.e. he may commit suicide not because of lack of wealth but because of extreme depression or failure in love.
House no. 6	Such a man is a murderer (as Moon is Mercury's enemy), may have to face lot of troubles even though he may be very rich.
House no. 7	Worst results of both the planets like sand in milk; though rich, yet unhappy; mother may either die or become blind; may also suffer from fits of insanity & depression.
House no. 8	The same bad results as are mentioned in house no. 4 above.
House no. 10	Bad results regarding wife & children; if no.8 is malefic, one may meet a tragic death; worst life.
House no. 12	Saturn's effect will be poisonous, even though it may be exalted in the horoscope.

Moon–Saturn

(Weapon which may strike back like a boomerang – tortoise – sour milk – a motor vehicle – bloody well; poisonous milk)

When both of them are combined, it will be like a blind horse or a house being flooded by the waters of the river; if one is exalted, the other is malefic & hence, the results of both the planets are bad. Remedy lies through Sun. Both will be considered together till 34th year; Ketu's effect will be bad.

When Saturn's effect is good, Moon will give bad effect up to 50%; if Moon is good, Saturn will be three times malefic.

Good effects

Association with a relative of his own age (may be uncle or nephew or brother-in-law etc.), will confer good results regarding wealth and Saturn will also help.

House no. 1	The same benefic effect as mentioned in Sun-Saturn (combined) in house no. 10.
House no. 2	Best effect, if one takes interest in acts of charity and philanthropy such as providing wells, water pumps etc. If malefic, may be killed with a weapon.
House no. 3	Exceedingly rich, if benefic, otherwise, coffers without money.

House no. 4	Moon will confer the best results now; if Sun also helps, parents will shower their blessings; Saturn will be like a helpful benign snake; will be cured of physical deformity by a snake's bite; but he will be like a poisonous snake for others. For malefic effect, refer to house no. 4 under 'Bad effects'.
House no. 6	Will have his own income and houses; for malefic results, refer to house no. 6 under 'Bad effects'.
House no. 9	Good income, but bad effect of Moon; may even be blind; bad family life.
House no. 12	Will not care for money; selfish; unhappy married life.

Bad effects

Lustful conduct will spell ruin. Moon is the heart which is enticed by the beautiful locks and glitter in the eyes of a woman & it is this infatuation with a beautiful woman that may cause ruin and even death.

Such a man's wealth will be enjoyed by his wife, her relatives (in-laws), friends & other relatives (brother-in-law etc.). Whenever Moon's enemy planets occupy house no. 1 in the Annual chart, there will be incidences of theft or loss of money. Saturn's business, relatives or articles etc. will give bad effects; will earn a bad name for accumulating his wealth i.e. even his hard-earned money will bring bad name to him. Saturn's house will give sorrows instead of happiness. If Moon is exalted, it will give wealth. Saturn will be like a dirty treasurer who will not allow the owner to use his own wealth; his wealth will be of no use to him.

Such a person may have a squint in his eyes or may even be blind of an eye; he is like a poisonous snake which may bite anyone; selfish.

House no. 1	The same malefic effect as mentioned in Sun-Saturn no.1.
House no. 2	May die in an accident or with a weapon.
House no. 3	Thieves will break into his house, but will find empty boxes and coffers. (Remedy as for Saturn for wealth & for as Ketu regarding son & if Ketu is also malefic, bury red alum in the earth).
House no. 4	Man will be like a bloody well for others; may die by drowning at night when Sun is not in no.1, 7, 10 & if it is in no.1, 7, & 10, may not be drowned at night. His wealth will be used by others including his wife and beloved; woman's extravagant or lavish living. Illicit relations or flirting with others may be the cause of ruin. (Remedy: Offer milk to snake, it may help. If he is of loose character, he will suffer from the cataract of the eye or lose his eyesight; especially when Mercury is in no.4. He may die away from his ancestral home; when no.10 is occupied by the enemies of Moon or when he occupies a house where remainder is 4, he will be poor, ill-fated, beast of burden (i.e. donkey like) and will live from hand to mouth. (Remedy lies in Moon no.4 & Saturn no.4. Father may be shot dead).

House no. 5	The same effect as mentioned in Sun-Saturn no.1; bad for wealth & children; worst fate. In distress or during bad days, whole life will be like a volcano. Saturn will be like a mountain of smoke & Moon will be like a muddy ocean. In short, most ill-fated person. Mother's or his eyesight will be affected, whenever he kills snake. Saturn's big box of iron will be the cause of ruin and utter destruction; even the house may be auctioned. (Remedy: Do not keep Moon's articles in boxes of iron; keep 'dry dates' in these iron boxes).
House no. 6	Proverbial three dogs (i.e. a parasitic brother in sister's house, a parasitic grandson in maternal uncle's house & a parasitic son-in-law) are all hated and hence are the cause of utter ruin. Both Moon & Saturn will give worst results regarding their articles and business and relatives and will be ruined and they may also cause destruction.
House no. 7	Disease of the eyes; may even become blind; quarrel with Venus i.e. wife & everything connected with her will be the cause of ruin; worst family life. Must not take milk with black pepper at night; it may cause diseases of the lungs, T.B. or heart ailments which may result in loss of money or eyesight. Before 42nd year, one of the parents may die (9th, 18th, 36th year) at his birth place. His wealth will be the cause of bad name or notoriety like the 'Langur' (black-faced monkey) and Saturn will be the cause of death.
House no. 8	During Saturn's period (i.e. 9th, 18th, 36th year) one may suffer from mishaps from Saturn's articles (i.e. weapons, animals, snake etc.); bad eyesight during old age; may lose eyesight, but will never be completely blind.
House no. 9	Moon's worst effect will be like the poison in milk i.e. disturbed & depressed life; wound marks on the body; even divine 'Amrita' will be poisoned by Moon.
House no. 10	Will lose all wealth; coffers may be full, but will soon be empty; ill fated; lustful ways will be his undoing.
House no. 12	Unhappy married life.

Remedies:

(a) Take water with lemon or an iota of sugar with water.
(b) Offer milk to snake on Lord Shiva's phallus (Shivalinga).
(c) Throw coconut, almond, mustard, til and curd after the Lunar eclipse in running water or throw them in a deserted place if no running water is available for 43 days.
(d) Keep a plate of silver filled with water in an iron box (except when Moon-Saturn are in no.5).
(e) When they are in no.5, keep dry dates in the iron box.

Moon–Rahu

When both of them are together in any house, especially house no. 4, such a horoscope (native) will be noble and inclined towards religion; Rahu's earthquake can only be stopped by Moon and it does not move beyond the house in which Moon is placed.

Moon-Rahu combined gives bad effect on the house in which they are placed. If they are placed in no.1 to 6, it may have bad effect on mother's life; but will not be bad for self. If they are in no.7 to 12, there will be bad effect on mother's life; if ever they give malefic effect, it will adversely affect both mother & son and that too up to 24th day or 24th month or 24th year.

If both are in no.2, one may be poor, or may face humiliation or may earn bad name and may even abscond; but will never be arrested.

Good effects

If Saturn is exalted/benefic in the horoscope, Rahu's effect will be the best.

House no. 7	If Sun & Venus are exalted in no.11, domestic life and career will not be bad; otherwise in-laws will be ruined.
House no. 9	Ancestral house & comforts associated with it will be revived; wealth will be regained; otherwise partial lunar eclipse.
House no. 11 (Mercury in no.3 & Jupiter in no.2)	Take a thin wire of gold; heat it and extinguish its heat in milk; thereafter take that milk; it will help in the birth of children.

Bad effects

Fear of death till 24th or 42nd year (Rahu's period); skin diseases & allergies e.g. eczema, dermatitis etc. white & black spots on the body (which is not leucoderma). In-laws will be financially ruined; Moon's effect will be dim i.e. partial lunar eclipse, imaginary fears & superstitions may make him temporarily mad or he may be prone to strange behaviour.

Rahu's tremors are controlled by Moon and Rahu's malefic effect is removed by Ketu.

House no. 3	Bad effect of Mercury & Ketu till 34th year.
House no. 7	In-laws will be ruined.
House no. 9	Partial lunar eclipse; Moon's effect will be dim.
House no. 12	Bad effect on Moon & all things connected with it i.e. mother, heart, brain etc., but also bad effect on Venus i.e. spouse.

Remedies:

(a) Throw coconut, almonds, mustard, til, banana & curd in running water during lunar eclipse.

(b) Rahu's tremors are controlled by Moon and Rahu's malefic effect is removed by Ketu. If Ketu is also malefic, remedy lies in Mars or Jupiter or Moon and if they are also bad, final remedy lies in Mercury.

Moon–Ketu

(Complete lunar eclipse – blind horse – stale & sour milk)

When Moon is being destroyed because of adverse effect or is being destroyed by Mercury or both of them (i.e. Moon-Ketu) are in no.6, there will be complete lunar eclipse. Mother, though noble and religious-minded, will be defamed & may earn bad name; their malefic effect will be visible on wealth & life; regarding other matters, it will be as mentioned in Moon-Rahu i.e. read Moon-Ketu instead of Moon-Rahu for bad effects.

If Mercury is exalted, it will not be a lunar eclipse and Moon will give its good effect from 24th to 48th year. Bad period of lunar eclipse usually lasts for one year and total period is 24 years.

Good effects

If Sun, Jupiter, Mars are exalted or benefic, Moon-Ketu will give good effect. When it is helped or aspected by Mars, everything will be fine till 28th year.

Bad effects

Worst fate like that of a stale or sour milk or blind horse or a lame mother; mother's health & son's life will be doubtful i.e. grandson will not live with grandmother. Naturally grandmother should not see her grandson for 80-86 days i.e. 40-43 days before and after the birth of the child; otherwise bad effect on both.

Both Jupiter & Moon (i.e. father & mother) will not help; bad results of travels on land & sea. If Moon – Ketu are in no.2, both will be malefic and Sun's effect will be malefic till 45th year. Both Moon (mind) and Ketu (Son) will not give good effect.

House no. 1 & 8	Both will destroy the man, his peace of mind & wealth.
House no. 2	May suffer from pneumonia, gout or may be on death bed; lunar eclipse. (Remedy: Let the new born child wear silver ring on the feet).
House no. 4	Religious-minded; no adverse effect of wicked planets.
House no. 6	Worst lunar eclipse; bad for mother & son; both may even die.
House no. 9	Bad effect of both; but individual effect will be good.
House no. 12	May earn a lot, but will have nothing in the end.
Other Houses	Individual effect.

Remedies:

(a) Do not urinate at a place or spot where someone has already urinated.

(b) Do not take milk at night.

(c) Keep black and white and red-coloured things; donate articles concerning Mercury i.e. Moong.

(d) One may suffer from gout or arthritis or urinary troubles and disruption in studies. Donate 3 bananas everyday for 48 days in a temple, it will help.

(e) Throw coconut, almonds, mustard, bananas, til & curd in running water on the lunar eclipse day.

OOO

Venus – Mars

{Tandoor of mud (a fireplace made of mud for baking bread); sweet pomegranate; red mud; wife's wealth}.

Wealthy himself and in-laws; like a sweet pomegranate i.e. rich & comfortable life; travels for 20 years and comforts for 7 years; both the planets will give combined effect till 36th year; if Mars' effect is 1, then Venus' effect will be 1/3rd.

If Mars is malefic, its bad effect will be 4 parts, but Venus will still confer good effect and that will be 3 parts.

In fact, now when both of them are together, it will be the best effect of Moon; now even Mercury & Ketu will not behave as enemies. When Venus & Mercury are in different houses and Mars-Mercury together are in earlier houses in the horoscope and Venus in later houses, in that case, Mercury will help Mars & Venus both i.e. man will definitely have a son even though Mars-Mercury are in no.3 (Mercury in no.3 is like poison) and Venus in no.9 (Venus in no.9 is like malefic Mars).

Relationship between Malefic Mars (Mangalik) and Venus

Worst effect; Venus is destroyed; may cause tragic death; fear of death & fire for 17 years and sickness for 4 years; life full of sorrows and miseries. Remedy is the same as for malefic Mars.

Good effects

If both are aspected by Jupiter	Best effect; rich & comfortable life; sweet domestic life.
If both are aspected by Jupiter & Moon	Best effect regarding wealth; noble and thorough gentleman.
House no. 2	Very rich in-laws; may inherit from them; wife will bring hefty dowry; may even live with in-laws; he will earn a lot from in-laws.
House no. 3	His brothers and sisters will be benefited by his wealth.
House no. 7	Large and happy family members for four generations; very rich, but self-made; will help other members of family.
House no. 8	Himself rich and will have the courage to fight the enemies, but if malefic, ill-fated, a rumour-monger and a back-biter.
House no. 10	Wife's relatives will be rich; if the members of family of in-laws are dark complexioned, but his wife is fair-complexioned; he will enjoy all comforts i.e. rich, life of luxury and exalted status.
Other Houses	Individual effect.

Bad effects

(a) Both aspected by wicked planets i.e. Rahu-Ketu & Saturn.	Miserable life full of troubles and worries.
(b) If combined with malefic Mars (Mangalik)	Though Venus (woman) dominates all; yet in this case, Mars (malefic) destroys and dominates Venus; may cause even death; fear of fire, sickness and tragic death. (Remedy: As for the malefic Mars).
House no. 3	Man will be a womanizer and lustful.
House no. 4	Maternal uncles themselves will be ruined and will also ruin him; they may die by drowning; malefic Mars & Venus will be doubly malefic & lustful and in their quarrel, Mercury (sister-in-law) will be destroyed.
House no. 8	Back-biter, irresponsible, critic, rumour-monger; will destroy the man who helps him; but no harm will come to him.
House no. 9	Wife's health will be destroyed; her brothers should help her for better results. (Remedy: Wife should wear silver bangle with red colour).
House no. 10	Poor; quarrelsome; wife will be dark-complexioned and cunning like a snake; may even fight against brothers on the instigation of his wife; may even indulge in litigation over a trifle.
Other houses	Individual effect.

Venus–Mercury

(Semi-govt. job; artificial Sun; balance; sandy mud; water mill)

Both the planets are of equal strength and will confer the effect of Sun i.e. will be powerful like Sun; both will give the combined effect till 44th year. If Mercury-Venus aspect Mars or Mars-Mercury or Mars-Venus, Mars will poison the effect.

Good effects

As long as Venus-Mercury are not associated or aspected by Sun, results will be best; comfortable domestic life and lot of wealth. Man becomes rich; even Saturn gives good effect (except in no.4); semi-govt. job.

House no. 1	Semi-govt. job; if malefic, short-lived.
House no. 2	If of good character, results of both the planets will be exalted; rich businessman or broker.
House no. 3	Even if Moon is malefic, all relatives from mother's side will be helpful except the stepmother.

House no. 4	If Moon is exalted, no bad effect; otherwise the worst as mentioned in 'Bad effects' of house no. 4; wife's maternal uncle may help.
House no. 5	No bad effect on children.
House no. 6	'Rajayog' for self; daughters will occupy eminent position and will help father; exalted result of Mercury; women may help; comfortable family life.
Sun no. 2	Will earn a lot through printing press, publishing business, writings and from govt.
Saturn no. 2	Will earn a lot and will have honest income.
House no. 7	Exalted results, best domestic life; rich businessman or broker or middleman.
House no. 9	If no.1, 3, 6, 7, 9 & 11 are occupied by Moon or Ketu or Jupiter, Mercury will never give bad effect, even Venus will give good effect.
House no. 10	Good health and intelligent, provided no.2 is benefic or vacant; If no.2 is malefic, worst results.
House no. 12	Good health and long life.

Bad effects

He will be a womanizer and lustful.

House no. 1	Short-lived; deprived of vehicle.
House no. 2	Womanizer.
House no. 3	When Moon is malefic, stepmother will not help.
Aspected by Mars	Partnership in business with wife's relatives will ruin him; they will rather cheat him. Mercury no.3 usually destroys not only no.3, but also no.9, 4, 5 & 11; must not marry in the family of his first deceased wife. (Remedy: Donate goat). If one marries at the age of 17 or 34 years (Mercury's period) or 25 years (Venus' period), it will be bad for health and job.
House no. 4	Mercury (Musical instruments etc.) and Venus (Agricultural land etc.) will give bad effect; maternal uncles and in-laws will be good for nothing & worthless; doubtful character, mother's relatives will create problems in business; if Moon is benefic, there will be no bad effect.
House no. 5	Lustful conduct will destroy the wife.
House no. 6	If associated with Sun, opposition from women; problem in the birth of children, especially son.
House no. 7	If Moon is being adversely aspected or eclipsed by Rahu or Ketu, both Mercury and Venus will give bad effect; problem in marriage and birth of children. (Remedy: A pot of bronze will help).

House no. 8	Worst family life; (Venus is blind & Mercury is a leper – to be avoided); both sick; problem in marriage and birth of children; Venus (wife) will act foolishly; Mercury being malefic will ruin sisters and maternal uncles; perfect house of death; worst results indeed.
House no. 9	If Mercury is malefic, he will dash the hopes of elders till 17th year or the birth of first daughter; it will be like malefic Mars (worst results).
House no. 10	If no.8 is malefic, the effect of Venus-Mercury will be bad & poisonous.
House no. 11	Separation from relatives and the near and dear (Remedy as for Mercury).
Jupiter-Sun in no. 10	Bad effect; wash rosary of gold beads with milk for better results or remedy as for Moon for domestic happiness and official career.
Mars-Saturn in no. 8	Incidence of fire during the periods of Mars (28 years) & Saturn (36 years).
House no. 12	Both Mercury and Venus will be like the rabid dog or goat; bad domestic life after the birth of daughter; worst fate like the sand mixed in sugar; bad health of wife, but he may live up to 100 years; both the planets may cause ill health, if Mercury is retrograde (i.e. Saturn or Jupiter is not in no.2, 3, 12).

Venus–Saturn

(Luxurious life; black pepper & ghee; black but bright stone; mound of sand or earth).

Venus is the woman and Saturn is her eyesight; exalted results; comfortable and luxurious life; both will give combined effect till 52nd year in the ratio of 4 (Venus) : 3 (Saturn) for benefic effects; if results are bad, Saturn's share will be 1/3rd i.e. Saturn will not oppose the associated planet, but will help it till 52nd year. When Venus & Saturn are combined, Saturn refers to the native's father. In such a horoscope, Mars & Ketu are usually together; one will pray to God in his house; even Mercury will not be bad; & Rahu-Ketu will also help.

Good effects

Both aspecting Jupiter	Both will confer exalted results; father will help him; Saturn will secretly help him.
House no. 3	Both husband & wife will get everything without effort i.e. will be parasites upon others.
House no. 4	Individual effect; if Sun is in no.10, throw copper coin everyday for best results regarding income.
House no. 9	Best results; Venus will not be malefic like Mars; even such a person belongs to a family of ill-reputed and loose character family, life will be happy and will earn a lot.

275

Both in no. 9 or 12 & Jupiter in no. 5, 6, 10	Will have a lot of property and best domestic life.
House no. 10	Now Venus will be as powerful as Saturn; will lead a luxurious life in youth, but will be a preacher in old age i.e. a sinner becomes a saint in old age; will be saved from accidents and mishaps; lot of wealth.
Sun in House no. 4	Long life; lot of property; death will not be tragic.
House no. 12	Comfortable domestic life; will earn a lot through agricultural lands.
Mercury in House no. 6	Womanizer; but good domestic life; will be respected.
Jupiter in House no. 5 or 9 or 10	Rich; lot of property; happy family life; will loot others.
All other houses	Individual effect.

Bad effects

Mercury aspecting both	His relatives will enjoy his wealth or he may spend all his wealth on property.
Sun aspecting both	Heart-rending death. (Remedy: Fix an iron rod over the roof of the house to save yourself from lightning).
House no. 1	Worst results of "Kaag Rekha"; as mentioned in Saturn no.1; womanizer.
Mars in no.4, Sun in no.2 & Moon in no. 12	Lazy, indolent, poor, bundle of sorrows.
Sun-Rahu or Sun-Ketu in no. 7	Sickly; bad health; may suffer from tuberculosis (T.B.); life full of sorrows & sufferings.
Both in no. 1 along with Rahu / Ketu & Sun in no. 7	—— Same as Above ——
House no. 3	Others will enjoy wealth; Uncle (Saturn) will have illicit relations with women of loose character; or his wife may be a vagabond.
House no. 4	If Sun is in no.10, tragic & heart-rending death.
House no. 7	Relatives will join him in his business & will cheat him.
Moon in no. 1, Sun in no. 4	Impotent and coward; a good-for-nothing & worthless man.
Other Houses	Individual results.

Venus–Rahu

(A dark dust storm).

Without Mercury; Venus will be destroyed when Rahu-Venus are combined in the horoscope; both are enemies & in their fight, Venus will be the loser; there will be problems in the birth of a son; and domestic peace will be disturbed; not only will the spouse have bad health, but there will be late birth of a son. Their malefic effect will be visible when the person suffers from piles, or the disease of the anus.

Both of them in all the houses, even in no.2, will be malefic and Venus (wife) will be destroyed and domestic life will be disturbed.

Bad effects

Worst effect on the spouse's health; even loss of wealth; the first indication of their malefic effect appears on finger nails; such a man/woman becomes fond of keeping long nails and polishing them; Rahu will have its worst effect on health till 43rd year. One may have sleepless nights.

House no. 1	Wife may be mentally unsound; ill health.
House no. 3	Bad results of Mercury & Ketu till 34th year.
House no. 7	If both occupy this house, both Venus & Mercury will be destroyed; even one may lose life at 24th year, as Ketu in no.1 will also be malefic, mother & her relatives will be destroyed and Moon will also be completely destroyed. Lustful & selfish behaviour will destroy him.
House no. 12	Venus (wife) may be exalted, but her health will be impaired; husband will lose his wealth. (Remedy: Bury a blue flower in the evening to ward off bad days).

Remedies:

(a) Keep rice washed in milk and silver at home.

(b) Donate coconut or white butter in milk for 43 days.

(c) Woman should wear a silver ring or silver bangle on the right arm.

(d) Bury copper coin in a deserted place.

Venus–Ketu

Enemies till 40th year; if both of them are in exalted houses, the results are benefic; if they are in debilitating houses, results are malefic. (Remedy as for Jupiter).

Good effects

House no. 9	Although Venus in no.9 is malefic, yet both Venus & Ketu in this house will confer best results.
House no. 12	Wife will be bold & give birth to a large number of sons like a sow (female pig).
Other Houses	Individual results.

Bad effects

House no. 1	Problem in birth of children; may be issueless; when Mars is in no.4, man will be unhappy because of death of friends & children.
House no. 6	Worst fate; unfortunate; barren wife.
Other Houses	Individual effects.

Mars – Mercury

(Excuse for death; Mercury will be like partridge; red dress worn by the bride at the time of marriage; blood colour, which is not bright; red-coloured neck of wise parrot).

Both the planets will be considered combined till 45th year. If Mars is benefic, both the planets will confer equal but benefic effect; and if Mars is malefic (Mangalik), Mercury's bad effect will be twofold and life will be like sand in sugar.

Microscope; red coloured clothes of a girl; flower of a pomegranate; Jupiter's position – good or bad–will determine their effect. When Mars is malefic, Mercury will not reveal its separate effect till 17th year & if Mars is benefic, Mercury will be silent, but will oppose Mars secretly. When both of them are together in a horoscope in the earlier houses than Venus; Venus, even though placed in malefic houses, will confer exalted results.

Good effects

Son for 24 years; noble and eminent; wife will be intelligent and noble; her utterance will be like the words of God; will have a son when both of them are in the earlier houses than Venus.

House no. 1	Healthy; stout body; will spend on wife's relatives.
House no. 2	Rich; wealthy in-laws; will be helped financially by them provided house no.8 is vacant.
House no. 3	If elder brother is alive and helpful, he will lead a better life; will have blessings of parents.
Venus no. 9	Will be blessed with a son, although Venus in no.9 is malefic.
House no. 4	Will not face problems, but may create problems for others.
House no. 6	Individual but good effects of both (as mentioned in house no. 3 & house no.6 for both individually).
House no. 8	Usually Mars in Scorpio is debilitating and malefic, but in conjunction with Mercury, both will confer good results.

Bad effects

During malefic Mars, there will be fear of fire & death, loss of name & fame; humiliation; father will be unhappy; Mercury's effect will be bad; life full of worries, sickness, problems and may earn even bad name.

Remedy: As for debilitating Mars.

House no. 1	It is bad for brother; dearth of son; insipid & tasteless life. {Remedy: Bury a decanter filled with honey or sugar or fennel (saunf) in a deserted place and cover it with the leaves of 'Dhak' tree}.
House no. 3	Thief may commit theft in his house; may lose wealth; heart full of bad ideas.
House no. 4	Not a bad man, but may unwittingly or unknowingly create problems for others.
House no. 7	Worst results like sand in honey; disease of veins carrying blood; Mars (tiger) will destroy Venus (wife) i.e. bad domestic life, unnecessary fights and litigation, foul tongue; uses abusive language; full of dirty & mean thoughts.
House no. 8	Bad for maternal uncles, who may become poor and renounce the world; may even become sadhu; if they leave their native place and settle somewhere else, they may save themselves; otherwise may face problems in service leading to even dismissal; loss of money; loss in business; life worse than a dead body.
House no. 11	If addicted to wine, he may develop a squint in his eye; or Jupiter (father, gold, and teacher) & Saturn (houses) will have bad effect. (Remedy: As for Moon & Jupiter – or take water of the sacred Ganga in the morning).

Mars–Saturn

(Doctor, dacoit, soldier, coconut, almond, dry dates).

Rahu will now be exalted, wherever it may be positioned; in house no. 2, 5, 9, 12 (Jupiter's houses), their result is exalted and family life is very happy and comfortable; their combined effect will be visible till 40th year, in the ratio of 3 : 4. If Mars is malefic, its effect will be 1/3rd & if Mars is benefic, Saturn's bad effect will be 1/3rd. The total effect of these two planets will depend upon Rahu i.e. if Rahu is exalted, both will confer best results and if Rahu is malefic, both will also give malefic effect. Benefic Mars and Saturn combined will give the effect of exalted Rahu and will always be victorious over enemies. But Malefic Mars and Saturn combined give worst results regarding fate and wealth. Mars will be zero like Mercury, but will lend its strength to Saturn and will make it doubly powerful. The following chart will indicate which planet's effect will be visible:

Mars-Saturn in Houses	Indication	Effect of Another Planet
House no. 1	The day person joins govt. service.	Mars
House no. 2	His marriage & in-laws.	Venus (In conjunction with Jupiter)
House no. 3	His daughter's marriage or when she attains puberty.	Mercury
House no. 4	The day a person owns agricultural land.	Moon (Moon & Mars in No.10)

House no. 5	The day he becomes father (birth of a son).	Sun
House no. 6	When bitch conceives in his house or in front of house (bitch's pups).	Ketu
House no. 7	The day when the man enjoys conjugal relationship with wife.	Venus
House no. 8	Death trap.	Malefic Mars
House no. 9	Ancestral wealth and large family.	Jupiter
House no. 10	When snake appears during the day time in his house (do not kill it).	Saturn
House no. 11	Self-made rich, instead of inherited property. (Note: The results of both Mars-Saturn are bad in this house; theft in a sadhu's house; good income, but still under debt. {Remedy for Jupiter or Ketu, but Rahu's remedy will be the best i.e. wear sapphire (Rahu) & not diamond (Mercury), which will destroy him}.	Jupiter
House no. 12	Large family, but self-made and ancestral wealth.	Jupiter

Good effects

Both Mars-Saturn are like two dacoits, who have become friends; the old age will be comfortable like the glow of the evening twilight; bold, brave, health & terror for enemies; will get the share of his elder brothers; man having the temperament of both tiger (Mars) & snake (Saturn) i.e. will pardon the meek & humble and kill the cruel person. Because of lot of wealth, dacoits may rob his house.

House no. 1	Good results of both the planets from the day he joins service; long life; rich in-laws; travelling business will help; for malefic effect, refer to the bad effects of house no. 1.
House no. 2	Jupiter will give good effect just after his marriage; in-laws will be rich & make him rich also; may even get wealth & property from them.
House no. 3	Lot of property; bold and brave; but will become rich after daughter's marriage or after she attains puberty; for malefic effect, refer to bad effects of house no. 3.
House no. 4	Good results after getting agricultural land; otherwise bad results (as mentioned in Moon-Mars no.10).
House no. 5	Good luck after the birth of a son.
House no. 6	Good luck after the bitch conceives & gives birth to pups either in his house or in front of his house.

House no. 7	Good luck after marriage resulting in cordial romantic & conjugal relations with wife; everything including children, wealth & domestic happiness will be fine.
House no. 9	Good luck through Jupiter i.e. ancestral property; lot of wealth & royal upbringing for 60 years, provided Mercury is not associated.
House no. 10	Good luck through Saturn (whenever a snake appears in the house during the day time, do not kill it, it is, in fact, the harbinger of good fate); such a person is rich with a lot of property; eminent position; administrator, provided Rahu & Ketu are in good houses; if they are malefic, good results of Mars & Mercury will be visible after 42nd year; further, if no other planet is in house no.3, 4 and no.1, 8 are not occupied by Mercury & Ketu (Mars's enemies) and if no.3, 4 or 1, 8 are occupied by enemies, the planets so placed in these houses will themselves be destroyed and will not cause any harm to Mars-Saturn in no.10; wife will be lucky for him; in short, Saturn will never give bad effect; will be a terror for enemies; like a tiger, if provoked; four-cornered house will be auspicious.
Moon no. 4	Best luck; exalted status; administrator; dominating personality; good govt. job.
House no. 12	Individual and best results of both the planets; even Mercury, Rahu-Ketu will also give good results.

Bad effects

Worst results in respect of wealth; family life; life full of problems, illnesses & worries; may suffer from chronic diseases, but will have a long life; may suffer losses after losses, if he lends money without receipts.

Remedies:

(a) Must obtain receipt whenever he lends money.

(b) For bad health, adopt remedies as mentioned in malefic Mars no.4 and malefic Saturn.

(c) Keep the milk of mare which has just conceived in a glass of bottle, it will help in matters of wealth and will save him from theft and dacoits.

House no. 1	When Mercury is malefic, one may suffer a lot between 24 and 36 years; loss of wealth; suffer from blood-related diseases; wife's flirtation may ruin him; a black-eyed woman may be the cause of his ruin; a gray-eyed woman whether wife or beloved, becomes his associate and causes his ruin. (Remedy lies in Moon – Mother's advice and her blessings will be helpful).
House no. 2	When Moon & Rahu are in no.12, he may meet an accident or undergo loss of wealth, if he accompanies his mother or father-in-law in the evening, but there will be no such mishap during the day time.

House no. 3	Will be opposed by his own relatives; wife's relatives may poison him; unhappy married life; loss of wealth; unhappy with uncles (Saturn), younger brothers (Mars) and sons; may be even issueless.
House no. 4	If malefic, both the planets will give the worst results; may meet an accident or even death. Most malefic results as mentioned in Moon-Mars no.10. (Remedy lies in Moon – Seek mother's advice & blessings).
House no. 5	If Ketu is in no.1, will have a second son after 42 years.
House no. 6 (Ketu no. 2)	Ungrateful & selfish; may suffer from disease of the stomach. {Remedy: Donate sugar or sweets (Mars' articles) to the places of worship}.
House no. 7	Bad eyesight during old age; but not blind. (Remedy: Use of 'Charaita' may save from mental weakness in old age).
House no. 8	Trap of death; incidence of fire, death & disease; life full of troubles & miseries; both are like graveyard or cremation ground. In short, the worst results. (Remedy: Keep water of a well or handpump in the cremation ground, it will help).
House no. 9	If Mercury is also in no.9 or associated with Mars-Saturn; it will be the worst life indeed.
House no. 11	Though good income, yet still under debt; will be self-made rich & have good luck after he earns money himself; Jupiter will destroy the effect of both Mars & Saturn.

Mars–Rahu

(King-like status; king riding an elephant).

If Mars is the Mahout, Rahu is the elephant i.e. king riding an elephant; if Mars is bread & water, then Rahu is the hearth. When both of them are together, Rahu will not give the individual effect; rather Rahu becomes ineffective or zero. Rahu will not play mischief now.

Good effects

When both of them are in houses where Rahu is exalted (i.e. no.3 or 6) and when it is aspected by friends, such a man enjoys eminent status; he is like a king riding an elephant.

Bad effects

If one of them is in a malefic house, there will be white reddish spot on the body. Rahu is like an elephant which has gone mad and is out to kill his rider.

House no. 10 (Ketu in no.4 & Sun in no.6)	One may suffer from urinary troubles; or Ketu (son) may be malefic. (Remedy: Throw an earthen pot filled with barley or mustard in a river or running water).
All other Houses	Individual effect.

Remedy for malefic Rahu: One must take one's meal in the kitchen.

Mars–Ketu

(Tiger-like dog).

In a woman's horoscope, Mars-Ketu combined, will confer good results in the birth of children; his good period will start from the age of puberty and last till the 48th year. When Venus & Saturn are together or are in each other's aspect, Mars will be doubly benefic, otherwise, Mars may be malefic; in that case, remedy lies through Moon; by seven kinds of fruits in a deserted place, after washing them with seven kinds of milk of different kinds otherwise one may suffer from tremors of hands and feet or from, T.B., etc. from the 28th to the 48th years.

When there are two Ketus (one real and the other artificial Ketu, but exalted, i.e., Venus-Saturn combined or one malefic, Ketu, i.e., Moon-Saturn combined), Mars will be doubly benefic; even if Mars is malefic, Ketu will destroy the malicious Mars and make it noble.

Good effects

House no. 2	Prosperous; rich; officer; individual, but exalted effect of both.
House no. 9	Condition will change for better or worse after the 28th year; house no. 3 & 5 will be the deciding factors; if no.10 is benefic, best results. (Remedy: Bury rainwater in front of the house or fill up a pure silver cup with honey and bury it in the foundation of the house or keep it in the house. Ketu's remedy will also be helpful; or bury 'Ganga' water in the foundation or keep it, it will be auspicious).
House no. 10	Remedy as suggested for house no. 10.

Bad effects

Mars is the tiger & Ketu is the ferocious dog and in their fight, Mars' effect is secretly destroyed. Keep black & white dog and bitch for better results.

House no. 4 & 6	Worst effect of both; both will be malefic.
House no. 8	The same malefic effect as mentioned in malefic Mars no.4, Ketu no.8 & Mars-Ketu combined no.4.
House no. 10	Conditions will deteriorate after the 28th year. Mars will be malefic (mangalik) which will destroy everything till the 45th year; even Ketu will be bad i.e. son will be ruined or will not be born. (Remedy: (a) Bury a silver cup filled with honey in the foundation of the house or keep it in the house, or (b) Bury rain water in the foundation of the house, or (c) Remedy as for Ketu, or (d) Remedy as for Moon i.e. keep 'Ganga' water or bury it in the foundation of the house).
House no. 11	The same effect as mentioned in Mars alone in no.10 provided Mars is not malefic.
All other houses	Individual effect.

Mercury – Saturn

(Movable property i.e. money & household goods etc.; mango tree, flying snake; eagle-eyed).

Both will give combined effect till 40 or 79 years in the ratio of 4 : 5.

Good effects

No bad effect on children; wealth for 45 years; sons for 24 years; protection from enemies for 42 years; long & happy life of parents; lucky & compassionate; for others, he is both like a snake and eagle-eyed i.e. penetrating eyes like those of an eagle which suddenly pounces on its prey; flying snake – good for self, but bad for in-laws. Mercury with Saturn is like window-dressing or white wash i.e. outward show.

House no. 2, 12	Will earn a lot in hardware (Saturn) business; good health; sympathetic; fortunate; long & happy life of parents.
House no. 4	Mercury's effect will never be bad, even though Moon may also join them. Moon's effect will, of course, be malefic. (See house no. 4 under bad effects).
House no. 7	Rich & happy.
House no. 11	Richest man of the area, provided Rahu/Ketu is in the adjoining house; and Saturn is not adversely aspected by enemies from House no.3; (If Saturn is aspected by enemies from no.3, all will depend upon Saturn's position – good or bad); wealth for 45 years.

Bad effects

House no. 2, 12	If Mercury is malefic, father may die in an accident, or by taking wine or poison.
House no. 4	Murderer; Moon's effect will be malefic; such a person is like a poisonous snake for others.
House no. 7	Will be addicted to wine & drugs; lustful and ungrateful.
House no. 9	Bad fate till 34th year (Mercury's period); thereafter exalted results of Saturn no.9; will have the blessings of parents who will be noble and long-lived.

House no. 11	As per no.11 (good effect); but if no.3 adversely aspects Saturn in no.11, Saturn's position (good or bad) will be the deciding factor about fate.
All other Houses	Individual effect.

Mercury–Rahu

{Tiler – a small bird which is commonly found on the Banyan tree (Jupiter-Moon) and eats its fruit i.e. destroys the effect of Moon-Jupiter}.

When Mercury-Rahu are together, Mercury will be like the trunk of an elephant; when both of them are not together, and are positioned in malefic houses separately, (i.e. Mercury in no.3, 8, 9, 12) & Rahu in no.1, 5, 7, 8, 11, it will be like a jail, mental hospital, deserted place & graveyard. {Remedy: Articles (regarding Moon) may be donated to a cremation ground or graveyard, bring water from the cremation ground and keep it, it will be helpful.

When both of them are associated with Jupiter, all the three will be malefic. If they are together in house no. 1 to 6, results are benefic; & from 7-12 (except no.11) results are malefic.

Rahu is elephant's body & Mercury is its trunk, hence best results.

Good effects

House no. 2, 3, 5, 6 (own signs or friendly signs)	Best results for self & helpful to others.
House no. 7, 10, 11	Dirty hawk i.e. good for self & malefic for others.
House no. 1, 4, 8, 9	Bad for self, but not so bad for others.

Bad effects

Whenever Jupiter aspects them or they are in no.9, 11, 12, bad effect on eye (squint etc.) or tongue.

House no. 1	Problems in the birth of a son.
House no. 3	Bad results of Ketu & Mercury till 34th year; sister, though rich, may become widow.
House no. 1, 4, 8, 9	Worst results.
House no. 11	Sisters may be rich, but will become widow after seven days or seven months or seven years after marriage. (Remedy: Close the hearth or fire place, if it is towards the west, before girl's marriage).
House no. 12	Most malefic for self & also for in-laws and maternal grandmother (Rahu); life full of sorrows & sufferings; may shout like a mad man in a mental hospital or jail. {Remedy: Make 100 small balls (golis) of mud and take one marble daily to the place of worship for 100 days continuously}.

Mercury–Ketu

{A ferocious animal (named Birri) who can scare & frighten even the elephant}.

Ketu is the dog and Mercury is its tail; and both of them are enemies; if both of them are combined, Ketu will be the most malefic; there will be ups and downs in the life, but not death;

{Remedy lies through Mars (i.e. donate sugar or masur daal); if both aspect each other, fate like that of a mad dog}.

Both are malefic; Mercury will be like the tail of a mad dog. Ketu alone in no.4 is pious and noble, but with Mercury, Ketu (sons), Moon (mother) and Mercury will be destroyed; but for wealth, it is 'Rajayog' (exalted effect). Bad results regarding travels on land & ocean; when Mars is in no.12, Mercury-Ketu cannot have bad effect on no.1; during the malefic effect of Mercury-Ketu, remedy lies in Moon.

Good effects

House no. 6	Though both are enemies, yet there will be no clash between the two, provided they are not adversely aspected by an enemy planet.

Bad effects

House no. 2	If both are not aspected and no.12 is not occupied by enemies; the results are benefic; otherwise bad; one is benefic and the other is malefic. Ketu's life depends upon Mercury i.e. its head.
Moon-Rahu in House no. 8	Sister & maternal uncles will be destroyed; may be lame or suffer from Ketu's diseases (i.e. urinary troubles; arthritis etc.).
House no. 3	Worst effect of both.
House no. 6	If Ketu becomes malefic because of adverse effect from no.2, Ketu will give malefic results, but if Mercury becomes malefic, worst results for Mercury & others.
House no. 12	May also suffer from problems of legs, urinary tract, waist, feet, spinal cord etc., between the 'age' of 17 and 34; both Mercury & Ketu will be destroyed.
All Other Houses	Individual effects.

Good effects

House no. 9	Although Venus in no.9 is malefic, yet both Venus-Ketu in this house will confer best results.
House no. 12	Wife will be bold; will give birth to a large number of sons like a sow (female pig).
Other Houses	Individual results.

Bad effects

House no. 1	Problems in birth of children; may be issueless; when Mars is in no.4, man will be unhappy because of dearth of friends & children.
House no. 6	Worst fate; unfortunate; barren wife.
Other Houses	Individual results.

ooo

Saturn – Rahu

(Lord of Death; death trap; sapphire at snake's hood).

Saturn is the lord of death, who rides the elephant (i.e. Rahu); it is malefic between 26 and 29 years; thereafter it is like the helpful and benign snake ('Ichchha-dhari nag' in Hindi).

If Saturn is the snake, Rahu is the precious sapphire on its hood; when both of them are together, it is like a benign and helpful snake which does not bite and which is the lord of its own life and death. If Saturn is iron, Rahu is the flint ('Chakmak stone'). In no.8, this is like the death trap'. In no.9, both of them are exalted; it will bless the man with a king-like status.

If there is an ordinary black spot which is just bigger than a mole, Rahu will give just ordinary effect; if it is just an average black mole which can be covered by the thumb, it is 'Padam' and if it is bigger than 'Padam', it is called 'Lahsun' and if it eclipses all the planets then worst results (i.e. poor life and may even be short-lived; in the other words, such a person will be like a beggar till 39 years). If this 'Lahsun' is above naval, it will be bad for man and if it is below naval, it will destroy wealth till 39th year. When both Saturn & Rahu are in separate houses and aspect each other, results are malefic; if Saturn aspects Rahu, Rahu will seethe with anger & jealousy and will act against Saturn. If Rahu aspects Saturn, Rahu will be malefic.

Good effects

If there is 'Padam' on the right side and is hidden from view, it will confer best results; and if Saturn-Rahu combined are not aspected by any planet, whether friend or foe, results are exalted and further no other planet should be associated with them i.e. they remain together without any aspect or association; the results will be benefic & best. 'Padam' in no.1 to 4 confers king-like status; from no.5 to 8, most eminent status i.e. like a 'Maharaja' and from 9 to 12, one is 'Yogi' i.e. a mystic & spiritualist.

House no. 2	Saturn will be benefic and a helpful snake, if there is a black spot resembling a snake on the left hand. Saturn will now not adversely affect the in-laws.
House no. 3	If Moon is in no.11, throw rice in the river for peace of mind.
House no. 9	Most exalted; royal upbringing and wealth.
House no. 12	Good results if there is a serpent-like spot on the right hand, but he is secretive and clever.
Other Houses	Individual effects.

Bad effects

'Lahsun' spot on the body will destroy everything; may be even short-lived; and if long-lived, he will be like a poor beggar till 39 years; everything including life and wealth will be eclipsed & destroyed. (Remedy lies in malefic Mars and malefic Saturn).

House no. 7	Worst domestic life (even though he may be clever because of Saturn); if Venus is in no.4, 8 or 9 i.e. malefic houses, the worst results in married life and problems in the birth of a son.
House no. 9	If one develops illicit relations with women of loose character, his ancestral house (Jupiter) will be destroyed (i.e. father may have asthma and his gold may be destroyed).
Other Houses	Individual effect.

Saturn–Ketu

(Ketu will be the angel of goodness).

Such a person will have sons; both combined confer exalted results, but fate's benefic results are available after 40 years. If a third planet joins them, then all the three will be malefic; such a person is full of determination & perseverance.

Good effects

House no. 6	Best effect; there will be a line starting from neck up to the anus; age not less than 70 years.
House no. 8	If separately placed, they may be malefic i.e. trap of death; now both will be benefic & there will be protection from death; but such a man is egoist and haughty (malefic Mars).
House no. 9	Most exalted; royal upbringing & wealth; most comfortable & long life; life full of luxuries and pleasures for many generations.
Other Houses	Individual effects.

Rahu – Ketu

According to the ancient Hindu astrology, Rahu & Ketu cannot occupy the same house, but from the point of view of aspect, they will be considered together. Both of them face each other in the birth chart i.e. they are opposite to each other at 180°; but as regards aspect, they can be regarded together. Both of them will be considered together in the later houses i.e. if Rahu is in no.1 & Ketu in no.7, both will be deemed to be together in no.7. In short, node in no.1 to 6 will merge its effect into no.7 to no.12 (except house no. 5 & 11, where each node will have its individual effect confined to that house only). Bad reputation, evil deeds and bad times (Rahu's misdeeds) will be revealed by Mercury; and good times and deeds (Ketu's virtues) will be revealed by Jupiter.

Both Rahu & Ketu meet each other on the thoroughfare i.e. it is their rendezvous (meeting place). Rahu acts on the sly; whereas Ketu will act openly; but both of them are wicked planets – when Ketu is in the earlier houses & Rahu in later houses, Ketu will be zero & Rahu will usually be malefic, but not always.

Rahu alongwith Jupiter has been assigned no.12 (sky) & Ketu along with Mercury has been assigned no.6 (underworld) & both are the agents of Saturn (whose headquarter is house no. 8). Both these nodes can just act as walls i.e. may eclipse Sun or Moon, creating problems for sometime, but after the eclipse, the affected planet will regain its lustre & glory.

Whichever node (i.e. Rahu/Ketu) is in the earlier house, it will merge its effect in the later house i.e. the node in no. 1-6 will merge its effect in no.7-12 (except no.5 & 11, which do not aspect each other).

Rahu is the shadow of head & Ketu is the shadow of body. In a human body, the portion above the naval is controlled by Rahu; whereas the portion below the naval to feet is dominated by Ketu. Rahu's headquarter is the chin & Ketu's capital is feet; both meet at thumb or the forehead (which is no.2 of birth chart) or the anus (no.8 of birth chart).

Both Rahu & Ketu revolve around Mercury i.e. their effect (good or bad) is determined by Mercury's position. When both of them are in no.4 or are in conjunction with Moon, such a horoscope is good & inclined to religion & spirituality and there will be no malefic effect of wicked planets on such a horoscope. In fact, all planets become noble.

When both the nodes merge into each other i.e. no.1 merging into no.7 etc. as explained earlier, the house in which they are deemed to be together becomes malefic and all things and relatives concerning that house are destroyed. This condition is not applicable to house no. 6 & 12 where they confer individual effect (whether good or bad). Rahu's bad effect usually lasts for one year and Ketu's for two years, thus making it a total of three years. If both the planets are malefic, and start giving bad effect (when there is neither solar eclipse nor lunar eclipse in the horoscope), their total period of malevolence will be upto 45 years (Rahu 42 years; Ketu 48 years & average 45 years). In other words, the black period will last till 48th year to the maximum and thereafter everything will be fine and beautiful. This malefic period of 48 years will start from the day when either of the nodes occupies house no. 1 in the annual chart. Example: Rahu/Ketu in no.1 in the birth chart will occupy house no. 1 in the annual chart during the first year; thus the malefic period will commence from 1st year of life and will continue till 42nd year for Rahu; or 48th year for Ketu and combined effect of both will last till 45th year. In the case of house no. 6, it may start from 9th year and in the case of house no. 9, it will start from 6th year.

Rahu's malefic effect will be visible from finger nails and that of Ketu from the nails of the feet; both may start affecting the nails nine months before the actual commencement of malefic period. If the finger nails of the right hand become dirty & get spoilt, Rahu will confer malefic effect for 6 years & in case of dirty finger nails of left hand, Rahu's malefic effect will be visible for 18 years or may extend to 42nd year.

Similarly, in the case of malefic Ketu, if the nails of right feet get spoilt, Ketu will give bad effect for 3 years and in the case of nails of left feet, it will give malefic effect for 7 years which may extend to even 48th year.

Solar or Lunar Eclipse

Rahu completely eclipses Sun, whereas Ketu eclipses Moon. In other words, Rahu destroys Sun and Ketu destroys Moon during the period of eclipses. Sun is the Lord of Day and lightens the Moon; or Sun is fire and Moon is water. Sun is all anger and heat, but Moon provides peace and controls the anger & fire. Sun is completely blackened by the molten lava of Rahu, but it is controlled & frozen by the Moon. In short, Rahu may eclipse Sun, but it simply bedims Moon; & on the other hand, Ketu completely eclipses Moon, but only bedims Sun.

When Sun-Rahu are together in no.9, 12 or Sun is aspected by Rahu, there will be complete solar eclipse; and when Moon-Ketu are in no.6, there will be complete lunar eclipse. Rahu's (solar eclipse) periods will be for two years and Ketu's period (lunar eclipse) will be of one year and total malefic period is three years.

{Remedy: Donate articles concerning Venus-Mercury (combined) or (individually)}.

Rahu & Ketu are great friends and are of equal power. They aspect each other (100%) and reverse the effect of the planet so aspected:

When Sun or Moon is with Rahu				When Sun or Moon is with Ketu			
H.No.	With Ketu	With Sun	With Moon	H.No.	With Rahu	With Sun	With Moon
1	Friend	Benefic	Benefic	7	Friend	Dim	Exalted
2	Equal Power	Half	Benefic	8	Equal Power	Half	Dim
3	Exalted	Benefic	Benefic	9	Exalted	Benefic	Benefic
4	Friend	Benefic	Half	10	Friend	Dim	Half
5	Equal Power	Benefic	Benefic	11	Equal Power	Half	Half
6	Exalted	Benefic	Benefic	12	Exalted	Benefic	Half

7	Friend	Half	Exalted	1	Friend	Benefic	Dim
8	Equal Power	Benefic	Half	2	Equal Power	Half	Benefic
9	Malefic	Eclipse	Eclipse	3	Malefic	Half	Half
10	Friend	Dim	Half	4	Friend	Benefic	Half
11	Equal power	Benefic	Half	5	Equal Power	Benefic	Benefic
12	Malefic	Eclipse	Half	6	Malefic	Half	Eclipse

Rahu-Ketu relationship has been interpreted differently by different astrologers. Some call Rahu as an earthquake tremor and Ketu as the accompanying storm. Others think that they are the angels writing the book of fate (good or bad). Some are of the opinion that they are symbol of day and night. The consensus of opinion is in the favour of Rahu (as snake's hood) and Ketu as its tail or Rahu as the mad elephant and Ketu as the naughty boy or pig. It is, however, a fact that two wicked planets mislead a man to evil ways. Rahu eclipses Sun, but its tremors are checked by Moon. In short, these two represent the forces of evil. There is a saying that a secret no longer remains a secret, if it is divulged to someone and a woman who becomes a vagabond, is also not dependable, so is the case with Rahu & Ketu. They are evil persons, as they are the agents of Saturn. Further, if Rahu or Ketu is in no.8, Saturn may be deemed to be in no.8, though it may be occupying some other house. The result will depend upon the placement of Saturn (good or bad).

It may also be noted that Ketu is Rahu's alter-ego or a serf or a slave. It always follows Rahu's commands and willingly submits to Rahu's will. There is a Persian saying, which means "I (i.e. Ketu) have offered services and powers to you (i.e. Rahu); now all depends upon you, whether to increase or decrease my powers, I will act under your behest."

Remedies:

(a) If you want to assess the effect of Rahu, adopt remedy for Moon i.e. keep a pure piece of silver with you. This will help.

(b) If you want to know the intentions of Ketu, adopt remedy as for Sun i.e. keep a piece of copper with you or feed monkeys with jaggery or throw copper or wheat or jaggery into running water. This will help.

(c) If Rahu/Ketu is in no.1, remedy lies in Sun i.e. keep a piece of copper; or throw copper or wheat or jaggery in the running water or feed monkeys with jaggery.

(d) If Rahu/Ketu is in no.4, adopt remedy for Jupiter i.e. keep gold or saffron or throw gram dal, saffron etc. in running water.

(e) For Rahu/Ketu in no.7, adopt remedy for Saturn i.e. donate 'Urad' (black pulses) or coconut or almond or iron articles, such as iron tong or iron plate.

(f) For Rahu/Ketu in no.10, adopt remedy for Mars, donate or throw 'Masur' pulses or sugar in running water. Keep red handkerchief.

Effects of Rahu–Ketu in various Houses

House in which Rahu is placed	House in which Ketu is placed	Effect
1	7	Rain & storm at birth; malefic effect till 40th year on self (1st house).
2	8	Ketu will confer benefic results till 25th year; thereafter malefic.
3	9	Most exalted 'Raashi' (sign) results on the man.
4	10	Moon's effect will be bad between 24 and 28 years; thereafter good.
5	11	Very bad results, as both are enemies.
6	12	Most exalted 'Raashi' (sign) results.
7	1	Bad effect on 7th house i.e. spouse.
8	2	Rahu malefic, but Ketu exalted.
9	3	Most malefic; unhappy with thankless brothers & relatives; bad for father & in-laws.
10	4	Bad health; good for father, but bad for mother.
11	5	Bad for sons, but good for himself.
12	6	Worst effects, as both are the most malefic.

Saturn–Rahu–Ketu, their nature & effects

(Three dare-devils; personification of evil; the most diabolical & wicked planets).

All these three planets are called three wicked musketeers or evil incarnates. They are wicked planets which are full of evil & sins. Rahu-Ketu are the agents of Saturn; they may not be as powerful as Saturn, but they imbibe the sinful qualities of Saturn – their master. House no.8 is their headquarter.

Evil Nature

(1) Whenever an enemy planet, if alone, occupies the house opposite to them, that planet is completely ruined.

(2) When two or more enemy planets are aspected by them, they are doubly destroyed. Saturn, Rahu, Ketu become doubly strong & their wickedness also accentuates.

(3) Whenever an enemy planet along with a friend of these wicked planets is aspected by them, both the friend & enemy are completely destroyed i.e. they do not discriminate between a foe and a friend and annihilate both.

(4) If any third planet (Jupiter, Moon or Mercury) joins any of these two wicked planets, all the three are destroyed (e.g. Ketu, Saturn, Jupiter – children will die).

(5) When two wicked planets (i.e. Saturn-Rahu or Saturn-Ketu) are together in any house, results will be exalted for the native.

When the wicked planets give malefic results, Jupiter will also become malefic and harmful.

OOO

Combination of Three Planets

(1) **Jupiter-Sun-Moon:** Best results; exalted status; a successful businessman; eminent writer; will help others.

(2) **Jupiter-Sun-Venus:** Benefic effect concerning Venus and its articles, relatives & business; best luck after marriage; wife will be good-looking, noble & well-mannered.

(3) **Jupiter-Sun-Mars:** Most exalted; brave like a lion (Jupiter), tiger (Sun) & panther (Mars); will have the power of riding all the three animals i.e. tiger, lion & panther. Eminent status, best luck; will have the power of dominating the bravest of enemies; will have the power of life & death over others; all the three planets confer most exalted results. Even his father, uncles & elder brothers will be very powerful & dominating; even his copper will turn into gold; in short, the best combination in the horoscope.

(4) **Jupiter-Sun-Mercury:** "Perfect Rajayog", if all benefic.

    (a) **All the three in no.5:** "Rajayog"; Jupiter & Sun will be dormant; their fate i.e. father's & son's, will be unreliable; they may not be financially very sound, but still there will be no dearth of money & religious ceremonies in their house. Even if he is a prisoner, he will be a 'Royal Prisoner'.

    (b) **All the three in no.2 & Venus in no.3:** May not marry his beloved; but the girl who loves & likes him, will marry him.

    (c) **All the three in no.2 & Mars & Saturn in no.1; Moon in no.10:** Usually, planets in no.2 give their individual effect & when Saturn is in no.1 & 7 or 10 is not vacant, it is a case of 'Kaag Rekha' i.e. when such a person digs the foundation of his house, there may be danger to his father's life. Remedy: As for Mercury house no. 2.

(5) **Jupiter-Sun-Saturn:** The man will earn fame & name, if all the three are in no.6. Even if all the three are in no.5, there will be no adverse effect on children (house no. 5).

(6) **Jupiter-Sun-Rahu:** Worst effect of all the three (except in no.5); even if he is a king, he may be treated like a thief i.e. no one respects such a person.

(7) **Jupiter-Sun-Ketu:** Sun's effect will be the worst (except in no.5).

(8) **Jupiter-Moon-Mars:** Best effect of all the three planets like the combined presence of 'Peepal', 'Neem', & 'Banyan' trees.

(9) **Jupiter-Moon-Venus:** May experience ups & downs in life; sometimes very rich & prosperous & sometimes very poor. When all the three are benefic (except in no.7), they will confer exalted results i.e. milk will gush out even from mud. Mother will be a pious and noble lady, but there will be loss of wealth after marriage.

(a) **All the three in no.7:** Person is like a butterfly hovering around women or a moth fluttering its wings around a candle. If Sun is malefic, he is a frustrated lover & may be destroyed because of unrequited love.

(b) **All the three in no.2 & Mars is malefic & combust:** Person may be deprived of a son. In such a case, Moon opposes Venus i.e. man may be lustful & womanizer & may squander his wealth on keeps, prostitutes & women of low character.

(c) **All the three in no.2 with exalted Mars:** A successful lover; exalted results.

(10) **Jupiter-Moon-Mercury:** Will earn a lot from business & inheritances; best results of all the three (except in no.2, 3, 4); Mercury will now be helpful, but may have to face troubles in spite of being a rich man.

All the three in no.2	Mercury will endanger father's life; but still rich.
All the three in no.3	Worst effects of all the three.
All the three in no.4	Danger to mother's life; but still a rich man.

Remedy: As for Jupiter.

(11) **Jupiter-Moon-Saturn:** All the three planets will confer best & friendly results (except in house no. 2 & 9); Jupiter & Saturn will especially be the most friendly & exalted. Such a man will be a 'philosophers' stone' for others i.e. he will be helpful to others like a sincere friend and will have parents' blessings for a long time.

All the three in no.2	Now no.8, howsoever, malefic, will not adversely aspect these planets & Moon will never be malefic, when all the three are in no.2.
All the three in no.9	Moon's effect will be malefic; worst fate like a man caught in a whirlpool.
All the three in no.11	Mother or grandmother or aunt may commit suicide or may be killed.

(12) **Jupiter-Moon-Rahu:** Jupiter may be silent, but will not disappear; now Jupiter & Moon will not be malefic except in house no. 12, where both Jupiter & Moon will be malefic; in other houses, men & women (i.e. Venus & Moon) may have problems in mutual relationships.

(13) **Jupiter-Moon-Ketu:** Worst results of all the three like an asthmatic patient gasping for breath amid cold winds; travel will be harmful.

(14) **Jupiter-Venus-Mars:** It will be a malefic Venus which will deprive the man of children, especially son; lustful & luxurious, but troublesome life.

(15) **Jupiter-Venus-Mercury:** Problems in marriage & domestic life.

All the three in no.7	May not have lot of wealth, but will have comfortable living; Venus & Mercury will be helpful; Jupiter will be like yellow gas, howsoever poisonous it may be.

(16) **Jupiter-Venus-Saturn:** Most exalted results if in no.9; in other houses, they will be like a benefic & helpful snake; but his wife will outwardly be humble, docile, full of false smiles, but cunning & sly like a cat & will be the root cause of all clashes & quarrels in the family. Shakespeare has rightly said, "a man may smile & smile and yet be a villain."

(17) **Jupiter-Mars-Mercury:** Worst results of all the three; especially when they are aspected by or associated with Rahu.

Remedy: Worship virgins, who have not attained puberty, by offering almonds at their feet, or feed goats with grams (black or white) during day time.

If all the three are in house no.8 along with Rahu in no.11 and Ketu in no.5, sons will suffer from asthma & arthritis.

Remedy: Keep gold on person.

(18) **Jupiter-Mars-Saturn:** There will be dearth of male members (except in house no. 2); Jupiter will be malefic; may sell his ancestral property, but will have self-earned wealth; will be under debt, even though he may have sufficient income, he will be like 'Dr. Jeykyl & Mr. Hyde' i.e. a man with split personality who runs with hare and hunts the hounds; ring leader of thieves & dacoits; mean thoughts & diseases will be the cause of his ruin.

All the three in no.2	Though Jupiter may now be the leader of thieves & dacoits, yet the native will be rich.

(19) **Jupiter-Mars-Ketu:** His fate & Ketu will be malefic till 45th year, but a lame brother will be helpful, though poor.

Remedy: Place yellow flowers (Jupiter's colour) on a black stone (Saturn's colour) – it will help.

(20) **Jupiter-Mercury-Saturn:** If Mercury is malefic, all the three (except in no.12) will give worst results & such a man will be poor & his life will be full of sufferings; will be ruined if foul-mouthed (especially in no.7); but if Mercury is exalted, life will be full of comforts, luxuries & pleasures.

In House no. 12	Most exalted effect regarding wealth, comforts & pleasures; Mercury will confer exalted results like 'Divine Amrita' (the elixir of life) & will protect the native's life, property, wealth & family.

(21) **Jupiter-Mercury-Rahu:** Although rich, yet miserly & close-fisted (especially when they are in no.12); will never be poor.

(22) **Jupiter-Mercury-Ketu:** Helpful & benefic fate (especially in no.2); rich & comfortable domestic life.

(23) **Jupiter-Saturn-Rahu:** Dearth of menfolk (especially in no.12) except in no.2. Now Jupiter will be like a sadhu who will be a thief; Rahu will be a cheat & Saturn a poisonous snake. In short, all the three will spread poison & ill will all around. Such a person should never live separately from his parents & brothers, otherwise he will be completely ruined.

In House no. 2	Father, grandfather (Jupiter) or father-in-law (Rahu) or uncle (Saturn) may commit suicide; especially if their ancestral house is near a cremation ground or a graveyard towards south.

(24) **Jupiter-Saturn-Ketu:** Problems (even death) in respect of sons; worst results regarding Ketu & things connected with it.

(25) **Jupiter-Rahu-Ketu:** Worst luck; may have to face problems & enemies; may suffer from vagaries of fate howsoever clever & shrewd he may be; in short, may face humiliation, bad fate & character assassination.

(26) **Sun-Moon-Venus:** Sometimes very rich & sometimes very poor (especially in no.9); but will be a thorough gentleman, humane & kind-hearted.

(27) **Sun-Moon-Mercury:** Father & his wealth may be destroyed in 17th or 34th year (Mercury's period); even mother or grandmother may die of snake bite; especially when Jupiter-Saturn-Rahu (all the three combined or individually) are in no.3.

Ketu in no.1 or 7, or 2, or 10	Sun & Mercury will confer good results.
Ketu in no.3 & Rahu in no.2	May pick quarrel with sisters in a moonlit night.
Ketu in no.8 & Saturn in no.6	Must not ride a horse or a vehicle belonging to in-laws, when wife is pregnant, he may lose his life.

(28) **Sun-Moon-Rahu:** Worst fate regarding mother & wealth; unhappy mother.

All the three in no.5	Sun will confer exalted results; bad for children, but will not be issueless. Remedy lies through Mercury.

(29) **Sun-Moon-Ketu:** Worst effect of Ketu; restless days & sleepless nights, despite being a multimillionaire.

All the three in no.5	Sun will confer benefic results, but Moon & Ketu will be destroyed; worst for children, but will not be issueless. Remedy lies through Mercury.

(30) **Sun-Mercury-Venus:** Sun & Mercury will conspire to destroy Venus; Ketu's position, whether good or bad, will decide about domestic happiness or otherwise. If Ketu is exalted & helps Mercury (e.g. Ketu no.12 & Mercury no.3) results will be good; if Ketu is debilitating & malefic, one may not have any son or the birth of a son may be delayed till old age or even beyond 40th year. If all these three planets are in a woman's horoscope in any house, she may suffer physically & financially after the birth of a son; similar fate awaits her after the birth of a daughter also, if all these planets are in a man's horoscope. The prime reason for this dismal fate is her bitter tongue or illicit relations with a cousin, whether real or concocted, this may result in character assassination & bad name for the woman, but may or may not end in divorce. It is also likely that one may suffer from disease of tongue.

Remedy: Throw mustard oil or wine in a drain for 43 days.

All in House no. 8	Marriage in 17th or 34th year will result in death of the spouse in an accident.
All in no.3 & Saturn in no.12	Bury almonds in the foundation of the house or under a dark room in the house; it will be auspicious for male children.
All in no.9 in Annual chart	Feed a beggar with 7 chapatis.
All in no.10 in Annual chart	Marriage of sister-in-law to a relative of the native will be inauspicious.
Moon in no.9	Worst results regarding Moon & Mercury.

Remedies:

(a) Wear silver ring.

(b) If there is a bundle of 'Nawar' in the house, it should be immediately removed to ward off the evil effect of these planets.

(c) At the time of marriage or marriage anniversary, fill a pot of copper with 'Moong' (green lentil) and put a copper lid over it and throw it gently into a river or stream.

(31) **Sun-Venus-Saturn:** Divorce or separation because of some misunderstanding between couple.

Remedy: (1) Red-colour floor is inauspicious, avoid it.

(2) Bury an earthen pot (filled with red-coloured stones washed in milk) in a deserted place; it will help in removing misunderstanding.

(32) **Sun-Venus-Rahu:** Sickly & unhappy wife; especially when all the three occupy house no. 1.

(33) **Sun-Venus-Ketu:** Both Sun & Ketu will give worst results, especially when they are in no.1; wife will be sickly, depressed, unhappy & even mad, if she lives in the husband's ancestral home.

(34) **Sun-Mars-Mercury:** Will have the courage to fight against enemies; self-respecting & full of determination.

(35) **Sun-Mars-Saturn:** Rich; but when all the three are in no.11, person is a liar, obstinate & unfortunate.

(36) **Sun-Mercury-Saturn:** No clash between Sun (father) & Saturn (son); will confer good results individually even in malefic houses.

All the three in no.2, 5, 9, 12	Malefic effect of Jupiter.
All the three in no.8 & Jupiter in no.2	Refer to good effect of Jupiter in house no.2.

If Sun occupies a good house, one will earn a lot in respect of business & profession concerning Mercury & if Saturn is in an exalted house, one will earn a lot of wealth.

(37) **Sun-Mercury-Rahu:** More marriages; bad in respect of sons, provided Venus is not associated with another planet. There will, however, be no bad effect on his job; there will be, of course, bad effect on Mercury & things associated with it i.e. bad for daughter, her husband, sister etc. Remedy lies through Moon.

(38) **Sun-Mercury-Ketu:** Profession & relatives associated with Ketu i.e. nephews & nieces will squander his wealth & will be thankless & ungrateful i.e. if the native helps them, they will forget his favours, but will always remember his disfavours.

(39) **Moon-Venus-Mercury:** No bad effect of Sun & Venus; no problem in employment; age will not be more than 85 years.

All in no.4	Long life of self & family members.
All in no.5	Life span of two years.
All in no.7	Problems regarding marriage & children; marriage may take place after 34th year & there will be worst results in respect of birth of sons, if marriage takes place earlier. Moon & Mars, both will confer harmful effects; mother will be unhappy or may be the cause of grief; bad effects in respect of govt. employment or business.

Remedies:

For Moon	Pray to your family deity.
For Mars	Gayatri Paath.
Far Rahu	Donate money on the marriage of some poor girl i.e Kanyadaan.
For Ketu	Donate banana.
For Mercury	Durga Paath.
Most Important Remedy	Feed a parrot or black-coloured fish between every Friday night and Saturday morning for 40 weeks regularly. This will help.

(40) **Moon-Venus-Saturn:** Worst fate for self; if he follows the advice that God helps those who help themselves, he may be wealthy; his wealth may be enjoyed by his children; death in a foreign land; otherwise he will outwardly show off his wealth, but empty from within like a mound of mud, even his in-laws may earn bad name for no fault of theirs.

(41) **Moon-Mars-Mercury:** Good health & wealth if all are in no.1, 4, 5, but bad for wealth & health, if they are in no.10 & 11 (i.e. Saturn's homes or signs).

(42) **Moon-Mars-Saturn:** All the three (except in no.11) will confer worst results & his wealth will be squandered by brothers, uncles etc.; may lose eyesight in old age; may suffer from leucoderma or leprosy; such a man is short-tempered, but a dominating haughty officer; will earn from a govt. job.

All in no.11	Best results regarding job.
All in no.3, 4, 8	Worst results; losses in business & wealth; very bad times indeed.

(43) **Moon-Mars-Rahu:** If the child is born upside down i.e. feet coming out earlier than the head, bad for father's life; may even be a posthumous child.

Remedy: Prepare pudding (halwa) in milk; take it yourself & serve others.

(44) **Moon-Mars-Ketu:** Now both Moon & Jupiter will be malefic; and Ketu (son) will also confer bad results; may be deprived of a son till 48th year especially when all the three are in no.7 & Venus is also malefic.

(45) **Moon-Mercury-Saturn:** Except in no.4, it is the horoscope of a murderer; all the three will confer bloody results; but he will be rich & a dare devil.

In no.4	Maternal uncles will be destroyed, but poverty will not be the cause of their death.

Such a person may suffer from fits, swoons, hysteria, depression & disease of the heart.

Remedy: For swoons & fits of depression, water the mango tree with milk; it will cure him/her Mercury & Saturn (Neem, Mango tree) and Moon & Mercury cause heart disease & fits of depression.

(46) **Moon-Mercury-Rahu:** Father may die by drowning, but there will no adverse effect on mother.

(47) **Moon-Saturn-Rahu:** Saturn may give malefic effect during 33rd to 36th years or during 39th year. He is a shameless & lustful person and consequently may lose his child. Unhappy wife & mother.

(48) **Venus-Mars-Mercury:** Bad in respect of marriage, children (sons) & his own life (i.e. may even be short-lived), when all the three are in no.3.

(49) **Venus-Mars-Saturn:** Best combination in respect of wealth, domestic happiness, sons, life and all comforts; long-lived; will receive divine help when in trouble; enemies will be vanquished; may even come out unscathed from jaws of death; happiness & comforts from father. In fact, most exalted combination.

(50) **Venus-Mercury-Saturn:** Complete happiness in respect of wealth, long life of sons & domestic harmony; best combination of planets; in order to brighten the effect further, he must feed a black dog or black cow and must not allow his own black dog or black cow to be fed by others. Skylights (ventilators) in his house will be an invitation to thieves, hence they should be removed.

(51) **Venus-Mercury-Rahu:** More than one marriage, but still unhappy married life when they are in no.7.

(52) **Venus-Mercury-Ketu:** Malefic effect of all the three, especially in no.7; problems regarding marriage & children, especially sons.

(53) **Venus-Saturn-Ketu:** Lustful; may have love affair with two women simultaneously.

(54) **Venus-Rahu-Ketu:** Bad for domestic life.

(55) **Mars-Mercury-Saturn:** Saturn is doubly malefic; bad health, loss of wealth, bad eyesight, impure blood; even malefic fate etc.; maternal uncles will be ruined; those maternal uncles, who survive, must live away from ancestral house.

In no.6	Wash snake on Shiva's Phallus in a temple with milk or donate 'chana daal' (yellow pulses) & yellow articles to a temple. It will help.
In no.2 or 12	Distribute sweets (Bataasha) at a place of worship.

(56) **Mars-Saturn-Ketu:** Malefic mars (Mangalik) will be at its worst form; house (Saturn) will be in fact partly cemented & partly of mud, with a Neem tree (Mars) & dog (Ketu).

(57) **Mars-Saturn-Any other Planet:** All the three malefic; their effect will be disastrous & poisonous.

(58) **Mercury-Saturn-Rahu:** The same as mentioned in Venus-Mercury-Rahu.

(59) **Mercury-Rahu-Ketu:** Worst death & fate when in no.1; may ruin all blood relatives; deprived of a son; tragic & miserable death; if Saturn is in no.8, Mercury-Rahu & Ketu will confer individual effect, as Saturn will keep a watch on them.

OOO

Travels & Transfers

Orders for travels & transfers

Moon is the lord of sea travels; Jupiter is the lord of air travels; whereas Venus is the lord of travel on land. But Ketu has the supreme authority to order travels over sea, air & land.

Travel/transfer upto 100 days are not considered travel/transfer at all. Travels under the following conditions are considered inauspicious:

Days	Direction	Planets according to Annual chart
Tuesday & Wednesday	North	Ketu-Mars or Ketu or Ketu-Mercury in no.6.
Friday-Sunday	West	Ketu-Sun or Ketu or Ketu-Saturn in no.10 or 11.
Monday & Saturday	East	Ketu-Moon or Ketu or Ketu-Saturn in no.1 or 5.
Thursday	South	Ketu or Jupiter-Ketu in no.3.

Whenever Moon or Ketu occupies benefic houses according to Annual chart or Ketu is in earlier houses & Moon is in the later house i.e. adjacent house, travel will never be bad but according to one's desire; provided Moon is not malefic. The final verdict will, however, lie with Ketu's position in the Annual chart as under:

Ketu in the Annual chart	Result
House no. 1	Be ready for travel; orders for transfer may be issued & one may be ready to shift lock, stock & barrel, but ultimately he will not undertake the journey. Even if the person has already left, he will have to return within 100 days. It may just be temporary transfer for about 100 days, provided house no. 7 is vacant.
House no. 2	Transfer with promotion & gain; both transfer & promotion will take place simultaneously; otherwise not, provided it is not adversely aspected by house no. 8.
House no. 3	Transfer to a place away from kith & kin, if Ketu is dormant.
House no. 4	Probably there will be no transfer; if ever it takes place, it will be a place where mother resides. Transfer will not be bad, provided house no. 10 is not malefic.

House no. 5	There will be no transfer; there is likelihood of change of room or inter-departmental change; if ever, it takes place, it will be beneficial, if Jupiter is exalted.
House no. 6	Transfer orders will be cancelled once, provided Ketu is awake.
House no. 7	Definite transfer or travel to the native place, but not promotion. If a person does not undertake the journey willingly, he may be shifted in a critical condition. In short, transfer is a must & will be beneficial if house no. 1 is not malefic & Ketu is awake.
House no. 8	Transfer against one's will & choice, if no.11 is not occupied by Ketu's enemies (i.e. Moon & Mars). It is likely that one may suffer from the disease of the ears, spinal cord, legs, arthritis, gout etc. Remedy lies in Moon i.e. feed the dog with milk & simultaneously donate milk to a house of worship for 15 days continuously. Or else seek help from house no. 2 by adopting remedy for a planet in that house.
House no. 9	Most auspicious transfer; travel to the native place willingly & cheerfully; best placement, provided it is not adversely aspected by house no. 3.
House no. 10	Doubtful; if Saturn is exalted, transfer will be doubly beneficial; if Saturn is malefic, transfer is doubly malefic. House no. 2 will be helpful; give 'Argh' of milk & water to the rising Sun i.e. worship the rising Sun with water & milk, it will help.
House no. 11	Orders for transfer will be issued, but will never reach the individual; transfer will be only on paper. If transfer ever takes place, it will be 11 times beneficial, provided house no. 3 does not adversely aspect it.
House no. 12	Happy times in the company of family members; promotion is certain, but not the transfer. If transfer ever takes place, it will be very beneficial. Ketu will confer its most exalted result, provided it is not adversely aspected or poisoned by house no. 2 & 6 i.e. if no.2 & no.6 are exalted.

OOO

Marriage

Timing of Marriage

In order to find out the year or month when a person is likely to be engaged or married, the positions of Venus, Mercury & Saturn (all friends) are to be thoroughly taken into consideration along with their friendly aspects in the Annual chart. Saturn, Venus & Mercury are friends and they should be thoroughly studied before predicting marriage yoga; of course, Ketu's position may also be considered as it is a great friend of Saturn & Venus, but Mercury & Ketu together are enemies i.e. one is exalted and the other is malefic. The following positions of these planets may be examined in Annual chart:

(1) If Saturn favourably aspects Venus; or Venus & Mercury favourably aspect each other or Saturn & Venus aspect each other and above all, Saturn occupies the 1st or 7th house, marriage yoga is formed.

(2) When Mercury & Venus are separately positioned in the horoscope; and both of them favourably aspect each other, marriage time may be predicted, provided Mercury is not in no.12, where it is malefic & destroy the 6th house.

(3) Even if Venus or Mercury is malefic in the horoscope and Jupiter, Sun or Mars are associated with Venus or Moon, marriage may be predicted when Saturn helps Venus or Saturn occupies 1st house.

(4) If Venus or Mercury occupies the 1st house, marriage may be predicted.

(5) If Venus or Mercury occupies house no. 2, or 10 to 12 (except Mercury in no.12), marriage yoga is formed.

(6) If Venus or Mercury is positioned in house no. 7 (provided Moon, Sun or Rahu should not be in no.3 or 11), marriage may be predicted.

If Venus or Mercury occupies the same house in which they are placed in the Birth chart, marriage may be predicted.

Here is an example:
Birth Chart   (Date of Birth : 10-09-1972)

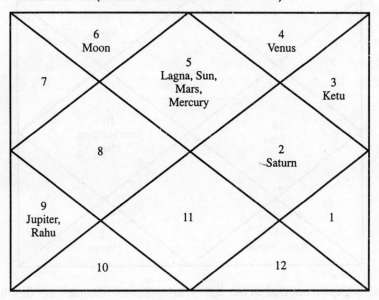

Convert it as under, taking the Ascendant (Lagna) as the 1st house.

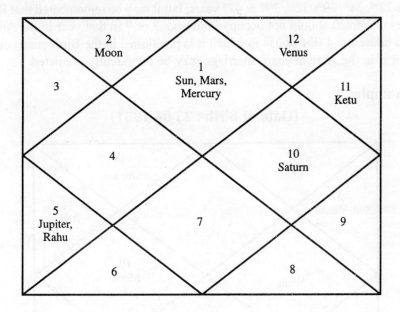

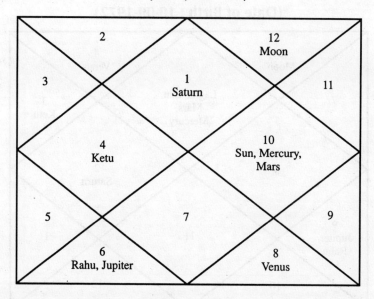

This lady was engaged/married in her 22nd year as Saturn occupies the first house.

In the case of Venus no.4 (whether alone or in association with other planets) marriage may be predicted in the 22nd, 24th, 29th, 32nd, 39th & 47th years; but it may be remembered that Rahu or Moon or Sun (enemies of Venus) should not occupy house no. 2 or 7 in that year in the Annual chart. If Venus occupies house no. 4 (the house in which it is positioned in the Birth chart) or house no. 7, of whose lord it is in the Annual chart, marriage may be confidently predicted.

Here is an example:
Birth Chart   **(Date of Birth : 23-06-1951)**

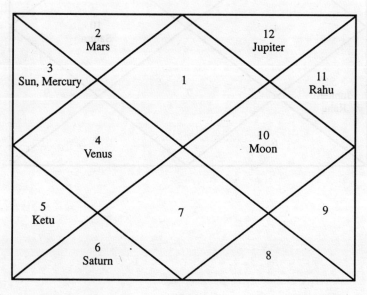

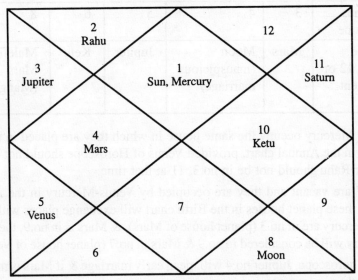

The native got married in his 27th year as Venus-Saturn aspected each other & Mercury aspected the 7th house. It was a perfect yoga for marriage, but Rahu's placement in no.2 was not taken into account, hence domestic problems, especially in the birth of a male child; so marriage should have been solemnized in the 29th year, as Venus occupies house no. 4 (i.e. the house of the Birth chart) in the Annual chart.

Inauspicious marriage yoga for consideration

(1) Marriage will be inauspicious during 24th or 27th year, if Moon is in no.1; and it is also inauspicious during 21st year, if Rahu is in no.7. In other words, a planet which destroys Venus or its house, will render the marriage inauspicious.

(2) If Venus is good or benefic or exalted, one should not have any misgivings about marriage; but this is not applicable if Saturn is in no.6 & Venus is in no.2 (in that case, Saturn will destroy Venus).

But if Mercury in no.9, 10, 12 is malefic, marriage may have bad effect regarding children & domestic happiness, especially when Rahu/Ketu are in no.1 or 7.

Note: When Venus & Mercury are destroyed or are malefic, reference may be made to Moon in place of Venus & benefic male planets in place of Mercury in the horoscope.

Auspicious time for marriage according to the Annual Chart

Name of the Planet	House No.				
Venus, Mercury combined or alone	1	2	10	11	12
Saturn at that time in no.1, 2, 10, 12 or	5 or 9	6 or 10	2 or 6	3 or 7	4 or 8
But Mercury should not occupy	7	8	4	5	6

Name of the Planet	House No.					
Mercury & Venus combined or alone	3	4	5	6	8	9
And at that time in no.2, 10, 11, 12 or in their permanent houses are	Mars	Moon (inauspicious marriage)	Jupiter	Ketu	Malefic Mars (Mangalik)	Jupiter

(3) When Venus, Mercury occupy the same house in which they are placed in the horoscope, or are in no.1, 7 in the Annual chart, provided Venus of Horoscope should not be of no.1 to 6 & Sun, Moon or Rahu should not be in no.3, 11 at that time.

(4) When no.2, 7 are vacant and they are occupied by Venus-Mercury in the Annual chart, the permanent of these planet houses in the Birth chart will exchange places with Venus-Mercury e.g. Venus/Mercury are in no.3 (planet house of Mars), & Mars is in no.9, then in the 17th year, Venus-Mercury will be considered in no.9 & Mars in no.7 (planet house of Venus & Mercury).

(5) In a woman's horoscope, Jupiter no.4 will mean early marriage & if Mars is malefic along with Jupiter, her father-in-law may not survive.

(6) When Rahu is in no.1 or 7 or is in direct aspect or clash with Venus, marriage at the age of 21 years will be meaningless & inauspicious; so is the case with Sun-Venus combination, when marriage between 22 and 25 years (especially 22nd & 25th year) will be meaningless. For remedy, refer to Sun-Venus combination.

(7) Father, whose Moon is in no.11, must not perform 'Kanyadaan' (giving the hand of daughter to the bridegroom) in the early morning (time reserved for Ketu which is Moon's enemy), otherwise either of the two will pass through bad days. This condition also applies to the bride-groom whose Moon is in no.11.

(8) Man with Saturn in no.7 must marry early (may be before the age of 22 years), otherwise he may lose eyesight or it may be badly affected.

(9) Jupiter in no.1 & 7th house vacant, early marriage is auspicious.

Marriage Agreement

In almost every Hindu family, an astrologer is consulted on the eve of engagement regarding the compatibility of the horoscopes of both the girl & the boy. If the astrologer tallies the horoscopes, the parents give their consent and marriage is solemnized. The traditional astrologer tallies the birth chart on the basis of a ready-reckoner printed in all Panchangs & Jantris (ephemerides). These ready-reckoners vouch safe for the compatibility of the birth charts on the basis of 'Nakshatras', 'Raashis' & 'Gunas' – but many a time it is found that these charts give disappointing results. It is therefore recommended that besides tallying the horoscope on the traditional basis, the astrologers must also tally the planets and their placement and aspects. Further 'Mangalik' or malefic Mars may also be taken into consideration.

It is also recommended that the Annual chart of the prospective husband & wife for a few years may also be prepared & results be computed to see whether their life will be good or bad; or whether both will have a long life or whether there will be death or separation.

Following is the example:

Birth Chart (April, 1974)

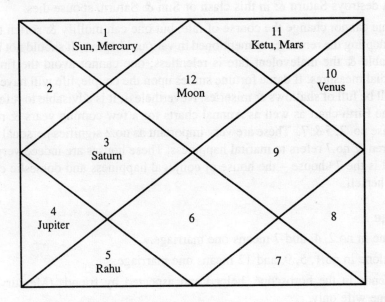

Annual Chart – 26th year

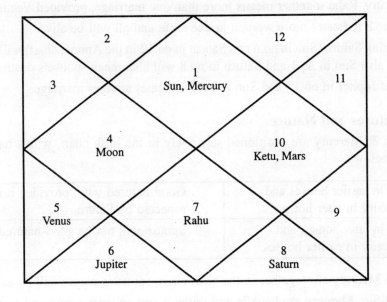

During the 26th year, she lost her husband in an accident, though she & her son survived. She inherited a lot of property from her deceased husband, but could not bear the shock. She should have, in fact, married the man after 26th year. Please refer to Sun no.1 & Saturn no.8 – death of spouse; as Sun destroys Saturn & in this clash of Sun & Saturn, spouse dies.

It is true one cannot change the course of fate, but one can mollify & soften the malevolence of planets by adopting the remedies as mentioned in various chapters. It should not be forgotten that death is inevitable & the malevolent fate is relentless; one cannot avoid the final hour, despite adopting remedial measures. If dame fortune smiles upon the couple, life will have smooth sailing, otherwise it will be full of shallows & miseries. Nevertheless, it is advisable to refer to the position of planets in the Birth chart as well as Annual charts for a few coming years & reference should be made to house no. 2, 5 & 7. These are very important as no.2 signifies personal happiness; no.5 indicates children & no.7 refers to marital happiness. These houses are indeed very important, but most important is the 7th house – the house of conjugal happiness and domestic comforts, whose Lord is Venus herself.

One Marriage

(1) Venus alone in no.2, 4, and 7 means one marriage.

(2) Mercury alone in no.1, 5, 9, and 12 means one marriage.

(3) Exalted Venus in the horoscope, helped and aspected by friends (Mercury, Saturn, Ketu) signifies one wife only.

More than One Marriage

(1) Debilitated Venus indicates more than one marriage.

(2) Sun, Mercury, Rahu together means more than one marriage, provided Venus is not alone.

(3) Mercury no.8 indicates more women in one's life and all will be alive.

(4) Sun aspecting Saturn (Sun in no.6 and Saturn in no.12 in the Annual chart) will cause spouse's death and also Sun in no.1 and Saturn in no.8 will also mean spouse's death.

(5) Debilitated Jupiter in no.10 and Sun in no.5 indicates another marriage.

Spouse's Features and Nature

(1) When Sun & Mercury are positioned separately in the birth chart, wife's nature will be as indicated below:

Sun in earlier houses and Mercury in later houses	Good-natured wife, provided it is not aspected by Saturn.
Sun in later houses and Mercury in earlier houses	Spouse will not be good-natured.

(2) If Sun and Mercury are together in the birth chart, spouse's nature will be as under:

   (a) When Sun-Mercury are benefic and without any adverse aspect and also not joined by Saturn or enemy planets, spouse will be good-natured.

(b) When Sun-Mercury are adversely aspected or joined by enemy planets, spouse will be cunning and sly like a snake.

One Living Spouse and Happy Domestic Life

(1) Mercury and Venus are exalted with friendly aspects.

(2) Saturn aspecting Sun.

(3) Saturn & Venus helping each other and without any inimical aspect.

(4) Mercury in house no. 1 or 6 and Venus benefic.

In all above cases, there will be one living spouse full of family bliss and happiness.

Spouse's Death

(1) One loses one's spouse when Mercury and Venus are aspected and destroyed by enemy planets; or

(2) Sun & Ketu are malefically joined with or destroy Mercury through adverse aspect.

Impotent Man

(1) Saturn in no.7 and Moon in no.1.

(2) Sun in no.4 and Venus in no.5, these configurations of planets make a man impotent.

Infertile Woman

(1) Venus alone in no.2 or 6, without any aspect or association with any other planet. Such a woman cannot produce a child, although she may be full of all womanly qualities and bringer of good fortune to her husband.

Couple will have a Son

(1) Exalted Venus in no.2 or 6 and helped by Jupiter or Sun.

(2) Sun in no.6 and a friend in no.12.

(3) Rahu in no.3. Such a man will be blessed with a son.

Mutual Relationship between Husband & Wife

Domestic Life

Benefic/Exalted Venus & aspected or helped by a friend.	Long life of wife & comfortable domestic life.
Benefic/Exalted Mercury & aspected or helped by a friend.	Long life of husband & comfortable domestic life.
Benefic/Exalted Venus & Mercury and aspected or helped by a friend.	Long life of both wife & husband and comfortable domestic life.

Mercury-Saturn together or Jupiter alone in no.10	Husband unhappy
Venus' enemies in no.7 (i.e. Rahu, Moon, Sun) or Moon-Saturn combined or Mercury-Moon combined or benefic Mercury, but malefic Venus or Mercury-Venus or Mercury-Venus associated with or aspected by Moon-Mars-divorce or separation.	Wife unhappy.

Mutual Understanding & Relationship

Relationship between Venus & Mercury will determine mutual fate of husband & wife (good or bad) as mentioned below:

Venus-Mercury associated with Jupiter	Will determine name, fame and good fate.
Venus-Mercury associated with Sun	Ordinary life.
Venus-Mercury associated with Moon	Will determine wealth, peace & life.
Venus-Mercury associated with Mars	Will determine the life of son.
Venus-Mercury associated with Saturn	Will determine property, house etc.
Venus-Mercury associated with Rahu	Will determine sorrow, poverty, enemies, death etc.
Venus-Mercury associated with Ketu	Will determine luxury, comforts, prosperity etc.

Birth of a Child

When Moon or Mars or Venus or Ketu or Mercury occupies house no. 1 in the Annual chart, provided house no. 5 is not occupied by any debilitated planet, birth of a child may be predicted. In case house no. 5 is occupied by a debilitated or wicked planet, there may be problems in the birth of a child. Further, if a male planet occupies house no. 1 or 5, or Ketu house no. 11 or Mars or Venus or Ketu or Mercury house no. 2 in the Annual chart, man will be blessed with a son. If Ketu is exalted in the Annual chart, son will be born and if Mercury is exalted, daughter will be born.

Note: If there are problems and wife conceives after an abortion etc., the following may be adopted for the welfare of the child and mother:

(1) Tie a red thread on the woman's wrist about 43 days before the expected birth of child.

(2) On the birth of the child this red thread may be tied to the child's wrist and the woman may tie another one.

(3) At the time of labour pains, let the woman touch two new glasses containing milk and sugar, which may be donated to a place of worship later. This will make the delivery easy and painless.

Chapter No. 32

Profession

Exalted Planets

1. **Exalted Jupiter:** Man of letters, educated, scholar, preacher & teacher, treasurer, reliable, God-fearing, good-doer, minister or advisor, noble & pious, aviation, law & allied profession.
2. **Exalted Sun:** King, emperor, controlling & dominating all; administrator, judge etc., ruler of body & soul, writing, audit & accounts, armed forces.
3. **Exalted Moon:** Prince of Wales, viceroy, respected advisor, competent & powerful minister, royal representative, ambassador, education, navy, sea voyages.
4. **Exalted Mercury:** Writer, deed writer, doctor, mathematician, industrialist, businessman, astrologer, astronomer, accountant general, speculator, investments.
5. **Exalted Mars:** Commander-in-chief, general of army or police officer, managing director, head of an organization or industrial house, wealthy, dominating, imperious, exalted status, public works.
6. **Exalted Venus:** Jeweller, trader, fond of music, poetry & beautiful women, agriculturist, affectionate householder, animal husbandry.
7. **Exalted Saturn:** Engineer, railway engineer, timber merchant, builder, iron merchant, landlord, and head of panchayat, rich estate holder, incharge of treasury & lands, machinery, medical, iron merchant.
8. **Exalted Rahu:** Incharge of jails, spying network, police, and electricity.
9. **Exalted Ketu:** Incharge of tourism, travels & transfers.

Debilitating Planets

1. **Debilitating Jupiter:** Poor sadhu, atheist, indulges in self-praise, devoid of religious traditions, hypocrite.
2. **Debilitating Sun:** Ordinary mason, faithful subject, servant, obeying others, rival.
3. **Debilitating Moon:** Poor spy, unreliable, full of mean thoughts, fits, depression, madness.
4. **Debilitating Mars:** Thief, poor, rioter, instigator, dacoit, butcher, bad-doer, notorious, drunkard, bad reputation.
5. **Debilitating Mercury:** Useless talker, chatter box, foul-mouthed, idiot, talks rot, cheap and useless learning, flatterer.
6. **Debilitating Venus:** Lover of prostitutes, sinful, lustful, companion of sinner & mean people, unreliable.
7. **Debilitating Saturn:** Illiterate, labourer, ordinary worker, miserly, slave, obedient servant, and full of mean thoughts.
8. **Debilitating Rahu & Ketu:** Mean, cheap & dirty profession.

OOO

313

Combination of Four Planets

(1) **Jupiter-Sun-Mars-Moon:** Will earn international acclaim, name & fame; will also have the most exalted effect of Jupiter no.2.

(2) **Jupiter-Sun-Venus-Mars:** Eminent position & a great scholar, will have the strength of three lions; fortunate, bold & large-hearted; royal blood.

(3) **Jupiter-Sun-Venus-Mercury:** All in house no. 3 with no.11 vacant – Must worship the rising Sun for better fate.

(4) **Jupiter-Moon-Mercury-Saturn:**

All in no.4	Bad health; wicked conduct & company of rogues.
All in no.6	Good health; good company; wealthy and will earn name & fame.

(5) **Jupiter-Moon-Mercury-Rahu:** Worst fate till 42nd year (Rahu's span); the house which they occupy is destroyed & all the four planets become malefic; but after 42nd year, all will become friends & confer best results.

(6) **Jupiter-Mercury-Saturn-Rahu:** His wealth will be destroyed in business, if they are in no.12; but money received from father-in-law (Rahu) & uncles (Saturn) will benefit him financially.

(7) **Sun-Moon-Venus-Mercury:** Exalted position of parents; a thorough gentleman doing good to all.

(8) **Sun-Moon-Mars-Saturn:** All these four planets in no.2, 6, 8 & 12 will confer best results.

(9) **Sun-Moon-Mercury-Ketu:** Father may die by drowning or die as a poor & unfortunate man.

(10) **Sun-Venus-Mercury-Saturn:** Will earn for others, especially all are in no.4. May have two wives who will be characterless & issueless; they will take pleasure in lustful conduct; in fact, useless life and may die a bad death.

(11) **Sun-Mars-Mercury-Saturn:** If all the four are malefic in the house they occupy, man is like a torn & damaged kite; if all the four are combust & destroyed, such a man has the courage to fight against enemies; if all are benefic, such a man becomes rich after robbing & cheating others.

(12) **Moon-Venus-Mars-Mercury:** Bad results, but will confer good effect after daughter's marriage.

(13) **Moon-Venus-Mars-Saturn:** Good position in a good job; comfortable life, especially when they are in no.2.

(14) **Moon-Venus-Mercury-Saturn:** Births & deaths will take place alternately or simultaneously in the family.

(15) **Venus-Mars-Mercury-Rahu/Ketu:** May face opposition from people in the marriage; may also lose wealth, especially when all are in no.7.

(16) **Mars-Mercury-Saturn-Rahu:** No bad effect on the house occupied by these planets; if Sun occupies the adjoining house, one of his brothers may be rich and the other issueless; loss of wealth; incidence of theft in the house; if Mercury is malefic, daughters will be sickly & unhappy.

Remedy: Fix a flat silver wire under the threshold; it must be of same length as the threshold.

Combination of Five Planets

The best combination of 5 planets is the one without Mercury, but it becomes all the more exalted if Rahu/Ketu is present:

(1) A 'Panchayat' of 5 planets with male, female & wicked planets (except Mercury) confers the most exalted results; such a person is fortunate, administrator, long-lived and father of eminent children having comfortable married life; in short, such a person enjoys all pleasures of the world, even though he may be a duffer & good for nothing fellows.

(2) If 'Panchayat' consists of Jupiter, Sun, Venus, Mercury & Saturn and all are in no.1 to 6, they will confer exalted results. If all are in no.7 to 12, the effect will be that of no.(1) above; but such a person will be self made rich & prosperous and will cross all hurdles, though he may feel scared.

(3) A 'Panchayat' of any five planets will confer best results in all respects. Even if such a person is a rogue & a devil, he will be better off than others.

(4) A 'Panchayat' without Saturn or Rahu or Ketu (wicked planets) is useless if that person is good & noble. In other words, the 'Panchayat' must have a wicked planet or the man himself should be wicked & devil-like so that others may respect him out of fear; otherwise a good man will be robbed & exploited by others.

Remedy: He must donate articles associated with wicked planets:

    (a) For Rahu: Barley or coconut.

    (b) For Ketu: Bananas

    (c) For Saturn: Almonds and iron articles, such as iron tong etc.

All Seven Planets Together

Although Rahu & Ketu cannot be together, yet one merges its effect into the other (e.g. Rahu in no.1 merges into Ketu in no.7). Naturally, if Rahu/Ketu are in earlier houses & all the rest are in later houses, it will confer 'Rajayog' i.e. eminent status.

All planets in no.2	Will be an administrator & ruler.
All planets in no.3	King-like status.
All planets in no.8	Eminent position, ruler, but egoist & selfish.
All planets in no.9	Exalted status, will help friends.

ooo

Chapter No. 34

Health & Sickness

(1) When Sun or Moon is associated with Venus, Mercury or wicked planets, such as Saturn, Rahu, Ketu in the Birth chart, one may suffer ill health, if the above named planets occupy house no. 1, 6, 7, 8, and 10 in the Annual chart.

(2) House no. 10 will be hit hard by the poisonous darts of house no. 5 or 6 and planets in house no. 10 will strike at the very roots of no.5.

(3) If house no. 3 & 9 are malefic, no.5 will naturally give bad effect, but when no.9 is occupied by Sun or Moon, no.5 will no longer be malefic, but will confer good results.

(4) House no. 3 occupied by malefic planets will cause illness and if it is vacant, malefic no.8 will be the root cause of troubles and health problems. If no.8 is also vacant, malefic no.5 will indicate sickness and ill health. If no.5 is vacant, no.11 will cause illness and if no.11 is also vacant, no.3 will give worst results. If all the above houses viz. 3, 8, 5, 11 are vacant in the Annual chart, no.4 will hold the secret.

(5) House no. 8 refers to disease, whereas house no. 2 is the excuse for that disease and house no. 10 will be the most malefic and give worst results.

(6) House no. 5 will indicate expenses to be incurred on illness; no.3 will pass the 'decree' for death, as planets in no.3 save the man from the malefic effect of house no. 8, provided it (no.3) is not made malefic by an adverse aspect of an enemy planet in no.11.

(7) Whenever house no. 2 is occupied by mutually opposed planets and if they are adversely aspected by enemy planet from no.8, man may suffer from illness, but its intensity will depend upon planet in house no. 10. If no.10 is vacant, the mutually inimical planets in no.2 will not cause any harm.

(8) Malefic planets in no.3 or any other house will cause mishap whenever they occupy no.3 or 9 in the Annual chart. The cause of mischief or mishap in such a case will be Rahu-Ketu. Their mischief can be prevented by adopting remedies for the planets in no.8. Perfect remedy lies in house no. 5 and if house no. 5 is vacant, there is nothing to worry.

In short, if house no. 3 is the pretext for disease and death, house no. 5 acts as the saving grace. House no. 5 instils new life even into dying body. The foundation for both these houses (i.e. no.3 and 5) is no.9. If no.3 and no.5 are vacant, the combined verdict of no.2, 6, 8, and 12 will be the deciding factor. The final appeal will, however, lie with Moon. Further, if Moon, the final arbitrator, is in no.4, even Rahu-Ketu, though occupying no.2-8, or no.6-12, will not adversely affect life. If Jupiter is debilitated, house no. 5 will be destroyed. (Refer to permanent house no. 5).

Planet in No. (in the Annual chart)	Disease or accident	Planet of House No. responsible for this	House which will help i.e. 'saving grace'
3	Sudden accident, injury or loss	1	Will be helped by no.11.
3	Will clash & betray	6	Will be helped by no.7.
3	Will maliciously strike	8	Common wall of assistance – no.2.
5	Sudden accident, or injury or loss	7	Will be helped by no.1.
5	Will deceive	8	Will be helped by no.1.
5	Will maliciously destroy & strike	10	Common wall of assistance – no.4.

Note: The above houses are according to Annual chart (refer to chart of friendship, enmity etc. at page no. 64).

Planets Causing Diseases

Here is the list of diseases and the malefic planets which cause the disease and their remedies. In the case of combined planets, remedy regarding the malefic planets is resorted to e.g. in case of Jupiter-Rahu. During bad period, Rahu's remedy is to be adopted.

If there are recurring cases of sickness and ill health in the house, following remedies are suggested:

(1) Donate ripe yellow pumpkin to the place of worship off and on.

(2) Keep two copper coins under the pillow and throw them into cremation ground or graveyard or a deserted place off and on. One will receive divine help.

S.No.	Name of the Planet (malefic)	Name of Disease
1	Jupiter	Asthma, lung disease.
2	Sun	Irregular heart-beat (when not helped by Moon); epilepsy; insanity; blood pressure (Mercury in no.12 and Sun in no.6); froth from mouth; loss of sensation.
3	Moon	Heart problem; epilepsy; eye-ailment; heart problem; irregular beating of heart; fits; restlessness.
4	Mars	Disease of stomach and intestine; ulcer; diarrhoea; cholera; liver troubles.
5	Mars (malefic)	Ulcer; boils; problem in uterus.
6	Venus	Skin disease; eczema; ringworm; boils etc. (pierce the nose).

7	Mercury	Small pox; disease concerning brain; insensitive to smell; ailments of teeth and veins; if Mercury is in no.12 and Sun is in no.6, blood pressure.
8	Saturn	Eye ailments; cough; asthma (throw coconut in the river).
9	Rahu	Fever; brain disease; plague; accidents; sudden loss.
10	Ketu	Arthritis; venereal disease; boils; cancer; urinary troubles; ear ailments; spinal cord; hernia; sciatica; dislocation of limbs; early ejection of semen.
11	Jupiter-Rahu or Jupiter-Mercury or Sun-Venus	Asthma; T.B.
12	Moon-Rahu	Pneumonia; madness.
13	Mars-Saturn	Leprosy; bursting of skin; impure blood.
14	Venus-Rahu	Impotence.
15	Jupiter-Mars (Debilitated)	Jaundice.
16	Moon-Mercury (clash with Mars)	Glands.
17	Mars-Ketu (both malefic)	Tremors in hands, feet and head; palsy; T.B., etc.

Note : For greater details, please refer to my book *Horoscope Reading* published by Pustak Mahal Publishers, Daryaganj, New Delhi.

ooo

318

Home – Sweet Home

If Saturn happens to give benefic effect on account of its priority association with or a friendly aspect of Rahu-Ketu, one will build houses. If it gives malefic effect because of clash with or adverse aspect of Rahu-Ketu, one may sell or destroy the house. In other words, whenever Saturn in conjunction with Rahu-Ketu becomes benefic, house will be constructed and conversely if the effect is malefic, house will be sold. Although Saturn may be associated with Rahu-Ketu it is opposed by them.

Example

Birth Chart   (23-11-1969)

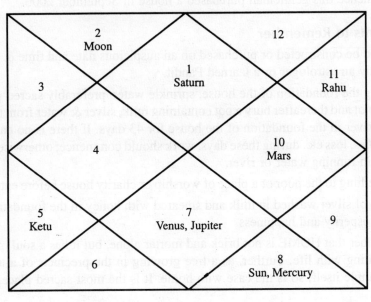

Note: Based on the chart the following positions are visible:
- House 1: Saturn
- House 2: Moon
- House 3: (empty)
- House 4: (empty)
- House 5: Ketu
- House 6: (empty)
- House 7: Venus, Jupiter
- House 8: Sun, Mercury
- House 9: (empty)
- House 10: Mars
- House 11: Rahu
- House 12: (empty)

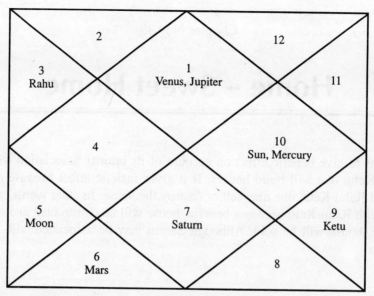

Saturn is aspecting Ketu (100%) and Rahu is aspecting Ketu (100%) and Saturn (50% – but a friendly aspect), hence this gentleman purchased a house in September 2000.

Important Points to Remember

(a) House should be constructed or purchased on an auspicious date and time & Nakshatra to be determined by an astrologer or a learned Pandit.

(b) Before laying the foundation of the house, sprinkle water, preferably sacred water, on all the sides of the plot and thereafter bury a pot containing milk, silver & water from the Ganges river or any holy river in the foundation of the house for 43 days. If there is no bad effect such as illness, troubles, loss etc. during these days, work should commence; otherwise remove the pot and place it in running water or river.

(c) Donate something to the poor or a place of worship or charity house before entering the house.

(d) Bury a piece of silver washed in milk and smeared with honey in the foundation of the house for peace, prosperity and happiness.

Please remember that HOME is not brick and mortar alone, but it has a soul of its own. It is a living thing pulsating with life. Further, as a tree growing in the precincts of a temple becomes sacred like the temple itself, so is the case with home. It is the most sacred place.

Effect of Saturn (in the horoscope) on House

Saturn in no.1	Very bad, when Saturn is debilitating; it will cause losses and destruction. However, when exalted Saturn is in no.7 and no.10 is vacant, it will confer good results concerning home.
Saturn in no.2	One must construct houses as he wishes; should not be prevented from constructing houses. Houses will be auspicious.
Saturn in no.3	One must keep or feed dogs.
Saturn in no.4	If one constructs a house, it will have bad effect on maternal uncles.
Saturn in no.5	Bad for children, if house is constructed before the age of 48 years; afterwards it is auspicious. Houses constructed by children will bring good luck. In such a case, one must donate things associated with Saturn (e.g. iron, almonds, buffalo, black lentils etc.).
Saturn in no.6	House should be constructed after 36 to 39 years; otherwise it will bring bad luck to the relatives of his daughter.
Saturn in no.7	One will have good number of newly-built houses, but must keep the threshold of the old house; it will be auspicious.
Saturn in no.8	When one starts construction of a house, there will be death in the family; Saturn's effect, good or bad, will depend upon Rahu's/Ketu's position.
Saturn in no.9	Should not construct a house when wife is pregnant; will have at least three houses; he may die after the construction of the third house.
Saturn in no.10	As long as he does not construct a house, he will have a lot of wealth. The moment he starts construction, he will lose his wealth.
Saturn in no.11	Will construct a house quite late i.e. after 55 years.
Saturn in no.12	Snake and monkey never build houses or holes; but whenever they desire, they get a house. So is the case with Saturn no.12. Such a man shall construct the house, as & when he wishes. He should not be discouraged.

Corners of a House

Before commencing work on a house, first find out the auspicious time and date. Measure the whole of the land/plot along with its corners. Rectangular/square plots having four corners are the most auspicious.

The following corners are considered inauspicious:

(1) **Eight-cornered plot:** Will get the malefic effect of Saturn no.8 i.e. will cause disease & death in the household.

(2) **Eighteen-cornered plot:** Will cause loss of gold & silver i.e. Jupiter & Moon.

(3) **Three/Thirteen-cornered plot:** Will give worst effect of malefic Mars i.e. relatives, brothers etc. may be destroyed; incidence of fire or death.

(4) **Fish-like corners (just like the raised under-belly of a fish):** Worst results; may see deaths in the family; may die issueless.

(5) **Armless-cornered plot (just like the armless or amputated arms):** May see deaths; if a marriage is performed in such a house, man/woman may lose the spouse.

(6) **Five-cornered plot:** Children will suffer & may be even destroyed.

Advice to the Owner

After measuring and seeing all the corners of the plot and before starting construction of the house, one must inspect the whole area and also the inner measurements of every room. The owner must measure the area with his own arms or measuring rod of 17" or 18" or 19". Length of the arm is to be taken from the elbow bone to the ringfinger or from the elbow bone to the middle finger.

Formula: $\{(\text{Length} + \text{Width}) \times 3 - 1\}/8$

The remainder will give the effect.

Example: Suppose length is 45 arms and width is 21 arms, the final result will be as under:

$45+21 = 66$; multiply by 3, the result is $66 \times 3 = 198$; deduct 1 from it; the resultant figure is 197. Now divide it by 8, the remainder comes to $197/8 = 24 — 5$ (remainder is 5). Obviously, if the remainder is in odd no. i.e. 1, 3, 5, 7, the results are auspicious and if the remainder is in even no. i.e. 2, 4, 6, 8, the results are inauspicious, for which the remedies may be adopted as under:

Even Remainder	Remedy
2	Jupiter-Venus in no.6 or Ketu in no.6
4	Saturn-Moon in no.4
6	Sun-Saturn in no.6
8	Mars-Saturn in no.8

Resultant Effect on the House

Remainder no.1	The effect will be that of Sun-Jupiter. Best results. Exalted status; king-like status.
Remainder no.2	Jupiter-Venus in no.6 or Ketu in no.6 – like stray dog; poor.
Remainder no.3	Jupiter-Mars in no.3 – tiger-like. Best for business; auspicious for men, but bad for children & ladies; victorious over enemies; a great rise in worldly affairs.
Remainder no.4	Saturn-Moon in no.4 – like a donkey; will work day & night and get almost nothing as wages.
Remainder no.5	Sun-Jupiter in no.5 – cow-like. All family members will be happy & comfortable; Venus will confer exalted results. Best fate. Even if the front is shorter than the backyard, results will be good.
Remainder no.6	Sun-Saturn in no.6; Ketu will give bad results; will be deprived of parental love; friends will deceive him; in fact, life will be full of difficulties & unhappy events.
Remainder no.7	Moon-Venus in no.7; elephant-like; all comforts of vehicles; even Rahu (in-laws) will be helpful.

Remainder no.8	Mars-Saturn in no.8; like an eagle or kite (bird of prey which feeds on dead animals); house of death; cremation ground or graveyard; Saturn's headquarter; end of all worldly affairs.

Main Gate for Entrance

(1) If the main gate for entrance is towards 'East', it would be the most auspicious; as one can watch people going to & fro on the main highway.

(2) The next best is towards the 'West'.

(3) Entrance gate towards 'North' or hill side is good for undertaking long travel, meditation or doing good deeds.

(4) Entrance gate towards 'South' is the most inauspicious, especially for a person with Saturn in no.3. It is bad not only for women folk, but men also. It is just like a cremation ground where everything is destroyed in fire. For such an owner, remedy lies in Mercury i.e. he should donate things associated with Mercury.

Direction of Beams

Its direction should be parallel to the main entrance door; it represents Venus, the lord of marital happiness and is, therefore, the most auspicious. If the beam is over the chest of a person who is asleep on a cot, it spells disaster, disease and trouble. (It will be the beam of malefic Saturn).

Directions for Sleeping

While sleeping at night, one must keep the pillow towards 'East'; it will be the most auspicious. During the day man's brain works & Sun helps; while during night soul exercises full control & Moon helps. The direction of the feet towards south-eastern side is ill-omened and inauspicious.

More Points to Remember

(1) If there is a 'Peepal' tree (sacred for the Hindus) in the premises of the houses or near it (but not in the walls of the houses), serve it by watering it daily.

(2) The presence of a 'keekar' tree in the premises of the house is inauspicious for children. Remedy lies in watering it on Saturday night off and on or for 43 days continuously. It will save the man from the evil effects of Saturn.

(3) Do not build a house at far end of a blind alley. It will be bad for children and may create problems and troubles.

Interior of the House

The following things will give auspicious results in the interior of the house:

(1) **Drawing & Living Room:** Should be in the middle of the eastern wall.

(2) **Fire i.e. Kitchen:** Should be towards south or south-eastern corner of the house.

(3) **Water or Meditation Room:** Should be towards the north-eastern corner or hill side of the house.

(4) **Place for Goddess Laxmi (wealth) i.e. bedroom for marital happiness & property:** Should be towards south or south-western corner of the house. It will be auspicious.

(5) **Empty Space i.e. Guest Room:** Should be towards the hill or north-western corner of the house.

(6) **Direction of Fireplace (Kitchen):** Should be towards eastern side.

The following figure will explain the above points:

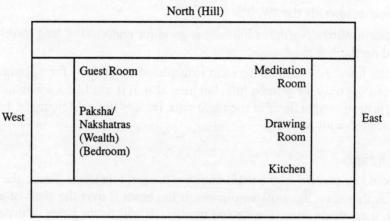

Pakshas: In Hindu astrology, every month is divided into two halves – one is called 'Krishna Paksha' ('Badi' in Urdu and 'dark fortnight' in English) and the other is called 'Shukla Paksha' ('Shadi' in Urdu & 'Full Moon'/'bright half' in English). 'Krishna Paksha' commences after 'Poornima' (15th day of Full Moon) and 'Shukla Paksha' commences after 'Amavasya' (15th day of dark fortnight).

Nakshatras (Constellation or Lunar Mansions or Asterisms): According to Hindu astrology, Zodiac is divided into 27 Nakshatras or constellations, each extending 13°–20° of arc. They are in groups of three & each is ruled by a planet i.e. 9 planets × 3 = 27 constellations. While constructing a house, favourable & auspicious Pakshas & Nakshatras may be taken into consideration.

The two figures on the next page show that every direction or corner of the house is reserved for a particular planet and articles associated with such planets are also indicated. For example, if a space reserved for a particular planet is filled with articles pertaining to its enemy, results will not be good for the owner. Suppose house no. 4 (North-eastern corner) is reserved for Moon and if someone keeps an iron box (Saturn's article) in that corner, the Moon's result will be bad.

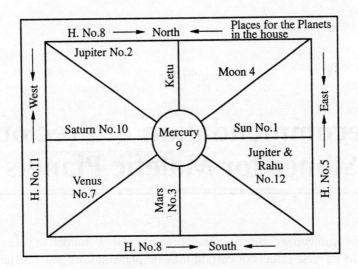

Places for the Planets in the house

- H. No.8 → North ←
- Jupiter No.2
- Ketu
- Moon 4
- West
- East
- Saturn No.10
- Mercury 9
- Sun No.1
- Jupiter & Rahu No.12
- H. No.11
- H. No.5
- Venus No.7
- Mars No.3
- H. No.8 → South ←

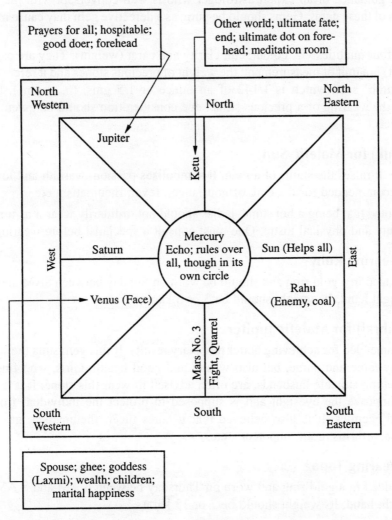

Prayers for all; hospitable; good doer; forehead

Other world; ultimate fate; end; ultimate dot on forehead; meditation room

North Western	North	North Eastern
Jupiter	Ketu	
West — Saturn	Mercury Echo; rules over all, though in its own circle	Sun (Helps all) — East
Venus (Face)		Rahu (Enemy, coal)
South Western	Mars No. 3 — Fight, Quarrel — South	South Eastern

Spouse; ghee; goddess (Laxmi); wealth; children; marital happiness

○○○

Chapter No. 36

Recommendation of Precious Stones for Malefic Planets

Astrologers often recommend wearing of certain precious stones studded in gold or silver or copper rings to ward off the adverse effects of certain malefic planets. Care must be taken to wear these gems under the guidance of an expert astrologer who is well conversant with the efficacious or injurious effects of these gems. Gems should be pure, as a defective gem may cause more harm than good.

A gem has four qualities viz. colour, cut, clarity and carat (weight). They are called four 'Cs'. A carat (or karat) is a unit of measurement, the weight of precious stones and it refers to the uniform weight of a 'carob' seed which is 1/142 of an ounce or 1/5 gms. (0.29 gms). Further, while recommending the wearing of a precious stone, due consideration should be given to the malefic planet and aspects.

1. Ruby (Manik) for Malefic Sun

It is a hot stone. It raises the status of a man. It symbolizes passion, warmth and love. It is red in colour and is recommended for the cure of gout, ulcer, fever, rheumatism etc.

It may be noted that being a hot stone, ladies should not ordinarily wear it as it may adversely affect their beauty and physical lustre. One must consult a specialist before wearing it.

Method of Wearing Ruby

It should be studded in a gold ring and should be worn on Sunday between 8AM and 10AM in the ring finger of right hand. Its weight should be 3 or 5 karat.

2. Topaz (Pukhraj) for Malefic Jupiter

It is often recommended for achieving better monetary results. If this gem suits the wearer, he may achieve not only fame and name, but also wealth and good health. Girls, who find obstacles in marriage and getting suitable husbands, are often advised to wear this stone. It is a cold gem and is believed to improve the eyesight and is supposed to protect the individual from calamities, misfortunes and enemies. It is also believed that it cures ulcer, rheumatism, gastric problems, jaundice, asthma, arthritis, gout, impotency etc.

Method of Wearing Topaz

It should be studded in a gold ring and worn on Thursday between 6 AM and 8 AM in the index finger of the right hand. Its weight should be 7 or 13 karat.

3. Pearl (Moti) for Malefic Moon

It is the best and most useful gem for ladies, as it calms their emotions and protects them from evil effects of malefic Moon. It also ensures a happy domestic life as it strengthens mental power and protects the ladies from tantrums such as hysteria, sorrows, fits, insomnia etc. Being a cold gem, it soothes the ruffled feelings and rash temperament.

It is also recommended for the cure of eye-troubles, heart ailments, T.B., hysteria, epilepsy, constipation, disorders of the uterus etc. It also enhances the body lustre of woman, makes her young and attractive, as it imparts sexual strength so as to make conjugal life happy and full of bliss.

Method of Wearing Pearl (Milky White)

It should be studded in a silver ring and should be worn on Monday or Poornmashi (bright fortnight) day between 10 AM to 11 AM washed in milk or sacred water of Ganges in the ring finger of right hand. Its weight should be 2 or 4 or 6 or 9 Karat.

4. Diamond (Heera) or Curd-like Pearl for Malefic Venus

A person wearing this stone leads a life of luxury, as it confers fame, name, wealth, all comforts and peace of mind. Being a hot gem it bestows great sexual powers. It is recommended for the cure of urinary troubles, diabetes, skin problems, V.D. etc.

Method of Wearing Diamond or Curd-like Pearl

It should be studded in a gold ring and should be worn in the middle finger of right hand on Friday between 1 PM and 3 PM or on 'Amavasya' (dark fortnight). Its weight should be between ½ and ¼ of a karat or gram.

5. Red Coral (Moonga) for Malefic Mars

It instills courage and cures blood-related diseases. Being red in colour, it is also recommended for material comforts and happiness. It cures fever, cough, bile, smallpox, loss of sexual strength, measles and headaches etc.

Method of Wearing Red Coral

It should be studded in a gold or silver ring and should be worn in the ring finger of the right hand on Tuesday between 11 AM and 1 PM. Its weight should be 9 or 11 or 12 karat.

6. Emerald (Panna) for Malefic Mercury

It enhances brain power, intelligence, memory, communication skills, and speech. Being a hot gem, it is recommended for the cure of wavering nature or indecisiveness, loss of memory, stammering, fear of evil spirits, asthma, dysentery, diarrhoea, ulcer, gastric troubles etc.

Warning: Mercury is an eunuch or effeminate; hence, the newly-wed couples must not wear this gem as it may impair their sexual powers.

Method of Wearing Emerald

It should be studded in a gold ring and should be worn on Wednesday between 4 PM and 6 PM in the little finger of right hand. Its weight should be 3 or 5 or 7 or 10 karat.

7. Sapphire (Neelam) for Malefic Saturn

Before wearing this stone, utmost care should be taken. Consult a specialist, as it can adversely affect the fortunes of a man. It must be tested for its efficacy and genuineness. If it suits a person, it offsets the evil effects of Saturn and can bring forth health, wealth, fortune, security, longevity of life. It is believed that it cures fits, loss of sexual power; baldness; mental problems etc.

Ordinarily, sapphire should not be worn. We would advise donation of iron articles or almonds to public places or charity and wandering sadhus for better results. If it is absolutely necessary, it may be worn under the supervision of an expert astrologer.

Method of Wearing Sapphire

It should be studded in gold or 'Panchdhatu' (five metals) in the middle finger of right hand on Saturday, just after the appearance of stars. Its weight should be 5 or 7 karat.

8. Hessonite (Gomed) or Neelam for Malefic Rahu

It must be used with great caution. It offsets the problems and diseases caused by Rahu and Saturn. If it suits a person, it confers success and victory over enemies. It cures insanity, mental disorders, stomach ailments etc.

Method of Wearing Hessonite

If absolutely necessary, it may be worn in the middle finger of right hand studded in silver under the strict supervision of an astrologer on Thursday evening. Its weight should be 6 or 11 or 13 karat. We would advise donation of sarson (mustard), barley and coconut for 43 days.

9. Cat's Eye (Lahsunya or Vaidrya) for Malefic Ketu

It must be worn after consulting an astrologer; otherwise it may cause discomfort and restlessness. It is recommended as a cure for the disease and evil effects of Ketu and Mars i.e. it cures mental worries, insanity, craze for something bad and saves the man from hidden enemies and sudden accidents and losses. It also confers unexpected wealth in investments in stocks, speculations, gambling etc.

Method of Wearing Cat's Eye

It should be worn in the middle finger studded in gold on Sunday, two hours before sunrise. Its weight should be 3 or 5 or 7 karat. We would advise donation of banana for 48 days or else donation of black and white blanket once in a year.

Warning: Injudicious and haphazard wearing of precious stones should be avoided at all costs.

Chapter No. 37

Person's Age

(1) House no. 11 determines the age of children; no.6 determines mother's age; no.10 refers to father's age and man's own age is determined by house no. 8. Finally, moon protects life.

(2) **Danger to Life (Short-lived)** $8 \times 8 = 64$ years is the maximum age because of the following combinations in the Birth chart. 8th day, 8th month or 8th year will be malefic and one may face danger to one's life when:

   (a) Jupiter is surrounded by enemy planets.

   (b) Jupiter is combined with Mercury and Venus in no.9.

   (c) No.9 is occupied by enemies of the Jupiter i.e. Rahu, Mercury & Venus.

   (d) Moon & Rahu are in no.7 or no.8.

   (e) Mercury is in no.9.

   (f) Jupiter is in no.6, 8, 10, 11; Venus and Mars are in no.7; Mercury, Venus and Moon are in no.5 — Age – 2 years.

Such a person may face danger to his life i.e. illness etc. during 8th, 16th, 32nd, 40th, 48th, 56th, 64th years of his life.

Life Span of an Individual

Total Life Span	Planets in Various Houses
12 days	Moon in no.6 – Sun in no.10 – Moon-Ketu in no.6.
One year	Sun-Saturn combined in Jupiter's permanent house, when male planets are not in association with or helpful.
9 years	Sun-Moon combined in no.11.
10 years	Moon-Ketu in no.1.
12 years	Moon in no.5, Sun in no.11, when male planets are not in association with or helpful. If Saturn is in no.5, he will have a long life, as Sun & Saturn will be friends now.
15 years	Moon-Rahu in no.1.
20 years	Jupiter-Rahu in no.2 or Jupiter-Mercury in no.6.

22 years	Sun-Rahu in no.10 or 11, when no.8 is occupied by malefic (leading to death) planets and simultaneously Sun-Rahu are jointly placed in no.10 and Saturn along with a female planet in no.2 or Sun-Rahu jointly in no.11 and Saturn is malefic in house of death; person will have a long life if Saturn is in no.3, 5, or 6.
25 years	Moon-Rahu in no.6 or malefic Mars (Mars-Mercury in no.6, or Venus and Ketu are both debilitating).
30 years	Mercury-Jupiter in no.2 or Jupiter-Rahu in no.3.
35 years	Moon-Mercury-Rahu jointly placed.
40 years	Jupiter-Rahu in no.9 or 12 or a lot of hair on forehead.
45 years	Mercury-Ketu in no.12 or Rahu-Jupiter in no.6.
50 years	Moon-Rahu in no.5, provided both of them are not aspected by any planet or malefic planets in no.2 or 7.
56 years	Moon-Rahu-Mercury jointly in no.2 or 5.
60 years	Moon-Mercury in no.2.
70 years	Jupiter-Ketu in no.9 or Saturn-Ketu in no.6 or Moon-Saturn in no.7.
75 years	Moon-Rahu in no.9 or Moon in no.9.
80 years	Moon-Jupiter in no.4 or Moon in no.3-6 will have lot of wealth.
85 years	Exalted Moon in no.7.
90 years	Exalted Moon in no.1, 8, 10, 11.
96 years	Exalted Moon in no.2 or 4.
100 years	Jupiter-Ketu in no.12 and exalted Moon or Moon-Jupiter in no.5 or Mars in no.1, 2, 7 and Sun in no.4, or exalted male planets or helpful to Moon or exalted Moon, Sun and Jupiter.
120 years	Moon-Jupiter in no.12.

Reasons for Death

Planets & House No.	Reason for Death
Moon, Saturn, Mars in no.5 or 8; malefic Mars & Venus in no.5 or 8 – but not associated with or aspected by Sun or Moon.	May die in battlefield, while fighting.
Saturn-Venus combined in no.10 and Sun in no.4.	Heart-rending death.
Exalted Sun in no.1 alone and not associated with or aspected by any other planet.	Natural, but sudden death.
Moon-Mercury jointly in no.3 or 6, or Moon-Saturn jointly in no.7 or Moon-malefic Mars are jointly in no.7 or 10.	Death by shock.

Mercury in no.12, Saturn in no.7 or Moon-Mercury combined and debilitating Sun or Moon-Mercury jointly in no.4.	Likely to commit suicide.
Mercury & Rahu together or Ketu aspected by or associated with Saturn.	May die of snake-bite or electrocution.
Mercury-Saturn jointly in no.4 or Mercury-Moon-Saturn and malefic Sun.	May commit murder.
Saturn in no.3; Mercury in no.11 or Saturn-Sun in no.10, Mercury in no.8.	May die in jail or police custody.
Venus in no.1, Sun in no.7 along with enemy planets or wicked planets or Sun-Venus combined in no.3 in Birth chart or Annual chart.	May die of tuberculosis or pneumonia or asthma.
Sun-Mercury-Moon combined in no.4.	Fatal accident.
Moon-Rahu in no.4.	Death by drowning or strangulation or hanging or suffocation.
Sun-Saturn in no.7 or Sun-Saturn-Mercury in no.7.	May be assassinated or shot dead.
Mercury-Jupiter in mutual aspect or clash.	Paralysis of limbs or brain.

Moon, its Signs (Raashi) and total life period

Day of Death	Sign (Raashi)	Lord of the Raashi	Age
Wednesday	1 (Aries)	Mars	90 years
Friday	2 (Taurus)	Venus	96 years
Wednesday	3 (Gemini)	Mercury	80 years
Friday	4 (Cancer)	Moon	85 or 96 years
Tuesday	5 (Leo)	Sun	100 years
Sunday	6 (Virgo)	Ketu and Mercury	80 years
Friday	7 (Libra)	Venus	85 years
Wednesday	8 (Scorpio)	Mars	90 years
Thursday	9 (Sagittarius)	Jupiter	75 years
Tuesday	10 (Capricorn)	Saturn	90 years
Saturday	11 (Aquarius)	Saturn	90 years
Thursday	12 (Pisces)	Rahu-Jupiter	90 years

Final Annual Chart

(a) Venus & wicked planets become all the more wicked and malefic.

(b) Mercury, Rahu-Ketu combine together somehow or the other.

(c) House no. 3 is vacant or occupied by malefic planets and no.6 and 8 become all the more malefic, either both of them and individually.

(d) There are vacant kendras i.e. 1, 4, 7, 10 in Annual chart or they are not occupied by planets of kendras of the Birth chart.

(e) Moon is debilitated and loses its life-saving powers.

(f) No.4 is poisoning or destroying no.8 through no.2.

(g) Mercury is in no.3, 8, 9, 12.

(h) Saturn destroys Moon through Ketu (feet) and Rahu (head).

(i) Rahu is in no.8 and Moon becomes debilitating.

Final Hour (Ultimate End)

The moving finger writes and having writtten,

Moves on, nor will our piety nor wit,

Shall lure it back to cancel half a line,

Nor all your tears wash out a word of it.

(Omar Khayam)

When death strikes, all remedies and efforts prove futile.

Moon is the lord of life. Ultimate end of man's life depends upon Moon's position and the planets in no.8, 12. Moon's position in the Birth chart is known. If there is a malefic planet in no.8 and it is adversely aspected by no.12, that will be the red signal for the end of life.

Whenever Mercury and Rahu or Ketu are together; it will be a signal for impending death. Moon-Saturn in no.4 will cause man's death in a foreign land. When Jupiter is in no.2 and Ketu is in no.6, man will have a premonition of his death.

Birthday and Time of Birth of an individual will never be the day and time of death. Further, planet in no.3 occupying no.3 in the Annual chart will not be the year of death.

Before predicting death, house no. 6 (house of underworld and compassion); house no. 8 (house of death and brutal justice) and house no. 12 (heaven and justice) should be thoroughly studied.

We may, however, sound a note of warning – **"Never predict Death"**. Time and date will not be correct. Only God knows the exact time of death. When it is universally known that death will finally close the chapter of life, one must not feel scared; rather one should accept the final hour with stoic resignation. Longfellow has rightly said, *"Dust thout art, to dust returnest, Was not spoken of soul!"*

Lord in the Holy Gita says, "The soul is never born or dies; for it is unknown, eternal, everlasting and primeval; even though the body is slain, the soul is not."

Body is perishable, but the soul is eternal. May God bless the whole human race, and animals and birds with prosperity, peace and amity!

Let me quote the following beautiful lines from Allan Seeger:

"I have a rendezvous with death, at some disputed barricade —
And I to my pledged word am true, I shall not fail that rendezvous."

Final Chart – A Few Case Studies

Case Study No.1: Mr. ABC was born on 9-12-1927. His Birth Chart was as under:

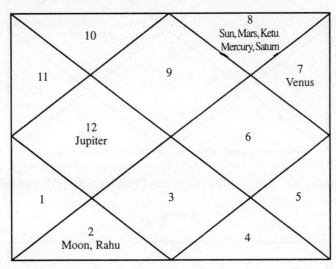

His Annual Chart during 74th year i.e. 9-12-2000 to 8-12-2001 was as under:

74th Year

Here Moon, Rahu become the most malefic (see Moon-Rahu no.12) and Mercury/Ketu becomes the planet of deception (see the chart of deception on page 67). He died of a massive heart attack on 22-08-2001. He was passing through the Mahadasha of Mercury with the intervening dasha of Saturn from 28-6-1999 to 7-3-2002.

Case Study No.2: Miss XYZ was born on 4-6-1979. Her birth chart was as under:

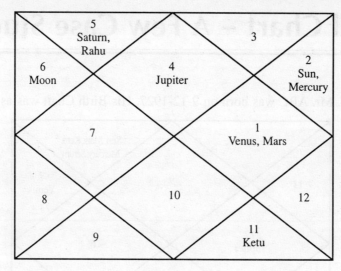

Her Annual Chart during her 23rd year i.e. from 4-6-2001 to 3-6-2002 was as under:

23rd Year

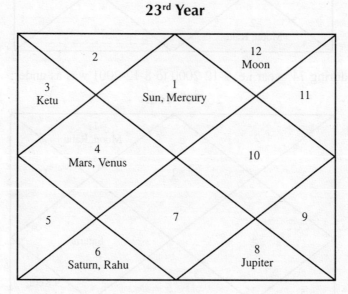

She commited suicide on 10-8-2001. Ketu & Jupiter are malefic; Saturn-Rahu are destroying Moon (see the chart of deception on page 67); Mars-Venus move from 10th house to 4th house (sudden attack); hence the most malefic Annual Chart.

Mahadashas, Artificial Planets & Remedies

I. Introduction About Mahadasha According To Lal Kitab

Like the Mahadasha cycle of 120 years in the ancient Astrological system, Lal Kitab also refers to the same span i.e. 120 years of the wheel of Mahadasha but the order in which the planets occupy a particular Mahadasha is different. It is as under:

Jupiter: 16 Yrs., Sun: 6 Yrs., Moon: 10 Yrs.,

Venus: 20 Yrs., Mars: 7 Yrs., Mercury: 17 Yrs.

Saturn: 19 Yrs., Rahu: 18 Yrs., Ketu: 7 Yrs.

Total Span: 120 years.

1. Planets which will remain dormant or asleep for years indicated against each

Mahadasha Planet →	Jupiter	Sun	Moon	Venus	Mars	Mercury	Saturn	Rahu	Ketu
Planets which will be asleep	Saturn 6 Yrs.	Malefic Mars 6 Yrs.	Jupiter 2 Yrs.	Jupiter 6 Yrs. Mars 6 Yrs.	Venus 1 Yr. Saturn 6 Yrs.	Jupiter 6 Yrs. Mars 6 Yrs.	Jupiter 16 Yrs. Ketu 3 Yrs.	Jupiter 8 Yrs. Sun nil	Jupiter 6 Yrs. Sun nil
	Rahu 6 Yrs.	–	Mars 6 Yrs.	Mercury 2 Yrs.	–	Saturn 5 Yrs.	–	Moon 1 Yr.	Mercury nil
	Ketu 3 Yrs.	–	Saturn 2 Yrs.	Saturn 6 Yrs.	Rahu nil	Ketu nil	–	Venus 3 Yrs. Mars 6 Yrs.	Saturn 1 Yr.
Total	15 Yrs	6 Yrs.	10 Yrs.	20 Yrs.	7 Yrs.	17 Yrs.	19 Yrs.	18 Yrs.	7 Yrs.

The planets noted above will remain dormant in the same order as indicated in the above chart. The planets, against which 'nil' is written, will be neutral.

Note: Jupiter's main period extends to 16 years, as its Mahadasha commences from the second year. It, in fact, reserves the first year as 'Guru Dakshina' i.e. 'offering to the teacher'. Out of the remaining 15 years, it accepts as 'Guru Dakshina' one year from Saturn, Rahu and Ketu each, second year from Saturn's period of six years i.e. 2, 3, 4, 5, 6, 7, eighth year from Rahu's years i.e. 8, 9, 10, 11, 12, 13 and finally Ketu's fourteenth year from years 14, 15, 16. Thus, the first, second, eighth and fourteenth years are Jupiter's 'Guru Dakshina' years and tenth year is his personal property. *For details, please refer to the first stanza under Jupiter (pages 111 & 112).*

2. Planets which will not be affected by a particular Mahadasha

S. No.	Mahadasha of a Planet	Planets which will not be affected or which maintain their own power and entity
1.	Jupiter	Except wicked planets all other planets will remain as they are.
2.	Sun	Except malefic Mars, all other planets will maintain their power.
3.	Moon	Mercury, Venus, Sun, Rahu, Ketu.
4.	Venus	Sun, Moon, Rahu, Ketu.
5.	Mars	Sun, Moon, Jupiter, Ketu & Mercury (Rahu will be ineffective).
6.	Mercury	Sun, Moon, Venus, Rahu (Ketu will be ineffective).
7.	Saturn	Sun, Moon, Mars, Mercury, Venus, Rahu.
8.	Rahu	Saturn, Mercury, Ketu (Sun will be zero).
9.	Ketu	Moon, Venus, Mars, Rahu (Sun and Mercury will be ineffective).

Note: Mahadasha cycle of 120 years as propounded by our ancient seers is perfect and should be preferred. Let me cite the following instance:

A gentleman was passing through his Main period of Rahu with the sub-period of Ketu and sub-sub-period of Moon (Rahu – Ketu – Moon). It works out to month – 1, days – 1.5. During this period, he had the worst nightmare of his life. He lost his job and was in a state of depression. But after the expiry of this period, he got another job and everything was fine. Moon during this period was afflicted with two most malefic planets i.e. Rahu and Ketu.

I was able to predict the same result through the annual chart of that year.

Example

Birth Chart

(Date of Birth : 23-11-1969)

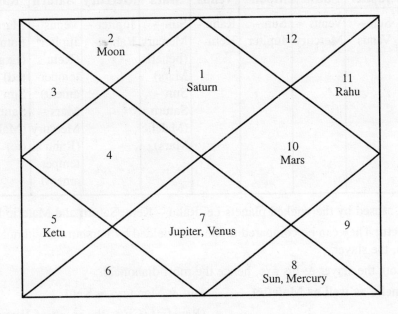

Here 'Ketu' is destroying Moon & Rahu being in 4th house, causes loss of job and depression too.

Annual Chart of 33rd year

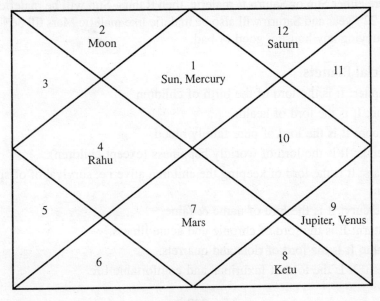

I would, therefore, advise that Mahadasha cycle as enunciated by our ancient sages should also be consulted to arrive at exact results. *Kindly refer to pages 38 & 39 for details.*

II. Information Regarding Artificial Planets

Planets →	Jupiter	Sun	Moon	Venus	Mars	Mercury	Saturn	Rahu	Ketu
Artificial Planets	Sun – Venus	Venus – Mercury	Sun – Jupiter	Rahu – Ketu	Sun – Mercury (benefic Mars) Sun – Saturn (Malefic Mars)	Jupiter – Rahu	Venus – Jupiter (Ketu's temperament) Mars – Mercury (Rahu's temperament)	Mars – Saturn (Exalted) Sun – Saturn (Malefic)	Venus – Saturn (Exalted) Moon – Saturn (Malefic)

Note: Death is caused by the wicked planets i.e. Rahu – Ketu, Saturn and Malefic Mars.

a. **Rahu – Ketu:** They can be compared to the axe wielded by Parshuram without its owner i.e. Parshuram, the slayer.

b. **Saturn:** Both the slayer & his axe, hence the most diabolical.

c. **Mars (Benefic as well as Malefic)**   Sun & Mercury → Ketu
(Benefic) (Gives the result of Venus)
Sun & Saturn → Rahu
(Malefic)

Sun – Saturn: (Day & night together) constitute Mercury only. If they are malefic or are in such houses where either Sun or Saturn is malefic, then Rahu – Sun will be malefic or will be like malefic Mars till 22nd year and Saturn will also be malefic like malefic Mars till 36th year, no matter they may be occupying any house – good or bad.

Effect of Artificial Planets

1. Artificial Jupiter: It is the lord of the birth of children.
2. Artificial Sun: It is the lord of health.
3. Artificial Moon: It is the lord of pure family blood.
4. Artificial Venus: It is the lord of worldly happiness (except children).
5. Artificial Mars: It is the lord of keeping the children alive i.e. survival of offsprings and also of vegetation.
6. Artificial Mercury: It is the lord of name & fame.
7. Artificial Saturn: It is the lord of chronic and acute illness.
8. Artificial Rahu: It is the lord of riots and quarrels.
9. Artificial Ketu: It is the lord of luxurious and comfortable life.

III. Remedies for Planets

It is said that diamond cuts diamond and the greater rogue dominates the lesser one. Here are a few examples:

(a) **Mercury:** The green-coloured emerald slays and destroys all, but it is destroyed by a very soft element called tin foil (कलेई in Hindi or fusible alloy) which is used in soldering. It creates a hole in the green emerald. Similarly, wicked planets destroy other wicked planets.

(b) **Malefic Rahu:** Its malefic effect is mitigated by adopting remedy for Ketu.

(c) **Malefic Ketu:** Its malefic effect is minimized by adopting remedy for Rahu.

(d) **Malefic Venus:** Feed a cow with a part of your food.

(e) **Malefic Saturn:** Loss in wealth indicates Saturn's malefic effect. Feed a cow with a part of your food and for the benefit of children, feed a dog with a part of your food.

(f) In every planet's artificial situation, there are two planets. When a particular planet becomes malefic, then take away one of the two artificial planets which may confer better results. For example, when Saturn becomes malefic, take away Jupiter from its artificial components of Jupiter – Venus (refer to Chart on page 3) and add Mercury to the remaining planet i.e. Venus. Now it is a benefic combination of Venus – Mercury. This will transform malefic Saturn into a benefic one.

(g) Besides these remedies, adopt other remedies according to 'Lal Kitab'. As regards the artificial condition of a planet, two planets are considered together; out of these two, remove the planet which gives bad effect.

Example: (i) When Venus becomes malefic, then remove Rahu from its combination of Ketu – Rahu as artificial planets (refer to Chart on page 338) and now Ketu remains. Thus, to make Venus benefic, take the help of Rahu in order to make it benefic.

Example: (ii) In order to make both Mercury and Jupiter benefic, green-coloured things pertaining to Mercury will be helpful i.e. *keep gold ornaments in green-coloured paper.*

Example: (iii) The remedy for Mercury – Venus – Saturn combination is to offer three morsels of your own food to cow, crow and dog. It will confer best results regarding name, fame, wealth, glory and welfare of children.

IV. Remedy for Malefic Mars

1. To ward off the worst effect of malefic Mars, keep 'Mrigshala' – the skin of deer.

   Mars – Mercury: Mars (malefic) and Saturn's poisonous fang OR Mars – Mercury and Saturn (all combined) need skin of deer to offset the worst effect of the above combinations and malefic Mars. The poisonous snake never touches or goes near the skins of the deer, that is why sadhus prefer to squat on them.

2. Worship Moon for removing the worst effect of malefic Mars. Adopt remedy for Moon according to its placement in a particular house.

3. Moon and Malefic Mars both spring from Lord Shiva. The former is *the lord of life*, whereas the latter is the *lord of death and destruction*. Moon is life-giving and confers all benefits upon an individual. Malefic Mars is like the gallows or the noose of a halter around one's neck. That's why, worshipping of Moon as the sole remedy for malefic Mars is recommended i.e.

donate sweet tandoori bread for 43 days every year. It may be noted that where there is Moon, there will be no malefic Mars and vice-versa.

V. Remedy for Malefic Rahu

1. Bury jaw (Barley - नौ) in a closed place under some weight.

                                OR

2. Wash barley with milk and throw them into the river.

3. If one suffers from T.B. or from prolonged illness, wash Barley in cow's urine and keep them wrapped in red-coloured cloth.

4. Clean your teeth with cow's urine.

Note: Take the help of exalted planet as a remedy for controlling the malefic planets.

Years of Personal Influence of Planets during Mahadasha

S.No.	Planet	Mahadasha Years	Years of Personal Influence
1	Jupiter	16	10th Year (This is in addition to 1st year (as Guru Dakshina); 2nd, 8th and 14th years of Mahadasha.
2	Sun	6	All odd years of Mahadasha, i.e., 1st, 3rd & 5th years.
3	Moon	10	All even years, i.e., 2nd, 4th, 6th, 8th and 10th years.
4	Venus	20	11th year of Mahadasha
5	Mars	7	4th year of Mahadasha
6	Mercury (both exalted & malefic	17	5th year of Mahadasha
7	Saturn	19	6th year of Mahadasha
8	Rahu	18	7th year of Mahadasha
9	Ketu	7	3rd Year of Mahadasha

Effects of Planets in Various Houses:

S.No.	Planet, if alone & not aspected by others*	House in which it is bad**	House in which it is good***
1	Jupiter	6,7,1,11 (Ketu will help debilitating Jupiter)	1,2,3,4,5,8,9,12
2	Sun	6,7,10	1,2,3,4,5,8,9,11,12
3	Moon	6,8,10,11,12	1,2,3,4,5,7,9
4	Venus	1,6,9	2,3,4,5,7,8,10,11,12

5.	Mars	4,8	1,2,3,5,6,7,9,10,11,12
6.	Mercury	3,8,9,10,11,12 (Mercury is not always bad in 9 & 11)	1,2,4,5,6,7
7.	Saturn	1,4,5,6	2,3,7,8,9,10,11,12
8.	Rahu	1,2,5,7,8,9,10,11,12	3,4,6
9.	Ketu	3,4,5,6,8	1,2,7,9,10,11,12

*The planet is not aspected by any other planet and is alone for all intents and purposes.

**When the planet occupies the house in which it is considered debilitating or is placed in the enemy house and is malefic according to the Raashi (sign).

***When it occupies its own house or a friendly house and is considered exalted or benefic according to the Raashi (sign).

Closed Palm and Horoscope:

Child is the knot that ties together the Mercury (Sky) and the Jupiter (Air). Naturally, every knot of child's palm refers to his fate in terms of all the nine planets. Here is the birth chart in table form:

House No.	Planet	Features
1	Sun	Body
2	Moon	Mother
3		Brothers & Relatives
4	Jupiter	Wealth
5		Children
6	Rahu & Mercury	Wife's & own relatives
7	Saturn	Property
8		Disease & death
9		Ancestors; religion
10	Mars	Food
11		Income concerning Birth date
12	Venus-Ketu	Woman; marital happiness

(a) House No. 1-7; 4-10: Inherited wealth and property.

(b) House No. 9, 11, 12: Childhood & parent's monetary position.

(c) House No. 2,3,5,6: Old age & children

(d) House No. 8: Sickness; death & bad times; road to the other world. It looks backwards & not forwards and is the noose of the gallows.

Aspects:

1. 100% aspects: 1-7, 4-10 (Wealth brought at the time of birth).
2. 50% aspects: 3-11, 5-9 (Wealth & conditions created with the help of others).
3. 25% aspects: 2-6-12 (Things obtained from relatives)

"To assess effect of a planet in a House without the Raashis (Signs)":

First find out whether the planet is good or bad, though it may be occupying any House in the Birth Chart. It will have the same effect as per its placement in the horoscope. Suppose, Jupiter and Venus are weak and malefic in the horoscope, they will have an adverse or bad effect on House No.2 as per the following chart:

House No.											
1	2	3	4	5	6	7	8	9	10	11	12
Mercury Sun, Mars, Saturn	Jupiter Venus	Mercury Saturn, Mars	Jupiter Sun's relationship with Moon	Jupiter Sun, Rahu, Ketu connection	Mercury Ketu, Venus	Venus Mercury	Mars Relationship of Saturn-Moon	Jupiter Personal influence	Saturn Rahu-Ketu's relationship from right & left	Saturn With Jupiter	Rahu Jupiter's relationship with Saturn

Remarks: In every house we will find the individual effect of planets given here-in:

नर ग्रह बोलते जुफ़्त (even) के घर में

नारी बोलते ताक़ (odd) में है।

बुध है बोलता 3-6 में तो

पापी 2 में नहीं बोलते हैं॥

Male planets may be placed anywhere, but its effect will be visible on even nos. Houses in the horoscope, i.e., 2,4,6,8,10 & 12; whereas, the effect of female planets will be visible on odd nos. of houses, i.e., nos. 1,3,5,7,9 and 11. Mercury affects house nos. 3 and 6. The sinners (Saturn, Rahu & Ketu) adversely affect every house except house no. 2, which is the House of God, and temple of Great Guru.

Ordinarily, when Ketu is benefic or exalted in a horoscope, in such a horoscope, Mercury / Rahu will be debilitating OR will be surrounded by Male planets / Female planets. In a horoscope, where Mercury is exalted, Ketu will be debilitating or weak. But if both of them are of equal strength, then the boy and girl (Ketu & Mercury) will be of equal power. If the son and daughter (twins) are born together from the same womb, the boy will be destroyed or weak. If Mercury occupies No.6 or is in conjunction with Ketu, Ketu will be destroyed, i.e., it will be malefic; but Mercury will not be malefic. If Rahu & Mercury are together in No. 12, then Mercury will be malefic but Rahu will be benefic.

Planets (exalted / malefic) occupying 1st House in the Annual Chart:

(a) When the planets having equal powers, i.e., neutral planets are malefic, through the main planet which is not malefic, then such a planet occupies the 1st House in the annual chart, and it will also become malefic during that month. It will be deemed to have entered the Mahadasha.

342

(b) If the main planet itself is malefic and the others having equal powers are malefic, such a planet while occupying House No. 1 or on birthday, everything will be topsy-turvy and bad. It will be deemed to have entered its Mahadasha. During that period, friendly planets will not help, but enemy planets will harm and sprinkle salt on the wounds.

*Note: For catalogue of "equal power / neutral planets", please refer to Page No. 59-60.

Mahadasha Years	Name of Planets	House No.	Planets of equal powers in House No.	Such planets in Birth Chart – Bad years	No. of bad years during Mahadasha	Malefic years of Mahadasha
16	Jupiter	10	Rahu 9-12 Ketu 3-6 Saturn-1	20, 21, 22 years	3 years out of 16 years	11, 12, 13th years
6	Sun	7	Mercury-12	12th year of life	One year out of 6 years	6th year
10	Moon	8	Venus-6 Saturn-1 Mars-4 Jupiter-10	17th year of life of 10 years	One year out	10th year
20	Venus	6	Mars-4 Jupiter-10	9, 11, 12, 13, 17, 18, 21, 25, 27 years	8 years out of 20 years	1, 3, 4, 5, 9, 10 12, 17, 19th year
7	Mars	4	Venus-6 Saturn-1 Rahu 9, 12	4, 5, 6, 9 years	4 years out of 7 years	1, 2, 3, 6th year
17	Mercury	12	Saturn-1 Ketu 3, 6 Jupiter-10	12, 14, 15, 17, 22, 24, 28 years	7 years out of 17 years	1, 3, 4, 6,11, 13, 17th year
19	Saturn	1	Jupiter-10 Ketu-3,6	1, 2, 11, 13 years	4 years out of 19 years	1, 2, 11, 13th year
18	Rahu	9	Jupiter-10 Moon-8	6, 8, 9, 10, 14, 15, 16, 17, 18, 20, 22	11 years out of 18 years	1, 3, 4, 5, 9, 10 11, 12, 13, 15th year
	Rahu	12	Jupiter-10 Moon - 8	12, 14, 16, 17. 20, 22, 23, 24, 28, 29		
7	Ketu	3	Jupiter-10 Saturn-1 Mercury-12 Sun-7 As above	3, 4, 6	3 years out of 7 years	1, 2, 4th year
	Ketu	6		9, 12, 13		1, 4, 5th year

Note:

(i) The chart below explains the position of malefic but "equal power planets and their malefic effect".

(ii) During Mahadasha aspects of Jupiter, Mars and Saturn will be different as explained in the Note No. (i), (ii) & (iii) under the next charts.

The time of Mahadasha according to Planets

Houses occupied by malefic but equal power planets /neutral planets giving malefic results.

Planet Mahadasha	1	2	3	4	5	6	7	8	9	10	11	12
Jupiter	Saturn		Ketu			Ketu			Rahu	Jupiter		Rahu
Sun							Sun					Mercury
Moon	Saturn			Mars		Venus		Moon		Jupiter		
Venus				Mars		Venus				Jupiter		
Mars	Saturn			Mars		Venus			Rahu			Rahu
Mercury	Saturn		Ketu	Mars		Ketu				Jupiter		Mercury
Saturn	Saturn		Ketu			Ketu				Jupiter		
Rahu								Moon	Rahu	Jupiter		Rahu
Ketu	Saturn		Ketu			Ketu	Sun			Jupiter		Mercury

Note:

(i) During the Mahadasha, if Mars is in no.4, it will aspect H.No.7 and 11.

(ii) During the Mahadasha, if Jupiter is in No.10, it will aspect H.No.2 and 6.

(iii) During the Mahadasha, if Saturn is in No.1, it will aspect H. No.3 and 10.

(iv) If during the movement of the planets enumerated in the above chart, the following placements of the following planets will nullify the malefic effects:

(a) Moon in H. No.2

(b) Rahu in H.No.3

(c) Rahu & Mercury in H.No.6 (individually or collectively)

(d) Ketu & Venus in H. No.12 (individually or collectively)

(e) Auspicious Planets in H.No.4

In the above cases, there will be no malefic Mahadasha.

Another Mahadasha Chart

1 Venus	2 Raashi No. 12 ends	3 Sun	4 Moon	5 Ketu	6 Mars	7 Mercury	8 Saturn	9 Rahu	10 Death Planet in No. 8	11 Ancestral Planet in No. 9	12 Jupiter
1	2	3	4	5	6	7	8	9	10	11	12
13	14	15	16	17	18	19	20	21	22	23	24
25	26	27	28	29	30	31	32	33	34	35	36
37	38	39	40								

From the above chart, it is clear that no.1 indicates the 1st year of Mahadasha, No.2 indicates the 2nd year of Mahadasha, etc., though Mahadasha of a planet may commence from any year of life.

Example: Suppose, the Mahadasha of Venus of an individual starts from the 23rd year, substitute no.1 with 23, No.2 with 24 and so on and so forth. Another point to be noted is that the Mahadasha of Venus ends at the 20th year and the planet occupying no. 20 in the above chart is Saturn; hence, in the 20th year of the Mahadasha of Venus, we will have mixed results of both the planets, i.e. Venus and Saturn.

Practical Palmistry

—Dr. Narayan Dutt Shrimali

Palmistry is an important organ of the science of astrology, which can forecast the future of an individual authentically. Human existence confronts many hurdles and uncertainties; hence, man suffers from indecision and is unable to concentrate on his goals.

Of all the sciences of the world, Palmistry has come to the rescue of modern man because it can not only tell us about the past, it can also predict the future. A palm is a treasure of vitality and working power of a human being from the materialistic point of view and is the source of all activities of life from the astrological point of view. By means of our palm we know our past and believe it, we understand the present and try to mould ourselves by acquainting ourselves with the future, so that we may remain constantly active.

*Demy Size • Pages: 365 • Price: Rs. **80/-** • Postage: Rs. 15/-*

Palmistry for Beginners

—Richard Webster

Discover how the ancient science of palmistry — which has been used as an accurate tool for self-knowledge for thousands of years — can lead you to a better understanding of yourself and others.

Learn how to assess a palm at a glance, determine compatibility between couples, help people choose their ideal career— and gain a greater understanding of yourself. The book will enable complete novice to learn how to read palms as quickly as possible, but it will also serve as a valuable reference for experts. Whether you are interested in taking up palmistry professionally or just for fun, you will find this book an exceptionally easy-to-use guide to the fascinating language of the palm.

* Gain new insights into the personalities, talents and ambitions of yourself and everyone you meet.
* Locate specific palm lines easily with the 181 clear, large-sized hand drawings.
* Determine your friends', family's and your own future in the areas of health, money, travel, romance and children.
* Learn what career you would be best at and enjoy the most.
* Find out what loop pattern, lines, shape of hand and length of fingers mean.
* Learn how to assess a palm at a glance.
* Easily discover whether two people are compatible or not.
* Receive the most comprehensive explanation of dermatoglyphics (the study of skin patterns) found in any palmistry book.

*Demy Size • Pages: 282 • Price: Rs. **88/-** • Postage: Rs. 15/-*

Explore the Power of ASTROLOGY

—Dr. A.P. Parashar, Dr. V.K. Parashar

Backed by years of astrological experience, Dr Ambika Prasad Parashar and his son Dr Vinod Kumar Parashar offer a fresh perspective on each Sun sign and the signs of other planets when they transit different houses in a chart (kundali). Examining the main areas of life – relationships, finances, family, career, health, love and personal characteristics – the authors probe the gifts of the Sun signs interwoven with the influence of other planets' aspects and transits in the houses. The book tells readers how things operate in life due to astrological influences, so that they can approach life from a new perspective to discover the right vocation and attain great success, happiness, love and peace. Case studies of prominent persons are dealt with extensively to help readers understand the planetary influences and other signs that indicate foreign travel, property, love, money, position, luck and other factors in life. The book also throws ample light on how to compute one's own lagna (rising sign) and make one's own chart, if required.

Demy Size • Pages: 200 • Price: Rs. 96/- • Postage: Rs. 15/-

Explore the Power of Astrology—TRIKONA

—Dr. A.P. Parashar, Dr. V.K. Parashar

Inspired by their first book, **Explore the Power of Astrology** Dr. Ambika Prasad Parashar and his son Dr. Vinod Kumar Parashar once again offer a fresh and advanced perspective on the three important angles (houses) of the chart (kundali) traditionally known as TRIKONA, which are, the ascendant, the fifth and the ninth houses. These three houses deal with the most important areas of one's life, such as, the self, individual temperament, appearance and level of self-awareness; creativity, children and romance; religion and philosophy, extensive journeys including foreign travel, higher education, publishing and language, respectively. The book deals very extensively how these three houses influence one's life constantly and how the planets, when own these houses, influence individual's life. The authors have also analysed 36 case studies in relation to these three houses and have discussed elaborately how planets play their role in the growth of human beings.

Demy Size • Pages: 208 • Price: Rs. 125/- • Postage: Rs. 15/-